GLOBAL LANGUAGE JUSTICE

Global Language Justice

Edited by Lydia H. Liu
and
Anupama Rao
with
Charlotte A. Silverman

Columbia University Press
New York

Columbia University Press
Publishers Since 1893
New York   Chichester, West Sussex
cup.columbia.edu

Copyright © 2024 Columbia University Press
All rights reserved

Library of Congress Cataloging-in-Publication Data
Names: Liu, Lydia He, editor. | Rao, Anupama, editor. | Silverman, Charlotte A., editor.
Title: Global language justice / edited by Lydia H. Liu and Anupama Rao, with Charlotte A Silverman.
Description: New York : Columbia University Press, 2023. | Includes index. Identifiers: LCCN 2023016256 | ISBN 9780231210386 (hardback) | ISBN 9780231210393 (trade paperback) | ISBN 9780231558396 (ebook)
Subjects: LCSH: Sociolinguistics. | Social justice. | LCGFT: Essays.
Classification: LCC P40 .G58 2023 | DDC 306.44—dc23/eng/20230721
LC record available at https://lccn.loc.gov/2023016256

Cover design: Milenda Nan Ok Lee
Covert art: Xu Bing, *Gravitational Arena* installation view, Museum of Art Pudong (MAP), Shanghai. Copyright © 2023 Xu Bing.

CONTENTS

POEMS AND ARTWORKS vii

ACKNOWLEDGMENTS ix

Introduction
The Lifeworld of Languages:
Rethinking *Logos*, *Oikos*, and *Techné* 1
LYDIA H. LIU AND ANUPAMA RAO

Chapter One
Equality or Diversity: Language, Rights, Justice 36
L. MARIA BO

Chapter Two
Global Language Justice Inside the Doughnut:
A Planetary Perspective 68
SUZANNE ROMAINE

Chapter Three
The Asylum Trial: Translating Justice at the Borders of Europe 98
TOMMASO MANFREDINI

Chapter Four
Challenging "Extinction" Through Modern Miami
Language Practices   126
WESLEY Y. LEONARD

Chapter Five
Indigenous Languages Between Erasure and Disinvention   166
DANIEL KAUFMAN AND ROSS PERLIN

Chapter Six
Linguistic Democracy and the Algerian Hirak   194
MADELEINE DOBIE

Chapter Seven
Digital Vitality for Linguistic Diversity:
The Script Encoding Initiative   220
DEBORAH ANDERSON

Chapter Eight
Language Justice in the Digital Sphere   244
ISABELLE A. ZAUGG

Chapter Nine
EXIT: An Interview   275
LAURA KURGAN AND CHARLOTTE A. SILVERMAN

CONTRIBUTORS   293

INDEX   299

POEMS AND ARTWORKS

Orlando White, "Ats'íísts'in" 35
Bei Dao, "February" 66
Zhai Yongming, "Becoming a Child" 96
Abhay Xaxa, "I Am Not Your Data" 125
"Vachanas", trans. Manu V. Devadevan 159
Mohammed Bennis, "Words" 192
Xu Bing, *Square Word Calligraphy* 243
Diller Scofidio + Renfro, Mark Hansen, Laura Kurgan, and Ben Rubin, Overview of *EXIT* 274

ACKNOWLEDGMENTS

This book was inspired by many stimulating conversations and surprising encounters of minds over a period of four years. The idea of doing some research on global language justice began in a Sawyer Seminar initiative led by the Institute for Comparative Literature and Society (ICLS) at Columbia University. We are grateful to the Andrew W. Mellon Foundation for its generous support from the fall of 2017 through the middle of the Covid-19 pandemic. During this time, we organized numerous lectures, workshops, and symposia to which we invited colleagues, students, writers, poets, translators, and activists to speak to us about linguistic diversity and biodiversity with a view to approaching language justice as the humanistic equivalent of environmental justice.

Our discussions converged eventually around the limitations of the discourse of linguistic rights, the role of technology in the advancement or erasure of languages and scripts, and the tensions between respect for diversity and demands for equality in regard to Indigenous languages and social justice. Most of the contributors to this book were involved at one point or another in the discussions organized through the Sawyer Seminar. Isabelle Zaugg joined us as a Mellon postdoctoral fellow and played a leading role in the programming associated with the Sawyer Seminar; she also taught innovative courses that explored the role of linguistic diversity in digital technology. Her research on digitally disadvantaged languages around the world and on Ethiopia's national language, Amharic, in particular, has been eye-opening. Just as important is Deborah Anderson's Script Encoding Initiative. Her work shows how the Unicode Standard—the protocol underlying the ability to access webpages, conduct internet searches, text on phones, send email, and post social media messages—has become such a central concern for linguistic diversity. Their contributions show that the issue of digital vitality is a cornerstone in the study of global language justice. L. Maria Bo was first involved in the Sawyer Seminar as a graduate fellow and then continued as a key interlocutor after she joined the faculty of ICLS as the director of undergraduate studies. Her chapter helps frame some of the fundamental questions of this volume through a philosophical critique of linguistic rights.

Suzanne Romaine has been one of the pioneers in the contemporary scholarship on biodiversity and linguistic diversity, and she has contributed a great deal to our discussions as well as a chapter in this book. Daniel Kaufman and Ross Perlin have done exemplary work at the Endangered Language Alliance in New York and regularly participated in the Sawyer Seminar. Their work, including the coauthored chapter in our volume, has taught us much about migration, survival, and linguistic diversity in metropolitan centers. Madeleine Dobie's new research on contemporary Algeria focuses on the meaning of democracy and political participation from the angle of linguistic polarization and its colonial past. Tommaso Manfredini shines a unique light on the questionable practices of translation and their legal ramifications for asylum seekers and refugees on the southern border of the European Union. We thank all the contributors for their participation in the Sawyer Seminar and their enormous patience with our editorial work.

We read Wesley Leonard's seminal work on Indigenous languages after the Sawyer Seminar, and we are honored to include it in this volume. As editors, we would like to extend our gratitude to Leonard and to the American Indian Studies Center, UCLA © 2011, Regents of the University of California, for permitting us to reprint his essay "Challenging 'Extinction' Through Modern Miami Language Practices," which originally appeared in the *American Indian Culture and Research Journal* (vol. 35, no. 2) in 2011.

We are also very much indebted to the other scholars and activists who contributed to and expanded the scope of our discussions as invited speakers and workshop participants. Special thanks go to Philippe Van Parijs,

ACKNOWLEDGMENTS

Souleymane Bachir Diagne, Moira Inghilleri, Mary Louise Pratt, Moira Paz, Maya Hess (and her amazing work at Red-T), Michele Moody-Adams, Simona Škrabec, Carol Benson, Elise Pestre, Sareeta Amrute, Anish Gawande, Jane Anderson, Marissa Johnson-Valenzuela, Anshuman Pandey, William R. Frey, and Daan van Esch. Their scholarship and theoretical reflections have been incredibly valuable as we consider global language justice. In 2017, Laura Kurgan and Lydia H. Liu created a seminar called "Conflict Urbanism: Language Justice" at Columbia University in an effort to involve undergraduate students in the development of research projects on global language justice.

Around 2018, our work began to intersect with the International Year of Indigenous Languages, declared for 2019 by the United Nations, and some members of our group attended the seventeenth session of the United Nations Permanent Forum for Indigenous Languages. Working with Elsa Stamatopoulou, director of the Indigenous Peoples' Rights Program at Columbia University's Institute for the Study of Human Rights, we decided to convene a symposium on Global Language Justice for Indigenous Languages jointly with UNESCO, the Secretariat of the United Nations Permanent Forum on Indigenous Issues, and the Permanent Mission of Ecuador to the United Nations, New York. In April 2018, we hosted members of the First Nations; representatives of Indigenous peoples from New Zealand, Europe, and North America; linguistic rights activists; and UN officials. Those who spoke at our symposium were Chief Wilton Littlechild, Chief Clara Soaring Hawk, Tania Ka'ai, Miryam Yataco, Luis Males, Mariam Aboubakrine, Dmitrii Harakka-Zaitsev, Irmgarda Kasinskaite-Buddeberg, Billy Noseworthy, Aili Keskitalo, Kanerahtens Skidders, Angel Vicente-Ferrer, and Romina Quezada Morales. Isabelle Zaugg, Atefeh Akbari, Maria Bo, and Amanda Earl also made important contributions to these discussions. The success of the meeting was the result of Elsa Stamatopoulou's tireless efforts devoted to the cause of Indigenous issues worldwide.

Those exciting intellectual engagements would not have been possible without the active participation and contributions from our graduate fellows over the four-year period: Maria Bo, Alexandra V. Méndez, Atefeh Akbari, Chloe Estep, Amy Zhang, and Charlotte Silverman. Each of them was devoted to the project and played key roles in programming and assisting in hosting workshops and conferences. Bo founded the blogsite *Explorations in Global Language Justice* (https://languagejustice.wordpress.com/), which has published numerous incisive observations, pieces, reports, and student essays, in addition to contributing to this volume. Charlotte Silverman has worked with us as an editorial assistant, and her intellectual acuity and careful editing have been crucial in every step of the manuscript preparation.

Sarah Monks, assistant director of ICLS, supported the Sawyer Seminar and our publication effort throughout. From budget planning to conference and workshop organization and publicity, the impact of the Sawyer Seminar and this ensuing volume are a testament to her meticulous attention to detail. We are very appreciative of her dedication to the project and the hard work of Kelly Lemons and other staff members at ICLS who provided assistance. Jim Cheng, Chengzhi Wang, and Ria Koopmans-de Bruijn of the C. V. Starr East Asian Library and Lauren E. DeVoe of the Butler Library at Columbia University provided their generous support and timely assistance. We are deeply indebted to them. We also thank Samantha Rose DeNinno and Adeline Chum for providing additional help at short notice.

Over the years, our collective project has received grants from partner institutes and centers as well as from the Arts and Sciences administration at Columbia University, including the Office of the Executive Vice-President, Dean of the Humanities, Institute for Social and Economic Research and Policy, and Data Science Institute. We are grateful, in particular, to David Madigan, Sarah Cole, and Sharon Marcus for their support and encouragement. Apart from the Mellon grant, our project received an award from the Collaboratory Fellows Fund of the Data Science Institute to foster rigorous interdisciplinary exchange between the humanities and computer science. That award enabled Isabelle Zaugg and Smaranda Muresan, a computer scientist, to design and teach a new course titled "Multilingual Technologies and Language Diversity." Students from their classes contributed essays to the *Explorations in Global Language Justice* blog and became participants in our project.

Our decision to include bilingual poems and artworks in the book came from the recognition that poetic voices and art embody our vision of global language justice in concrete form. As early as the inaugural event of the Sawyer Seminar, we were very fortunate to have some of the finest contemporary poets join us and engage with the wider multilingual communities in the city of New York. We thank all the poets, their translators, and the Poets House for taking part and inspiring us: in particular, Anne Waldman (United States), Raúl Zurita (Chile), Anna Deeny Morales

ACKNOWLEDGMENTS

(United States), Sharmistha Mohanty (India), Bei Dao (China), Eliot Weinberger (United States), Orlando White (Diné, United States), Mohammed Bennis (Morocco), Zhai Yongming (China), Daouda Ndiaye (Senegal), and Nabaneeta Dev Sen (India).

We would like to acknowledge the generosity of poet Mohammed Bennis and his translator Camilo Gomez-Rivas, poet Ouyang Jianghe and his translator Austin Woerner, and poet Zhai Yongming and her translator Andrea Lingenfelter for giving us permission to reprint their poems here. Indigenous poet Orlando White's poem "Ats'íísts'in" was previously published in *Bone Light* (Copyright © 2009 by Orlando White) and is reprinted here with the permission of The Permissions Company, LLC on behalf of Red Hen Press, redhen.org. Bei Dao's poem "February," translated by David Hinton with Yanbing Chen, appeared originally in *Landscape Over Zero* and is reprinted here by permission of New Directions Publishing Corp. (copyright © 1995, 1996 by Zhao Zhenkai; translation copyright © 1995, 1996 by David Hinton with Yanbing Chen). The Indigenous poet Abhay Xaxa, a member of the Kurukh tribe who was born and brought up in Chattisgarh, India, died tragically of a heart attack in March 2020. His poem "I Am Not Your Data" was published first by *Round Table India* and later by *Adivasi Resurgence* and is included here to convey Xaxa's distinctive critical voice, his unceasing commitment to Adivasi land reform, and his imagining of political solidarities through a radical utopianism. We are indebted to Manu V. Devadevan for his skillful translation of the Kannada vachanas. We thank the great artist Xu Bing and his studio for permission to reproduce a portion of his seminal creation, *Square Word Calligraphy*, and for permission to use his art work on our book cover, which teaches us how to think imaginatively about script, image, and difference.

At the culmination of the Sawyer Seminar, this book represents a collective endeavor that aims to transform ourselves even as we seek to transform society. It is our expectation that the book will help shape the thinking of those whom it has touched for years to come and will continue to catalyze conversations that bring us closer to a just world.

FIGURE 0.1. *EXIT* exhibition: An audience view. Diller Scofidio + Renfro, Mark Hansen, Laura Kurgan, and Ben Rubin, in collaboration with Robert Gerard Pietrusko and Stewart Smith, *EXIT*, 2008–2015. Immersive audiovisual installation based on an idea by Paul Virilio (45 min.). View of the installation at the Palais de Tokyo, Paris, 2015. Collection Fondation Cartier pour l'art contemporain, Paris. Photo by Luc Boegley.

FIGURE 0.2. *EXIT* exhibition: Satellite images. Diller Scofidio + Renfro, Mark Hansen, Laura Kurgan, and Ben Rubin, in collaboration with Robert Gerard Pietrusko and Stewart Smith, *EXIT*, 2008–2015. Immersive audiovisual installation based on an idea by Paul Virilio (45 min.). View of the installation at the Palais de Tokyo, Paris, 2015. Collection Fondation Cartier pour l'art contemporain, Paris. Photo by Luc Boegley.

GLOBAL LANGUAGE JUSTICE

Introduction

THE LIFEWORLD OF LANGUAGES: RETHINKING *LOGOS, OIKOS,* AND *TECHNÉ*

LYDIA H. LIU AND ANUPAMA RAO

There are visible disappearances and invisible disappearances, each demanding a different kind of attention. As the world becomes increasingly captivated by appearances and by advanced technologies that enable such appearances, high-resolution satellite pictures of Earth showing the ongoing effects of tropical deforestation and climate catastrophe never cease to shock us. Such images are powerful because they make things almost tangible, allowing reflection, critique, and action, while simultaneously presuming to be an objective picture of the world accessible or imaginable from the distance of outer space. Slipping below the radar screen, however, are a large number of invisible and silent disappearances; their traces are not readily available for thought or action, yet they have every reason to be included in the ongoing debates on climate change and environmental justice. We are speaking here of the lifeworld of languages whose stories of survival, death, and revival across the world's cultures may shine a new light on the ecological conditions of the planet and help reframe our conversation about what it means to talk about justice in planetary terms.

To speak of a lifeworld of languages is to take stock of the fact that ecological devastation aligns with the silent disappearance of thousands of human languages we are witnessing in our lifetime. It is to extend our awareness of crisis, catastrophe, and extinction, which typically attach to discussions about climate and ecology, to the situation in which many languages have already become extinct within the past several decades and thousands more are on their way to becoming marginal or superfluous to contemporary life. Working across scales to knit together different orders of explanation may provide coherence to our understanding of the complex distributions of cause and effect, action and reaction, structure and movement in our political present. To speak of a lifeworld of human languages is also to reckon with the persistence of injustice and with our conceptions of justice and their limitations: Can we demand language justice the way others have demanded environmental justice, economic justice, and social justice? Are these demands interlinked, conflictual, or interdependent at fundamental levels? If ethical imperatives compel people and governments to take responsibility for climate change, how is it possible not to reflect on the degradation of the humanity of a large number of marginalized communities that have been uprooted or forcibly removed from their habitats by the same forces of capitalist expansion, armed conflicts, and developmentalism that are destroying the living conditions of the planet?

The links among ecological degradation, mass displacement, involuntary human migration, and the loss of vibrant language communities began to attract urgent attention after UNESCO and the United Nations Permanent Forum on Indigenous Issues took on the task of monitoring the deteriorating processes. In 2016, the UN warned that no less than 40 percent of the roughly 6,700 languages of the world—Suzanne Romaine and others estimate up to 7,100+ languages—were in danger of disappearing in the twenty-first century.[1] Soon after, the UN moved to proclaim 2019 the International Year of Indigenous Languages and called on state and nonstate actors to take immediate action.[2] More recently, the General Assembly has launched the UN Global Task Force for Making a Decade of Action for Indigenous Languages and has formally announced the decade of 2022–2032 as the International Decade of the Indigenous Languages (IDIL2022–2032). Xing Qu, deputy director-general of UNESCO, explains that this task force is dedicated to "identifying concrete, long-term and sustainable measures to protect and promote indigenous languages in all levels of society" as the UN seeks to develop an international framework for inclusion, openness, participation, and multistakeholder engagement in the IDIL2022–2032.[3]

It must be pointed out, however, that in the decades leading up to the launch of the IDIL2022–2032, many international organizations, NGOs,

THE LIFEWORLD OF LANGUAGES: RETHINKING *LOGOS*, *OIKOS*, AND *TECHNÉ*

and activists had already developed standard-setting tools for the promotion and protection of Indigenous communities and their cultures. Some of these mechanisms—such as the Universal Declaration of Linguistic Rights (1996), the Universal Declaration on Cultural Diversity and its Action Plan (2001), the Convention for the Safeguarding of the Intangible Cultural Heritage (2003), the Recommendation Concerning the Promotion and Use of Multilingualism and Universal Access to Cyberspace (2003), and the Convention on the Protection and Promotion of the Diversity of Cultural Expressions (2005)— were designed specifically to protect linguistic diversity.[4] Unfortunately, many of these tools have not led to robust reinforcement of linguistic diversity or have found only extremely limited applications.[5] This could be attributed to the fact that the problems they are intended to address penetrate deeper than those with which we are equipped to cope, intellectually or legally—hence, the perceived need to reflect, reorient, and reframe the question of linguistic diversity in the midst of our planet's ecological catastrophe.

BEYOND LANGUAGE EXTINCTION

Our volume seeks to reflect on these pressing questions by investigating the lifeworld of languages—always in the plural—as being intrinsic to the larger ecological, political, and socioeconomic processes that cut across developed and developing societies. Rather than treating language as a tool of communication or a linguistic matter at the starting point of our discussion, even though languages can be analyzed in these ways, we are centrally concerned with the evolving and open-ended processes that have been central to how language communities come into being, disperse, intermingle, disappear, or revive and, conversely, with how the relationships among languages—never reducible to the speakers of particular languages, who might be bilingual, multilingual, or translingual—shape ecological, political, and socioeconomic processes. These may include, for example, discriminatory public policies, unjust social practices in education, and unequal distributions of language-based resources such as access to digital technology, health care, and social services in general.

Unlike biological diversity, linguistic diversity has been defended as a matter of democratic inclusiveness and egalitarianism, but the value of such diversity has not gone uncontested precisely on the ground of social justice.

4
THE LIFEWORLD OF LANGUAGES: RETHINKING *LOGOS, OIKOS,* AND *TECHNÉ*

Who is supposed to bear the cost of providing bilingual education or maintaining diversity for the benefit of all society? Furthermore, is linguistic diversity valuable in itself, or is it just one of the means to achieve something else we value?[6] In light of these questions, the relationship between linguistic diversity and the spread of a global lingua franca like English proves particularly vexing as we reexamine the ecological and technological infrastructure of that relationship through the lens of digital vitality. More critical, however, is the fundamental issue of whether the lifeworld of languages itself is worth sustaining—along with its diversity, multiplicity, messiness, and unpredictability—as the planet undergoes unprecedented ecological transformations. If the answer is yes, we must then articulate the implications of that worth clearly and coherently to be able to grasp the contours of a ravaged linguistic landscape that literally forces our attention to language death and language loss. In this book, we approach the task by seeking to develop a new set of concepts to address the fundamentals in the lifeworld of languages, focusing in particular on what has happened to the situation of *logos, oikos,* and *techné* in our times: namely, the growing entanglement of language, ecology/economy, and craft/technology with vital worldwide consequences.

Sociolinguistic and ethnographic studies have shown that the diversity of languages and species is heavily concentrated in the tropics, where animal and plant species are being lost at an exponential rate and where a large percentage of the world's languages are fast disappearing. The temptation to attribute the accelerated language extinctions to the forces defining the Anthropocene or the post-1945 Great Acceleration is undoubtedly strong, but in view of the available research, it strikes us as premature to consider the Anthropocene as a viable paradigm to explain the specific timeline of disappearing and extinct Indigenous languages until credible evidence emerges in favor of such an argument.[7]

In chapter 4, Wesley Leonard challenges the articulation of language extinction, a conclusion ironically reiterated by linguists and ethnographers who mourn the loss of languages but pay scant attention to the ceaseless transformation and adaptability of these languages through interaction with English, French, and other languages. Those who reflect on settler colonialism and language loss tend to romanticize a time when native languages existed as linguistic wholes and were somehow frozen in the past. In his analysis of the cultural practices relating to *myaamia*, the Indigenous language of the Miami people, Leonard suggests that as long as Native American language systems are reified in these terms, the dynamism that characterizes language reclamation as an essential aspect of broader claims to political selfhood and multicultural identity will continue to be ignored or denigrated as inauthentic. He writes: "If the language isn't allowed to change in order to reflect our contemporary circumstances as a multilingual and multicultural people, the reclamation sought by the Miami people truly might have only a 1 percent chance of occurring because we will have accepted the dominant discourse, which says our language is extinct and cannot change."

As has happened with other Native American languages, *myaamia* is experiencing a surprising resurgence precisely when the discourse of language loss and extinction is prevalent among the experts, indicating a redefinition of the relationships among history, power, and language is under way. Leonard argues that tropes of language purity must be challenged in favor of "recognizing and legitimizing 'newer' Miami practices, especially those that contain elements from the many other communities of practice to which Miami people belong." His essential contribution teaches us that the desire for (language) authenticity and policies of cultural extinction are connected logics that leave little room for recognizing Native American agency and creative exploration. Genocide, forced removal, and the retraining of the tongue are conjoint processes that structure both the politics of language reclamation, which has enabled the resurgence of *myaamia* today, and its inherent novelty as a linguistic form that is responsive to histories of encounter, violence, and cultural mixing: that is, the complex multicultural realities that shape contemporary Miami existence. Thus, Leonard insists on making a place for *modern Indigenous languages* as both sign and symptom of a powerful claim to Native Americans' historical existence and their flourishing in the contemporary world.

In that spirit, what we seek to do collectively in this book is to explore the transformative conditions of the lifeworld of languages in order to arrive at a clearer understanding of our current predicaments. Insofar as the conditions we examine are multiple, our book chooses to focus on the sites (and boundaries) of displacement and migration, refugee crises, and the megacity and its multilingualism as well as on the related questions of linguistic rights, the digital divide, and the legal and political institutions that impede or assist in the effort to meet these challenges on the ground.

That is to say, the focus of our book is not the endangerment of Indigenous languages and their reclamation, a task that others have pursued with vision, skill, and great courage, including many of our authors (Suzanne Romaine, David Kaufman, Ross Perlin, Wesley Leonard, and Deborah Anderson), who have done exemplary work in that regard. Rather, we are setting out to explore the contractionary yet interconnected loci of ecological and socioeconomic changes that accelerate the decline and death of Indigenous languages but that could also give rise to new possibilities through population movement, unexpected encounters, technological innovation, and social transformation. The new possibilities might include, for example, the arrival and gathering of Indigenous languages on the foreign shore, in megacities like New York and Mumbai. One might imagine a scenario where a child born in the summer of 2021 of refugee parents who fled from Kabul at the close of the twenty-year American war in Afghanistan would find herself settling down in New York City with her family. What would it take for a child like her to flourish like other, albeit more fortunate, American children of her generation? Would she grow up bilingual or translingual without fear, shame, or stigma attached to her parents' native tongue? With these questions in mind, we begin to touch on some of the core concerns this book attempts to bring to the fore.

To contemplate the goal of global language justice, one must begin by reflecting on the lifeworld of languages itself and trying to discern the patterns of its evolving transformations. To be precise, we have decided to frame the lifeworld of languages in the three distinct but intersecting registers of *logos*, *oikos*, and *techné* in a series of ongoing dialogues with philosophers, theorists of social justice, and language rights advocates as well as among the contributors to this volume. Although the discussions of *logos* and *oikos* are not unfamiliar to those who demand language justice and write about it in the tradition of Western legal and philosophical discourse, much more theoretical work is needed to articulate the *logos* and *oikos* to the exigency of *techné* in clear and robust terms, especially as we are confronted with a certain future where digital technology is becoming ubiquitous and indispensable to the sustainability of languages.

ON THE ECOLOGY OF LANGUAGES

Consider some of the well-known sociological explanations of language survival and decline. In the unequal relations that characterize human society, languages are closely bound up with social distinction, political rule, economic hierarchy, and the production of national/ethnic unities or divisions. With linguistic asymmetries traversing communities and nations, a dominant language can confer prestige on some groups, opening the door to economic opportunities and other social advantages, and can withhold it from others, especially from Indigenous and ethnic minority groups. It is not difficult to grasp, writes Nancy C. Dorian, why "speakers abandon their native tongue in adaptation to an environment where use of that language is no longer advantageous to them. This much about language death is simple and uncontroversial. The more complex, and thus obscure, issue is '*What* brings about the decreased efficacy of a language in a community?'"[8] This question is key. If language death is neither inevitable nor strictly correlated to the community's desire to adopt a language that offers more socioeconomic advantages than does their native tongue, this suggests that the sociological explanation of linguistic hierarchy and language death requires further explanation and historical elaboration.

When Indigenous peoples abandon their native tongue, whose efficacy has not been questioned for millennia, it often happens that they are also abandoning their ancestral habitat, though not necessarily by choice. Indigenous peoples become doubly exiled from their land/livelihood and from their language, and in the many cases we have examined, language loss cannot be separated from Indigenous peoples' escape, flight, and forced migration as a consequence of colonial dispossession, deforestation, war, or climate change.[9] With the recent discovery of hundreds of unmarked graves of children at Catholic Church–run boarding schools in Canada, the memories of how Indigenous children were subjected to cultural genocides have received renewed attention in mainstream media. The truth is that Indigenous peoples have never ceased to call for reckoning with their double losses of land/livelihood and language. When Clara Soaring Hawk, Deer Clan chief of the Ramapough Lenape Nation, officiated at the opening for the symposium Global Justice for Indigenous Languages held at Columbia University in the spring of 2018, she gave a blessing in both Lenape and English and asked her audience to remember the Lenape people on whose traditional land, Manhattan, Columbia University stands.[10] She and the other Indigenous speakers at the symposium told their personal stories of the double losses they have suffered in the United States and Canada. When these losses are scaled up to planetary portions, as they should be, the ecological implications of the global displacement of

Indigenous peoples become apparent. It is estimated that Indigenous peoples speak around 60 percent of the world's languages and live on lands containing about 80 percent of the world's biodiversity.[11] The entanglement of biodiversity and linguistic diversity suggests that the decline of the one will not leave the other intact, so it seems we can no longer ignore what has been happening to Indigenous communities as we confront the ecological disaster.

"Where have all the languages gone?" Daniel Nettle and Suzanne Romaine have raised the question in their investigation of how biodiversity and linguistic diversity cooccur in some of the most vulnerable areas of the planet's ecosystem. In *Vanishing Voices: The Extinction of the World's Languages*, these authors observe that languages are not self-sustaining and the causes of language death are not linguistic but must be sought elsewhere. "To understand why languages are born, and why they die, then, entails looking not just at the languages themselves, but at all aspects of the lives of the people who speak them."[12] This is where an ecological conception of language can help. Starting with the etymon *ecology*, which derives from the Greek root οἶκος or *oikos*, meaning "home," "house," or "household," Nettle and Romaine argue that "a language can only thrive to the extent that there is a functioning community speaking it, and passing it on from parent to child at home. A community can only function where there is a decent environment to live in, and a sustainable economic system."[13] The logic of their argument seems obvious enough; yet not so obvious is the implied notion that our conception of language should be regrounded in the *oikos*, not exclusively in the λόγος or *logos*, as is commonly the case when people debate the meaning of words and concepts in discourse.

And what does this regrounding mean for an ecology of languages? It means that the *oikos* and *logos* must be reordered and reworked to allow for a concept of ecology capacious enough to reconnect the livelihood and economic well-being of a community's members back to the languages they speak as they navigate their environment. This is especially urgent for speakers of Indigenous languages trying to survive in precarious conditions and applies to other small-language groups and immigrant communities as well. Until we recognize the profound indebtedness of the *logos* to the *oikos*, many of the vital connections and interdependencies in the lifeworld of languages will remain invisible. The moment we begin to make the philosophical move of rearticulating the *logos* to the *oikos* in this order

THE LIFEWORLD OF LANGUAGES: RETHINKING *LOGOS*, *OIKOS*, AND *TECHNÉ*

(to which we will add a third element, *techné*, in the discussion of digital vitality later), formerly obscure connections and, in particular, those hiding in plain sight emerge into view. For example, the "economic" in Nettle and Romaine's "sustainable economic system" will be rearticulated, more than ever before, to the *eco-* in *ecology* not least because these terms share the same original etymon *oikos*; more important, the rearticulation raises the genuine possibility of transforming the very idea of economy to make it relevant again to people's livelihood in their original environment or in their newly adopted homes. It is the task of our book to render the obscure and rising connections between *oikos* and *logos* visible, audible, and tangible for reflection, critique, and action.

In chapter 2, Romaine undertakes precisely such a task, as do our other authors in this book. Is a sustainable economic system practical or conceivable without reckoning with the reality of the world's linguistic diversity? The answer is no. Reworking Kate Raworth's conceit of doughnut economics or the planetary model for the twenty-first century, Romaine reinserts the missing link of language in the doughnut hole to demonstrate the ways linguistic diversity, as encouraged by multilingual language policies in education, can be central to the goals of social justice and inclusive economic growth. This is made abundantly clear by her critical reassessment of the unfulfilled promises of the ambitious UN Millennium Development Goals and Education for All Goals as well as the other major international agendas that are attempting to combat extreme poverty, poor health, lack of education, and the deteriorating environment. Romaine observes a strong overlap between the geographies of educational disadvantage and linguistic diversity, where the most linguistically diverse countries host 72 percent of out-of-school children worldwide. Citing research on Africa, she warns that future education that relies mainly on international languages at the expense of local vernaculars and Indigenous languages will end up reproducing rather than reducing inequalities and could lead to pernicious consequences, if not total failure, in the attempt to achieve the goals of public health, legal protection, and human rights.

Today, few people will deny that equal access to education is fundamental to the flourishing of modern society, but some will contest the centrality of linguistic diversity in social justice programs and even view it as an obstacle to development in the Third World. In her book *Linguistic Diversity and Social Justice*, Ingrid Piller observes that in social science studies, there is always a way of positing negative correlation between the number of sizable language groups and a country's gross domestic product that favors the idea that the greater a country's linguistic diversity, the greater its poverty. When searching for a practical solution to bring its population out of poverty and create job opportunities, that country will therefore vastly prefer a policy of linguistic assimilation over one of diversity. In response to this calculus of cost and benefit, Piller offers an astute analysis: "The fact that high levels of linguistic diversity and disadvantage co-occur does not mean that there is a causal relationship between the two nor does it mean that changing the language variable toward linguistic assimilation will have the desired development outcomes."[14] Her own research suggests that the negative correlation turns out to be a self-fulfilling prophecy, where the link between the dominant language—such as Global English—and socioeconomic development has actively been pursued to promote neoliberal capitalist agendas. What happens on the ground is that a link becomes "causal" and most effective when developmental aids and other financial resources are diverted to the promotion of English-language learning in conjunction with the socioeconomic programs and initiatives of the West.

Looking at the economic aid practices and other assistance to the Third World, we begin to glimpse a partial answer to Dorian's earlier question: "*What* brings about the decreased efficacy of a language in a community?" Take Cambodia, for example. Stephen Clayton's study shows that external aid spending began to prioritize English-language teaching over basic literacy education in the 1990s, the consequence being that English quickly became indispensable for accessing foreign intervention in the form of donors and international aid. UN organizations like the United Nations Transitional Authority provided foreign aid in the Thai-Cambodia border region to run refugee camps and programs in reconstruction, development, and democratization. These aid agencies poured millions of dollars in English-language teaching aid into Cambodia even as the majority of the adult population was mired in poverty and could not enjoy basic literacy education.[15] Bear in mind that this neoliberal model of development has been replicated in many parts of the world, where targeted investment in English-language teaching aid is deemed essential rather than superfluous to the economic aid packages from the West. What it suggests is that the linguistic divide has not been separated nor is it separable from the economic divide, often to the detriment of Indigenous languages and their environment.

THE LIFEWORLD OF LANGUAGES: RETHINKING *LOGOS, OIKOS,* AND *TECHNÉ*

Neoliberal developmentalism has presented unique challenges to linguistic diversity that go beyond the global spread of English—a subject we will take up later—to include the illusion of linguistic choice, where the conditions of one's choice are invariably left out of the calculus. Be it violent colonial dispossession, military conflict, predatory capitalism, or neoliberal foreign intervention, these conditions are always discursive and always already language specific in the sense that they involve a mode of address in time and place to articulate, transform, or remold relations of power among different groups of people. There is not much room for choice when one (dominant) language group enters into a discursive relationship with another to the point of dictating what they can possibly say and do to each other or what language one must learn to speak in order to adjudicate matters of vital concern. In times of ecological devastation and climate change, this mode of address could jeopardize an Indigenous community's chances of survival in relation to what is left of their land, water, forest, and other resources.

This brings us back to the idea of rearticulating the *logos* to the *oikos* in the effort to reframe language death and language loss as a problem of economy and ecology. It is important, however, that our engagement with the problem be dialectical as well as critical so as not to lose sight of transformative possibilities, for the lifeworld of languages is not only planetary in scale but also dynamic in time and place. In conjunction with language loss, we have been witnessing a steep upsurge in border crossings and migrations by Indigenous peoples and other vulnerable populations uprooted and displaced by political and socioeconomic forces and ecological devastation to their livelihood. In 2008, the UN estimated there were 16 million displaced people, and that figure jumped almost fourfold in 2015. By the end of 2021, more than 89.3 million people fled their homes, of which 27.1 million were refugees and 4.6 million were asylum seekers, according to *Global Trends: Forced Displacement in 2021*, a report of the UN Refugee Agency.[16] Today, the 50 million climate-displaced people outnumber those fleeing political persecution. The UN International Organization for Migration estimates that 1.5 billion people could be forced to leave their homes over the next thirty years, whereas other scientific projections put the number of environmental migrants at 3 billion by 2070, after the global population reaches its predicted peak.[17] This developing situation is going to have immeasurable impact on multiple fronts because, in their flight to the foreign shore, refugees and Indigenous peoples face intensified struggles for access to educational resources, technologies, legal protection, and social goods, raising a different set of issues than does the crisis of endangered languages.

The massive movement of Indigenous peoples and immigrants around the globe suggests a need for us to reflect on how the *logos* is rearticulated to the *oikos* time and again in dynamic and changing multilingual situations and how, for instance, asylum seekers, refugees, and displaced ethnic minorities cope with the silences, invisibility, monolingualism, nonrecognition, racism, and other discriminatory practices. For instance, Tommaso Manfredini devotes his chapter in this volume to investigating the struggles in asylum adjudication processes on the borders of the EU member states. His research raises the issue of linguistic recognition and shows how nonrecognition can compromise the integrity of international legal procedures. From his writing, we learn that the crucial first step in the asylum application is to establish a credible narrative, during which the asylum seeker presents oral testimony that is taken down, translated, and transcribed in the language of the host country. Manfredini's research indicates that this process is extremely fraught, as asylum seekers hail from such diverse linguistic and geographic backgrounds that some languages or dialects cannot even be identified or named and some topographic boundaries remain unmarked on commonly used maps. Nevertheless, the politics of translation renders the languages of asylum seekers transparent and invisible to the judicial authority that itself remains monolingual.

Manfredini's work raises two important questions with regard to language and social justice in general: First, what are the linguistic conditions governing access to legal protection? Second, can justice be imagined in the absence of linguistic diversity? People who work at the front lines of refugee crises or asylum assistance, including activists, translators, and those representing NGOs and international organizations, are likely to assert that justice will not be achieved in the absence of linguistic diversity. However, these questions, especially that about the linguistic conditions governing legal access to justice, cannot be sufficiently addressed through experience alone, as they both touch on the fundamental premises of political philosophy concerning human rights, equality, and nondiscrimination. The notion of linguistic rights in particular has been evoked regularly to justify the legal protection of minority languages and linguistic diversity, but it has encountered numerous difficulties, including repeated failure to find support in courts of law. Is this notion sufficiently defensible or conceptually coherent to play a role in maintaining linguistic diversity? Is the value of linguistic diversity itself self-evident? What options exist to challenge English dominance and monolinguality? These questions are explored by L. Maria Bo, Madeleine Dobie, and David Kaufman and Ross Perlin in their chapters.

DIVERSITY, EQUALITY, JUSTICE

Regulatory regimes, with their power to name, define, categorize, enumerate, and, ultimately, include and exclude, function as a bridge between the social critique of language hierarchies, on the one hand, and efforts to sustain language communities as a cultural resource, on the other. Manfredini's analysis of the failures of linguistic commensuration at the European border alerts us to the power of law in framing models of redress. The objectifying power of the law is secured through iterative practices of petitioning, testifying, and narrating. The failure to narrate produces a bureaucratic crisis for those within the asylum adjudication process. Meanwhile, it activates another sort of existential crisis about loss, displacement, and belonging for asylum seekers and refugees, who routinely confront unfamiliar legal regimes and police powers at the border.

In their research, Kaufman and Perlin suggest that identificatory practices are inherently comparative and hierarchical. Within the United States, for example, both the U.S. Census and the American Community Survey address linguistic diversity through the prism of English as a developmental norm: English is the public language of civic intercourse and the unspoken standard against which other languages and dialects are measured. Kaufman and Perlin go on to offer a powerful critique of how the reification of the idea of *language* enables models of linguistic diversity that merely confirm dominant distinctions among language, dialect, slang, and Indigenous languages. Though bureaucratic models of language diversity are ultimately tautologous, they adjudicate definitions of language and linguistic rights. In the process, they miss out on the everyday practices of translanguaging, on encounters of mutual intelligibility that reflect language justice in action. (We will return to this issue of creative responses to linguistic enclaving and nonrecognition later.)

In matters of legislation, recognition of linguistic diversity prioritizes the plurality and flourishing of languages, whereas ideas about equal treatment attach to the rights of language speakers. The protection of linguistic diversity is more akin to demands for the recognition of difference that secures commitments to multiculturalism in Western democracies. Although multiculturalism privileges diversity as a common good and commits to the equal protection of difference, it does so without necessarily committing to eradicating inequality arising from *historical relations* of domination, subordination, and hierarchy. Demands for equality, however, often attach to the differential treatment of language speakers who suffer marginalization and discrimination that denies them access to social services and other public goods, whether it is the right to bilingual education, interpreters, adequate housing, or medical care, due to their inability (or their refusal) to communicate in the dominant language. The equality principle, too, faces a tension between individual and group rights, which troubles liberal theories of rights derived from models of individual freedom and autonomy. Anxieties about group recognition occupy a spectrum—from fears about political polarization and identitarian politics to concerns about democratic functioning within groups.

However, clarifying the difference between ideas of linguistic diversity, which privilege discourses of protection and focus on the sheer multiplicity of communicative cultures, and the democratic commitment to equal rights is a useful first step. It explains the confusion of categories that often prevails in legal contexts when linguistic rights are refused or foreclosed. Are nonnormative language cultures in jeopardy, or do the *users* of those languages suffer social discrimination and political marginalization? What form of collective rights is being demanded? Animating this paradox is an underlying tension between viewing language as fundamental to being human (human beings as communicative animals if you will) versus our understanding of language as the (collective) resource of communities. As a subset of human rights, linguistic rights are embedded in a strained understanding of the relationship between language and human existence, where language is both an object of protection and that which is constitutive of the human subject. Our current conjuncture, which is characterized by the ongoing disappearance of minority and Indigenous languages as a consequence of environmental and economic crises of scale, brings the two ideas about language into close proximity and demands their mutual resolution.

THE LIFEWORLD OF LANGUAGES: RETHINKING *LOGOS*, *OIKOS*, AND *TECHNÉ*

The situation of ongoing crisis and imminent catastrophe explains the belated attention to linguistic rights *as such* that is articulated by the 1996 Universal Declaration of Linguistic Rights (UDLR), which was ratified in Barcelona by PEN International. In chapter 1, Bo takes a critical look at the work of PEN International as it seeks to protect marginalized writers and argue for their autonomy and right to freedom from censorship. Over 220 linguists, lawyers, writers, and activists representing ninety states, five continents, and over forty languages came together under its auspices to ratify the UDLR, which establishes that linguistic rights include the right to "the use of one's own language both in private and in public," the right to "maintain and develop one's own culture," and the right "of an equitable presence of their language and culture in the communications media" of any given territory (Article 3.1–3.2). From the start, linguistic rights were conceived in a broad manner, covering everything from instrumental ideas about communication to poetry, art, and works of imagination. Bo reminds us that there is a longer history to the protection of linguistic rights as an essential aspect of human dignity and the inalienable rights of all persons, including the 1992 Declaration on the Rights of Persons Belonging to National or Ethnic, Religious and Linguistic Minorities; the 1950 European Convention on Human Rights; and even the 1948 Universal Declaration of Human Rights itself. She notes that even though they mention linguistic rights as an aspect of minority protections, none of these documents "fully defines linguistic rights or focuses on what their significance is and what they entail."

The international human rights regime has developed in much the same manner that the British sociologist T. H. Marshall noted in his 1950 lecture "Citizenship and Social Class." There Marshall described the development of civil, political, and social citizenship within nation-states as an evolutionary sequence, each an expansion of rights en route to substantive equality, starting with suffrage and equal protection before the law but culminating in ideas about social citizenship as the right to economic security and cultural well-being.[18] If we have arrived at linguistic rights as the logical entailment of a longer-term global history of human rights, this is because human rights are themselves conditioned by the philosophy of rights and its history that had roots in a classic liberal model of rights to autonomy and private property that form the basis of social contract theory, but that is today radically transformed by demands for group rights, whether religious rights, protection of sexual identities, or respectful recognition of language communities.

Now, the rational, speaking subject forms the basis of contract theories predicated on the individual's right to own property through the fruits of their own labor. Indeed, property ownership functions as the organizing template for the imagination of rights. This is why children, mentally ill persons, enslaved persons, women, and other of various races were initially precluded from the imagination of (individual) rights and autonomy. At the heart of the fiction of contract lies the individual capable of entering into contract. However, as Bo notes, an individuated model of rights relies ultimately on "a linguistic reality, deeply tied to communication and relationship with others—rather than a purely individual, rational reality—that determines the natural locus of rights in human society." Not for nothing is the idea of contract qualified by the term *social*: being in language with others is at the origins of the individual's right to consent to the social contract. This is the fundamental instability at the heart of contract theory itself.

Modern commentators on liberal thought puzzle over the extension of rights to the collective. Or else they seek to undercut the original predication of rights on the right to property through territorial enclosure via one's labor. (Lockean liberalism assumes the link between labor and the enclosure of private property.) That is, many political philosophers today seek to unthink the troubling porosity of property and personhood that lies at the heart of the liberal rights regime. At the same time, they are uncomfortable with Marxist critiques of private ownership of property and the political means to challenge it through the revolutionary struggles and activism of the working classes.

As an alternative, Dobie discusses the model of deliberative democracy as a rich resource for rethinking democratic rights. In, chapter 6, she focuses on the work of the political philosopher Seyla Benhabib as a way to think about language processually, where "regular collective deliberation conducted rationally and fairly among equal individuals can determine what is in the common interest more flexibly and with greater nuance than a model in which the state is charged with interpreting and enforcing a corpus of rights. In addition, rather than steering people toward the defense of their rights, open public discussion informs them about other points of view and makes room for changes of opinion." Dobie notes that "deliberative

THE LIFEWORLD OF LANGUAGES: RETHINKING *LOGOS, OIKOS,* AND *TECHNÉ*

democracy raises its own set of questions, not least of which is how to achieve the conditions of free, fair, and rational discussion." For example, Benhabib's model of deliberation is itself indebted to the idea of the communicative subject (and of communicative action) as outlined by someone like Habermas. Deliberation presumes that we are all on the same page with regard to our ideas of social etiquette, civil discourse, and equal dialogue. Interpersonal communication is imagined as transparent and smooth, without the speed bumps introduced by the actual act of translation.

However, translation is neither transparent nor transactional: it is never merely a matter of finding equivalents for words and concepts between languages, since no language exists as a signifying whole. In their attention to translanguaging and communicative acts that prioritize mutual intelligibility, Kaufman and Perlin discuss practices of "making do," of inhabiting multiple language communities simultaneously across language and dialect in a city like New York. Like Laura Kurgan, they are practitioners of mapping as an alternative mode of visualization, which allows us to see how displaced communities, refugees, asylum seekers, and survivors of political and ecological violence are reshaping the world as well as cities like New York. Kurgan describes the transformative effects of making people see the planetary consequence of forced migration and climate crisis in a museum context as an act of engaged pedagogy and an act of creative border crossing.

In chapter 5, Kaufman and Perlin note that in New York, these same linguistic communities that have been displaced by mass violence, economic crisis, and environmental degradation undergo a sort of spatial compression. This requires them to live cheek by jowl with other groups that are similarly vulnerable and violated through acts of friendship, agonistic intimacy, or sheer indifference. Language loss in one part of the world is met by formation of hybrid linguistic communities elsewhere. One of their important findings is that more than seven hundred languages are spoken at least by one individual in the New York metropolitan area. These hybrid linguistic communities engage the state in one language, mobilize a standardized dialect to communicate with members from their own nation-states in other contexts, and retain fugitive practices of language use and innovation in yet other situations. Deploying strategic essentialism of this sort is a tool of survival. It is an index of linguistic vitality and an important example of translation under conditions of political and economic precarity.

The late political theorist Iris Marion Young has argued that debates about group rights tend to convert questions of historical injustice, which are essentially political questions, into demands for distributive justice predicated on perfecting policy design.[19] She goes on to state that this functions as a form of depoliticization. However, we might explore the idea of group rights in a slightly different manner. Dobie's chapter offers a rich meditation on the politics of multilinguality in this regard. The concept of group rights approaches identity in one of two ways: as either *relational* or *embodied*. That is, there are aspects of personhood that evoke repulsion, violence, and social exclusion, while other acts of exclusion are contextual. This tension captures social contradictions at the discursive level, where "the terms of exclusion on which discrimination is premised are at once refused and reproduced in the demands for inclusion."[20] Simply put, this involves emphasizing race to undo racial exclusion, to speak as an "untouchable" to demand the annihilation of caste, or to speak in the mother tongue in order to claim language rights. We should recall that this relationship between embodied and relational identities has different consequences for law and for politics: courts typically require making compelling arguments in standard legal language to succeed, while demands for rights and recognition in the public sphere reprise political agonism in creative and productive ways.

The politics of colonization/decolonization is complexly ramified and connected to the rights (and the public presence) of language communities in Algeria. In her chapter, Dobie views the practice of language justice through the resignification of linguistic practice as well as the established hierarchies of French, Modern Standard Arabic (*fusha*), a regional Arabic dialect (*darija*), and Amazigh or Berber dialects (which tend to predominate in the Algerian diaspora in France), as these occurred during the prodemocracy movement, or *hirak*, that began in February 2019. She argues that "colonial dynamics" have "undoubtedly shaped the depiction of the Amazigh and Kabyle movements as cosmopolitan and secular and the countervailing depiction of the Algerian state, and to some extent the Arabic language, as provincial and Islamic." However, it is the *recalibration* of those hierarchies that is noteworthy. Dobie's close and careful reading of the *hirak* as an ongoing event reveals its capacity to reshuffle the logic of political competition between Arabs and Berbers and their differential relationship to France and to French. By rejecting party identity and the commitment to any one political ideology, the *hirak* inaugurates struggle without end as the means and ends of contemporary politics. The fact that the movement's signs and symbols are truly polyvocal and take recourse to multi- and translingual forms of protest suggests a novel conception of embodied and relational identities, with the practice of group formation as both ephemeral and episodic. Again, translation moves across political stasis, desedimenting the signs and symbols through linguistic innovation and the production of new forms.

In her discussion of translation as practice and as method, Bo suggests that the idea of equal rights in our existing multilingual world hinges on the prospect that equivalent concepts can be found or created in another tongue. Drawing on the work of the Native American philosopher Vine Deloria Jr., Bo submits the concept of *equal rights* to the multilingual test as she seeks to illustrate the irreconcilable tensions in our reliance on equal rights to argue for linguistic justice.[21] Does diversity contradict equality? If so, this contradiction would be difficult to resolve. Even where collectives are deemed as stable rights-bearers, the concept of rights runs the danger of reifying the groups as much as it protects them. The historical trajectory of different communities, with their own experiences of precarity and marginalization, means that one might need to think of different ways to parse the problem of equality for diverse linguistic communities: parity across difference, rather than a model of competing equalities, might be required for the robust practice of language justice. In translation, we are borne across the boundaries of language, subjecting ourselves to alterity, incommensurability, and radical difference in ways that cannot easily be made equivalent. We are reminded of Manu Devadevan's spare translation of the medieval verse "The Vachanas"—printed in this volume—as an act of poesis across the social divide. The verse of subaltern worlding has brought the everyday language of the laboring classes and castes or the worldly language of artisans, peasants, and prostitutes into view. Here the articulation of the everyday and the philosophical achieves a momentary exuberance in the radical suture of hand, voice, and head.

DIGITAL VITALITY

Looking beyond the second decade of the twenty-first century, it is no longer possible for us to speak of linguistic diversity without confronting something we all know: namely, English has emerged as the global lingua franca of our times. This recent transformation, though deeply rooted in the colonial history of the British Empire, bears some distinct hallmarks of postwar American technocratic and military/industrial dominance on the planet. In our earlier discussion, we briefly touched on some aspects of this transformation during the U.S.-led export of neoliberal growth models to Third World countries, where millions of foreign aid dollars were poured into English-language teaching by international agencies at the expense of basic literacy programs in local languages. This is not an isolated case in Cambodia or in other war-torn developing nations but has had reverberations with vast consequences across international commerce, education, scientific research, technological innovation, financial investment, popular media, global affairs, and much more.

Not only has the worldwide demand for English kept pace with the opening of neoliberal capitalist markets over the past several decades, but also their mutual reinforcement is buttressed by the explosion of for-profit education markets where English-language learning has evolved into one of the most lucrative global industries. In China alone, the English-language training market was valued at $48.4 billion in 2021 and is estimated to grow to $119.2 billion in 2026, with incremental growth worth $70.8 billion in five years.[22] The New Oriental Education and Technology Group, a leading private tutoring company in China founded in 1993, went from 800,000 students enrolled in its English classes in 2005 to a staggering 10.6 million students in 2020, and the company was worth $11 billion on the eve of Beijing's sweeping clampdown on private tutoring services in July 2021.[23] On the other hand, in India, the historical association of English as the language of command and its ongoing association with caste and class privilege mean that access to English has long constituted the dividing line between inherited privilege and aspiration. In the complex multilingual contexts that obtain across southern Asia, one finds oneself confronting two sets of interlinked demands for language justice: demands to undo the dominance of English versus the other national languages and to support minority and Indigenous languages, languages without script, regional dialects, and so forth. The social politics of language is such that Dalit and lower-caste communities have prioritized learning English to effect a detour around associations between language, caste, class, and identity. The fact that desire for English is rarely complemented by access to learning English has resulted in a phenomenal rise in charlatan enterprises that claim to teach English, promising lucrative jobs at call centers and success in the civil service examinations at exorbitant prices. The retreat of the state from primary and secondary education and the ruinous infrastructure of government schools have reprised casted logics of access to English, which has come to be viewed instrumentally as an access route to livelihood and survival and as an escape from historical discrimination and the daily humiliations of caste.

In these contexts, the calculus of cost and benefit with respect to the value of linguistic diversity—i.e., who should bear the cost of multilingual education, in the abstract—sounds a little hollow because the question, however reasonable, is already skewed and contaminated by the massive investments that have been dedicated to English-language training for decades. On this extremely uneven playing field, we believe that the calculus of cost and benefit is part of the problem rather than a starting point for any discussion of linguistic diversity, the global lingua franca, and justice.

Nevertheless, one must be careful about imputing causal links between the simultaneous rise of English as a lingua franca and the decline of Indigenous languages. One thing we have learned about the politics of language in world history is that the shift in lingua franca has occurred not just once but many times across Europe, Asia, and other parts of the world since antiquity. Interestingly, there is no evidence to suggest that the arrival of each new lingua franca occasioned massive language deaths or led to the decline of linguistic diversity. Even in the face of modern ethnonationalism, which insists on building ethnic identities on the basis of a shared language or dialect, linguistic diversity has coexisted for a long time with either a regional lingua franca or a global lingua franca in India, China, Europe, Africa, the Americas, and indeed the entire world, where multilingualism, not monolingualism, has been the norm rather than the exception.[24] So the real question in our current predicament is not whether we should want a global lingua franca or should resist it, but rather where Global English stands in relation to linguistic diversity and to the lifeworld of languages in general.

Philippe Van Parijs has analyzed the tensions between linguistic diversity and the global lingua franca in the context of his extensive research on the ascendance of English as a lingua franca in Europe and on the EU language policies on multilingualism and linguistic diversity. Responding to the widespread fear that the adoption of English as a lingua franca could pose a threat to the pursuit of social justice across diverse linguistic communities, he concedes the point but argues that the solution cannot be a defensive retreat to "shrill whispering in provincial dialects"; instead, nonnative speakers of English should grab the "global megaphone" unapologetically and bend the instrument to their own purpose.[25] This is based, of course, on the assumption that the speakers share his normative premise that justice must be conceived as global egalitarian justice across multilingual entities, not at the level of small monolingual nation-states. One of the difficulties he notes, however, is that "the megaphone cannot be connected directly to the domestic wiring. They will need to keep switching linguistic codes as they move back and forth between domestic and international audiences."[26] This is an interesting point. Van Parijs might be speaking in metaphors when he refers to the megaphone, wiring, and code switching, but in our view, these are more than fortuitous figures of speech. Whether he intended it or not, the metaphors place Global English squarely in the realm of information technology, and this curious conjunction inadvertently reveals the limitations of *lingua franca* as a concept. We must unpack the idea to understand where Global English stands in relation to information technology.

People have long understood the lingua franca as a language used for communication among people who speak mutually unintelligible mother tongues. The examples they often use to illustrate this include Latin in medieval Europe, Spanish in Latin America, English or Hindi in modern India, and Mandarin in modern China.[27] Today, English appears to be assuming this role in the world, but the differences are significant enough to warrant not thinking of Global English as a mere case of lingua franca. It is not by accident that Global English often operates on the basis of human-machine interfaces and code switches in a literal sense, and its technological advantage is not the same thing as unmediated and face-to-face communication in English-speaking countries, former British colonies, and scientific communities.[28] The question we raised earlier as to where Global English stands in relation to linguistic diversity touches only tangentially on the role of the lingua franca in Van Parijs's sense of the global megaphone.

Among the areas of the world where the English language is not spoken as a lingua franca is East Asia. Here modern Mandarin, Japanese, and Korean are the lingua francas on mainland China, Japan, and Korea, respectively.

The writing systems of these countries use a block script called the *Hanzi*, which are coded in Unicode as the CJK characters for computer use. This means that the *Hanzi* script has a digital presence in Unicode, and it also means that the script is both subordinated to the imperial infrastructure of information technology and enabled to thrive in the digital world. This sort of contradiction is familiar, and it runs through nearly all discourses of inclusion, equality, and justice and must be confronted, as we have done in our analysis of group rights, where the demand for inclusion may at the same time refuse and reproduce the terms of exclusion on which discrimination is based. What Isabelle Zaugg calls the "double-edged sword" of digital inclusion in chapter 8 points exactly to this predicament.

What we wish to emphasize, though, is that Global English would not be what it is today without the support of an elaborate infrastructure of information technology that enables it to do what it does with efficiency while denying the same privilege to most other languages. For this reason, we need to engage in a sustained discussion of the global digital divide and ask that such a discussion happen, first and foremost, at the level of technological infrastructure. Insofar as this book is concerned, the technological infrastructure of informatics is the first step in our exploration of how the digital divide affects the state of linguistic diversity in our hypermediated and hyperconnected world. The contributions by Deborah Anderson and Zaugg are bringing some of these issues into sharp focus, and their work on script encoding, digital presence, and the possibility of digital vitality is pushing our understanding of linguistic diversity and the global lingua franca in a new direction.

In her work on script encoding, Anderson brings up the issue of digital presence and argues that the digital presence of a language is crucial, if not necessary, for its linguistic survival in the contemporary world. And what is digital presence? At the infrastructural level, it means that the script of a given language is included in Unicode and that fonts and keyboards are designed accordingly and made available to users who can easily type, search, and send written materials across the platforms. At the present moment, Unicode is the most widely accepted information technology standard for the consistent encoding and representation of text in the world's scripts. If a language does not have a digital presence in Unicode, younger generations in that language community will be prevented from using its script on digital devices, and in time, that could lead to what some critics call digital language death.[29] But before going further into a discussion of digital presence, we must address some conceptual distinctions with respect to script, language, and code.

In ordinary parlance, people use the terms *script* and *alphabet* interchangeably, which can generate some confusion, and this confusion tends to be exacerbated by yet more levels of confusion, such as that between *script* and *writing*, that between *language* and *writing*, or even that between *word* and its (written) *image*—all of which run deeper than most of us realize.[30] Without having made an effort to grasp these basic distinctions and their relationships, what script encoding does for Unicode and why this is important for information technology are likely to elude our understanding completely.

To clear up the initial confusion, we simply note that there are fewer scripts in the world than there are writing systems and that writing systems are language specific, whereas scripts typically are not. For instance, when ancient Greeks adapted the conventional Phoenician Semitic consonantal alphabet and Cypriote syllabary to their spoken language, what they had imported into Greek was not a writing system but rather foreign scripts out of which they created their own writing system. The Devanagari script is used in India for a variety of languages, such as Hindi, Nepali, and Marathi; alternatively, Hindi and Urdu are virtually the same spoken language, but Hindi is written in Devanagari script, whereas Urdu is written in Perso-Arabic script.[31] Anderson has noted in her chapter that the Santali language of India and surrounding countries can be written in several scripts: Bangla, Devanagari, Latin, Odia, and Ol Chiki. The Hanzi script is another case of a script that has been adopted over the millennia—here used to create multiple writing systems across Asia, such as Japanese, classical Korean, and Vietnamese, along with other scripts and writing systems still used in mainland China. Yet its fortunes began to plummet in favor of the Latin/Roman script in the early twentieth century when it came under attack during the Romaji movement in Japan and the vigorous romanization and latinization campaigns in China.[32] Unlike in Turkey, Vietnam, and other countries where the script conversion ultimately succeeded in eradicating the old scripts and remaking their writing systems in the image of Latin/Roman script, the latter never took hold sufficiently in Japan and China to remold their original writing systems, although it does have a presence there—and certainly a digital presence.[33]

THE LIFEWORLD OF LANGUAGES: RETHINKING *LOGOS*, *OIKOS*, AND *TECHNÉ*

In the course of Christian evangelization and European colonialism, the Latin or Roman script was adapted to the writing systems of a vast number of languages across Africa, Asia, and the Americas. That history has simultaneously propelled a powerful and enduring theory of evolutionary development that places so-called primitive pictographic, syllabic, and ideographic scripts at the bottom of the universal linguistic hierarchy while obscuring the process whereby the phonetic alphabet itself evolved into one of the dominant imperial technologies. The critique of phonocentrism by philosopher Jacques Derrida has helped dismantle the metaphysical ground of logocentrism in the Western philosophical tradition, although strangely his deconstructionist privileging of writing ends up leaving the *techné* of script—along with its multilingual historicity and materiality—unaccounted for.[34] As can be seen, what we are trying to develop in this book is a novel theoretical framework that can better explain how the *logos* articulates to the *oikos*, on the one hand, and to the *techné* (script making included), on the other. This is not to privilege *techné* or any of the other terms for the sake of theory but to call attention to the technological infrastructure of script making and to the political struggles surrounding their multilingual stakes. One of the questions that follow in the wake of deconstruction is how informatics and digital media have transformed the phonetic alphabet from the earlier mistaken notion of visual representation (of speech sounds) to that of universally applicable technological code capable of transcending all languages. Hence, we need to explore the *techné* of script making and its implications for the life and death of many languages.

It is in the expansion of the American Empire after World War II and in the advent of its information technologies that we begin to observe how the English alphabet became consolidated as the universal code of communication systems. Claude Shannon, the pioneering information theorist, was responsible for inventing what he called "Printed English," which he used interchangeably with "statistical English" as he laid the mathematical foundation for the information machine. His invention helped introduce a profound distinction between the English language as a global lingua franca and Printed English/Global English as script technology.[35] The failure to grasp this historical distinction is what has led to much of the confusion surrounding Global English, which cannot easily be resolved through redefinitions. In our own usage, we will leave the vague notion of a global lingua franca behind and maintain the historical distinction as outlined here. That is to say, we will restrict the sense of Global English to Shannon's Printed English for the purpose of reexamining the role of script in the technological infrastructure of informatics as well as the challenges it poses to the future of linguistic diversity.

In order to explore the technological infrastructure of informatics and its implications for linguistic diversity, it is impossible not to take note of Unicode. When the first version of Unicode was published in 1993, it accommodated only 23 scripts. There has been steady progress in the inclusion of minority scripts, and by 2022, Unicode version 15.0 published as many as 161 scripts, although Anderson estimates that over 140 scripts are yet to be included. The Script Encoding Initiative, a project she founded at the University of California, Berkeley, in 2002, responds to requests to prepare proposals to encode scripts and script elements not yet supported in Unicode. These requests tend to come from language communities that want a digital presence for their scripts, many of which are minority scripts from southern Asia, Africa, and the Middle East. The examples in Anderson's chapter show how incorporating a script into Unicode has increased the representation of the languages that use it in the digital realm, and this occasionally leads to the revitalization of Indigenous languages, as illustrated by Osage script. The new script of the Osage Nation, published in Unicode in 2016, has enabled members of this Native American community to navigate the digital world using an Osage font and keyboard. Leonard has discussed the *s*-wedge (š), a symbol in *myaamia* that does not exist on QWERTY keyboards even though the Indigenous language adopted the Roman script. It represents a voiceless postalveolar fricative and is written as *sh* in English orthography. American Indians who use *myaamia* have resorted to substituting the dollar sign for the *s*-wedge in computer-mediated communication.

In that sense, the digital presence of individual scripts may be taken as a measure of our unspoken assumptions about whose lives and languages actually matter in social life, online and offline. However, even after the script of a digitally disadvantaged language achieves a formal presence in Unicode, it still encounters formidable difficulty on multiple fronts for being a low-resource language. Zaugg explains in her chapter that languages are classified as digital resources in natural language processing and are ranked from high to low. Her study of the digital vitality of Ethiopian and Eritrean languages shows that speakers of low-resource languages must make some difficult choices that their counterparts speaking high-resource languages with robust digital corpora never have to face. She argues further that while digital inclusion provides benefits to language communities that have been historically marginalized and excluded, the same digital tools designed to support a language can also be used to surveil and coerce its speaker communities and endanger those who face displacement, state-sanctioned violence, and criminalization.

Those are some of the contradictory conditions of life that users of low-resource languages are experiencing on a daily basis and know intimately well. It seems that the social contradictions we have been discussing thus far—like equality and diversity, inclusion and exclusion, legibility and illegibility, and vitality and death—are now being fully extended and amplified in the digital sphere. Reflecting on the future of digital support and its implications for the vitality or death of languages, Zaugg concludes that its impact "is likely to play a growing role as communities across the world increasingly rely on digital communication. Minoritized and Indigenous language speakers stand to lose the most from language extinction, but loss of language diversity impacts us all." Indeed, the more deeply the infrastructure of information technology penetrates every aspect of our social and ecological life in the foreseeable future, the more thoroughly the social contradictions in which we live will be mediated and transformed by the same technologies.

We began by noting the planetary conditions of ecological harm, climate catastrophe, and the other conditions of upheaval that are consequential to the life and death of languages in our time. The correlation between ecological catastrophe and language endangerment is urgent and real. It is indexed by the mass expulsions of our time that are caused by complex biopolitical assemblages—e.g., deforestation, water wars, unrestricted mining, land grabs, imperial warfare, famine, and drought. The death of a vibrant ecosystem of languages, the rise of Global English, and the complex reconstitution of linguistic communities are the invisible work of neoliberal capital to be sure, but they are also a visible reminder that the asylum seeker, the ecological refugee, and the gendered care worker are on the front lines of remaking linguistic communities and revivifying the lifeworld of languages. The chapters that follow contain a wealth of research and analytical methods that will help readers navigate and explore the roots of the current predicament of languages as embedded in the developing relationship of *logos*, *oikos*, and *techné*.

We must not forget, however, that the reworking of justice requires poetic imagination, the kind embodied by the powerful poems and artworks we include in the book. In an equally imaginative vein, Amartya Sen writes: "The neighbourhood that is constructed by our relations with distant people is something that has pervasive relevance to the understanding of justice in general, particularly so in the contemporary world."[36] Indeed, it is only when we try to bring remote regions of the planet closer and rethink them as our own multilingual neighborhood that we begin to awaken to the linguistic preconditions of justice. This book strives to elaborate on Sen's notion of justice as the authors attempt to train us to listen differently across mutual (un)intelligibility and differences, to recognize that our shared future in the planetary neighborhood rests on embracing the languages and cultures of distant peoples, to discover the truth of the lifeworld of languages, and to find hope and beauty again in the midst of crisis and catastrophe.

NOTES

1. United Nations Permanent Forum on Indigenous Issues, "Indigenous Languages" (background paper, UNPFII, New York), accessed March 20, 2021.x, www.un.org/esa/socdev/unpfii/documents/2016/Docs-updates/backgrounderL2.pdf. See also United Nations Permanent Forum on Indigenous Issues, "Indigenous Languages: Preservation and Revitalization: Articles 13, 14 and 16 of the United Nations Declaration on the Rights of Indigenous Peoples," PFII/2016/EGM (concept note, UNPFII, New York, 2016), https://www.un.org/esa/socdev/unpfii/documents/2016/egm/Concept_Note_EGMLanguages_FINAL_rev.pdf. For different estimates, see note 11.
2. The editors of and some of the contributors to this book were involved in organizing or participating in the conferences that took place at UN Headquarters in New York and at Columbia University.
3. UNESCO is leading this effort in cooperation with the United Nations Department of Economic and Social Affairs (UNDESA) and other agencies, including the Office of the High Commissioner for Human Rights (OHCHR). United Nations Educational, Scientific, and Cultural Organization, "UNESCO Launches the Global Task Force for Making a Decade of Action for Indigenous Languages," March 22, 2021, https://en.unesco.org/news/unesco-launches-global-task-force-making-decade-action-Indigenous-languages.
4. The UN Permanent Forum on Indigenous Issues has identified other useful tools such as the Convention Against Discrimination in Education (1960); the International Convention on the Elimination of All Forms of Racial Discrimination (1965);

the United Nations International Covenant on Civil and Political Rights (1966); the International Covenant on Economic, Social and Cultural Rights (1966); the Convention Concerning the Protection of the World Cultural and Natural Heritage (1972); and the Convention on the Rights of the Child (1989).
5. See Moria Paz, "The Failed Promise of Language Rights: A Critique of the International Language Rights Regime," *Harvard International Law Journal* 54, no. 1 (2013): 157–218. See also L. Maria Bo's chapter in this book, which interrogates the philosophical and legal grounding of linguistic rights as a concept.
6. See Phillip Van Parijs, *Linguistic Justice for Europe and for the World* (Oxford: Oxford University Press, 2011), 175.
7. Dipesh Chakrabarty introduces a distinction between the *globe* and the *planet* in his attempt to reframe the current debate on the Anthropocene. However, this distinction is highly language dependent (as opposed to statistical or imaging methods, for example) and should be subjected to the test of multilingualism, translingualism, and translation, a method we emphasize in this book. See Dipesh Chakrabarty, *The Climate of History in a Planetary Age* (Chicago: University of Chicago Press, 2021). See also J. R. McNeill and Peter Engelke, *The Great Acceleration: An Environmental History of the Anthropocene Since 1945* (Cambridge, MA: Harvard University Press, 2014).
8. Nancy C. Dorian, "Western Language Ideologies and Small Language Prospects," in *Endangered Languages: Language Loss and Community Response*, ed. Lenore A. Grenoble and Lindsay Whaley (Cambridge: Cambridge University Press, 1998), 22 (emphasis in original).
9. Daniel Nettle and Suzanne Romaine discuss three kinds of language losses: population loss, forced shift, and voluntary shift, all of which are related to land loss to some degree. See Daniel Nettle and Suzanne Romaine, *Vanishing Voices: The Extinction of the World's Languages* (Oxford: Oxford University Press, 2000), 92.
10. The symposium was convened by the Institute for Comparative Literature and Society at Columbia University, in collaboration with UNESCO and the United Nations Permanent Forum on Indigenous Issues, at Columbia University on April 21, 2018. Clara Soaring Hawk's remarks on April 21, 2018, are available at https://podcasts.apple.com/us/podcast/chief-clara-soaring-hawk-opening-ceremony-for-global/id506431392?i=1000416666397.
11. Precise extinction rates and endangerment risk have been difficult to ascertain and can vary widely according to methods. For an explanation of the criteria used by researchers, see Suzanne Romaine, "Language Endangerment and Language Death: The Future of Language Diversity," in *The Routledge Handbook of Ecolinguistics*, ed. Alwin Fill and Hermine Penz (New York: Routledge, 2018), 40–55.
12. Nettle and Romaine, *Vanishing Voices*, 79.
13. Nettle and Romaine, *Vanishing Voices*, 79.
14. Ingrid Piller, *Linguistic Diversity and Social Justice: An Introduction to Applied Sociolinguistics* (Oxford: Oxford University Press, 2016), 167–168.
15. Stephen Clayton, "The Problem of 'Choice' and the Construction of the Demand for English in Cambodia," *Language Policy* 7, no. 2 (2008): 143–164.
16. United Nations High Commissioner for Refugees, *Global Trends: Forced Displacement in 2021* (Geneva: UNHCR, 2021), https://www.unhcr.org/62a9d1494/global-trends-report-2021.

17. Gaia Vince, *Nomad Century: How Climate Migration Will Shape Our World* (New York: Flatiron Books, 2022), 64, 69. Gerald J. Roche has characterized the current crisis impacting the world's languages as a moment of both emergency and indeterminacy that opens up the possibility of new forms of multilingualism. See Roche, "The World's Languages in Crisis (Redux): Toward a Radical Reimagining for Global Linguistic Justice," *Emancipations: A Journal of Critical Social Analysis* 1, no. 2 (2022): Article 8.
18. T. H. Marshall, *Citizenship and Social Class, and Other Essays* (Cambridge: Cambridge University Press, 1950).
19. Iris Marion Young, *Justice and the Politics of Difference* (Princeton, NJ: Princeton University Press, 2011).
20. Joan Scott, "The Conundrum of Equality" (Occasional Paper no. 2, Institute for Advanced Study, Princeton, NJ, March 1999), 3.
21. Vine Deloria's aunt, Ella Cara Deloria, was among Franz Boas's most important female students, along with women like Zora Neale Hurston. Deloria met Boas while she was at Teachers College and worked with him until his death in 1942; she also worked with two of his other students, Margaret Mead and Ruth Benedict. Deloria utilized her fluency in the Sioux dialects of Dakota and Lakota to challenge earlier linguistic and ethnographic studies of the Sioux Nation and to coauthor *Dakota Grammar* (1941) with Boas. She was his only student to do so. When Deloria died in 1971, she left behind a large archive of Sioux language notes and ethnological observations. Her legacy was formalized as the Ella C. Deloria Project at the University of South Dakota, where she taught.
22. The numbers we cite are from the 2023 TechNavio market research report called *English Language Training Market in China by End-user and Learning methods – Forecast and Analysis 2022–2026*, p. 25.
23. See James Palmer, "Why China Is Cracking Down on Private Tutoring," *Foreign Policy*, July 28, 2021, https://foreignpolicy.com/2021/07/28/china-private-tutoring-education-regulation-crackdown/.
24. For a recent comprehensive overview, see Nicholas Ostler, *Empires of the Word: A Language History of the World* (New York: HarperCollins, 2005).
25. Philippe Van Parijs, *Linguistic Justice for Europe and for the World*, 33.
26. Van Parijs, *Linguistic Justice for Europe and for the World*, 34.
27. See, for example, Van Parijs's definition of *lingua franca* in *Linguistic Justice for Europe and for the World*, 9.
28. For the ascendance of Global English as a hegemonic language of science in postwar scientific communities of the world, see Michael D. Gordin, *Scientific Babel: How Science Was Done Before and After Global English* (Chicago: University of Chicago Press, 2015).
29. See András Kornai, "Digital Language Death," *PLoS ONE* 8, no. 10 (October 22, 2013), https://doi.org/10.1371/journal.pone.0077056.
30. For a critique of the mutual exclusion of word and image in Western linguistic and art theories, see W. J. T. Mitchell, *Picture Theory: Essays on Verbal and Visual Representation* (Chicago: University of Chicago Press, 1994), ch. 1–3.
31. Peter T. Daniels and William Bright, eds., *The World's Writing Systems* (Oxford: Oxford University Press, 1996), 384–390.

32. To clarify, this is not directly related to the simplification of written Chinese characters that came about much later in the wake of the failed romanization campaign. The pinyin alphabet with its twenty-one consonants and fifteen vowels/diphthongs is written in the Latin script and is used to transcribe the sounds of written Chinese characters. It does not comprise a writing system in China; however, members of the Zhuang ethnic minority speak a different language and use the Latin script for their own writing system. For recent studies of romanization movements in China, see Yurou Zhong, *Chinese Grammatology: Script Revolution and Literary Modernity, 1916–1958* (New York: Columbia University Press, 2019); Jing Tsu, *Kingdom of Characters: The Language Revolution That Made China Modern* (New York: Riverhead, 2022); and Uluğ Kuzuoğlu, *Codes of Modernity: Chinese Scripts in the Global Information Age* (New York: Columbia University Press, 2023).
33. For a discussion of modern Turkish script reform, see Nergis Ertürk, *Grammatology and Literary Modernity in Turkey* (Oxford: Oxford University Press, 2011).
34. See Jacques Derrida, *Of Grammatology*, trans. Gayatri Chakravorty Spivak (Baltimore, MD: Johns Hopkins University Press, 1976).
35. On Claude Shannon's pathbreaking invention, see Lydia H. Liu, *The Freudian Robot: Digital Media and the Future of the Unconscious* (Chicago: University of Chicago Press, 2010), ch. 2, 39–98.
36. Amartya Sen, *The Idea of Justice* (Cambridge, MA: Belknap Press of Harvard University Press, 2009), 172.

WORKS CITED

Boas, Franz, and Ella Deloria. *Dakota Grammar*. Washington, DC: U.S. Government Printing Office, 1941.

Chakrabarty, Dipesh. *The Climate of History in a Planetary Age*. Chicago: University of Chicago Press, 2021.

Clayton, Stephen. "The Problem of 'Choice' and the Construction of the Demand for English in Cambodia." *Language Policy* 7, no. 2 (2008): 143–164.

Daniels, Peter T., and William Bright, eds. *The World's Writing Systems*. Oxford: Oxford University Press, 1996.

Derrida, Jacques. *Of Grammatology*. Trans. Gayatri Chakravorty Spivak. Baltimore, MD: Johns Hopkins University Press, 1976.

Dorian, Nancy C. "Western Language Ideologies and Small Language Prospects." In *Endangered Languages: Language Loss and Community Response*, ed. Lenore A. Grenoble and Lindsay Whaley (Cambridge: Cambridge University Press, 1998).

Ertürk, Nergis. *Grammatology and Literary Modernity in Turkey*. Oxford: Oxford University Press, 2011.

Gordin, Michael D. *Scientific Babel: How Science Was Done Before and After Global English*. Chicago: University of Chicago Press, 2015.

Grenoble, Lenore A., and Lindsay Whaley, eds. *Endangered Languages: Language Loss and Community Response*. Cambridge: Cambridge University Press, 1998.

Kornai, András. "Digital Language Death." *PLoS ONE* 8, no. 10 (October 22, 2013). https://doi.org/10.1371/journal.pone.0077056.

Kuzuoğlu, Uluğ. *Codes of Modernity: Chinese Scripts in the Global Information Age.* New York: Columbia University Press, 2023.

Liu, Lydia H. *The Freudian Robot: Digital Media and the Future of the Unconscious.* Chicago: University of Chicago Press, 2010.

Marshall, T. H. *Citizenship and Social Class, and Other Essays.* Cambridge: Cambridge University Press, 1950.

McNeil, J. R., and Peter Engelke. *The Great Acceleration: An Environmental History of the Anthropocene Since 1945.* Cambridge, MA: Harvard University Press, 2014.

Mitchell, W. J. T. *Picture Theory: Essays on Verbal and Visual Representation.* Chicago: University of Chicago Press, 1994.

Nettle, Daniel, and Suzanne Romaine. *Vanishing Voices: The Extinction of the World's Languages.* Oxford: Oxford University Press, 2000.

Ostler, Nicholas. *Empires of the Word: A Language History of the World.* New York: HarperCollins, 2005.

Palmer, James. "Why China Is Cracking Down on Private Tutoring." *Foreign Policy*, July 28, 2021. https://foreignpolicy.com/2021/07/28/china-private-tutoring-education-regulation-crackdown/.

Paz, Moira. "The Failed Promise of Language Rights: A Critique of the International Language Rights Regime." *Harvard International Law Journal* 54, no. 1 (2013): 157–218.

Piller, Ingrid. *Linguistic Diversity and Social Justice: An Introduction to Applied Sociolinguistics.* Oxford: Oxford University Press, 2016.

Roche, Gerald J. "The World's Languages in Crisis (Redux): Toward a Radical Reimagining for Global Linguistic Justice." *Emancipations: A Journal of Critical Social Analysis* 1 no. 2 (2022), Article 8. https://scholarsjunction.msstate.edu/emancipations/vol1/iss2/8.

Romaine, Suzanne. "Language Endangerment and Language Death: The Future of Language Diversity." In *The Routledge Handbook of Ecolinguistics*, ed. Alwin Fill and Hermine Penz, 40–55. New York: Routledge, 2018.

Scott, Joan. "The Conundrum of Equality." Occasional Paper no. 2. Institute for Advanced Study, Princeton, NJ, March 1999.

Sen, Amartya. *The Idea of Justice.* Cambridge, MA: Belknap Press of Harvard University Press, 2009.

Soaring Eagle, Clara. Remarks at the symposium Global Justice for Indigenous Languages, Institute for Comparative Literature and Society in collaboration with UNESCO and United Nations Permanent Forum on Indigenous Issues, Columbia University, New York, April 21, 2018. https://podcasts.apple.com/us/podcast/chief-clara-soaring-hawk-opening-ceremony-for-global/id506431392?i=1000416666397.

TechNavio. *English Language Training Market in China* by End-user and Learning methods: Forecast and Analysis 2022–2026. Infiniti Research Limited.

Tsu, Jing. *Kingdom of Characters: The Language Revolution That Made China Modern.* New York: Riverhead, 2022.

United Nations Educational, Scientific, and Cultural Organization, Convention Concerning the Protection of the World Cultural and Natural Heritage, November 16, 1972. https://whc.unesco.org/en/conventiontext/.

United Nations Educational, Scientific, and Cultural Organization. "UNESCO Launches the Global Task Force for Making a Decade of Action for Indigenous Languages," March 22, 2021. https://en.unesco.org/news/unesco-launches-global-task-force-making-decade-action-Indigenous-languages.

United Nations General Assembly. Convention Against Discrimination in Education, December 14, 1960. http://portal.unesco.org/en/ev.php-URL_ID=12949&URL_DO =DO_TOPIC&URL_SECTION=201.html.
United Nations General Assembly. Convention on the Rights of the Child, November 20, 1989. https://www.ohchr.org/en/professionalinterest/pages/crc.aspx.
United Nations General Assembly. International Covenant on Civil and Political Rights, December 16, 1966. https://www.ohchr.org/en/professionalinterest/pages/ccpr.aspx.
United Nations General Assembly. International Covenant on Economic, Social and Cultural Rights, 1966. https://www.ohchr.org/en/professionalinterest/pages/cescr.aspx.
United Nations General Assembly. International Convention on the Elimination of All Forms of Racial Discrimination, December 21, 1965. https://www.ohchr.org/en /professionalinterest/pages/cerd.aspx.
United Nations High Commissioner for Refugees. *Global Trends: Forced Displacement in 2020*. Geneva: UNHCR, 2021. https://www.unhcr.org/60b638e37/unhcr-global-trends -2020.
United Nations Permanent Forum on Indigenous Issues. "Indigenous Languages." Background paper, UNPFII, New York. Accessed March 22, 2021. https://www.un.org /esa/socdev/unpfii/documents/2016/Docs-updates/backgrounderL2.pdf.
United Nations Permanent Forum on Indigenous Issues. "Indigenous Languages: Preservation and Revitalization: Articles 13, 14 and 16 of the United Nations Declaration on the Rights of Indigenous Peoples." Concept Note, PFII/2016/EGM. UNPFII, New York, 2016. https://www.un.org/esa/socdev/unpfii/documents/2016/egm/Concept _Note_EGMLanguages_FINAL_rev.pdf.
Van Parijs, Philippe. *Linguistic Justice for Europe and for the World*. Oxford: Oxford University Press, 2011.
Vince, Gaia. *Nomad Century: How Climate Migration Will Shape Our World*. New York: Flatiron Books, 2022.
Young, Iris Marion. *Justice and the Politics of Difference*. Princeton, NJ: Princeton University Press, 2011.
Zhong, Yurou. *Chinese Grammatology: Script Revolution and Literary Modernity, 1916–1958*. New York: Columbia University Press, 2019.

Ats'íísts'in

ORLANDO WHITE

Below the skull there is a part of a letter
shaped like a bone. But the skull is not a skull;
it is a black dot with white teeth. And the piece
of the letter under it is not really a bone,
rather a dark spine. This is not the end of language.
When it was alive it had a ribcage;
each rib taken out by small pincers
the way strands of eyelash are removed
from eyelids. And the dot used to have eyes—
white like two grains of salt. But they were dissolved
by two drops of ink. The way a letter fades
on the page after many years of reading
or how it soaks into a fingerprint and forgets itself.
The way a word tries to breathe inside
a closed book; the way a letter shivers when
a page is turned. Because underneath sound
there is thought. Language, a complete structure
within the white coffin of paper. If you shake it
and listen, it will move, rattle like bones on the page.

Chapter One

EQUALITY OR DIVERSITY

Language, Rights, Justice

L. MARIA BO

Linguistic rights have received increasing attention in the process of reframing human rights in the period following World War II. They were officially enumerated in the 1996 Universal Declaration of Linguistic Rights (UDLR), a watershed document ratified in Barcelona by PEN International. The UDLR states that linguistic rights include the right to "the use of one's own language both in private and in public," the right to "maintain and develop one's own culture," and the right "of an equitable presence of their language and culture in the communications media" of any given territory.[1] The document came together at a meeting of over 200 linguists, lawyers, writers, and activists who represented ninety states, five continents, and over forty languages. What they produced is at once a literary work, a legal pronouncement, and a philosophical treatise, one that "promises a future of coexistence and peace thanks to the recognition of the right that each linguistic community has to shape its own life in its own language in all fields."[2] Quickly gaining the widespread support of such activists and luminaries as Nelson Mandela, Desmond Tutu, and the Dalai Lama, the document was seen as a much-needed benchmark that marginalized writers and linguistic communities could use to argue for autonomy and accountability.

The UDLR is far from the first document seeking to ensure linguistic rights.[3] It draws from earlier pronouncements like the 1992 Declaration on the Rights of Persons Belonging to National or Ethnic, Religious and

Linguistic Minorities; the 1950 European Convention on Human Rights; and even the 1948 Universal Declaration of Human Rights (UDHR) itself; all of these mention linguistic rights as part of what contributes to human thriving, but none fully defines linguistic rights or focuses on what their significance is and what they entail.[4] The UDLR seeks to do just that, especially by outlining the policy implications of having human rights extend to language. To this end, the UDLR specifically assures linguistic minorities—whether they be migrants, ethnic minorities, or Indigenous peoples of a territory—access to infrastructure that linguistic majorities largely take for granted. Indeed, the UDLR takes as its premise the "basic principle of the equality of all peoples and languages," such that linguistic equality—and not just equality of persons—becomes itself a matter of cultural and political importance. Dispensing with arbitrary titles like "official, regional, or minority languages," the UDLR asserts that "neither economic, social, religious, cultural, demographic, etc. features nor linguistic features justify any sort of discrimination; therefore, all linguistic communities are subject to the same rights."[5] Throughout the document, the dominant principle is thus one of equality.

When it comes to seeking justice for the unrepresented or marginalized, we are hard-pressed in the Western, post-Enlightenment world to imagine anything other than equality as the baseline to be achieved. Equality—at least of worth and opportunity—is the basis for our notions of impartiality and fair play, for our picture of a just society. Thus, we see these key phrases in the American Declaration of Independence: "that all men are created equal, that they are endowed by their Creator with certain unalienable Rights"; and in the French Rights of Man and Citizen: "Men are born and remain free and equal in rights." Though more complicated in its origins,[6] the UDHR has similar language, insisting on "recognition of the inherent dignity and of the equal and inalienable rights of all members of the human family [as] the foundation of freedom, justice and peace in the world." This equality in dignity eventually became the "first generation" of human rights, to be later supplemented by a "second generation" of largely economic and social rights. As Miroslav Kusy writes:

> In the first generation of human rights, the primary place belongs to the right to life . . . but in the second generation of rights we take a radical new step forward. For the citizen it is no longer enough to be granted the right to

life as such; he or she also wants to have it defined by dignified conditions of living: by the right to work, by a maximum of eight hours work per day, to social security, to a secure retirement, etc. In this way, the second generation of human rights promotes and protects the basic economic, social, and cultural conditions of life in dignity.[7]

Kusy's progression of rights is typically seen as a march forward of social justice. It is a familiar narrative of progress, one that consequently feels difficult to question. What problem could there be in acknowledging that a discussion of justice begins with *equals*, that it is only through attaining equal rights that we find the basic conditions necessary for building a just world? This narrative matters all the more when considering those rights specifically articulated for marginalized minorities, such as the right to one's culture or language. Typically considered part of the "third generation" of human rights—that is, *rights of solidarity* to protect certain threatened groups—linguistic rights were included obliquely in the UDHR to protect minority groups specifically and linguistic diversity more generally. Linguistic rights come into play when courts are required to provide a translator for someone on trial, when official forms are not provided in a minority language, and when a child is forced to learn a language in school that their community cannot support or sustain. In the UDLR, language becomes the flexion point for ensuring the basic conditions of social, economic, and political development, particularly for the marginalized. And yet, as the introduction to this volume states, there remains a fundamental lack of clarity as to what is being protected: "Are nonnormative language cultures in jeopardy, or do the *users* of those languages suffer social discrimination and political marginalization? What form of collective rights is being demanded?"

The creators of the UDLR are not alone in placing this emphasis on language—or in realizing the intractability of theorizing what its social and political implications are. Political theorists Alan Patten and Will Kymlicka have shown that language policy—which answers such questions as what languages would be the "official" ones in post-USSR Eastern Europe and what languages merit institutional support in an increasingly multilingual United States—intersects with some of the biggest questions concerning democracy, citizenship, immigration, and political participation in the late twentieth and early twenty-first centuries.[8] Add to these the concerns of linguistic diversity—currently in massive decline, alongside ecological diversity, as experts predict the loss of nearly 90 percent of the world's languages within the next fifty years[9]—and the need for effective language policy becomes all the more pressing. Seen in this light, the need for a third generation of rights of solidarity is incontestable, particularly if equal participation and access are what we wish to achieve.

But what if "the equality of all peoples and languages" is not necessarily the right place to start when it comes to regulating or preserving language even in the face of very real encroachment by globalization, colonial legacies, and shortsighted educational policies? Could it be that the insistence on equality fundamentally limits our understanding of linguistic justice, even though it seems essential to realizing it? Linguistic rights are supposed to retroactively "affirm and protect" the more fundamental rights to life and dignity;[10] but as many have mentioned before, one of the problems with rights—presuming all to be definitionally inherent and inviolable—is that they leave no clear method for prioritization. To put demands for linguistic equity into the language of rights makes language as sacrosanct as one's access to food, health care, and education. In his classic work of political theory, *Spheres of Justice*, Michael Walzer writes that "the effort to produce a complete account of justice or a defense of equality by multiplying rights soon makes a farce of what it multiplies.... Men and women do indeed have rights beyond life and liberty, but these do not follow from our common humanity; they follow from shared conceptions of social goods; they are local and particular in character."[11] Walzer's emphasis on the particular contexts that determine rights, as opposed to universal declarations, is critical, as I discuss later. As many scholars have shown, including in the introduction to this volume, language is one of the most basic of social goods: without the right to language, one's rights to education, medical care, legal protection, and more can be, and often are, seriously compromised. Language, as a fundamental access point to political and social existence, thus demands to have a place in rights discourse. And yet simply declaring equal linguistic rights for all may hamper this project from the outset, through an impulse as much for conformity as for diversity.

In his contribution to this volume, Tommaso Manfredini writes that "a focus on *rights* cannot be divorced from a focus on the linguistic conditions that mediate access to justice and the protection of those rights." Indeed, attending to the specific language of one's right to language is politically necessary if we want to take seriously the rights documents themselves. The UDLR, for instance, was written first in Spanish and Catalán before being translated into over twenty languages.[12] Emerging from the act of translating—literally "carrying over"—are comparable documents whose stakes for correspondence are high. After all, it is the universal translatability of *human rights* that fuels their philosophical and political weight; rights should be understandable in every human tongue if they are to be the common denominator of what constitutes the *human*. This is all the more true for linguistic rights, which declare the fundamental communicability of all the world's languages, no matter how diverse. At the same time, the accurate translation of human rights documents is precisely what holds governing bodies universally accountable to the same standard. A document in the declaration or convention model thus fuses together linguistic equivalence and political equality as mutually constitutive practices: the message of "political equality for all" hinges on the reality that equivalent concepts can be found (or created) in another tongue. More than other rights, linguistic rights by nature demand our attention to the practical intersection of political concepts in a multilingual world.

This chapter explores whether the political notion of equal rights can hold when the translations thereof are not equivalent, thus loosening fundamental western European political concepts even while articulating them. Manfredini's contribution to this volume states that translating such documents is not a "transparent [operation] even when we assume the utmost good faith and competence of all parties involved. And yet such translations are treated as such, or, rather, they are treated as neutral and unaltering steps in the transmission of meaning." This constitutes a translation problem that has been little discussed in rights discourse. But perhaps the lack of equivalent translations can also lead us beyond the trap of political equality. In what follows, I first provide a backdrop of rights discourse in social contract theory, including the pivotal role of the linguistic community in the formation of social contract theory and the questions this raises about how rights are predisposed toward individualism. I then examine some outspoken critiques of rights discourse from the very Indigenous writers that linguistic rights are supposed to protect. Turning to the work of Western Sioux philosopher Vine Deloria Jr., I critique how western European political theory—and American studies with it—has consistently conflated equality with justice across languages and cultures, a move that

EQUALITY OR DIVERSITY

has ultimately limited our ability to redress linguistic grievances and imagine new forms of political coexistence. I then analyze different translations of the UDLR to see how the ideals of this document hold up when put through the practical necessities of translation. Far from simply highlighting the document's uneven translations, I argue that the many translations of *equality* in the UDLR can chart new paths to justice by redefining our freedoms, so that language can become the source of its own emancipation.

INDIVIDUAL WRONGS AND RIGHTS

In a 2018 interview, Carles Torner, then head of PEN International and one of the principal movers behind the authorship of the UDLR, stated that the biggest debate in the drafting process involved "a consensus about the linguistic community [rather than the individual] being the subject of right."[13] Article 1 of the UDLR defines "a *language community* [as] any human society established historically in a particular territorial space, whether this space be recognized or not, which identifies itself as a people and has developed a common language as a natural means of communication and cultural cohesion among its members." Torner goes on to explain to his interviewer, Peter MacDonald, the political significance of this expansion from the individual rights-bearer: "Maybe the most important contribution of the *Declaration* is that it considers the collective and individual dimensions of linguistic rights inseparable. The principle is that language is collectively constituted within a community and it is within this community that we all make a personal use of it. The practice of individual linguistic rights, to be effective, asks for the collective rights of all communities to be respected by everyone."

For Torner, making the community the primary rights-bearer, from which the individual gains his/her rights, runs directly against the grain of typical rights discourse. He is not wrong: rights have long been the bastion of political individualism. Assured through social contract theory, rights were the definitive assertion of the Everyman's dignity against the oppression of tyrannical regimes. Individual rights—whether to life (Thomas Hobbes), property (John Locke), or freedom (Jean-Jacques Rousseau)—were guaranteed by a binding social contract, formed when a group of rational actors reached consensus on its content.[14] It was a root belief in the individual's rational capacity that not only repudiated feudal hierarchies, making all individuals equal to each other, but also made the individual, the limit of reason, the inviolable rights-bearer. In this line of thinking, the group existed only as a vehicle to protect the rights of the individual.

That the modern rights tradition is based largely on the Enlightenment social contract theories of Hobbes, Locke, and Rousseau is well-known. What has been insufficiently studied, however, is the fact that even these canonical social contract theories—in particular, Hobbes's and Rousseau's—were themselves based on theories of language. The philosopher Philip Pettit has noted that Hobbes's view of language was foundational to his earliest conceptions of the social contract framework and the very nature of politics. As Pettit writes, Hobbes's big idea was that "human minds are made by words. . . . Language is an invented technology, not a natural inheritance, . . . and it is a technology that transformed our kind, introducing a deep cleavage between us and otherwise comparable animals."[15] It was language that allowed humans to develop rational thought and eventually engage in collective action to end their solitary life, which was famously "nasty, brutish, and short." Unlike Platonists, Aristotelians, and even Hobbes's contemporaries like Descartes, Hobbes averred that language was not a by-product or result of rational thought but the precursor to it. In other words, if rationality is what premises equal rights under the social contract, rationality is itself premised on a shared use of language. As Hobbes himself claims, without language "there had been amongst men, neither commonwealth, nor society, nor contract, nor peace, no more than amongst lions, bears, and wolves."[16] To participate in human community in any meaningful way thus meant to be *en*languaged, from which the social contract could then gain shape and validity. That context also explicitly and early on excluded the nonhuman. For Hobbes, language did not simply allow individuals to form into a political collective called the social contract; language itself *was* the original social contract.

Hobbes's reliance on language means that, at their most basic level, political communities based on social contracts essentially *are* linguistic communities. It is the fact of shared language that makes the social contract ontologically viable, and from this, there is no point of return: i.e., there is no retroactive retreat from a mutual sociolinguistic existence back to a "state of nature." Hobbes's notion of language is thus fundamental for the speech acts of institutional power that instantiate the moral and legal claims of political governance. Indeed, language in Hobbes's formulation is the essential linchpin that transforms a *nation*—a group of people affiliated through shared history, territory, or cultural characteristics—into a *state*, a working government capable of taking collective action on behalf of its constituents.

This linguistic underpinning of the social contract, as well as the state created therefrom, provides a real philosophical basis for Torner's questioning of whether the individual or the collective is the ultimate rights-bearer. This question is a necessary corrective to a concept of individualism, which has been unevenly applied from the start. Western philosophy's belief in the sanctity of the individual has ever sat uneasily beside imperialist campaigns in Asia, Africa, and the Middle East that grossly violated the rights to reason and self-governance, which the Enlightenment championed as the rights of all.[17] Even within Europe, there was rigid policing of who counted as citizens, and thus were privy to rights, and who did not (non-landowning men, women, children, and ethnic or religious others). The American context is no better. As Radha D'Souza notes in *What's Wrong with Rights*, the Enlightenment "mythology of rights should have broken down first and foremost in the US," where colonial brutality against Indigenous peoples and slave labor were not only practiced but also legalized.[18] Indeed, rights discourse in these early American contexts was often used *against* the oppressed and marginalized rather than *for* them.[19] Simultaneously driving global economic exploitation *and* championing the inalienable rights of the individual, the United States is thick with contradictions around its notion of *equality*. This is especially true when, as Mary Glendon writes, "the language of rights is the language of no compromise," whereby the absolutism of individual freedoms allows well-intentioned rights like the right to privacy to devolve into the individual's "right to be left alone."[20] These tensions returned with a vengeance in Covid-19-ravaged 2020, as the world looked on in rank disbelief as Americans protested infringements on their rights for being required to wear face coverings in public in the midst of a global pandemic. Rights, especially those localized in the individual, have all too often brought about a particularly heedless and self-centered form of equality.

I argue that these occurrences are not so much a failure of equal rights discourse as a fulfillment of it—for these examples highlight the tension between individual and collective that has plagued rights discourse from the beginning. Some scholars have argued that there is no fundamental tension between individual and collective: for example, Michael Freeman writes that "it is a mistake to believe that liberal democracy has favoured the individual over the collective. Rather, it has given the individual a special status within a particular collectivity, the nation-state."[21] However, the fact remains that group/collective rights have been far more difficult to justify than individual rights. This is partly due to rights' dependence on equality: while it may be easy in a liberal framework to affirm the fundamental equality of rational individuals, rationality is a much harder criterion to utilize to justify equality between groups—and especially between groups with greater or lesser numbers, abilities, or resources.[22] To date, whether and how collectives can be rights-bearers is itself a thorny question at the heart of political debate in an increasingly globalized world.

Uncovering the linguistic basis of Hobbes's social contract thus complicates an easy understanding of equality as narrowly construed between individuals. Hobbes's linguistic community does not explicitly make the collective the rights-bearer, but it does rely on the communal construction of language rather than individual reason as the underlying basis for equality. Here I mean language in the abstract: it is a linguistic reality, deeply tied to communication and relationship with others—rather than a purely individual, rational reality—that determines the natural locus of rights in human society. Hobbes's theory also constitutes a profound reversal of political foundations. We typically construe rights as the most foundational good, where other facets of political and material existence find their basis: one has the right *to* live one's life, *to* vote, *to* own property, etc., where rights are the access point that allows one to engage meaningfully in the world. However, understanding language as the original social contract makes language the precursor to rights; instead of discussing the right to language, therefore, we should be discussing the pathway that language carves out in defining rights.

Put this way, the UDLR's logic of linguistic rights, construed as communal as opposed to individual, does not extend to questioning the deeper underpinnings of the rights regime. It settles for according rights to language rather than questioning the linguistic basis of rights themselves. It also does not question the long-standing foundation of property in rights discourse. Torner notes the impossibility of acknowledging a linguistic community—and, by extension, the UDLR itself—as a matter of land:

CARLES TORNER: Well, we all knew that by acknowledging *collective* rights, the idea of the "language community" as a rights-bearing entity, we were condemning the *Declaration*, ensuring it would not become a text adopted by UNESCO too soon. . . .

PETER MACDONALD: Because [doing so] would inevitably put you on a collision course with state power?

CARLES TORNER: Of course. As soon as you define any kind of collective right, as soon as you define the right of, say, the Mapuche linguistic community, or the Maoris, to be educated in their language, the next step is land. . . . I understand this politically, but I still defend it as a real success to have put the concept of linguistic community . . . at the heart of the *Declaration*.[23]

Torner's position conflates language use and territorial rights, which is understandable given his Catalonian background and the long-standing struggle of that linguistic community for political autonomy. Conceptually, this makes sense: if language is the original social contract, then linguistic communities can come dangerously close to challenging the larger social contract of the state. Nevertheless, practical examples abound of linguistic communities existing in all manner of configurations within and under the modern nation-state. Dialect-speaking communities in China and India, tribal groups in Australia and Africa, the Québécois French, the Welsh in the UK—all exist without aspirations of claiming statehood and the right to territory within the modern nation in which they find themselves. Land, construed as rights to territory, is not the inevitable outcome or goal of speaking a certain language.

Owning territory is, however, deeply tied to a framework of rights in which the rights-bearer has been historically landowning. Consider Locke's definition of owning private property, as opposed to common property, as the entry point to the social contract;[24] Locke concludes that it is one's labor that turns what is *common* property into *private* property. Torner's conflation of language and landownership thus turns language into a type of labor, a reflexive guarantor of territory, a move that veers uncomfortably close to what Walzer calls "simple equality." Walzer writes poignantly that "equality taken literally is an ideal ripe for betrayal," by which he means that the easy equation of material benefits and social mechanics presents enormous problems for a regime based on equality.[25] For Walzer, believing that equality requires equivalence across all social spheres is a created and selective tautology that is self-defeating;[26] instead, he asserts that complex equality is needed to recognize that the mere existence of differences is not only inevitable but also unproblematic in itself for justice:

> Monopoly is not inappropriate. . . . There is nothing wrong, for example, with the grip that persuasive and helpful men and women (politicians) establish on political power. But the use of political power to gain access to other goods is a tyrannical use. . . . In formal terms, complex equality means that no citizen's standing in one sphere or with regard to one social good can be undercut by his standing in some other sphere, with regard to some other good. Thus, citizen X may be chosen over citizen Y for political office, and then the two of them will be unequal in the sphere of politics. But they will not be unequal generally so long as X's office gives him no advantages over Y in any other sphere—superior medical care, access to better schools for his children, entrepreneurial opportunities, and so on. So long as office is not a dominant good, is not generally convertible, office holders will stand, or at least can stand, in a relation of equality to the men and women they govern.[27]

Walzer highlights the paramount boundaries between social goods: ironically, equality is most threatened when one views various social spheres and values as equivalent, making advantage in one fungible with advantage in another. Accordingly, rights "are only of limited help in thinking about distributive justice," as they tend to flatten the field of social goods with the more rights that are created.[28] When rights to language are threatening because they are construed as coterminous with rights to land, it is precisely this fallacy of equal rights that is afoot. Failing to distinguish between complex equality and simple equivalences plagues collective rights as much as individual ones, stalemating language rights at their very conception.

I am in no way saying that we should get rid of the concepts of *rights* and *equality* altogether. The lack of these concepts has historically left the vulnerable defenseless and led to authoritarianism and abuse the world over. But it is imperative that we understand the tensions in using rights to argue for linguistic justice. Is there a way for us to conceive of a larger network of relationships where even collective needs are defined not in terms of entitlement from others but rather in terms of cooperation *with* them? Perhaps understanding the place of language in shaping these relationships can help us to break out of a conformity shaped by easy equivalents, in which different groups—and even different members of a group—are assumed to want the same thing.

VINE DELORIA JR. AND ECOLOGICAL COVENANTS

The Native American writer and philosopher Vine Deloria Jr. sees the same problem that Walzer does in simple equality and locates it as much in linguistic equivalence as in political concept. Deloria's critique begins with individualism itself: "Can we continue to struggle for justice on an atomistic premise that society is merely a conglomerate of individuals who fall under the same set of laws? American society has never recognized that groups exist."[29] After dismissing the notion of the American melting pot, in which individual differences are evened out into a harmonious homogeny, he goes on to emphasize that what has been missing is precisely a robust sense of collective identity:

> Once we have rejected this melting pot, we can arrive at new definitions of social problems. In recognizing the integrity of the group we can understand the necessity for negotiations between groups. . . . Perhaps on this basis we can finally arrive at a society of laws and justice. The primary obstacle at present is the unwillingness or inability of the peoples of Western European descent to give up the idea that we are all the same—in every respect.[30]

For Deloria, the very notion of *the individual* projects a sameness of Western notions of individuality and all the legal implications thereof. In an individualistic framework, collective rights and needs barely register and thus cannot be well legislated. In fact, the legislation inevitably falters because the very conceptualization of society narrows precipitously to individual acts and behaviors rather than encompassing larger trends, needs, and patterns.[31]

A perfect example of this is Deloria's take on the Black Power movement of the 1960s. Widely recognized now as the father of the Red Power movement, Deloria does far more than simply advocate that Native Americans adopt the same framework as African Americans in order to understand either rights or equality. He writes poignantly that "when Black Power was first dominating discussions, many of us tried to speak meaningfully to blacks about Indian tribalism. Everything we said was passed off as a clumsy attempt to catch on to the coattails of the power movement and ride them to glory. No one would listen to OTHER ideas, such as the need for capital, the idea of the sovereignty of the group, and the necessity for grounding the movement in a land base peculiar to the local community group."[32] The underlying problem was that

> using a vocabulary that has definite meaning for whites and blacks does not remotely relate to other groups. Thus equality in a white-black context means that the black man should have equal legal rights and economic opportunities in his individual capacity as white citizens. In a Mexican-Anglo context the word equality may very well take on the sense that somewhere along the line Mexicans have been deprived of their rights to specific pieces of land guaranteed to them by treaties with Mexico. In an Indian-white context this specifically means the surrender by the white of his eternal quest for the key to turn an Indian into a Western European immigrant. The whole field of relationships between the different groups in society has been perverted by failing to understand the necessity to change words and meanings when dealing with different groups.[33]

Deloria's point is poignant: making equality equivalent across various groups of people, even within the same society, cuts off the potential for a robust understanding of justice. When equality is considered defined without attending to other meanings, perspectives, and languages, it risks precisely this conflation between equality and equivalence, with language masking the diversity of political goals. And yet that is precisely how equality tends to operate in the realm of rights: as an unquestioned baseline that leads to unintentioned conformity. The collective consciousness of Native Americans, Deloria avers, had much to contribute to that developed by African Americans—and that is the point: it is sometimes only on the level of groups that such crucial differences become visible. Only after considering collective needs can the right adjustments be made to laws that might otherwise be considered universal when they are based solely on the universality of the individual.

And yet, as mentioned above, the solution cannot be simply to make the collective, rather than the individual, the bearer of rights. Lionel Wee, following Jeremy Waldron, notes the homogenization that occurs when one tries to ascribe collective rights: a rights-bearing group must not only have clearly definable boundaries (who is in/out) but also tolerate little variance within it when it assumes that all members of said group should be identified with this right in the first place.[34] Internal group variation is especially problematic when discussing linguistic and cultural rights, which are typically accorded on the basis of a shared ethnic identity: establishing a group's rights to a certain linguistic pattern, code of dress, or hairstyle culturally essentializes such practices in a way that not all members of that group find tenable. Indeed, "given the need of boundary marking in a rights-based discourse, any language that has been enshrined as the object of a right (like the culture that it is supposed to be a part of) then acquires a solidity that can be significantly at odds with the actual experiences of its speakers. It is this that opens language rights advocates to charges of essentialism, despite the fact that some language rights advocates are acutely aware of the pitfalls of essentialism."[35] The need for internal consistency for this object leads to "a significant appeal to erasure" of inherent heterogeneity. Furthermore, Wee argues, rights have a strongly "comparative orientation," resulting in "the need to keep up with the Joneses, where if some group is given a particular right, then other groups must also be accorded comparable ones."[36] As Madeleine Dobie points out with regard to the Algerian context in her contribution to this volume, even when campaigns for minority linguistic rights have been successful, they have also "reinforced divisions between so-called Arabs and Berbers that were inherited from colonial ideology, and [their] actual impact on linguistic practice remains somewhat limited." Thus, even using collective language rights successfully tends to reify those collectives in harmful ways. This is partly what Deloria was describing with his discussion of inequivalent equalities: rights discourse does not readily permit different groups to have different equal rights. The discourse of rights thus runs the danger of essentializing and prescribing the possibilities of groups as much as it protects them.

For all these aforementioned reasons, Deloria develops an alternative to a rights-based system. He writes: "Developing a responsible self-discipline is not difficult, but it cannot be done in a society in which equality is perceived as sameness and conformity. Sitting Bull, looking with disdain at the white man's educational style, remarked that 'it is not necessary that eagles be crows.' We would do well to cast a critical glance at our ideas and expectations of democracy, brotherhood, and equality in the light of the demand for self-discipline."[37] At first blush, Deloria seems to be insisting that natural hierarchies exist and that those who are eagles are inherently better than those who are crows—but the fact that most eyes go immediately to hierarchies when reading this line demonstrates how confining the false binary in Western political theory is: one can adhere either to equality or to hierarchy, nothing in between. But what Deloria is suggesting is a different kind of *brotherhood*, one that works toward a deep understanding of how different life-forms in a particular space interrelate.

The starting point for Deloria is the larger ecosystem—the entire network of needs and ways of life—in a manner reminiscent of what the introduction to this volume calls the interrelationship between *logos* and *oikos*, language and ecology. As Suzanne Romaine states in her chapter in this volume, "Human well-being can exist only within both social and ecological limits," taking into account not just human activity but also the logics and rhythms of what various actors in a particular place, including nonhuman ones, need to stay in a sustainable balance with each other. According to Deloria, equality is not necessary to properly care for each other; in fact, insisting on equality can often get in the way. He writes: "Respect in the American Indian context does not mean the worship of other forms of life but involves two attitudes. One attitude is the acceptance of self-discipline by humans and their communities to act responsibly toward other forms of life [and also, one can presume, toward each other]. The other attitude is to seek to establish communications and covenants with other forms of life on a mutually agreeable basis."[38] The covenant that Deloria names here is explicitly *not* the social contract. Whereas a contract insists on equality or dignity based on mutual, rational agreement, a covenant presumes beings are equal in terms of dignity but not in terms of rights. This allows Nature and other creatures to count as keepers of the covenant and to make and keep agreements, just as people do. In a social contract world, reason creates the equality of its members, whereas in a covenantal world, the dignity and worth of all involved are the factors that allow the creation of the covenant. Ironically, it is only in the covenantal model that worth and dignity are not dependent on group consensus.

Furthermore, Deloria's ecology-based covenant has no basis in private property, least of all in land ownership. Instead, in a covenantal worldview, the land is a party to the ecological covenant. Deloria's ideas emphasize that reciprocity in the covenant and equality in the contract are not the same thing: when being responsible to another (including the land) and attending to their needs, equality is neither a prerequisite nor necessarily the desired goal. An eagle does not have to be a crow for them to find a way to coexist. Instead, insisting on equality can obscure the complex connections and differences that need to be taken into consideration in order to find the right balance among varied actors, needs, and desires. When compared to a simple equality, ecological responsibility is structured around a far deeper encounter with and awareness of the other. Deloria emphasizes awareness not just of others but also of the self's own needs, and thus of the self's dependence on others in covenantal living.

The question remains, then, whether rights discourse, with its insistence on equality, is the best way to talk about the complex realities of linguistic oppression and justice. Linguistic minorities in Europe, Africa, and the Americas have collaborated now for decades to insist on governmental aid and protection, sometimes with significant gain. These should not be diminished. And yet Moria Paz has shown through extensive research that, official language policies notwithstanding, no single *legal* case has ever been successfully made for someone based on linguistic rights alone: for the last two decades, claimants in courts have consistently demurred from insisting on linguistic rights in both Europe and the United States, opting instead to pursue their cases through claims of discrimination based on education and ethnic minority status.[39] In conclusion, Paz writes: "Rather than adopting a human rights approach to language claims, it may be better to break down this broad, overarching category of language rights into a collection of narrower, more particular interests, only some of which (and likely not most) are entitled to absolute protection under the law." Her reminder is prescient: "Those linguistic interests that we do not deem rights are not for this reason invalid or unworthy of protection; indeed an interest can be perfectly just, even if it is not framed in terms of human rights."[40] Breaking out of this rights framework could be what allows language the flexibility to be not just one in a litany of rights that are guaranteed to minorities but rather something elemental that allows minorities to have their own say.

Deloria writes that attention to the larger needs of the environment—for both human and nonhuman actors—could be a new form of "world-renewing," where "all possible elements of the universe must be brought within a harmony" rather than to equality.[41] In her contribution to this volume, Romaine agrees, stating that "we need to move beyond restrictive ideologies to embrace a new planetary perspective grounded in a firm commitment to genuine cultural and linguistic pluralism" if there is to be reimagining of language justice. But whereas Romaine emphasizes that simply enforcing "equal access" to English-language education in Africa and Asia will do nothing to lift "the bottom billion" out of poverty, Deloria's covenantal framework treats the environment not simply as a resource to be lived within or as an analogy for diversity but rather as an entry point into more flexible forms of thinking about language itself.

The author and artist Jenny Odell helpfully puts this concept into the framework of an encounter. Calling contemporary Western inattention to nature "a relatively recent problem of language," Odell finds a source of renewal in *Reinventing the Enemy's Language: Contemporary Native Women's Writings of North America*, by the Native American writer Gloria Bird. In this passage, Bird recalls the way her aunt talked about a mountain:

> In the long process of colonization, what has survived in spite of the disruption of native language is a particular way of perceiving the world. For example, my aunt once, when we were looking at what was left of Mount St. Helens, commented in English, "Poor thing." Later, I realized that she spoke of the mountain as a person. In our stories about the mountain range that runs from the Olympic Peninsula to the border between southern Oregon and northern California our relationship to the mountains as characters in the stories is one of human-to-human. What was contained in her simple comment on Mount St. Helens, Loowit, was sympathy and concern for the well-being of another human being—none of which she had to explain.[42]

While one could read this as a story premised on equality—where the aunt's comment reflects viewing Mount St. Helens as equal to a human being—ensuing paragraphs belie such a reading. Bird goes on to state:

> It is at this site [of dialogue with Loowit] where "reinventing" can occur to undo some of the damage that colonization has wrought. In becoming

attentive to the nuances of the English language and its ability to "capture" us, we can eliminate from our vocabulary terms of domination such as speaking of ourselves as a "minority" in relationship to a "dominant" culture, which will only serve to keep the power structure in place, unchallenged and unchanged.... In addition, the focus on what is being "lost" reinforces what we are told about ourselves, that we are dying, that our cultures are dying. Yet all around me I see evidence of the opposite.[43]

Importantly, Bird is not simply deconstructing harmful power dynamics between former colonizer and colonized so that the once disempowered now see themselves as equal in worth to the dominant culture. Instead, her focus on language centers on speaking *to* Loowit rather than for it, making dialogue rather than agreement the space of transformation. Indeed, the aunt's comment ("Poor thing") betrays the tension between naming Loowit as a "thing" in English and having an emotional connection that belies such language use. Here language is itself a subversive tool of connection and redefinition rather than one that merely "reinforces what we are told about ourselves." While linguistic rights may preserve languages, they can also become a way to limit languages and their possibilities for existence through the sheer language of survival. Bird's linguistic "reinvention" paradigm allows the Native perspective to reinhabit the English tongue—but not in the familiar terms of equal status. Rather, bringing that relationship of human to human into English creates a more holistic connection of sympathy and lamentation, spaces that are harder, but also more productive, reckonings with (at least one) Native reality.

Odell, a more mainstream American reader, goes on to write: "Reading this, I began to see that my reaction to the San Jacinto Mountains was something that Western culture and language gave me no way to conceptualize. It was a deep and hopeful suspicion that these forms were something more than rock, that they embodied something, that someone was there."[44] Perhaps the language for conceptualizing a covenantal world rather than a contractual one *cannot* come from within a Western language. There is no need to essentialize this difference, as if Native American (or Asian or African) languages are in some way simply more "natural" than Western ones. But it is the uneven contact between linguistic referents and cultural systems— Odell's realization of lack in her own English tongue—that prompted the spark of something new. While social contract theory is limited to seeing language itself as a human invention, the point of Bird's reflection is that the human-to-human relation to Loowit sees past the contractual requirement of language to a different way of understanding dignity.

In the final section, I propose that we need look no further than the inconsistencies of language itself, exposed through the process of translation, to find a path to a different kind of freedom that is not so trapped by equality's premise. Examining several translations of the UDLR raises powerful questions regarding linguistic equivalence and the political commensurability of rights. As I show, these linguistic inequalities need not represent or reinforce hierarchies, though at times they may; they can also resonate for us with that "deep and hopeful suspicion that these forms were something more."

TRANSLATING RIGHTS

The UDLR came together in Barcelona in June 1996, a joint effort of PEN International and a number of NGOs that involved over two hundred writers, activists, linguists, and policy makers. As I mentioned, the document was at once a literary work, a legal pronouncement, and a philosophical treatise. Starting with a fable and ending with poetry, the formal declaration consists of a list of stipulations and decrees on the rights of linguistic communities, in addition to a number of written testimonials and letters of support from relevant literary and political figures. The document drafted in Barcelona has since been presented to UNESCO but has yet to be ratified by the organization, perhaps for reasons mentioned earlier by Torner. A special follow-up committee is still working toward this ratification, even as PEN has gone on to collaborate with other organizations to articulate and ratify linguistic rights.

Regarding its own linguistic provenance, the UDLR is fairly clear as to its European origins. The original documents seem to have been prepared in Catalán and Spanish, while the English and French translations were produced therefrom.[45] On a more global scale, however, it is unclear into what languages the declaration has been translated and who the individuals are that completed these translations, despite the best efforts of the author to ascertain this information. These details matter, for though political equality and semantic equivalence are not the same thing, there are very real ways in which the "equivalent" versions of the UDLR manifest its political promise. On the most concrete level, translating the UDLR is what extends its reach and puts its claims to equality into the hands of linguistic minorities around the world so that they can vie for rights in their own contexts. More philosophically, if every language is considered equal (or should be made so), then translation into and out of that language often serves as the first step in acknowledging such equality. Like conferring legitimacy on a foreign government through successful economic or political exchange, translation's linguistic exchange manifests the political viability of all tongues to engage in active intercourse with each other.

Ideally, for this study I would have been able to examine translations of the UDLR in various Indigenous and endangered languages, the better to examine how its universality has been interpreted in as diverse a field of languages and contexts possible. This would have been especially helpful given the ecology-based argument that I have built largely on the work of Native American writers and thinkers. However, because of the limitations of both time and space (as I write, I am more place-bound than ever in pandemic lockdown in California), the sources I could find for linguistic comparison were those that were digitally available. That these are the western European (English, Spanish, and French) versions and, after some digging, the Chinese version is indicative of the still uneven visibility and accessibility of such a document, itself marked by the relative dominance of European languages in the discourse of rights.[46]

The collusion of European values and languages manifests even in some casual comparisons across translations. The original Spanish version of the UDLR, for instance, posits a goal of "hacer plenamente compatible el espacio comunicativo mundial con la participación equitativa de todos los pueblos, de todas las comunidades lingüísticas." This sentence is matched by the Catalán ("fer *plenament* compatible") and the French ("rendre *pleinement* compatible"), both of which stress the importance of the equitable participation of all in world communications. However, the English UDLR lists this goal without the adverb: it calls merely for "rendering the worldwide communications space *compatible* with the equitable participation of all peoples, language communities and individuals" in a new world order.[47] Though seemingly minor, this discrepancy between translations happens ironically at just the moment the text emphasizes a need for equitable participation. Indeed, this moment of difference points to the impossibility of the goal that the text is trying to name— to note how hard it is to make the world communications space "completely compatible" with the equitable participation of all within it.

Once the Chinese version, translated from the French, is taken into account, the lack of meaning equivalence becomes even clearer. The Chinese version states the goal thus: "From a cultural perspective, for worldwide communications space and the equal participation of all people groups, linguistic communities, and individuals *to become completely consistent/one with each other* (一致，*yizhi* in Mandarin) *in the development process*" [从文化角度使世界传播空间与各国人民、各语言社区和所有个人对发展进程的公平参与完全一致起来].⁴⁸ The Chinese phrase *yizhi* goes beyond making world communications "compatible" to making them "completely consistent," "of one accord," even "identical." It would seem that the less hegemonic power a language has, at least in relation to Western modes of thought (English → Spanish/French → Chinese), the stronger the insistence on a totally equal participation—so much so that the Chinese version requires absolute consistency, while the English version settles for "compatible" communication for all. All this is perhaps unsurprising, though one can argue (as I do) that these nuances are far from incidental when it comes to defining the linguistic rights supposed to be shared universally by all linguistic communities.

The nuances of translation can, however, open the path for other paradigms beyond that of a mere insistence on linguistic equivalence to foster political equality. This happens most effectively in the passages addressing the fraught relationships between individual and collective, language and land. While addressing the clash of territories or responsibilities in linguistic rights, Article 4 of the English UDLR states: "This Declaration considers . . . that *assimilation*, a term which is understood to mean acculturation in the host society, in such a way that the original cultural characteristics are replaced by the references, values, and forms of behaviour of the host society, must on no account be forced or induced and can only be the result of an entirely free choice."⁴⁹ It is a fairly close match to the Spanish version.⁵⁰ But whereas the Spanish and English versions emphasize the "entirely free choice" of the individual to adopt their linguistic and cultural expressions, the French version deviates significantly. Rather than declaring that *l'assimilation* is entirely free, the French translation states that this process "ne doit en aucun cas être forcée ou induite, mais bien le résultat d'un choix délibéré." The word *délibéré*—literally *de*-libéré, or "out of freedom"—suggests both the complete, unrestricted freedom that the English and Spanish versions advocate *and* its opposite. Meaning something close to the English word *deliberate*, *délibéré* emphasizes the restriction of careful, studied thought. Even more tellingly, while *délibéré* suggests something personal and willful (as in *délibéré en soi-même*), it more typically occurs as a matter of group discussion (*délibéré entre juges*, "deliberation between judges," or *une affaire en délibéré*, "a matter under advisement"). In the French version, the process of assimilation emphasizes less the absolute openness of one's freedom and more the pathways of and restrictions on one's choices.[51] It resonates with a group weighing in. The French version of an "entirely free choice" thus rescripts that founding principle of individual choice as something more specific and communal.

This emphasis on deliberation matters in light of what Patten and Kymlicka call the "deliberative turn" in democratic theory that has been growing since the 1990s. Succeeding a vote-centric view of democracy, the deliberative model emphasizes public discourse: "the decision-making process would draw forth the otherwise unarticulated knowledge and insights of citizens, and . . . citizens would test and discard those assumptions or beliefs which were found in public debate to be wrong or shortsighted or otherwise indefensible."[52] Wee agrees, stating that "deliberative democracy is emphatically not interested in simply allowing individuals to signal their preferences. Rather, it . . . [emphasizes] the principle of reciprocity . . . which demands that individuals impose on others and themselves the willingness to engage with the viewpoints of others to learn from such engagements.[53] Dobie's chapter in this volume provides a compelling example of multilingual deliberative democracy under way in Algeria, in which language is understood as an iterative "social practice" rather than a reified object that one needs rights to defend. As I see it, *deliberation* is a sign of actual linguistic context and relationship rather than just the promise of equality in rights or votes.

Language—a shared common language of debate—is a moving part of this deliberation process. Indeed, as has been evident in the UDLR, it is precisely the diversity of languages that can alert us to the latent debates (on the nature of *freedom*, say) that are already extant among English-, French-, and Spanish-speaking communities. The Chinese translation of *assimilation*, because it is made from the French UDLR, ends up adding further to the concept of deliberation: "相反，本宣言认为在任何情况下不应强迫或引

诱同化，它应是一种有意识选择的结果" (... [assimilation] should be a result of conscious choice).[54] The phrase "有意识 *you yishi*" refers to consciousness and awareness, though curiously enough its standard usage as a noun tends to be communal or systematic (as in 意识形态 "ideology" and 宗教意识 "religious awareness"), while as a verb it is typically used on a personal level to imply an awakening to a new idea or an epiphany (as in 他意识到了自己的责任 "he became aware of his responsibilities"). The aspect of careful discussion contained in the French *délibéré* then becomes, in translation, something that bridges the structures of collective thought with the internal choice of a person. In the Chinese version, this collective thought eschews the form of active debate and rather emphasizes the formation of latent cultural or ideological systems. Cultural assimilation for the Chinese reader thus again reshapes our notion of what it means to be "entirely free": to hold together personal epiphany and choice in the midst of the always present context of the individual's social background.

As the declaration moves into different languages, then, we see that it is not the same definition of freedom that is universally applied but an expansion of it: freedom takes on the larger ramifications of public debate and consideration, of both individual and collective awareness, that can be actively discussed while also ambiently present. While this disparity between the English and Spanish versions and the French and Chinese versions of the UDLR may seem like moments of mistranslation, this may be precisely what the process of universalization *should* look like: not repeating the exact same meaning(?) in endless succession but reforming these key concepts to fit different languages and traditions. Taken seriously, the translation of *freedom* here becomes what we make of it, such that what we *do* with languages shapes the actual rights that inhere. Importantly, it is the necessities of translation, representing languages' close relationship and communication with each other, that offer the opportunity for such small-scale epiphanies that can transform our thinking.

Where does this leave us, then, in terms of equality? If equality is not to be maintained by our mutual assent to one shared ideal, what could it be instead? The "problems" of translation begin to suggest that equality might be only a beginning rather than an end goal of justice. The translation process requires both the host and the guest languages to become othered, decentered, secondary to themselves. And when translation is not simply the matching of one tongue to the idea of another but rather the act of bringing linguistic fields together to reshape the idea itself, then translation becomes its own productive process. This is a good thing: the linguistic diversity I've identified in the UDLR's translations is not the same as political inequality, and yet my point is that this diversity is precisely what helps us to amplify our understanding of what political equality could be—for if the translations do nothing to influence the political rights they name, then we have lost the point of having equal rights in the first place. Those equal rights need to be open to interpretation, a looseness that sounds difficult and downright dangerous. And yet putting rights—even rights to language—above language itself risks making those rights applicable in only the most limited sense: as a concept defined in isolation by one political history, unable even to benefit from the diversity it proclaims, victimized by the conformity it seeks to hold at bay.

Rather than using equal linguistic rights to guarantee linguistic diversity, then, it may be that linguistic diversity is what continually and rightly challenges abstract notions of equality, requiring it to adapt—and not always equally. What we gain may be a more holistic, interconnected way forward into a future we make together.

NOTES

1. Universal Declaration of Linguistic Rights (UDLR), (English), trans. Beatriu Krayenbühl i Gusi. Universal Declaration of Linguistic Rights Follow-Up Committee, June 6–8, 1996, Article 3.1–3.2.
2. UDLR, trans. Beatriu Krayenbühl i Gusi, preface.
3. See Tove Skutnabb-Kangas and Robert Phillipson, "Linguistic Human Rights, Past and Present," in *Linguistic Human Rights: Overcoming Linguistic Discrimination*, ed. Tove Skutnabb-Kangas and Mart Rannut (Berlin: De Gruyter Mouton, 1995), 74–76, for a detailed breakdown of the five historical phases of linguistic rights and their development in the West over the centuries. The authors detail how early versions of linguistic rights were protections guaranteed first to religious and then to national minorities, usually in territories recently conquered by an external power. Among the protections guaranteed to these minorities was the right to conduct daily life and operations in their own language.
4. For instance, Article 22 of the Universal Declaration of Human Rights (UDHR) states: "Everyone, as a member of society, has the right to social security and is entitled to realization, through national effort and international co-operation and in accordance with the organization and resources of each State, of the economic, social and cultural rights indispensable for his dignity and the free development of his personality." Many have read the "right to language" into the "cultural rights indispensable for . . . dignity and the free development of . . . personality," though the connection has always been somewhat ambiguous.

5. United Nations General Assembly, The Universal Declaration of Human Rights (UDHR). New York: United Nations General Assembly, 1948, Article 22.
6. See Lydia Liu's discussion of P. C. Chang's contestation of the theological underpinnings of key texts from the Western canon and their notion of equality in "Shadows of Universalism: The Untold Story of Human Rights Around 1948," *Critical Inquiry* 40, no. 4 (2014): 385–417, https://www.jstor.org/stable/10.1086/676413. Liu details the involvement of Third World intellectuals in the UDHR's process of formation, which added new political dimensions to the notions of equality as originally articulated in the French and American revolutionary documents. Liu notes with regret that such contributions have been largely erased from our current understanding of the UDHR as a pure legacy of Western Enlightenment freedom and equality. It is this image of the UDHR—its conventional stature and understanding, as opposed to its complicated history—that I address in this chapter on the normative understandings of equal rights.
7. Miroslav Kusy, "Innate Dignity, Cultural Identity and Minority Language Rights," *International Journal on Minority and Group Rights* 6, no. 3 (1999): 302.
8. Alan Patten and Will Kymlicka, eds., *Language Rights and Political Theory* (Oxford: Oxford University Press, 2003).
9. See Daniel Nettle and Suzanne Romaine, *Vanishing Voices: The Extinction of the World's Languages* (Oxford: Oxford University Press, 2000).
10. Kusy, "Innate Dignity," 302.
11. Michael Walzer, *Spheres of Justice: A Defense of Pluralism and Equality* (New York: Basic Books, 1983), xv.
12. I discuss more of the translation process of the UDLR later in this chapter. In 2011, the UDLR was condensed into the 11-point Girona Manifesto, a simplified set of clear, actionable points embodied in the UDLR. In 2016, PEN International partnered with the Unrepresented Nations and Peoples Organization and others to produce another document: the Protocol to Ensure Language Rights, colloquially called the Donostia Protocol, which again asserted that "language rights must certainly be included among these basic human rights."
13. Carles Torner, "Linguistic Rights: An Interview with Carles Torner," interview by Peter MacDonald, Writers and Free Expression, November 22, 2018. https://writersandfreeexpression.com/2018/11/22/linguistic-rights-an-interview-with-carles-turner/.
14. As Hannah Arendt reminds us in "The Perplexities of the Rights of Man," "Equality, in contrast to all that is involved in mere existence, is not given us, but is the result of human organization insofar as it is guided by the principle of justice. We are not born equal; we become equal as members of a group on the strength of our decision to guarantee ourselves mutually equal rights." In other words, the individual exists as an individual only under the protection of a collective decision. To Arendt's point, Tommaso Manfredini's contribution to this volume avers that one becomes most conscious of one's need for collective belonging only when one becomes a refugee: thus shorn of a stable national identity, the refugee finds themself saddled with "the burden of proof . . . not only proof of being in danger but also proof that one is in danger as a member of a [persecuted] group." Individualism, it would seem, is taken for granted only as the locus of rights within a nationalistic framework. Hannah Arendt, "The Perplexities of the Rights of Man," in *The Origins of Totalitarianism* (New York: Harcourt Brace, 1973), 300.

15. Philip Pettit, *Made with Words: Hobbes on Language, Mind, and Politics* (Princeton, NJ: Princeton University Press, 2009), 2.
16. Thomas Hobbes, *Leviathan* (Oxford: Oxford University Press, 2009), ch. 4.1.
17. See Carl Schmitt's consideration of sovereign rights in *The Nomos of the Earth in the International Law of Jus Publicum Europaeum* (Candor, NY: Telos, 2006).
18. Radha D'Souza, *What's Wrong with Rights? Social Movements, Law and Liberal Imagination* (London: Pluto, 2018), 9.
19. Bringing rights discourse and "the light of civilization" to natives was often used as the justification for slavery and overseas colonization, such as in the Philippines at the turn of the twentieth century.
20. Mary Glendon, *Rights Talk: The Impoverishment of Political Discourse* (New York: Free Press, 1991), 9.
21. Michael Freeman, "Are There Collective Human Rights?," *Political Studies* 43, no. 1 (1995): 26–27. For more on this debate between the individual and the collective as rights-bearing entities, see Freeman, "Are There Collective Human Rights?"; Vernon Van Dyke, "The Individual, the State, and Ethnic Communities in Political Theory," *World Politics* 29, no. 3 (1977): 343–369, http://www.jstor.com/stable/2010001; Will Kymlicka, *Multicultural Citizenship* (Oxford: Oxford University Press, 1995); and Joshua Fishman, *Reversing Language Shift: Theoretical and Empirical Foundations of Assistance to Endangered Languages* (Bristol, England: Multilingual Matters, 1991). The most convincing argument for collective rights is that an individual's rights simply cannot be guaranteed if the group's are not protected, though this point merely instantiates again that the individual's rights are primary, while the group's rights are ancillary or utilitarian at best rather than inherent.
22. Thus, in *Just and Unjust Wars* (New York: Basic Books, 1977), Michael Walzer argues that individual collectives like nations have rights similar to those of individuals (by possessing rights to personal sovereignty and self-determination and also by being subject to forfeiting these rights when they violate other nations' rights). Even for Walzer, though, these rights inhere to the government of the nation, not to the people at large: "In the absence of a universal state, men and women are protected and their interests represented only by their own governments" (61). Even more tellingly, although these rights belong to governments, "they derive ultimately from the rights of individuals, and from them they take their force" (53), thus limiting Walzer's point on collective rights to the same subsidiary status as individual rights.
23. Torner, "Linguistic Rights," 9.
24. See John Locke's *The Second Treatise of Government* (Cambridge: Cambridge University Press, 1970). Locke's formulation adumbrates the point that the individual is defined *against* the group and specifically *by* their possessions.
25. Michael Walzer, *Spheres of Justice: A Defense of Pluralism and Equality* (New York: Basic Books, 1983), xi.
26. Lydia Liu's account of how translation produces the "same" word in another language in *Tokens of Exchange: The Problem of Translation in Global Circulations* (Durham, NC: Duke University Press, 1999), is a helpful analogy for what Walzer is arguing here. Liu's argument critiques Saussure for asserting that words possess independent equivalents in another tongue, without taking into account that this equivalence comes about only when other differences or possibilities for a translation have already been eliminated a priori in order to make the equivalence possible. Liu

writes that the notions of *sameness* and *difference* themselves "hardly [even make] sense until the languages in question are brought together in a reciprocal, differential, and antagonistic relationship by translation, etymology, and history" (33). Thus, the notion of sameness (and difference, for that matter) is *produced by* comparison rather than preceding it. In like manner, Walzer's critique of simple equality is that it presumes a preexisting sameness when this sameness is actually created by comparison rather than preceding it in an abstract ideal of *equality* as equivalence. Given this understanding, any kind of comparative justice must take into account both difference and sameness, as Walzer argues for in complex equality, since both are created by the same processes.

27. Walzer, *Spheres of Justice*, 19–20.
28. Walzer, *Spheres of Justice*, xv.
29. Vine Deloria Jr., *We Talk, You Listen* (New York: Macmillan, 1970), 106.
30. Deloria, *We Talk, You Listen*, 106–107.
31. A Marxist critique of this individualism runs through the works of Etienne Balibar, Judith Butler, and Ernesto Laclau, who fault the individual focus—and the rights that derive from it—for its blindness to the underlying relations between labor and capital. My critique differs from their communitarian alternatives by attending more directly to the role of language in shaping social relations and forming the basis of rights talk itself.
32. Deloria, *We Talk, You Listen*, 94–95 (emphasis in original).
33. Deloria, *We Talk, You Listen*, 87–88.
34. Wee's example of language policy in Singapore is telling. Singapore promotes a policy of multilingualism, in which the languages of the country's three dominant ethnic groups—Mandarin for Chinese, Tamil for Indians, and Malay for Malays—are all accorded official status and taught in schools alongside English. However, when Mandarin was designated the official language that the Singaporean Chinese community had a right to use, this action forcibly displaced the other ten Chinese dialects widely spoken by the Chinese population until the 1980s—other languages that, on a fairly arbitrary basis, did not enjoy this "right" of government sanction. That the Chinese population could have only one official language was at least partly due to the fact that the Malay community enjoyed only one dominant language and granting any more for another group would have troubled a hard-won truce in a pluralistic society. The result was a sharp decrease in linguistic diversity in order to make the Chinese community a rights-bearing entity. Lionel Wee, *Language Without Rights* (Oxford: Oxford University Press, 2011), 29–32.
35. Wee, *Language Without Rights*, 25.
36. Wee, *Language Without Rights*, 31–32.
37. Vine Deloria Jr., "If You Think About It, You Will See That It Is True," in *Spirit and Reason: The Vine Deloria Jr. Reader* (Golden, CO: Fulcrum, 1993), 51.
38. Deloria, "If You Think About It," 55.
39. The corpus of legal cases examined by Paz is impressive, encompassing all those submitted to the United Nations Human Rights Council between 1976 and 2012; to the European Court of Human Rights between 1959 and 2012; and to the Inter-American Court of Human Rights between 1979 and 2012.
40. Moria Paz, "The Failed Promise of Language Rights: A Critique of the International Language Rights Regime," *Harvard International Law Journal* 54, no. 1 (2013): 213.

41. Deloria, "If You Think About It," 55.
42. Gloria Bird, quoted in Jenny Odell, *How to Do Nothing: Resisting the Attention Economy* (Brooklyn, NY: Melville House, 2019), 24.
43. Bird, quoted in Odell, *How to Do Nothing*, 24–25.
44. Odell, *How to Do Nothing*, 146–147.
45. Between the Spanish and the Catalán versions, it is hard to identify a clear original. However, the English and French versions state that they were translated by Beatriu Krayenbühl i Gusi, a Catalonian linguist and writer.
46. The title page of the Chinese version of the UDLR asserts that the document has also been translated into Russian and Arabic, making the document available in all six official languages of the UN. Extensive internet searching, however, has not yielded easy access to those two latter versions of this document.
47. UDLR, trans. Beatriu Krayenbühl i Gusi, Article 4.
48. Shijie yuyuan quanli xuanyan [Universal Declaration of Linguistic Rights] (Chinese). Universal Declaration of Linguistic Rights Follow-Up Committee, June 6–8, 1996, 7 (emphasis added to English translation).
49. UDLR, trans. Beatriu Krayenbühl i Gusi, Article 4.
50. "Esta Declaración considera, en cambio, que la asimilación—entendida como la aculturación de las personas en la sociedad que las acoge, de tal manera que substituyan sus características culturales de origen por las referencias, los valores y los comportamientos propios de la sociedad receptora—no debe ser en ningún caso forzada o inducida, sino el resultado de una opción plenamente libre." Declaración Universal de Derechos Lingüísticos (Spanish). Universal Declaration of Linguistic Rights Follow-Up Committee, June 6–8, 1996.
51. Déclaration Universelle des Droits Linguistique (French), trans. Beatriu Krayenbühl i Gusi. Universal Declaration of Linguistic Rights Follow-Up Committee, June 6–8, 1996. https://www.pencatala.cat/wp-content/uploads/2016/02/dlr_frances.pdf
52. Patten and Kymlicka, *Language Rights and Political Theory*.
53. Wee, *Language Without Rights*, 164–165.
54. Shijie yuyuan quanli xuanyan [Universal Declaration of Linguistic Rights] (Chinese). Universal Declaration of Linguistic Rights Follow-Up Committee, June 6–8, 1996.

WORKS CITED

Arendt, Hannah. "The Perplexities of the Rights of Man." In *The Origins of Totalitarianism*. New York: Harcourt Brace, 1973.

Bird, Gloria, and Joy Harjo, eds. *Reinventing the Enemy's Language: Contemporary Native Women's Writings of North America*. New York: Norton, 1998.

Declaración Universal de Derechos Lingüísticos (Spanish). Universal Declaration of Linguistic Rights Follow-Up Committee, June 6–8, 1996. https://www.pencatala.cat/wp-content/uploads/2016/02/dlr_espanyol.pdf.

Déclaration Universelle des Droits Linguistique (French), trans. Beatriu Krayenbühl i Gusi. Universal Declaration of Linguistic Rights Follow-Up Committee, June 6–8, 1996. https://www.pencatala.cat/wp-content/uploads/2016/02/dlr_frances.pdf.

Deloria, Vine, Jr. "If You Think About It, You Will See That It Is True." In *Spirit and Reason: The Vine Deloria Jr. Reader*. Golden, CO: Fulcrum, 1993.

Deloria, Vine, Jr. *We Talk, You Listen: New Tribes, New Turf.* New York: Macmillan, 1970.
D'Souza, Radha. *What's Wrong with Rights? Social Movements, Law and Liberal Imaginations.* London: Pluto, 2018.
Fishman, Joshua. *Reversing Language Shift: Theoretical and Empirical Foundations of Assistance to Endangered Languages.* Bristol, England: Multilingual Matters, 1991.
Freeman, Michael. "Are There Collective Human Rights?" *Political Studies* 43, no. 1 (1995): 25–40.
Glendon, Mary Ann. *Rights Talk: The Impoverishment of Political Discourse.* New York: Free Press, 1991.
Hobbes, Thomas. *Leviathan.* Oxford: Oxford University Press, 2009.
Kusy, Miroslav. "Innate Dignity, Cultural Identity and Minority Language Rights." *International Journal on Minority and Group Rights* 6, no. 3 (1999): 299–306. https://www.jstor.org/stable/24674631.
Kymlicka, Will. *Multicultural Citizenship.* Oxford: Oxford University Press, 1995.
Liu, Lydia H. "Shadows of Universalism: The Untold Story of Human Rights Around 1948." *Critical Inquiry* 40, no. 4 (2014): 385–417. https://www.jstor.org/stable/10.1086/676413.
Liu, Lydia H., ed. *Tokens of Exchange: The Problem of Translation in Global Circulations.* Durham, NC: Duke University Press, 1999.
Locke, John. *The Second Treatise of Government.* Cambridge: Cambridge University Press, 1970.
Nettle, Daniel, and Suzanne Romaine. *Vanishing Voices: The Extinction of the World's Languages.* Oxford: Oxford University Press, 2000.
Odell, Jenny. *How to Do Nothing: Resisting the Attention Economy.* Brooklyn, NY: Melville House, 2019.
Patten, Alan, and Will Kymlicka, eds. *Language Rights and Political Theory.* Oxford: Oxford University Press, 2003.
Paz, Moria. "The Failed Promise of Language Rights: A Critique of the International Language Rights Regime." *Harvard International Law Journal* 54, no. 1 (2013): 157–218.
Pettit, Phillip. *Made with Words: Hobbes on Language, Mind, and Politics.* Princeton, NJ: Princeton University Press, 2009.
Protocol to Ensure Language Rights (Donostia Protocol). "Introduction." Donostia–San Sebastián, Spain, December 17, 2016. Available at https://protokoloa.eus/?lang=en.
Schmitt, Carl. *The Nomos of the Earth in the International Law of Jus Publicum Europaeum.* Candor, NY: Telos, 2006.
Shijie yuyuan quanli xuanyan [Universal Declaration of Linguistic Rights] (Chinese). Universal Declaration of Linguistic Rights Follow-Up Committee, June 6–8, 1996. https://web.archive.org/web/20150518094020/http://unesdoc.unesco.org/images/0010/001042/104267cb.pdf.
Skutnabb-Kangas, Tove, and Robert Phillipson. "Linguistic Human Rights, Past and Present." In *Linguistic Human Rights: Overcoming Linguistic Discrimination*, ed. Tove Skutnabb-Kangas and Mart Rannut. Berlin: De Gruyter Mouton, 1995.
Torner, Carles. "Linguistic Rights: An Interview with Carles Torner." Interview by Peter MacDonald. Writers and Free Expression, November 22, 2018. https://writersandfreeexpression.com/2018/11/22/linguistic-rights-an-interview-with-carles-turner/.

United Nations General Assembly. The Universal Declaration of Human Rights (UDHR). New York: United Nations General Assembly, 1948.

Universal Declaration of Linguistic Rights (English), trans. Beatriu Krayenbühl i Gusi. Universal Declaration of Linguistic Rights Follow-Up Committee, June 6–8, 1996. https://culturalrights.net/descargas/drets_culturals389.pdf.

Van Dyke, Vernon. "The Individual, the State, and Ethnic Communities in Political Theory." *World Politics* 29, no. 3 (1977): 343–369. http://www.jstor.com/stable/2010001.

Waldron, Jeremy. "Is Dignity the Foundation of Human Rights?" Public Law & Legal Theory Research Paper no. 12–73, NYU School of Law, New York, 2013.

Walzer, Michael. *Just and Unjust Wars*. New York: Basic Books, 1977.

Walzer, Michael. *Spheres of Justice: A Defense of Pluralism and Equality*. New York: Basic Books, 1983.

Walzer, Michael. *Thinking Politically: Essays in Political Theory*. New Haven, CT: Yale University Press, 2007.

Wee, Lionel. *Language Without Rights*. Oxford: Oxford University Press, 2011.

February
BEI DAO

night approaching perfection
I float amid languages
the brasses in death's music
full of ice

who's up over the crack in a day
singing, water turns bitter
bled flames pale
leaping like leopards toward stars
to dream
you need a form

in the cold morning
an awakened bird
comes closer to truth
as I and my poems sink together

february in the book:
certain movements and shadows

Translated by David Hinton with Yanbing Chen

二月
北岛

夜正趋于完美
我在语言中漂流
死亡的乐器
充满了冰

谁在日子的裂缝上
歌唱,水变苦
火焰失血
山猫般奔向星星
必有一种形式
才能做梦

在早晨的寒冷中
一只觉醒的鸟
更接近真理
而我和我的诗
一起下沉

书中的二月:
某些动作与阴影

Chapter Two

GLOBAL LANGUAGE JUSTICE INSIDE THE DOUGHNUT

A Planetary Perspective

SUZANNE ROMAINE

Even as global poverty levels continue falling, development agendas are failing to reach the most vulnerable. The United Nations Millennium Development Goals (MDGs) era, which ended in 2015, left nearly a billion extremely poor people living under the international poverty line (less than $1.25/day). The overwhelming majority of poor live in two regions—southern Asia and sub-Saharan Africa, where about 80 percent of the global total of extremely poor people live. The most disadvantaged children are those still furthest from achieving universal primary education completion, an unmet goal of another ambitious global agenda, Education for All (EFA). The poorest regions, not coincidentally, also have the highest number of out-of-school children and the lowest literacy rates.[1] At the end of 2017, 262 million children, young adolescents, and youth (comprising 18 percent of these age groups) remained out of school.[2] The poorest also tend to have the least access to the languages preferred at school: more than half of all out-of-school children live in regions where their own languages are not used in the classroom. Policies that discriminate against the languages of the marginalized poor severely compromise the power of education to improve their lives. They also increase the likelihood that language minorities will continue to constitute the majority of those still living in poverty. The crosscutting effects of linguistic diversity on all aspects of human welfare mean that global development agendas cannot reach the bottom billion until they speak to them in their own languages.

Examining progress toward global development goals in piecemeal fashion by focusing on one target or indicator at a time misses the larger picture of cumulative disadvantage that particular groups experience. Changing the normative perspective to make room for language requires teasing out and understanding numerous complex linkages among language, poverty, education, health, gender, and the environment that have been rendered invisible by prevailing models and discourses of development.[3] When we ask what language has to do with sustainable development, the short answer is *everything* if we look more specifically at who was left behind by the unfinished business and unkept promises of the MDGs and EFA. This is where language comes prominently into the picture. As the rich get richer, the poor do not remain merely poor: they become even poorer as they wind up in what Paul Collier called the "bottom billion" left behind by development.[4] Not only does a rising tide fail to lift all boats, but also it swamps the poorest and weakest of them in its backwash. As Ed Milliband, former UK Labour Party leader, observed: "Now the rising tide just seems to lift the yachts."[5] A vicious circle of intersecting disadvantages pushes language minorities into this bottom billion. Speaking a minority language constitutes an economic, social, and health risk because ethnolinguistic minorities comprise a large proportion of the bottom 20 percent still living in extreme poverty and suffering from poor health, lack of education, and deteriorating environments.

With nearly three-quarters of the world's 7,100+ languages concentrated in a small number of biodiversity "hotspots" inhabited by some of the poorest peoples, the fate of most of our planet's biological, linguistic, and cultural diversity lies in the hands of a small number of the world's poorest, who are most vulnerable to pressures of globalization and most marginalized by inequality of access to development.[6] Both languages and species are heavily concentrated through the tropics. Animal and plant species are being lost at a rate a thousand times greater than historical levels;[7] 25–90 percent of the world's languages may soon vanish.[8] Most are spoken by small groups and are unwritten, undocumented, and endemic—i.e., found nowhere else. With both species and languages facing similar threats and experiencing rapid declines in the same places, we are at a tipping point into a fundamentally less diverse world. What happens in these hotspots of biocultural diversity will determine the immediate welfare of millions—and ultimately the future diversity of life on earth.

Maintaining this biocultural diversity is inextricably linked to the survival of numerous small Indigenous communities, whose subsistence lifestyles depend on healthy ecosystems. Without such resources, they struggle to maintain their lifeways and cultural identities on which the continued transmission and vitality of their languages depend. Comprising 15 percent of the world's poor and one-third of the world's 900 million extremely poor rural people, Indigenous peoples live on lands containing about 80 percent of the world's biodiversity and speak around 60 percent of the world's languages, many at risk of extinction.[9] The poor are enmeshed in a vicious cycle where environmental degradation exacerbates poverty and poverty exacerbates environmental degradation. Climate change provides one of the clearest demonstrations of global inequality and injustice. The richest 10 percent of the global population is responsible for 52 percent of all total emissions, but the poorest communities, which contribute least to climate change, already feel the most severe impacts.[10]

This sums up in a nutshell where we are today. Proceeding without changes in policy and practice, especially in the education sector, makes it likely that linguistic minorities will remain the majority of those still living in poverty beyond 2030. The UN must do more than simply renew or repledge itself to the same framework. Nowhere is this clearer than in the UN's seventeen Sustainable Development Goals (SDGs), which replaced the expiring eight MDGs in 2016, setting the global development agenda until 2030. Meanwhile, the EFA agenda also ended with the launch of the Education 2030 Framework for Action, pledging to leave no one behind. SDG-4 aims to ensure equitable and inclusive quality education and lifelong learning for all by 2030.[11]

Bad policies, no matter how well funded, will not work. We need to move beyond restrictive ideologies to embrace a new planetary perspective grounded in a firm commitment to genuine cultural and linguistic pluralism as a foundation for global language justice. The next section introduces such a model based on a doughnut as a way of thinking about relationships between language and inequality in a linguistically diverse world and of explaining why language is the missing link in the global debate on sustainability, equity, and poverty.

CONCEPTUALIZING GLOBAL LANGUAGE JUSTICE INSIDE THE DOUGHNUT

Originally introduced by economist Kate Raworth, the doughnut is a visual metaphor for guiding sustainable development and depicting how human well-being can exist only within both social and ecological limits.[12] The innermost ring of the model is humanity's social foundation, inside which lie critical deprivations—e.g., poverty, hunger, illiteracy, and poor health. The outermost ring is the ecological ceiling, beyond which lie environmental degradations—e.g., biodiversity loss and climate change. Between the rings is the safe and just space where inclusive, sustainable development takes place, where we can meet the needs of all within the means of the planet. Raworth intends the doughnut primarily as a heuristic device to reframe twenty-first-century economic thinking by setting out a vision rather than a fully elaborated economic theory with specific pathways and policies. Although she does not mention language, I bring global language justice into the model by situating language inside the doughnut, thus moving beyond her vision in order to identify specific pathways and evidence-based policies for sustaining linguistic diversity (figure 2.1).

Thanks largely to development policies that push economic growth at the expense of the environment, we have already breached the doughnut's outer boundary in several places—e.g., climate change and biodiversity loss. Meanwhile, the bottom billion live inside the doughnut hole—i.e., below the minimum social foundation of well-being. The current economic system is failing the majority of people and the planet.

Raworth introduces another insightful metaphor in observing that "economics is the mother tongue of public policy. . . . It dominates our decision-making for the future, guides multi-billion-dollar investments, and shapes our responses to climate change, inequality, and other environmental and social challenges that define our times."[13] If economics is the mother tongue of public policy, it must be multilingual, and public policy in our linguistically diverse world must rest on explicit recognition of language as both a right and a means of inclusive, sustainable development. For me, this is the essence of global language justice.

GLOBAL LANGUAGE JUSTICE INSIDE THE DOUGHNUT

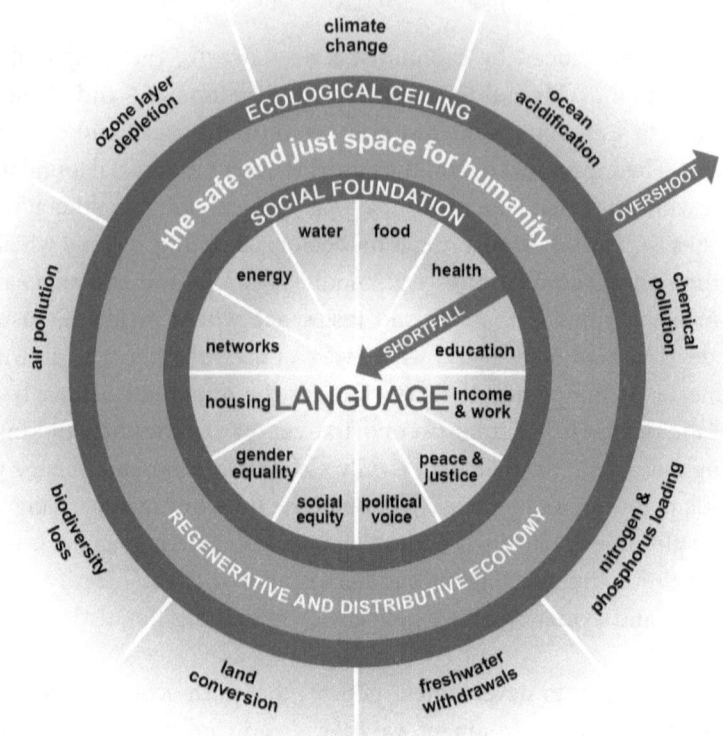

FIGURE 2.1. Global language justice inside the doughnut. Adapted from Kate Raworth, *Doughnut Economics: Seven Ways to Think Like a 21st-Century Economist* (White River Junction, VT: Chelsea Green, 2017), 51.

NO TRUE DEVELOPMENT WITHOUT LINGUISTIC DEVELOPMENT

True development cannot exist without linguistic development. With the most linguistically diverse countries hosting 72 percent of out-of-school children worldwide, a strong overlap exists between the geographies of educational disadvantage and linguistic diversity.[14] While virtually everyone acknowledges clear links between good education and a broad range of benefits impacting poverty, health, and gender inequality, there is limited recognition of the role language plays as an intervening variable in development. Most languages are currently excluded from education and other higher domains of public life. Failure to take language into account means that the goal of education for all translates into schooling for some.

The result is a lost generation of children in the poorest countries whose life chances are irreparably damaged by failure to protect their right to quality education. No country has achieved sustained economic growth without near universal primary education, but the vast majority of countries have failed to reach this goal. The global total of out-of-school children is 262 million: of these, 64 million (9 percent) are children of primary school age, 61 million (16 percent) are young adolescents of lower secondary school age, and 138 million (37 percent) are youth of upper secondary school age.[15] More than one-quarter of the world's out-of-school children are unlikely ever to enter school, including up to one-third in sub-Saharan Africa and up to one-quarter in southern and central Asia.[16] Following the 2008 global financial crisis, a sudden halt in education aid stalled progress in reducing these numbers.[17] This is especially true in sub-Saharan Africa, where the school-age population is growing faster than elsewhere; its share of the global out-of-school population of primary school age grew from 41 percent in 2000 to 54 percent in 2017.[18]

Focusing briefly on the African development landscape reveals how this vicious circle unfolds in the linguistically richest but economically poorest region on earth. As the second-largest and second-most-populous continent, with over one billion people, nearly one-third of the world's languages, and nearly one-third of the world's poor surviving on less than $1.25/day, Africa is particularly disadvantaged. The so-called Africanization of poverty underlines the enormity of the gap between Africa and developed countries on virtually all dimensions of human welfare. With the highest proportion of people (87 percent) without access to mother tongue education, some 90 percent of Africans have no knowledge of the official language of their country even though it is presumed to be the vehicle of communication between government and citizens.[19]

Ludwig Wittgenstein was not referring to Wikipedia when he wrote: "The limits of my language mean the limits of my world."[20] Nevertheless, with articles in only 317 (less than 4 percent) of the world's languages, Wikipedia is only as rich as your language; most content concerns a relatively small part of our planet. While African languages have many speakers, low literacy rates mean Africa has few readers and writers in any language. More than 50 million Hausa speakers have a scant 17,582 articles, while only 5 million Norwegian speakers have 595,452.[21] Even if the infrastructure existed and Africans could afford to access the internet, closing the digital divide means going the language last mile. Deborah Anderson and Isabelle Zaugg address the notion of justice and inequality in the digital sphere in this volume. Zaugg estimates that at least 95 percent of languages are digitally disadvantaged. Africa's marginalization from development processes is perpetuated by almost complete exclusion from the global flow of information, leaving most Africans disempowered and disenfranchised from political participation.

Girls are the first to be excluded. Gender disparities are among the most entrenched inequalities.[22] SDG-5 (achieve gender equality and empower all women and girls) builds on some targets beginning with the MDGs and EFA; very strong interlinkages exist between SDG-5 and the other SDGs. Gender parity in education has been seen as a crucial indicator of gender equality overall and was an intermediate goal to be achieved by 2005, well ahead of other goals. Globally, primary-school-age girls are still three times more likely than boys to be out of school, and 16 million girls will never enter school, including 9 million girls versus 6 million boys in sub-Saharan Africa. The poorest girls are almost nine times more likely never to have set foot in a classroom than the richest boys.[23] In Guinea and Niger in 2012, over 70 percent of the poorest girls had never attended primary school, compared with less than 20 percent of the richest boys. At the current rates of progress (or lack of it), the richest boys in sub-Saharan Africa will achieve universal primary education by 2021, but the poorest girls will not do so until 2086.[24]

Speaking a minority language and living in a rural area further compound female marginalization. Minority girls face numerous disadvantages, both as a group and as a subgroup of the disadvantaged. Nearly three-quarters of out-of-school girls belong to ethnic, religious, linguistic, or other minorities.[25] Fewer than half of poor rural females have basic literacy skills. Nigeria has a female youth literacy rate of only 58 percent, and 65 percent of Hausa speakers, comprising one-fifth of its population, have no education. Moreover, 97 percent of poor Hausa-speaking girls and over 90 percent of rural Hausa women between the ages of seventeen and twenty-two have fewer than two years of education.[26]

The push toward universal primary education in the context of the MDGs and EFA obscures an even greater crisis, especially for the poorest and most marginalized. Added to millions not in school are more than 617 million (or 6 out of 10) children and adolescents who have not achieved basic literacy and numeracy skills due to poor-quality schooling. This includes more than 387 million children of primary school age and 230 million adolescents of lower secondary school age. More than half (56 percent) of all children will not be able to read or handle mathematics with proficiency by the time they complete primary education. More than 85 percent of children in sub-Saharan Africa are not meeting the minimum standards; girls of primary school age are the most disadvantaged. Central and southern Asia have the second-highest proportion of those not learning.[27] In North America and Europe, 96 percent achieve the minimum benchmark for reading by grade 4. In sub-Saharan Africa, the region with the lowest youth literacy rate, only 40 percent do; even fewer do in southern and western Asia.[28] With "business as usual" progress, it would take a century or more for many developing countries to reach current OECD means set in international assessments like the Programme for International Student Assessment and Trends in International Mathematics and Science Study. Some countries would never catch up. This is true especially for the poorest and for girls.

THE COST OF BEING LEFT BEHIND

As a core component of the right to education and an indispensable prerequisite to lifelong learning, literacy is key to sustainable development. The Dakar Framework for Action stressed the importance of local languages for initial literacy.[29] Even a 10 percent increase in the share of students achieving basic literacy translates into an annual growth rate that is 0.3 percentage points higher than it would otherwise be.[30] Countries succeeding in raising literacy by 20–30 percent have also experienced GDP increases of 8–16 percent, with the strongest relationships in Africa.[31] Illiteracy is costly for illiterate individuals, who earn 30–42 percent less than their literate counterparts; for developing countries, which lose up to 2 percent of GDP; and for the global economy, which loses up to $1.2 trillion.[32]

No country has achieved continuous and rapid economic growth without first having at least 40 percent of adults able to read and write. EFA-4 aimed to increase adult literacy but was one of the most neglected goals. The global adult illiteracy rate fell only 23 percent by 2015, far short of the 50 percent target, which only 25 percent of countries achieved. This left 750 million adults, nearly two-thirds of them women, lacking basic literacy skills, a proportion unchanged since 1976, the earliest date available for the world total. In southern and western Asia and sub-Saharan Africa, 50 percent of women cannot read or write.[33] Adult illiteracy is a legacy of inequalities and restricted educational opportunities beginning in childhood. When schooling fails to ensure that all those completing primary school achieve sustained literacy, new illiterates continue to enter adulthood. If all children entering school after 2000 had left literate, we would have seen rapidly falling adult illiteracy. However, this proportion has not changed since 2009. An important reason is the increasing share of the population in sub-Saharan Africa, which has the highest illiteracy rate (41 percent) and the slowest progress, and it has not been able to deliver mother tongue education. Things will get even worse as the African population is expected to quadruple by 2100.[34]

The cost of being left behind by these inequities in accessing good-quality education is high indeed—as high as human life itself because health is related to every other aspect of development. Africa carries the highest burden of HIV/AIDS, malaria, and tuberculosis, accounting for more than half of all cases and deaths worldwide. HIV/AIDS continues to have severe impacts on women and girls, who in 2019 accounted for 48 percent of new HIV infections worldwide and 59 percent of new HIV infections in sub-Saharan Africa. For adolescent girls and young women (ages fifteen to twenty-four), HIV risks are especially pronounced, with adolescent girls (ages fifteen to nineteen) 4.5 times more likely to acquire HIV than their male counterparts. At the same time, knowledge about HIV prevention is alarmingly low among young women in sub-Saharan Africa, with only about one-third having comprehensive knowledge.[35] Because HIV/AIDS is the leading cause of death for women of reproductive age worldwide and remains the number one killer of adolescents in sub-Saharan Africa, this knowledge is critical to SDG-3 (ensure healthy lives and promote well-being for all at all ages).

From 2014 to 2016, the deadliest Ebola outbreak in history killed around 11,300 people, robbing a generation of children of a year's education and further undermining already weak health care systems in the three most affected countries: Sierra Leone, Liberia, and Guinea. The Ebola crisis was also very much a communications crisis.[36] The problem was indeed "how to spread the word," as a poster distributed by the Liberian government put it, especially in highly multilingual West Africa, with adult literacy rates below 48 percent and even lower for the poor, women, and those in rural areas. Officially, Sierra Leone and Liberia are English-speaking, while Guinea is French-speaking. In Liberia, however, only 20 percent speak English. Untranslated posters, flyers, banners, and billboards aimed at educating the public in fact serve only the minority elite because they are the ones who speak English. For the vast majority of West Africans, English information is of no more use than Swahili would be in Britain. One main criticism was the initial slow response when the disease took hold in spring 2014. Claudia Evers, Médecins Sans Frontières Ebola emergency coordinator in Guinea, said: "In the first nine months, if people had been given [these] proper messages, all this could have been prevented."[37] Information in languages and formats people can understand can help save lives in a crisis, but language is usually not seen as a priority in emergency responses. Misinformation, mistrust, fear, and panic spread quickly, leading people to hide their sick and bury bodies secretly.

Unfortunately, the Covid-19 pandemic has revealed the same failure to disseminate information in the languages spoken by the most vulnerable, even in developed countries such as the United States, where many do not speak English. The proportion of the population age five and above living in households where English is spoken less than "very well" has risen from 2.7 percent in 1980 to 8.2 percent in 2020.[38] In this volume, Daniel Kaufman and Ross Perlin state that they have found over seven hundred languages spoken at least by one individual in the New York metropolitan area, where the pandemic hit hard. Shahana Hanif, a Bangladeshi American representing New York City Council District 39, which encompasses Brooklyn's Kensington neighborhood and is home to one of the city's largest enclaves of Bangladeshi immigrants, said: "Information consistently reaches folks we want to target . . . last. . . . That sort of lethargy around language access is a deep failure. It is what makes access to language services and inclusive services life or death."[39] At Brigham and Women's Hospital, one of the best hospitals in Boston, staff noticed in March 2020, just weeks into the pandemic, that patients who spoke little English began surging into Boston hospitals and that those who didn't speak much, or any, English had a 35 percent greater chance of death.[40] In the EU, which has twenty-four official languages, the first communications addressing the Covid-19 pandemic were available only in English, which at the time was the native language of only 1–2 percent of the population.

MOTHER TONGUE-BASED MULTILINGUAL EDUCATION AS A FOUNDATION FOR AN EGALITARIAN THEORY OF SOCIAL JUSTICE

Globally, it is the poor who miss out on school.[41] Getting more of these children into school without changing the language of instruction will not solve the problem. Providing quality education to the poorest requires teaching them through the language they understand best.[42] Nevertheless, this commonsense principle is still the exception rather than the rule worldwide.

This is where my concept of global language justice inside the doughnut comes back into the picture. Deeply entrenched disparities in development outcomes of the type I have outlined reveal how far removed we are from satisfying the requirements of an egalitarian theory of social justice based on the premise that a society of equals is one where disadvantages do not cluster and there is no clear answer to the question of who is worse off.[43] Tackling these inequalities that are tied to socioeconomic status, gender, location, ethnicity, and language and that accumulate through life and compound over time is key to getting everyone inside the doughnut.[44] The most urgent task for an egalitarian theory of practice capable of offering guidance to policy makers is identifying the worst off and taking immediate steps to improve their position. We know who is worst off, and I have identified some key linguistic dimensions to these inequalities. Excluding up to 90 percent of the world's languages from education constitutes linguistic and social injustice. The group most impacted by injustices in language policy and planning, especially in education, is the rural poor (especially women and girls), who speak languages not represented in formal structures. As long as education relies mainly on international languages at the expense of local vernaculars, education will reproduce rather than reduce these inequalities, making sustainable and equitable development difficult, if not impossible, to achieve. Because language impacts the whole development enterprise, increasing linguistic diversity, especially through multilingual language policies in education, is key not only to progress with social justice but also to inclusive economic growth.

Children can more easily acquire literacy in languages they already know. This promotes more effective education, contributing to poverty reduction and to development, especially for girls and women. Mother tongue programs can produce competent readers in two to three years rather than the five or more years typical of many second-language programs. In countries where children average only five years of school and the poorest even fewer, mother tongue programs present the only possibility for the majority attending school to achieve even modest literacy. Many are still learning the alphabet in grade 3, rendering the first two grades lost years for learning content required by the curriculum. Early exit models in which the mother tongue instruction transitions to instruction in English or other international languages in grade 3 allow insufficient time for students to develop literacy in their own language, putting them at risk of never developing advanced skills that can later be transferred to learning to read English. The more developed children's literacy is in their mother tongues, the more prepared they will be to acquire second languages successfully. Submersion models plunging children into a second language with no instruction or support in their first are a recipe for persistent, if not permanent, underdevelopment. They will continue to produce a large underclass of almost 90 percent who will finish below the mean, with insufficient skills for doing little but manual labor.[45]

Many scholars blame bad language policies for leaving the majority of Africans behind. Neville Alexander claims that language policy in postcolonial Africa has been, with hardly any exception, an unmitigated disaster.[46] The perpetuation of colonial languages as official and/or national languages is one key reason "why the majority of African people are left on the edge of the road."[47] With very high repetition and dropout rates and fewer than 50 percent of African pupils remaining to the end of primary school, instruction through English (or other European languages like French and Portuguese) has done and can do little for most students; 80–90 percent of the population still has not learned European languages, despite more than five decades of such instruction.[48] Even in South Africa, where English has been a school subject for more than a hundred years and is widely spoken in larger society, proficiency is still very low among the poorest, predominantly Black population speaking African languages. Income inequality is also significantly higher in countries using colonial languages as the medium of instruction.[49]

Because language impacts the whole development enterprise, language matters more than ever to SDG-17 (create global partnerships for sustainable development). What prospects does the SDG agenda present for tackling these inequalities, especially those in education arising from unjust language policies that combine to trap the poorest in a cluster of disadvantages persisting across generations?

The Incheon Declaration, adopted at the 2015 World Education Forum, recognized inclusion and equity in and through education as the cornerstone of a transformative education agenda. Countries committed to "making the necessary changes in education policies" to address exclusion, marginalization, and inequities. To ensure that no one is left behind, they pledged that "no education target should be considered met unless met for all."[50] There is consensus at virtually every level, from the poorest family in the most remote village to the global policy leaders who are shaping the world's future development goals: education matters.[51] We must build on this consensus and open the school door to mother tongue teaching.

Quality education delivers monetary and nonmonetary returns benefiting individuals and communities, but educating children in languages they do not understand results in poor outcomes. Investing in the development of local languages in the context of high-quality, well-resourced, mother tongue–based multilingual education (MTBMLE) lays the foundation for sound economic policy promoting long-term sustainable development. It might seem easier and more cost-effective to immerse children as early as possible in the national and/or international languages they will eventually need for accessing wider opportunities and participating in national life beyond their communities, especially when school provides the only context for learning them. However, the added expenditure entailed in moving from a monolingual to a bilingual education system is much smaller than commonly believed. Where evaluations exist, they suggest additional costs of around 3–4 percent above the cost of monolingual schooling.

This estimate does not take into account the fact that using more of the children's first language will likely produce more effective learning of additional languages and reduce repetition and dropout rates, especially for girls, resulting in significant cost savings for education budgets.[52] If Zambia adopted Mambwe instead of English as its official language, it would move up forty-four positions on the UN's Human Development Index ranking, becoming similar to a country like Paraguay in human development levels.[53] In Ethiopia, mother tongue instruction introduced in 1994 has had positive effects at all schooling levels; the number of students completing six years or more of schooling increased 12 percent. Ability to read also correlated with a 25 percent increase in newspaper readership, which has been found to be positively correlated with measures of social capital and electoral participation.[54] In Senegal, newly implemented "simultaneous" bilingual education programs using the two most widely spoken national languages (Wolof and Pulaar) alongside French to teach literacy, mathematics, and science from the first year of primary school have produced superior performance compared to traditional monolingual French classes.[55]

Yet many countries continue to make poor choices based on ignorance, misguided political ideologies, poor governance, corruption, and military conflict.[56] Unsound policies that prevent quality education from reaching the most linguistically diverse populations have never realized a positive return on investment in educational, social, or economic terms despite significant financial and donor resources funneled into them. Failing to educate large numbers of young people results in unemployment, lost earnings, hopelessness, and instability. Being out of school has repercussions over the lifetime of individuals, over generations, and for societies as educational disadvantage is transferred from parents to children. Globally, for each additional year of schooling, earnings increase by 10 percent on average and even more for girls and poor regions like sub-Saharan Africa.[57] A one-year increase in average educational attainment of a country's population raises annual per capita GDP growth by 2–2.5 percent.[58]

UNESCO called for mother tongue education in a 1953 report on the use of vernacular languages and in other, more recent documents,[59] but estimates reveal that 2.3 billion people, nearly 40 percent of the world's population, still lack access to education in their own languages.[60] Intergovernmental and nongovernmental organizations are also doing sterling work, but relatively little coordination exists among donor responses. The World Bank, the biggest international donor to education, argued in 2005 that mother tongue education should be a part of its dialogue with educators and policy makers.[61] A more recent policy paper may signal its renewed interest in language with the recommendation that it should actively champion and lead the way on good language-of-instruction policies because they promote human capital accumulation and are therefore of acute concern to national policy makers and development partners.[62]

The Incheon Declaration mentions bi/multilingual education policies to address exclusion and encourages teaching and learning in home languages in multilingual contexts. It also recognizes the role of first languages in literacy. UNESCO's *Global Education Monitoring Report* adopted the proposal to measure the percentage of students in primary education whose first language is the language of instruction.[63] While acknowledging that tracking language of instruction is fraught with technical and political challenges, UNESCO stressed that countries and regions should tackle this issue head-on if no one is to be left behind.[64] Language policies need to be monitored; language of assessment matters too. Ministries of education need to conduct school censuses that include language data. We can also encourage researchers and NGOs doing household surveys of various kinds to collect language data. Surveys sometimes report languages spoken at home, but information is rarely collected on language of instruction at school—information crucial for understanding the impact of language barriers on school attendance. Because those furthest behind tend to belong to more than one disadvantaged group and suffer multiple, overlapping forms of marginalization, we still need better indicators to measure exclusion from education and to understand how poverty, gender, ethnicity, language, location, and other factors intersect.

We should also lobby ministries of education, policy makers, donors, and funders like the World Bank to convince them that money spent on MTBMLE is a wise investment for promoting long-term sustainable development. We should prioritize poor countries and earmark funds for MTBMLE. In December 2017, the World Bank gave Ethiopia $300,000 to improve its provision of quality education. Norway designated mother tongue education as one of its development policy priorities for 2017. Overall, however, aid to education has been declining and is far too low to meet 2030 targets. Aid would need to increase at least sixfold to fill the annual $39 billion gap.[65] With another global recession looming in 2023 due to the Covid-19 pandemic and other factors, I remain pessimistic about prospects for increased aid on a sufficiently large scale, even with targeted advocacy.

I am also not so naive as to imagine that simply increasing access to good-quality MTBMLE will provide a magic road to sustainable development. Political factors play a far greater role in selecting and implementing actual policies than do considerations of social justice or minority language rights. Language policy faces critical limitations as an agent of change when political, socioeconomic, and ideological currents flow in a contrary direction. Many countries will continue to make poor choices. Meanwhile, the global rush to adopt English as a medium of education at increasingly earlier ages virtually guarantees that most children in the poorest countries, especially in Africa and southern Asia, will be left behind.[66]

GETTING INSIDE THE DOUGHNUT

Although NGOs, governments, the World Bank, and even the United Nations have discussed doughnut economics, it has not really transformed the SDG agenda into a convincing road map for sustainable development. Currently, no country operates inside the doughnut's safe space, and we are far offtrack on SDG-4 and many other SDGs. There are many reasons for this, going far beyond this chapter's scope. I touch briefly here on only a few key issues.

The 2015 MDG report on Africa emphasized the need to focus on pathways and enablers rather than simply on outcomes.[67] Targets and indicators must be specific, measurable, realistic, and relevant. Targets with little chance of being met by 2030 are unlikely to receive political commitment, support, and cooperation from governments, donors, NGOs, and local communities. In addition, the SDGs, like the MDGs and EFA, are a voluntary agreement among nations without the force of international law. The more ambitious the proposed target is, the more unlikely it will be met. Many important concepts in the ten SDG-4 targets remain uncovered by the eleven indicators, and many important aspects of quality education remain difficult or impossible to measure.[68]

Looking briefly at SDG-4 illustrates why language matters. Target 4.1 is ambitious—and quite unrealistic—in aiming to ensure that all girls and boys complete free, equitable, and quality primary *and* secondary education. When only 52 percent of countries achieved universal primary education by 2015, ensuring universal secondary education by 2030 is clearly beyond the reach of most countries. At current trends and with no change in language policy, universal primary education will not be achieved until 2042 or beyond, with the poorest countries achieving this goal over one hundred years later than the richest. Even universal completion of lower secondary education is not projected to be reached in low- and middle-income countries until the latter half of the twenty-first century. No country has yet achieved universal completion of upper secondary education. Even at the fastest rate of progress, 10 percent of the countries in Europe and North America would not reach it by 2030.[69]

It is too soon to tell what long-term effects Covid-19 will have globally on education and other development goals. Official SDG statistics still reflect the prepandemic situation, and by October 2021, schools globally had been at least partially closed for 55 percent of their total days. Nevertheless, the quality of education for *all* learners across *all* countries has clearly been compromised, as the pandemic magnified existing challenges in literacy and learning. Minority language speakers risk being left further behind because emergency education tends to be provided only in major national or international languages. The massive shift to remote digital learning also underlines inequities in access and the need for linguistic diversity in the digital domain.[70]

Other SDG-4 targets express a utopian vision that most would probably endorse, but they are too vague, too complex, and too difficult to measure. Consider target 4.7: "By 2030, ensure that all learners acquire the knowledge and skills needed to promote sustainable development, including, among others, through education for sustainable development and sustainable lifestyles, human rights, gender equality, promotion of a culture of peace and non-violence, global citizenship and appreciation of cultural diversity and of culture's contribution to sustainable development."[71] Interestingly, this is one of the few places where cultural diversity and culture's contribution to sustainable development are mentioned.

Although it has become increasingly accepted that economic growth must be socially and environmentally sustainable, it must be linguistically and culturally sustainable as well. The conservation of biodiversity and cultural-linguistic diversity and the welfare of the poor are inextricably linked. Cultural-linguistic diversity is an important missing dimension in the proposed three-pillar model of sustainability, incorporating economic, social, and environmental components. Moreover, as the UN warned, global development agendas are unlikely to succeed unless underpinned by credible and committed means of implementation that take into account both financial and nonfinancial resources.[72]

Let's examine poverty reduction, the centerpiece of the MDGs and a goal central to the post-2015 agenda. MDG-1 promised to reduce poverty by half, while the much more ambitious SDG-1 proposes to eradicate extreme poverty, defined by the poverty line of $1.25 per person per day. There are at least two ways to accelerate poverty eradication: increase the growth rate of the global economy as a whole and increase the share of global growth of the poorest households. Introducing more baked goods into the discussion offers a way of evaluating these choices: we can either bake a bigger cake or cut it up in a different way. Anne Krueger, former World Bank chief economist and deputy director of the International Monetary Fund, endorsed the prevailing model of economic development when she said: "The solution is more rapid growth—not a switch of emphasis towards more redistribution. Poverty reduction is best achieved through making the cake bigger, not by trying to cut it up in a different way."[73]

During the MDG years of 2000–2015, inequality reached new extremes. Instead of an economy working for the prosperity of all, for future generations, and for the planet, we created "an economy for the 1 percent."[74] The poorest half of the world's population received just 1 percent of the total increase in global wealth, while half of that increase went to the top 1 percent. If inequality within countries had not grown during that period, an extra 200 million people would have escaped poverty. If economic growth had benefited the poor more than the rich, that number could have risen to 700 million. Instead of trickling down, income and wealth are being sucked upward at an alarming rate. Those in the richest 1 percent now have more wealth than the rest of the world combined. In 2015, just sixty-two people (fifty-three of them men) had the same wealth as the 3.6 billion people that make up the bottom half of humanity. The average wealth of each adult belonging to the richest 1 percent was $1.7 million, more than three hundred times greater than the wealth of the average person in the poorest 90 percent. This did not happen accidentally but resulted from policies favoring the dominant economic world order, which will never be inclusive or sustainable. Fraser Nelson, editor of *The Spectator*, a weekly conservative magazine published in Britain, ridiculed Oxfam for linking wealth and global poverty to convince us that "the poor are poor because the rich are rich: that wealth is a pie, and the powerful are helping themselves to an ever-larger slice."[75]

What happens if we continue to go for growth? Can we really have our cake or pie and eat it too? David Woodward estimated that at present growth levels, it would take at least a hundred years for the poorest two-thirds of humanity to receive $1.25/day.[76] For them to receive a more realistic $5/day would take two hundred years because the total poverty headcount would rise to 4.3 billion people, more than 60 percent of humanity. If we accelerated growth to try to eradicate poverty at the $1.25/day level by 2030, global GDP would need to increase by nearly fifteen times its 2010 level, and global per capita income would need to exceed $100,000. At the $5/day level, GDP would have to increase by 173 times its 2010 level, and global per capita income would have to be no less than $1.3 million. Baking a cake this huge would undermine SDG-12 (ensure responsible consumption and production) and SDG-13 (take urgent action to combat climate change and its impacts). It would entail unsustainable increases in global production and consumption that would cause irreparable damage to ecosystems.

Seen from the vantage of the doughnut, planetary boundaries represent an oven that is too small to bake a larger cake. Humanity is currently using nature 1.7 times faster than ecosystems can regenerate. This is akin to using 1.7 Earths. We would need at least 3.4 Earths to sustain this level of production and consumption. This also assumes that high-income countries would slow their present growth rates to zero. The losers would again be the poorest, whom we are trying to help and who live in areas most vulnerable to climate change but who are responsible for only around 10 percent of total global emissions while at the same time depending heavily on healthy ecosystems for their livelihoods.[77]

If we ask whether the SDG agenda is sustainable and in what way its vision of sustainable development differs from that of development, I conclude that the SDGs offer the disease as a cure: growth will solve the problems of poverty and the environmental crisis it has created in the first place. Relying on global growth to eradicate extreme poverty even by the highly restrictive $1.25/day definition is not viable without increasing the share of the benefits of global growth to the world's poorest by a factor of more than five. In other words, we would have to slice the cake or pie in a different way and decide how big a slice each of us can eat. In short, getting everyone within the doughnut's safe and just space is theoretically possible—but not without a radical rethinking of the SDGs and prevailing development theories.

Generally, the more social thresholds a country achieves, the more biophysical boundaries it transgresses.[78] No empirical evidence supports the notion that rich nations can make sufficiently dramatic reductions in resource use and emissions while simultaneously pursuing economic growth.[79] The only way of achieving a good life for all within planetary boundaries is for countries overshooting the doughnut's outer ring to significantly reduce their biophysical footprints.

RETHINKING DEVELOPMENT IN A PLANETARY PERSPECTIVE

The UN recognizes that inequalities in human development constitute a roadblock to achieving the SDG agenda, but time is running out.[80] We are almost halfway to the 2030 deadline. The need to rethink our approach to development is what prompted my exploration of the doughnut model to make room for linguistic diversity and global language justice. The doughnut highlights the importance of addressing environmental sustainability and social justice together. This idea is not new. In fact, it goes back to the Brundtland Commission, which recognized inequality as our planet's main environmental problem and early on offered a definition of sustainable development as "progress that meets the needs of the present without compromising the ability of future generations to meet their own needs."[81]

I have argued that linguistic diversity lies at the crossroads of a critical pathway to sustainable and equitable development. As long as globalization continues to drive growth by destroying the environment, all the while failing to lift the bottom billion, future generations will inherit a more impoverished and drastically less diverse world, and the future we want will be jeopardized by the flattening of cultural-linguistic diversity. Making room inside the doughnut for global language justice requires changing the normative framework of sustainable development so that linguistic diversity and multilingualism are included in the future we want.

NOTES

1. UNESCO Institute for Statistics (UIS), *One in Five Children, Adolescents and Youth Is Out of School*, Fact Sheet no. 48, UIS/FS/2018/ED/48 (Montreal: UIS, February 2018), 10, http://uis.unesco.org/sites/default/files/documents/fs48-one-five-children-adolescents-youth-out-school-2018-en.pdf.
2. UIS, *Meeting Commitments: Are Countries on Track to Achieve SDG-4?*, ED/GEMR/MRT/2019/HLPF/2 (Montreal: UIS, 2019), 3, https://unesdoc.unesco.org/ark:/48223/pf0000369009.
3. Suzanne Romaine, "Keeping the Promise of the Millennium Development Goals: Why Language Matters," *Applied Linguistics Review* 4, no. 1 (2013): 1–21.
4. Paul Collier, *The Bottom Billion: Why the Poorest Countries Are Failing and What Can Be Done About It* (Oxford: Oxford University Press, 2007).
5. Ed Miliband, Speech to the Labour Party Conference, Brighton, England, September 24, 2013, https://labourlist.org/2013/09/transcript-ed-milibands-2013-conference-speech/.

6. L. J. Gorenflo, Suzanne Romaine, R. A. Mittermeier, and Kristen Walker Painemilla, "Co-occurrence of Linguistic and Biological Diversity in Biodiversity Hotspots and High Biodiversity Wilderness Areas," *Proceedings of the National Academy of Sciences* 109, no. 21 (2012): 8032–8037.
7. Millennium Ecosystem Assessment, *Ecosystems and Human Well-Being: Multiscale Assessments* (Washington, DC: Island Press, 2005).
8. Daniel Nettle and Suzanne Romaine, *Vanishing Voices: The Extinction of the World's Languages* (New York: Oxford University Press, 2000).
9. Nettle and Romaine, *Vanishing Voices*.
10. Sivan Kartha, Eric Kempt-Benedict, Emily Ghosh, Anisha Nazareth, and Tim Gore, *The Carbon Inequality Era: An Assessment of the Global Distribution of Consumption Emissions Among Individuals from 1990 to 2015 and Beyond* (Oxford: Oxfam GB, 2020): 9, 27, https://oxfamilibrary.openrepository.com/handle/10546/621049; Thomas Wiedmann, Manfred Lenzen, Lorenz T. Keyßer, and Julia K. Steinberger, "Scientists' Warning on Affluence," *Nature Communications* 11, no. 1 (2020): 1–10.
11. UNESCO, *Education 2030: Incheon Declaration and Framework for Action* (Paris: UNESCO, 2015).
12. Kate Raworth, *Doughnut Economics: Seven Ways to Think Like a 21st-Century Economist* (White River Junction, VT: Chelsea Green Publishing, 2017).
13. Raworth, *Doughnut Economics*, 5.
14. Helen Pinnock, *Language and Education: The Missing Link* (London: Save the Children, 2009).
15. UIS, *Meeting Commitments*, 2.
16. UIS, *Literacy Rates Continue to Rise from One Generation to the Next*, Fact Sheet no. 45, FS/2017/LIT/45 (Montreal: UIS, 2017), 9, http://uis.unesco.org/sites/default/files/documents/fs45-literacy-rates-continue-rise-generation-to-next-en-2017_0.pdf.
17. UIS, *Meeting Commitments*, 2.
18. UIS, *Meeting Commitments*, 3.
19. United Nations Development Program (UNDP), *Human Development Report 2004: Cultural Liberty in Today's Diverse World* (New York: UNDP, 2004), 34.
20. Ludwig Wittgenstein, *Tractatus Logico-philosophicus*, trans. D. F. Pears and B. F. McGuinness (London: Routledge & Kegan Paul, 1961), 5–6.
21. Wikipedia, "List of Wikipedias" entry, accessed August 11, 2022, https://en.wikipedia.org/wiki/List_of_Wikipedias.
22. UNDP, *Human Development Report 2019: Beyond Income, Beyond Averages, Beyond Today; Inequalities in Human Development in the 21st Century* (New York: UNDP, 2019), 12.
23. UIS, *One in Five Children, Adolescents and Youth is Out of School*.
24. UNESCO and UNICEF, *Fixing the Broken Promise of Education for All* (Montreal: UNESCO, 2015), 56, 61.
25. Maureen Lewis and Marlaine Lockheed, *Inexcusable Absence: Why 60 Million Girls Still Aren't in School and What To Do About It* (Washington, DC: Center for Global Development, 2006).
26. UNESCO, *EFA Global Monitoring Report 2010: Reaching the Marginalized* (Paris: UNESCO and Oxford University Press, 2010), 60, 152, 167.

27. UIS, *More Than One-Half of Children and Adolescents Are Not Learning Worldwide*, Fact Sheet no. 46, UIS/FS/2017/ED/46 (Montreal: UIS, September 2017), 2, 7, http://uis.unesco.org/sites/default/files/documents/fs46-more-than-half-children-not-learning-en-2017.pdf.
28. UNESCO, *EFA Global Monitoring Report 2013–2014: Teaching and Learning; Achieving Quality for All* (Paris: UNESCO, 2014), 91.
29. UNESCO, *The Dakar Framework for Action: Education for All* (Paris: UNESCO, 2000).
30. Anthony Cree, Andrew Kay, and June Steward, *The Economic and Social Cost of Illiteracy: A Snapshot of Illiteracy in a Global Context* (Melbourne: World Literacy Foundation, 2012).
31. David Wheeler, "Human Resources Development and Economic Growth in Developing Countries: A Simultaneous Model" (World Bank Staff Working Paper no. 408, Washington, DC, 1980).
32. Cree, Kay, and Steward, *The Economic and Social Cost of Illiteracy*.
33. UIS, *Literacy Rates Continue to Rise*.
34. United Nations, *World Population Prospects: The 2017 Revision* (New York: United Nations, 2017).
35. Joint United Nations Program on HIV/AIDS (UNAIDS), *Evidence Review: Implementation of the 2016–2021 UNAIDS Strategy; On the Fast-Track to End AIDS* (Geneva: UNAIDS, 2020), 61, 65, https://www.unaids.org/sites/default/files/media_asset/PCB47_CRP3_Evidence_Review_EN.pdf.
36. See also Charles L. Briggs and Clara Mantini-Briggs, *Tell Me Why My Children Died: Rabies, Indigenous Knowledge, and Communicative Justice* (Durham, NC: Duke University Press, 2016). The authors use the term *communicative justice* in their investigation of connections between health and communicative inequities in epidemics among Indigenous communities in the eastern Venezuelan rain forest..
37. Quoted in Nadia Berger and Grace Tang, "Ebola: A Crisis of Language," *Humanitarian Exchange* 64 (2015): 35.
38. American Community Survey, "DP02: Selected Social Characteristics in the United States," U.S. Census Bureau, accessed August 11, 2022, https://data.census.gov/cedsci/table?tid=ACSDP5Y2020.DP02&hidePreview=true.
39. Quoted in Sara Dorn, "Language Barriers Compound COVID-19 Challenges Among Non-English Speakers," *City and State New York*, January 24, 2022, https://www.cityandstateny.com/policy/2022/01/language-barriers-compound-covid-19-challenges-among-non-english-speakers/361054/.
40. Martha Bebinger, "Hospital Adapts Language Plan After LEP Deaths," *Multilingual*, February 8, 2021. https://multilingual.com/hospital-adapts-language-plan-after-lep-deaths/.
41. UIS, *Literacy Rates Continue to Rise*, 4.
42. Stephen L. Walter and Carol Benson, "Language Policy and Medium of Instruction in Formal Education," in *The Cambridge Handbook of Language Policy*, ed. Bernard Spolsky (Cambridge: Cambridge University Press, 2012), 278–300.
43. Jonathan Wolff and Aver de-Shalit, *Disadvantage* (Oxford: Oxford University Press, 2007), 10.
44. See Bo's chapter in this volume for discussion of limitations in our understandings of equality in the quest for justice.

45. Stephen L. Walter, "The Language of Instruction Issue: Framing an Empirical Perspective," in *The Handbook of Educational Linguistics*, ed. Bernard Spolsky and Francis M. Hult (Oxford: Blackwell, 2008), 128–140.
46. Neville Alexander, "The Impact of the Hegemony of English on Access to and Quality of Education with Special Reference to South Africa," in *Language and Poverty*, ed. Wayne Harbert, Sally McConnell-Ginet, Amanda Miller, and John Whitman (Bristol, England: Multilingual Matters, 2008), 60.
47. Paulin G. Djité, "From Liturgy to Technology: Modernizing the Languages of Africa," *Language Problems and Language Planning* 32, no. 2 (2008): 133.
48. Hassana Alidou, Aliou Boly, Birgit Brock-Utne, Yaya S. Diallo, Kathleen Heugh, and H. Ekkehard Wolff, eds. *Optimizing Language and Education in Africa—The Language Factor* (Paris: Association for the Development of Education in Africa, 2006).
49. Gary Coyne, "Language Education Policies and Inequality in Africa: Cross-National Empirical Evidence," *Comparative Education Review* 59, no. 4 (2015): 619–637.
50. UNESCO, *Education 2030*, iv.
51. UNESCO/UNICEF. 2015. *Fixing the Broken promise of Education for All*. Montreal: UNESCO.
52. Carol Benson, *Girls, Educational Equity and Mother Tongue-Based Teaching*. (Bangkok: UNESCO, 2005).
53. David D. Laitin and Rajesh Ramachandran, "Language Policy and Human Development," *American Political Science Review* 110, no. 3 (2016): 458.
54. Rajesh Ramachandran, "Language Use in Education and Human Capital Formation: Evidence from the Ethiopian Educational Reform," *World Development* 98 (2017): 208.
55. Carol Benson, "An Innovative 'Simultaneous' Bilingual Approach in Senegal: Promoting Interlinguistic Transfer While Contributing to Policy Change," *International Journal of Bilingual Education and Bilingualism* 24, no. 5 (2020): 1399–1416, https://doi.org/10.1080/13670050.2020.1765968.
56. Suzanne Romaine, "Linguistic Diversity and Global English: The Pushmi-pullyu of Language Policy and Political Economy," in *Language Policy and Political Economy: English in a Global Context*, ed. Thomas Ricento (Oxford: Oxford University Press, 2015): 252–275.
57. Claudio E. Montenegro and Harry A. Patrinos, *Comparable Estimates of Returns to Schooling Around the World* (Policy Research Working Paper no. 7020, World Bank, Education Global Practice Group, Washington, DC. 2014); UNESCO, *Global Education Monitoring Report 2016: Education for People and Planet, Creating Sustainable Futures for All* (Paris: UNESCO, 2016), 58.
58. UNESCO, *EFA Global Monitoring Report 2013–2014*, 151.
59. UNESCO, *The Use of Vernacular Languages in Education* (Paris: UNESCO, 1953), and *Education in a Multilingual World* (Paris: UNESCO, 2003).
60. UNESCO, *If You Don't Understand, How Can You Learn?*, Policy Paper no. 24 (Paris: UNESCO, 2016).
61. Penelope Bender, Nadine Dutcher, David Klaus, Jane Shore, and Charlie Tesar. *In Their Own Language: Education for All*. Washington, DC: World Bank, 2005.
62. International Bank for Reconstruction and Development/The World Bank, *Loud and Clear: Effective Language of Instruction Policies for Learning* (Washington, DC: World Bank Group, 2021), 8.
63. UNESCO, *Education 2030*, iii.

64. UNESCO, *Global Education Monitoring Report 2016*, 255, 267–270.
65. UIS, *Meeting Commitments*, 11.
66. Romaine, "Linguistic Diversity and Global English."
67. United Nations, *Millennium Development Goals Report* (New York: United Nations. 2015), xviii.
68. UNESCO, *Global Education Monitoring Report 2016*, 170.
69. UNESCO, *Global Education Monitoring Report 2016*, 20, 150, 152.
70. International Bank for Reconstruction and Development/The World Bank, *Loud and Clear*, 28; see also Anderson and Zaugg in this volume.
71. UNESCO, *Education 2030*,.
72. United Nations, *Millennium Development Goals Report 2015*, xviii.
73. Anne O. Krueger, "Letting the Future In: India's Continuing Reform Agenda" (keynote speech to Stanford India Conference, Stanford, CA, June 4, 2004), https://www.imf.org/en/News/Articles/2015/09/28/04/53/sp060404.
74. Oxfam, *An Economy for the 1%: How Privilege and Power in the Economy Drive Extreme Inequality and How This Can Be Stopped* (Oxford: Oxfam, 2016).
75. Fraser Nelson, "What Oxfam Doesn't Want You to Know: Global Capitalism Means There's Less Poverty than Ever," *The Spectator*, January 19, 2015, https://www.spectator.co.uk/article/what-oxfam-doesn-t-want-you-to-know-global-capitalism-means-less-poverty-than-ever/.
76. David Woodward, "*Incrementum ad Absurdum*: Global Growth, Inequality and Poverty Eradication in a Carbon-Constrained World," *World Economic Review* 4 (2015): 43–62.
77. Global Footprint Network, "Ecological Footprint," accessed March 16, 2020, https://www.footprintnetwork.org/our-work/ecological-footprint/.
78. Daniel W. O'Neill, Andrew L. Fanning, William F. Lamb, and Julia K. Steinberger, "A Good Life for All Within Planetary Boundaries," *Nature Sustainability* 1 (2018): 88–95.
79. Jason Hickel, "Is It Possible to Achieve a Good Life for All Within Planetary Boundaries?," *Third World Quarterly* 40, no. 1 (2019): 30.
80. UNDP, *Human Development Report 2019*, 1.
81. World Commission on Environment and Development, *Our Common Future* (New York: Oxford University Press, 1987), 6.

WORKS CITED

Alexander, Neville. "The Impact of the Hegemony of English on Access to and Quality of Education with Special Reference to South Africa." In *Language and Poverty*, ed. Wayne Harbert, Sally McConnell-Ginet, Amanda Miller, and John Whitman, 53–67. Bristol, England: Multilingual Matters, 2008.

Alidou, Hassana, Aliou Boly, Birgit Brock-Utne, Yaya S. Diallo, Kathleen Heugh, and H. Ekkehard Wolff, eds. 2006. *Optimizing Language and Education in Africa—The Language Factor*. Paris: Association for the Development of Education in Africa.

American Community Survey. "DP02: Selected Social Characteristics in the United States." U.S. Census Bureau. Accessed August 11, 2022. https://data.census.gov/cedsci/table?tid=ACSDP5Y2020.DP02&hidePreview=true.

Bebinger, Martha. "Hospital Adapts Language Plan After LEP Deaths." *Multilingual*, February 8, 2021. Accessed August 11, 2022. https://multilingual.com/hospital-adapts-language-plan-after-lep-deaths/.

Bender, Penelope, Nadine Dutcher, David Klaus, Jane Shore, and Charlie Tesar. *In Their Own Language: Education for All*. Washington, DC: World Bank, 2005.

Benson, Carol. *Girls, Educational Equity and Mother Tongue–Based Teaching*. Bangkok: UNESCO, 2005.

Benson, Carol. "An Innovative 'Simultaneous' Bilingual Approach in Senegal: Promoting Interlinguistic Transfer While Contributing to Policy Change." *International Journal of Bilingual Education and Bilingualism* 24, no. 5 (2020): 1399–1416. https://doi.org/10.1080/13670050.2020.1765968.

Berger, Nadia, and Grace Tang. "Ebola: A Crisis of Language." *Humanitarian Exchange* no. 64 (2015): 33–35.

Briggs, Charles L., and Clara Mantini-Briggs. *Tell Me Why My Children Died: Rabies, Indigenous Knowledge, and Communicative Justice*. Durham, NC: Duke University Press, 2016.

Collier, Paul. *The Bottom Billion: Why the Poorest Countries Are Failing and What Can Be Done About It*. Oxford: Oxford University Press, 2007.

Coyne, Gary. "Language Education Policies and Inequality in Africa: Cross-National Empirical Evidence." *Comparative Education Review* 59, no. 4 (2015): 619–637.

Cree, Anthony, Andrew Kay, and June Steward. *The Economic and Social Cost of Illiteracy: A Snapshot of Illiteracy in a Global Context*. Melbourne: World Literacy Foundation, 2012.

Djité, Paulin G. "From Liturgy to Technology. Modernizing the Languages of Africa." *Language Problems and Language Planning* 32, no. 2 (2008): 133–152.

Dorn, Sara. "Language Barriers Compound COVID-19 Challenges Among Non-English Speakers." *City and State New York*, January 24, 2022, 18–20. https://www.cityandstateny.com/policy/2022/01/language-barriers-compound-covid-19-challenges-among-non-english-speakers/361054/.

Global Footprint Network. "Ecological Footprint." Accessed March 16, 2020. https://www.footprintnetwork.org/our-work/ecological-footprint/.

Gorenflo, L. J., Suzanne Romaine, R. A. Mittermeier, and Kristen Walker Painemilla. "Co-occurrence of Linguistic and Biological Diversity in Biodiversity Hotspots and High Biodiversity Wilderness Areas." *Proceedings of the National Academy of Sciences* 109, no. 21 (2012): 8032–8037.

Hickel, Jason. "Is It Possible to Achieve a Good Life for All Within Planetary Boundaries?" *Third World Quarterly* 40, no. 1 (2019): 18–35.

International Bank for Reconstruction and Development/The World Bank. *Loud and Clear: Effective Language of Instruction Policies for Learning*. Washington, DC: World Bank Group, 2021.

Joint United Nations Program on HIV/AIDS (UNAIDS). *Evidence Review: Implementation of the 2016–2021 UNAIDS Strategy; On the Fast-Track to End AIDS*. Geneva: UNAIDS, 2020. https://www.unaids.org/sites/default/files/media_asset/PCB47_CRP3_Evidence_Review_EN.pdf.

Kartha, Sivan, Eric Kempt-Benedict, Emily Ghosh, Anisha Nazareth, and Tim Gore. *The Carbon Inequality Era: An Assessment of the Global Distribution of Consumption*

Emissions Among Individuals from 1990 to 2015 and Beyond. Oxford: Oxfam GB, 2020. https://oxfamilibrary.openrepository.com/handle/10546/621049.

Krueger, Anne O. "Letting the Future In: India's Continuing Reform Agenda." Keynote speech to Stanford India Conference, Stanford, CA, June 4, 2004. https://www.imf.org/en/News/Articles/2015/09/28/04/53/sp060404.

Laitin, David D., and Rajesh Ramachandran. "Language Policy and Human Development." *American Political Science Review* 110, no. 3 (2016): 457–480.

Lewis, Maureen, and Marlaine Lockheed. *Inexcusable Absence: Why 60 Million Girls Still Aren't in School and What To Do About It.* Washington, DC: Center for Global Development, 2006.

Millennium Ecosystem Assessment. *Ecosystems and Human Well-Being: Multiscale Assessments.* Washington, DC: Island, 2005.

Milliband, Ed. Speech to the Labour Party Conference, Brighton, England, September 24, 2013. https://labourlist.org/2013/09/transcript-ed-milibands-2013-conference-speech/.

Montenegro, Claudio E., and Harry A. Patrinos. *Comparable Estimates of Returns to Schooling Around the World.* Policy Research Working Paper no. 7020, World Bank, Education Global Practice Group, Washington, DC, 2014.

Nelson, Fraser. "What Oxfam Doesn't Want You to Know: Global Capitalism Means There's Less Poverty than Ever." *The Spectator*, January 19, 2015. https://www.spectator.co.uk/article/what-oxfam-doesn-t-want-you-to-know-global-capitalism-means-less-poverty-than-ever/.

Nettle, Daniel, and Suzanne Romaine. *Vanishing Voices: The Extinction of the World's Languages.* New York: Oxford University Press, 2000.

O'Neill, Daniel W., Andrew L. Fanning, William F. Lamb, and Julia K. Steinberger. "A Good Life for All Within Planetary Boundaries." *Nature Sustainability* 1 (2018): 88–95.

Oxfam. *An Economy for the 1 Percent: How Privilege and Power in the Economy Drive Extreme Inequality and How This Can Be Stopped.* Oxford: Oxfam, 2016.

Pinnock, Helen. *Language and Education: The Missing Link.* London: Save the Children, 2009.

Ramachandran, Rajesh. "Language Use in Education and Human Capital Formation: Evidence from the Ethiopian Educational Reform." *World Development* 98 (2017): 195–213.

Raworth, Kate. *Doughnut Economics: Seven Ways to Think Like a 21st-Century Economist.* White River Junction, VT: Chelsea Green Publishing, 2017.

Romaine, Suzanne. "Keeping the Promise of the Millennium Development Goals: Why Language Matters." *Applied Linguistics Review* 4, no. 1 (2013): 1–21.

Romaine, Suzanne. "Linguistic Diversity and Global English: The Pushmi-pullyu of Language Policy and Political Economy." In *Language Policy and Political Economy: English in a Global Context*, ed. Thomas Ricento, 252–275. Oxford: Oxford University Press. 2015.

United Nations. *Millennium Development Goals Report 2015.* New York: United Nations, 2015.

United Nations. *World Population Prospects: The 2017 Revision.* New York: United Nations, 2017.

United Nations Development Program (UNDP). *Human Development Report 2004: Cultural Liberty in Today's Diverse World.* New York: UNDP, 2004.

UNDP. *Human Development Report 2015: Work for Human Development*. New York: UNDP, 2015.

UNDP. *Human Development Report 2019: Beyond Income, Beyond Averages, Beyond Today; Inequalities in Human Development in the 21st Century*. New York: UNDP, 2019.

United Nations Economic Commission for Africa, African Union, African Development Bank, and United Nations Development Program. *MDG Report 2015: Assessing Progress in Africa Toward the Millennium Development Goals*. Addis Ababa: United Nations Economic Commission for Africa et al., 2015.

United Nations Educational, Scientific, and Cultural Organization (UNESCO). *The Dakar Framework for Action: Education for All*. Paris: UNESCO, 2000.

UNESCO. *Education in a Multilingual World*. Paris: UNESCO, 2003.

UNESCO. *Education 2030: Incheon Declaration and Framework for Action*. Paris: UNESCO, 2015.

UNESCO. *EFA Global Monitoring Report 2010: Reaching the Marginalized*. Paris: UNESCO and Oxford University Press, 2010.

UNESCO. *EFA Global Monitoring Report 2013–2014: Teaching and Learning; Achieving Quality for All*. Paris: UNESCO, 2014.

UNESCO. *Global Education Monitoring Report 2016: Education for People and Planet; Creating Sustainable Futures for All*. Paris: UNESCO, 2016.

UNESCO. *If You Don't Understand, How Can You Learn?* Policy Paper no. 24. Paris: UNESCO, 2016.

UNESCO. *The Use of Vernacular Languages in Education*. Paris: UNESCO, 1953.

UNESCO and UNICEF. *Fixing the Broken Promise of Education for All*. Montreal: UNESCO, 2015.

UNESCO Institute for Statistics (UIS). *Literacy Rates Continue to Rise from One Generation to the Next*. Fact Sheet no. 45, FS/2017/LIT/45. Montreal: UIS, September 2017. http://uis.unesco.org/sites/default/files/documents/fs45-literacy-rates-continue-rise-generation-to-next-en-2017_0.pdf.

UIS. *Meeting Commitments: Are Countries on Track to Achieve SDG-4?* ED/GEMR/MRT/2019/HLPF/2, 2019. Montreal: UIS, 2019. https://unesdoc.unesco.org/ark:/48223/pf0000369009.

UIS. *More Than One-Half of Children and Adolescents Are Not Learning Worldwide*. Fact Sheet no. 46, UIS/FS/2017/ED/46. Montreal: UIS, September 2017. http://uis.unesco.org/sites/default/files/documents/fs46-more-than-half-children-not-learning-en-2017.pdf.

UIS. *One in Five Children, Adolescents and Youth Is Out of School*. Fact Sheet no. 48, UIS/FS/2018/ED/48. Montreal: UIS, February 2018. http://uis.unesco.org/sites/default/files/documents/fs48-one-five-children-adolescents-youth-out-school-2018-en.pdf.

UIS. *Reducing Global Poverty Through Universal Primary and Secondary Education*. Policy Paper no. 32 /Fact Sheet no. 44, 2017/ED/GEMR/MRT/PP/32. Montreal: UIS, June 2017. http://uis.unesco.org/sites/default/files/documents/reducing-global-poverty-through-universal-primary-secondary-education.pdf.

Walter, Stephen L. "The Language of Instruction Issue: Framing an Empirical Perspective." In *The Handbook of Educational Linguistics*, ed. Bernard Spolsky and Francis M. Hult, 129–146. Oxford: Blackwell, 2008.

Walter, Stephen L., and Carol Benson. "Language Policy and Medium of Instruction in Formal Education." In *The Cambridge Handbook of Language Policy*, ed. Bernard Spolsky, 278–300. Cambridge: Cambridge University Press, 2012.

Wheeler, David. "Human Resources Development and Economic Growth in Developing Countries: A Simultaneous Model." World Bank Staff Working Paper no. 408, Washington, DC, 1980.

Wiedmann, Thomas, Manfred Lenzen, Lorenz T. Keyßer, and Julia K. Steinberger. "Scientists' Warning on Affluence." *Nature Communications* 11, no. 1 (2020): 1–10.

Wikipedia. "List of Wikipedias" entry. Accessed August 11, 2022. https://en.wikipedia.org/wiki/List_of_Wikipedias.

Wittgenstein, Ludwig. *Tractatus Logico-philosophicus*. Trans. D. F. Pears and B. F. McGuinness. London: Routledge & Kegan Paul. 1961.

Wolff, Jonathan, and Aver de-Shalit. *Disadvantage*. Oxford: Oxford University Press, 2007.

Woodward, David. "*Incrementum ad Absurdum*: Global Growth, Inequality and Poverty Eradication in a Carbon-Constrained World." *World Economic Review* 4 (2015): 43–62.

World Commission on Environment and Development. *Our Common Future*. New York: Oxford University Press, 1987.

Becoming a Child

ZHAI YONGMING

at civitella I became a child

closing my eyes   my soul cast itself into five different roles
one went to mexico   one to new york
one went to england   one to brazil
and one was left   to ramble around italy

closing my ears   birdsong all around
it's the language of antiquity   and i understand
there are five thousand languages in the world   how many can one person master?
every two weeks   one of them dies
i fly after them like a bird
but they're dying faster than I can catch them
each with its own inherited codes   cycles and types

when humankind was newly born   we spoke but one language
as the world has grown larger   languages have grown hungrier
like black and white tigers devouring the weak   they have flooded the cities
morphed into computer languages   begun gnawing away our brains
when language becomes a kind of virus
humanity will be infected   the world will be sealed off
only children will be immune
five thousand languages will die   leaving but one

to become a child   is to change five thousand into one
to question the world with a child's mind
to speak like hands
to read like light
to connect like a shadow with nature soul to soul
i drop down to the grass to get closer to the sky
to become a child   is to become a language

Translated from Chinese by Andrea Lingenfelter

变成孩子

翟永明

在 civitella 我变成孩子

闭上眼睛　　我的灵魂分饰五角
一个去了墨西哥　一个去了纽约
一个去了英格兰　一个去了巴西
剩下的一个　在意大利倘佯

闭上耳朵　周围一片鸟叫

那是古代的语言　我能听懂
世界上有五千种语言　一个人能占有几种？
每两个星期　它们死一次
我象鸟一样追赶
赶不上它死亡的速度
它有自己的遗传密码　周期和种类

当人类刚刚出生时　　我们只说一种语言
世界变得越来越大　　语言也越来越饥饿
它们象弱肉强食的黑白老虎　　在城市中泛滥
变成计算机语言　　它开始吞噬我们的大脑
当语言成为一种病毒
人类将被感染　　世界将会封闭
只有孩子能免疫
五千语言将会死去　　只剩下一种

变成孩子　就是把五千变为一种
就是用孩子的心去询问世界
象手一样说话
象光一样阅读
象影子一样通灵通自然
我的视点低到草丛中去接近天空
变成孩子　就是变成一种语言

Chapter Three

THE ASYLUM TRIAL

Translating Justice at the Borders of Europe

TOMMASO MANFREDINI

There is a trial happening at the borders of the Global North. It takes place almost entirely outside the judicial system and only seldom reaches it, but its outcome has consequence for the lives of the people involved. This is the trial of those seeking protection from persecution, violence, and death.

In official documents, seeking and obtaining another state's protection appears to be a straightforward process, in which panels or commissions comprised of state representatives judge each person's case. Each case is built around a personal narrative of violence, fear, flight, and arrival involving events, actions, and movements through space and time that must *make sense* within prescribed legal parameters. In most of the Global North, commissions adjudicate the validity of each claim following the provisions of international refugee law[1] while also working to fulfill more or less explicit political goals, such as yearly quotas of admission.[2] In general, however, a successful narrative is one that tells a linear and (chronologically) plausible story that is at once uniquely personal and highly referential and that contains elements that are credible, recognizable, and verifiable as objectively *true*.[3]

In this chapter, I explore the domesticating practices of translation in the context of asylum seeking at the European Union's southern border to build on the discussion of language justice and linguistic rights foregrounded by editors Lydia Liu and Anupama Rao in their introduction to this volume and elaborated by L. Maria Bo and Madeleine Dobie in their contributions.

The EU's Asylum Procedures Directive provides asylum seekers with the right to file a claim regardless of their fluency in the language(s) of the state that receives the claim and mandates that each claim be translated into the official language(s) of the state in which the claim is filed to ensure fair and impartial review.[4] However, this right to translation does not require linguistic recognition. Rather, my chapter addresses the lack of linguistic recognition that characterizes translation practices in the asylum procedure in Italy. I use the concept of linguistic recognition to indicate a wide range of practices originating in the encounter between the often multiple languages of those seeking protection, on the one hand, and the institutional monolingualism of the Italian state, on the other. In this encounter, regimented by ideologies of linguistic domestication that attempt to reduce the incommensurability of foreignness to a recognizable Italian equivalent, the specificities, nuances, and rights of asylum seekers undergo a process of what Liu and Rao refer to in the introduction as "invisible and silent disappearances": that is, they are often flattened, curtailed, and misinterpreted by those authorities who listen, question, translate, and adjudicate. Thus, I take linguistic recognition to signify the right of a foreign language to be considered a rightful language of expression that is shared by humans enjoying the same basic rights—and as such to be supported by adequate means of translation—to be as important as the recognition of, and fluency in all the elements of that language—whether they be phonetic, grammatical, expressive, or cultural—that would ensure that the claim to protection be translated fairly. I focus here on some of the ways in which the absence of linguistic recognition can have immediate implications for asylum applicants, with sometimes profound or irreversible consequences for their livelihood. I will discuss the general lack of recognition—in the Italian asylum system, in particular—of foreign, nondominant languages from the Global South as means and communities of expression endowed with their own communicative and imaginative powers and not simply as vehicles for the transmission of information that is relevant to the demand for protection. Then I will sketch the implications that this lack of recognition has for the institutional practice of translation at various levels of the status determination procedure and the ways in which these mechanisms profoundly shape an asylum narrative and its outcome from intake to verdict.

First, an asylum seeker is a particularly vulnerable rights-bearing person. People become asylum seekers because they lost the protection of their own state, were forced to leave it, and cannot return to it, having only the "incomplete" provisions of refugee law—when applicable—and international human rights law as legal protections.[5] One could say, not so cynically, that they depend on little more than the benevolence of arrival states for the protection and enforcement of their rights. Second, even when the asylum seeker's quest for safety is successful and they obtain the protection of a state, that protection is understood to be temporary, even in the case of refugees. Third, refugee status depends simultaneously—and potentially contradictorily—on the asylum seeker's highly personal narrativization of their own experience of flight and on their membership in a distinct group, whether it be social, ethnic or political, as those categories are understood in the arrival state.[6]

The path to international protection is based on both technical and legal infrastructures that profess commitments to multilingual communication. In practice, however, their shortcomings become apparent. To function in a manner consistent with linguistic justice, these infrastructures must be underwritten by an ethics of translation as "recognition" of the other: linguistic recognition. When considering the question of justice in asylum procedures, we must therefore recognize that a focus on *rights* cannot be divorced from a focus on the linguistic conditions that mediate access to justice and the protection of those rights in transnational and multilingual settings.[7]

Similarly, three of the issues that lie at the core of language justice as a field of activism and inquiry—language diversity, linguistic pluralism, and language rights—are, in the case of asylum procedures, deeply intertwined and must be taken up together. In accordance with international refugee law, countries in the Global North have enacted legislation about the linguistic rights of persons seeking asylum, and to varying degrees, they accommodate and account for the language favored by the applicant. There is, however, a pervasive assimilationist force in the linguistic relationship between applicant and institution, one in which the person seeking protection is largely responsible for becoming intelligible to the state and for making the state intelligible to themselves.[8] This comes at the expense of what should be an institutional practice of linguistic equality and reciprocal literacy between the state granting protection and the individual seeking it.

In light of this, language recognition is as much the recognition of the asylum seeker's language within the spheres of adjudication and bureaucracy as it is the recognition of the Other in a linguistic setting of narration and translation in which all interlocutors have equal worth: the Other in and through their language.

WHO IS A REFUGEE?

The procedure for seeking asylum is regulated by international, regional, and national legal frameworks that can differ in life-changing ways, including in terms of the types of protection that can be granted in addition to asylum. These procedures all refer, however, to two foundational texts: the 1951 Convention Relating to the Status of Refugees (the 1951 Convention) and its 1967 Protocol.[9] In Article 1, A (2), the 1951 Convention provides the definition of a refugee that is generally used to assess an asylum claim to this day:

> For the purposes of the present Convention, the term 'refugee' shall apply to any person who . . . as a result of events occurring before 1 January 1951 and owing to well-founded fear of being persecuted for reasons of race, religion, nationality, membership of a particular social group or political opinion, is outside the country of his nationality and is unable or, owing to such fear, is unwilling to avail himself of the protection of that country; or who, not having a nationality and being outside the country of his former habitual residence as a result of such events, is unable or, owing to such fear, is unwilling to return to it.

Aside from phrases such as "well-founded fear of being persecuted" and "owing to such fear . . . [is unable] or unwilling to return to [their own country]," this definition contains an element instrumental for defining how an asylum claim must be formulated: this is the principle, and the necessity, of belonging to a group, which is expressed by the phrase "reasons of race, religion, nationality, membership of a particular social group." This automatically establishes two interrelated scales of representation: the first is individual, while the other is membership in a group that, for reasons named previously, is a target of violence and persecution. The burden of proof, which lies squarely with the applicant, entails not only being able to show proof of being in danger but also proof that one is in danger *as* a member of a group (or a political party). The applicant's narrative must meet both criteria: appearing at once personal *and* general enough to be credible while being relevant to the terms of the law.[10]

This general form for acceptable asylum narratives has a specific historical origin. The 1951 Convention definition is a result of the requirement to comply with a semantic field (the word choice of Article 1) that was drawn to encompass a specific form of persecution (against Jews), which occurred in a specific place (Europe) at a particular time (World War II and its immediate aftermath). Despite the extended scope provided by the 1967 Protocol, the constitutive elements of refugee status are to this day those provided by the 1951 Convention definition. Understandably, then, the discrepancy and distance between the geography, temporality, and general reality of the stories of those who seek protection in the Global North—one of the many "presents" of asylum—and the discursive landscape into which these stories are supposed to enter—which belongs, as both lexicon and logic, to the past—play an important role in the construction of an asylum narrative. Terms[11] such as *well-founded fear*, *harm*, and *persecution* demarcate, alone and in relation to each other, the space within which a personal story must fit to be considered worthy of protection. They work alongside the specific historical and geographical context in which the claim takes place to create the story's discursive space. This space is one of opportunity and of restriction and strictly enforced limits. If proven, each of these stories makes the claim eligible. Yet each term also provides a limit, a "fence" around a space within which a personal narrative should remain in order to be favorably received. This space is thus discursive and physical, since the personal narrative must develop logically in a specific way, with and against the limits posed by a pervasive and long-standing culture of suspicion that characterizes every step of the asylum process—and the interview, in particular.[12]

As a result of these constraints, the experience of asylum takes a specific shape on the page (figure 3.1).

ASYLUM AND THE EUROPEAN UNION

According to the United Nations High Commissioner for Refugees (UNHCR), there are currently 84.5 million forcibly displaced people worldwide, an increase of over 15 million in two years. Of these, 26 million

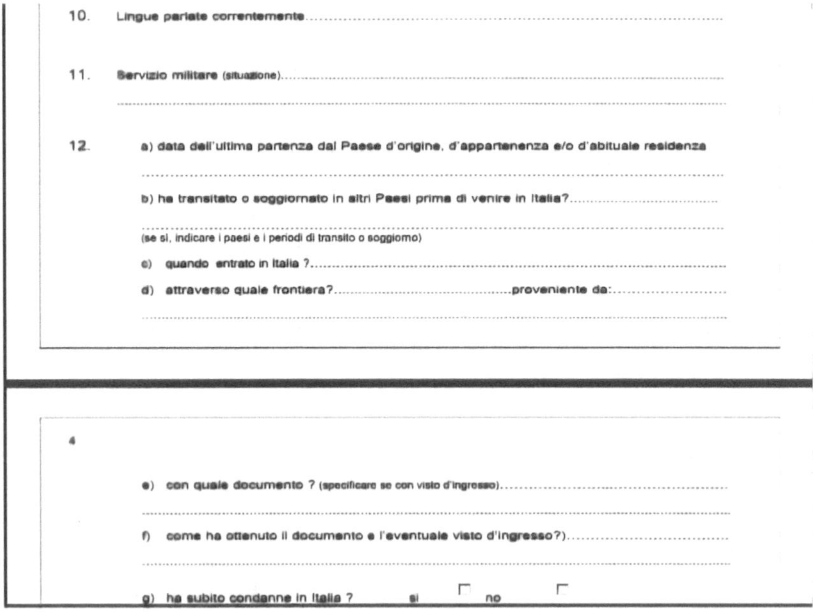

10. Lingue parlate correntemente ....

11. Servizio militare (situazione) ....

12. a) data dell'ultima partenza dal Paese d'origine, d'appartenenza e/o d'abituale residenza ....

b) ha transitato o soggiornato in altri Paesi prima di venire in Italia? ....

(se si, indicare i paesi e i periodi di transito o soggiorno)

c) quando entrato in Italia ? ....

d) attraverso quale frontiera? .... proveniente da: ....

4

e) con quale documento ? (specificare se con visto d'ingresso) ....

f) come ha ottenuto il documento e l'eventuale visto d'ingresso?) ....

g) ha subito condanne in Italia ? si ☐ no ☐

FIGURE 3.1. A sample of the C-3, the intake form that asylum seekers fill out in front of an Italian customs or police agent whereby they declare their intention to seek protection. In case of undetected entry, the asylum seeker is also making themself known to the state.

are refugees, and 4.2 million are asylum seekers. In 2019, shortly after this research was concluded, almost two-thirds of the world's refugees had fled four countries: Syria, South Sudan, Venezuela, and Afghanistan. The top receiving countries were Turkey, Colombia, Pakistan, and Uganda, and 85 percent of the world's displaced people were hosted in developing countries.[13] With the exception of Germany, which now hosts 2.2 million refugees since the start of Russia's invasion of Ukraine, Europe is nowhere represented in these numbers. Indeed, European asylum laws and procedures are some of the world's most restrictive. At the supranational level, EU asylum policies are a mix of international instruments of refugee and human rights law and regionally-specific regulations and jurisprudence. Member States can also implement their own legislation, although that is not supposed to limit the scope of the regional and international instruments to which they are signatories.[14] Despite recent attempts at reform that focus on border externalization, relocation, and return,[15] asylum policy within the EU space and among Member States is still governed by the Dublin Regulation,[16] which established the principle that anyone seeking international protection in the EU must do so in the first country of entry. The nature and topography of migratory flows to Europe in the past fifteen years have increasingly shown this framework to be ill-adapted and outdated, resulting in criticism both from proponents of stricter policies of relocation and redistribution and from those who decry the framework for its segmentation of European space and violent disruption of trajectories of human displacement.[17]

Nevertheless, the "first country" rule remains the principle for adjudicating jurisdiction over a claim.

(AT) THE BORDERS OF EUROPE

As a sovereign state with a supranational border, Italy's asylum system is a particularly interesting case study for reasons that are geographical, political, and linguistic. Since the early 2010s, Italy's southern shores, along with those of Greece and Spain, have been the main landing point for maritime entry into Europe. Due in part to the Dublin principle, as well as the lack of safe, alternative paths to lawful entrance, the soaring influx of people has corresponded to a growing number of demands for international protection that, for a time, significantly strained an underequipped and understaffed system. The linguistic relationship between the state and the people asking for its protection is also of interest: Italy's expansionist and colonial projects in the nineteenth and twentieth centuries were relatively unsuccessful, with the result that Italian never became a significant language of empire and was never powerful enough in postcolonial times to frame the relationship between Italy and its former colonies in a relevant way. Moreover, since World War II, there has never been a sustained effort to forcefully integrate foreign languages, including English, into public education curricula. This is an important trait in the context of asylum because it presents a system—and a group of administrators—whose ideology did not grow out of a particular postcolonial linguistic relationship between the metropole and its former empire. The Italian asylum system is ideologically monolingual in the sense that it does not account for the linguistic distance between the applicant and the state as a central aspect of asylum procedure. Neither does it consider this a relevant criterion for adjudicating a claim.

It is thus important to reconstruct the ways in which multilingualism is constantly negotiated and reduced to intelligibility in a single dominant language. This reconstruction, which pieces together various documents and moments that do not find their way onto the page, allows us to see how, between and across languages, the asylum procedure in general and the interview in particular are central, as moments and as sites, to a system that aims to restrict autonomous mobility and render it illegal.

In Italy, the asylum system has been at the center of political, scholarly, and humanitarian attention for more than a decade. Reflecting its history of emigration, Italy did not have a comprehensive immigration policy until the Martelli law (1991). In the period 1990–2013, the number of requests processed by the country's asylum system never reached more than 40,000 a year, which was in line with other EU countries.[18] After 2013, however, asylum requests doubled in the space of four years. There were 63,000 requests in 2014; 83,000 requests in 2015; 123,000 requests in 2016; and more than 130,000 asylum requests in 2017. They fell back to 53,000 in 2018, and the decreasing trend continued in 2019 (43,783 requests) and 2020 (26,963), only to climb back up in 2021, when 53,609 people requested asylum.[19]

In 2017, in the frenzy of what was being portrayed as a biblical invasion of asylum seekers who would bring the system to a breaking point, the government passed a sweeping reform, known as the Minniti law, that strengthened border control and restricted access to international protection.[20] In a purported effort to *streamline*[21] asylum procedures, the law introduced several controversial measures, such as decreasing the period in which to appeal the decision of the commission to thirty days and removing an intermediary level of appeal, leaving the Supreme Court (Corte di Cassazione) with the sole power to hear an appeal rejected by an ordinary tribunal.[22]

The Minniti law, which passed with the votes of a self-professed center-left government, provided the blueprint for the 2018 reform of "immigration, citizenship and security"—this time at the hands of the proudly racist and xenophobic Interior Minister Matteo Salvini.[23] His reforms put in place a set of stringent measures regarding migrant detention as well as health and citizenship rights. It also introduced an important modification to the types of protection that could be granted asylum seekers. Prior to this reform and in addition to the two statutory forms of protection sanctioned by the 1951 Convention—international protection (refugee status) and subsidiary protection, both lasting five years—Italy offered a residence permit "for humanitarian reasons" that lasted up to two years and could be renewed.[24] As a legal instrument, this humanitarian protection provision was heavily relied on for its suppleness. As opposed to the narrowly defined criteria of both refugee status and subsidiary protection—where the burden of proving "well-founded fear of persecution,"[25] often by a state or group; "a real risk of suffering serious harm"; or the danger of exposure to "torture or other inhuman or degrading or treatment"[26] may be insurmountable—humanitarian protection provided a much larger umbrella of acceptable reasons for protection. They had to be "serious and well-founded" but could be the result of age and health, political instability in the home country—such as institutional failure to sufficiently uphold human rights or prevent violence—or a natural or environmental catastrophe. Although replaced in 2018 by a provision of much narrower scope labeled *protezione speciale*, or "special protection," humanitarian protection has been largely reinstated by the most recent asylum law.[27]

An asylum claim is generally filed in the presence of a police officer. Then, often several months later, the applicant is notified of a date to appear in front of an asylum commission or board for the refugee status determination interview, also known as the RSD interview or simply "the interview." The RSD interview is central to asylum procedures across jurisdictions and possibly the most important moment of an asylum request. During the interview, the applicant sits in front of a panel of specifically trained experts, tells them their story, and answers their questions. Some asylum seekers are able to benefit from the help and advice of legal clinics, whose counsels, translators, and cultural mediators contribute to the formation of the applicant's narrative and train them for the moment when they will repeat it to the commission at the interview. In Italy, the interview's official transcript is called the *verbale*, and it is the document that certifies and legalizes the applicant's narrative.

The *verbale* reinforces the narrative rigidity inaugurated by the fill-in-the-blanks structure of the C-3 form, shown in figure 3.1. It is also a completely monolingual transcript of a multilingual conversation, born from constant and often rough, inattentive, or poorly informed translation involving at least two languages and three people.

The translation of matters pertaining to international law demands a hierarchization of languages or, rather, a hierarchization of versions.[28]

THE ASYLUM TRIAL

D. Ha compreso il contenuto di questo verbale, per come letto e poi tradotto dall'interprete nella lingua in cui si è svolta l'intervista? Ne conferma dunque i contenuti?
R. No.

Copia dello stesso verbale viene consegnata al richiedente, che sottoscrive in calce anche per ricevuta.

L'audizione ha termine alle ore 14.15.

Letto, confermato e sottoscritto,

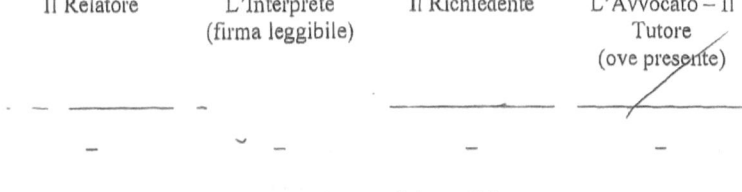

Si consegna copia del presente verbale di audizione all'interessato

(firma leggibile)

FIGURE 3.2. The last page of a *verbale*. Note how the interview's last question (starting at the top after "D.") asks the applicant whether they have understood the content of the *verbale* as it was read and translated to them by the interpreter. This points to a double translation occurring in rapid succession: during the interview, the commission officer almost simultaneously translates into Italian what will become the *verbale*, which is then translated back to the applicant in the language in which the interview took place. Never mind that the applicant refuses to certify its content (answers "No"): they sign, thus making this the legal version of their story.

There must be an original, and there must be a translation, and the two are not equal in value. An example of this ordering can be found in the "outer galaxy" of the refugee status determination procedure—namely, in the myriad of documents, briefs, pro memoria, and opinions that constitute the scaffolding and interpretative framework of the interview as a legal moment but which do not have the same textual and legal value as the interview transcript. The *Aide-Mémoire and Glossary of Case Processing Modalities, Terms and Concepts Applicable to Refugee Status Determination (RSD) Under UNHCR's Mandate* is a document accessible in four languages: English, French, Arabic, and Russian. By statute, all of the UN's official languages are equal. Here, however, each of the latter three versions of the *Aide-Mémoire* defers to the English version and does so in its own language. The French version, for instance, bears the following disclaimer: "En cas d'incohérence ou de discordance entre la version anglaise et la version française de la présente publication, la version anglaise fera foi."[29] In Arabic, the concept expressed by *faire foi* is conveyed by the word المرجع (*elmarj3*), which means "reference." Literally, the expression *faire foi* means to "make or create faith," where "faith" is to be understood as trust. Only one of these versions, the English, "makes faith" or "makes trust": i.e., only one of these versions is trustworthy in a context that implicitly demands the existence of a language as reference.

What I am trying to underscore is the relationship between translation and faith and between translation and trust that is constitutive of a complex system comprising multiple languages and versions and their need for representation in contrast with the need to order them by importance or by trustworthiness.[30] The need for an *original*, one that among all the successive and naturally diverging versions of itself has kept the "faith" with which it was originally endowed, is central for a global system of judgment such as asylum adjudication under UNHCR mandate. As it is framed and practiced in Italy, the RSD moment, from the intake forms to the interview, represents a specific instance of the global asylum order. If, on the surface, it seems to be resting on the same assumptions—namely, the equality of all languages before the law, the right to translation without the claim being penalized, etc.—it operates in a very specific way: it does not hierarchize languages; there is no original language "qui *fasse foi*." What does "make trust" is thus a document in the target language—Italian—that is a translation of a conversation among three people happening in at least one other language. The asylum seeker's signature, added at the end of the interview after a purported "reading and verification" (the statement that the document has been "read and verified" by the applicant *is in Italian*, as in Figure 3.2 above), is what originalizes the document; it is what "makes trust" and makes it trustworthy. It becomes the applicant's version of their story and, for the purposes of the commission, the official version of themselves.

Given the deeply asymmetrical power relationship between the applicant and the reviewing commission, the act of relegating translation to a mere procedural step, stripping it of its effective impact, is one of the ways in which "power enters into the process of cultural [and legal] translation." As the anthropologist Cristiana Giordano affirms, translation "becomes a form of listening and poses a fundamental epistemological question about what is knowable of the other language and what remains untranslatable (and unknown)."[31] The epistemological conditions surrounding the act of listening, alongside the strict formalization that guides the reception of the asylum narrative, influence the perception and judgment of truth and in turn the outcome of the claim. What remains largely unaddressed and uncontested, however, is the power of the state and its representatives to directly influence the form, length, pathos, and detail of the claimant's narrative. They do so through the enforcement of strict narrative codes and a system of knowledge production and interpretation that leaves little room for alternative polysemic signifiers, nonlinear plots, confused memories, and, above all, abstraction. In an example of both testimonial and "imposed" hermeneutical injustice, the general cultural and geopolitical unawareness on the part of the commission dramatically shrinks the realm of the true, the plausible, and therefore the acceptable.[32]

Simultaneously, the strict imposition of a "successful" narrative rewrites the claimant's relationship with their own story and past while assigning a different function to truth and lie. With particular reference to common European interviewing practices, it has been affirmed that "there can be no doubt that the politico-moral order of Schengen helps maintain arbitrary inequalities, and that the practice of deceiving or using 'tricks' to circumvent them, is by now part of postcolonial subjectivity and experience."[33] The *verbale* and the commission's decision, in particular, as moments in which the narrative is translated, transcribed, and reported, constitute layers that participate in the making of the narrative.[34] Ideally, from a critical point of view, all these layers would be equally accessible and legible. In my experience with asylum requests treated by the Centro Servizi Intergrati per l'Immigrazione, and particularly with the case study I present next, this was simply impossible. But a focus on a particular section of that process—the moment between the informal telling of the applicant's story and its official transcription and translation—shows that, despite procedural opacity and institutional concealment, bits and traces of the translation process that culminates in the *verbale* are carried through and can be made visible. It is important to stress, once again, that ultimately legal counsel and asylum seeker cannot reach a common space of mutual intelligibility without the translator's work and that a considerable amount of trust and power must therefore be bestowed on them for the conversation to go forward in any way. This at least partial unaccountability of the translator is also central to the way in which the commission interview is organized. There the translator not only enables the conversation but also is the one tasked with *rereading* the *verbale* to the applicant for official validation. These are not transparent operations, even when we assume the utmost good faith and competence of all parties involved. And yet such translations are treated as such, or, rather, they are treated as neutral and unaltering steps in the transmission of meaning and, by extension, in the construction of the asylum case. The study of the *textual residue*[35] and, in particular, of the layering of the narrative shows that translation means alteration and the production of something else, perhaps not Other in nature but different in a number of aspects that should be taken into account when the decision is based on the applicant's story. Translation builds the story that is eventually evaluated for protection, yet the implications of this "participation" are not deemed important anywhere along the chain of official documents. It is more likely to find a legal counsel who, at least in their own notes (which are never divulged), makes room for translation and its challenges. Interpreters are, of course, much more attuned and attentive, but in the RSD official documents, they tend to be *muted*, despite being central to the production of those same documents.

Applicant K

In late December 2018, Applicant K (A. K for brevity hereafter) was notified that his interview with the commission would take place the following day. We met in the office of the legal clinic that was helping him with his demand, located on the ground floor of the old city hospital. The building was surrounded by the thick fog of an early winter morning. A. K, a Pakistani national, came accompanied by a translator. We sat at a school desk in the back office of the clinic's archive room, on small plywood chairs that made our knees bend in acute angles. A. K and the interpreter sat on one side, the clinic's counsel and I on the other. The building's obsolete heating forced us to keep our winter coats on, and clouds of breath intermingled above the desk. Within the next few hours, A. K had to familiarize himself with the procedure for the interview, the next step in his asylum request, including the questions that would punctuate it and the challenges they might present. Most importantly, he had to understand the significance of his own story and of the way he was going to tell it.

THE ASYLUM TRIAL

After introducing me and asking for any objections to my staying in the room, the legal counsel briefly explained what international protection is ("You filed a request for international protection. Do you know what it is?") and the forms in which it could be granted. They sought to make sure that everything was clear to both A. K and the interpreter.[36] The counsel's introductory speech and the lead-up to the applicant's telling of their story are governed by formal rules. This preparation takes place for two primary reasons that seem at odds with one another. One reason is to prepare the applicant for the interview by simulating its conditions, while the other is to construct a safe space for the applicant in which they can, with the help of the counsel, reorder their past in a way that best follows the rules of the interview and fits the expectations of the commission hearing the claim. Questions such as "Do you know what the commission is?" and the recurrent advice to "tell *everything*"[37] are efforts to guide the applicant in such a manner.

Though he spoke no Italian and little English, A. K looked comfortable and at ease. So, I shared the counsel's surprise when he flatly stated that he preferred to keep his story for the asylum commission. The counsel gently but insistently attempted to emphasize the importance of trying to tell his story in advance of the official interview. "It is your right . . . , but I just want to remind you," the counsel said, "that we can make it better, together, identify its strengths."

In the counsel's record, the entire encounter with A. K fit into a single sentence: "The applicant decides to keep his story for the Commission." Yet our meeting lasted almost two hours, with most of the time spent attempting to locate A. K's village. His personal information redacted on an earlier intake form was wrong, so when the counsel read his place of birth and dwelling to him, A. K tried to correct it. As each of us attempted to find his actual birthplace on our own versions of Google Maps, it soon became clear that our finding his birthplace online was far more important to him than rectifying the form. On and through our screens, we *had* to find his home; there would be no reviewing his remaining personal information, let alone any discussion of his story, if we couldn't find it. We had to make his home exist in this foreign room, in this foreign situation, in this foreign country far away. His eyes lit up every time we mentioned a place or locale that was near his village or along a route there.

It turned out that A. K comes from a place that civilian satellites have a difficult time covering. He comes from a border, one of the most militarized ones in the world: Azad Jammu and Kashmir, or AJK. His village, he explained, is right in the heart of the region but also right on the superimposed border between India and Pakistan. Neither I nor the counsel spoke Urdu or were able to type it. The interpreter, sitting next to A. K and across the desk from us, did not seem to be able to find it either, perhaps due to the weak internet connection. We tried various spellings of his village: Ketli, Kori, Keri, Kary, Qari, Curry, Qeli—nothing. We zoomed in and out on the map; we asked him about rivers or signposts nearby. "Close to . . . ?" "No." What the internet was capable of representing was insufficient. Zooming in on the probable surroundings of A. K's village, roads were cut off and seemed to end nowhere; the map became blank. Though its area was viewable from far above, it was impossible to zoom in on the village itself. "K," I wanted to tell him, "your village does not exist on the internet." Suddenly, in Italian, he exclaimed: "Mia città *badarlan*!"³⁸

badarlan, badarlan . . .
. . . badarlan

All of a sudden, we realized: *borderland*. My city *borderland*. My mind immediately jumped to the opening scene in Gianfranco Rosi's documentary *Fuocoammare*,³⁹ where the searchlight from a coast guard helicopter scans a pitch-dark patch of Mediterranean Sea at night, searching for signs of a capsized vessel and for possible survivors. I told myself that the border—at 10,000 feet above and below sea level, in the mountains of Kashmir and deep in the high seas—is just as deadly and, to us listening to A. K from across the desk, just as mute. And whatever and whoever is on it is just as invisible, just as absent. In that repurposed hospital room, we could not agree on a way to search for A. K's village on Google Maps, on a way to spell its name that would yield results. We could not locate the village and write it into existence. The impossibility of locating his home, in this case, did not exactly equal complete absence—A. K exists and was right there in front of us—as much as it equaled absence of presence, absence of proof. His story had a vague point of origin, one that corresponded not with the precise coordinates of a defined place but to the more loose, tentative, and disputed ones of a perimeter. As a consequence, his story was already a step removed from being entirely verifiable—and therefore entirely credible. Later on, back in New York, when I read the *verbale* of his interview, some details emerged. But these details only reinforced this absence, only thickened the fog surrounding this uncertainty of place, provenance, and belonging. The examiner, insisting on locating A. K's village as precisely as possible, asked him to name the road they used in order to reach the closest town, which appears on Google Maps. "There's no main road," he said. "Only trails. There are no well-built roads."[40]

A. K's answer is important for two reasons. First, it encapsulates the operation of vertiginous synthesis and reduction that results from the interview and its act of simultaneous translation. Hidden behind this statement from A. K, invisible behind the line it occupies on the printed *verbale* in front of me, there is a lot of information. There are the several minutes of discussion about the mountains, lakes, and trails that surround his village, about the number and distribution of the houses on the land. There is our almost senseless search for his village on the internet and the strange impression that pervaded the room that finding the village online was actually very important. There is, invisible behind this single transcript statement, A. K's deep need to see, hear of, and tell us about home, even if it was only its name on a map. And as a consequence of this, also invisible behind the statement is the resulting impression that his leaving home wasn't simply leaving, that it wasn't "economic" or about a better paycheck. In A. K's attachment to proving the existence of his home through the internet, there were the restlessness and urgency that constitute the residue of flight—flight that is often the result of fear. And fear, if it is *visible*, must factor into the decision to grant international protection. I am not arguing here that the commission's decision in A. K's case hinged on the invisibility of this fear. I am, however, arguing that by making his fear more visible through a more articulated, plain, and thorough process of translation, the "facts" on which the decision was made would have been reconstructed differently.

The second reason why A. K's answer is important is its subtle power of estranging the reader, of sending them away from the context of the story. If A. K were to appeal the commission's decision, a judge would read the *verbale* before granting him a hearing. And even if it was followed by an in-person conversation, the judge's first encounter with A. K's story and case would be through the *verbale* of his interview with the commission. We cannot therefore underestimate the importance of the *verbale* in the process of an asylum request, both as a decisive document and as the transcription-translation of a decisive moment. The *verbale*, however, is often roughly or strangely translated in ways that undermine the coherence of the applicant's narrative, and the statement in question is a clear example of this. Keeping in mind that the examiner's question is asked in the context of their attempt to reconstruct the topography of a mountainous, impervious, sparsely populated, and highly militarized border zone between Pakistan and India, the problematic part of the way in which A. K's reply is translated is the phrase *strade pedonali*. In Italian, *strade pedonali* literally means "pedestrian streets," and the phrase is generally used in the context of old city centers that, after being plagued by excessive car traffic throughout the 1980s and 1990s, progressively started to interdict motorized vehicles. In pollution-prone and tourist-oriented Italy, where city centers are a constant battleground for motorists, business owners, and tired residents, the phrase cannot but send the reader's imagination somewhere else, somewhere closer to home, maybe toward the north, maybe just past the Alps. This phrase certainly has the strong potential to make the reader's mind at least fleetingly jump out of Kashmir and land in Lugano, Salzburg, or any other Cleanest City in Europe. Consequently, adopting this "commonsensical but . . . inappropriate local knowledge"[41]—deaf to and unable to bridge the linguistic and semantic distance with the applicant—in order to sustain a domesticating logic of translation has the power to lead the reader to think, even fleetingly or inadvertently, that it cannot be that bad where A. K grew up if there are pedestrian streets, a universally recognized sign of progress, civility, and peace.

Aspirations and work toward justice in the ideologies and practices of translation that shape the asylum procedure cannot, then, rest on the principles of domestication and equivalence that govern the state's understanding and translation of foreignness. As the example of *strade pedonali* shows, these principles obliterate foreignness and, with it, its "equal rights before the law"—that is, the right to have one's story conveyed, as much as possible, through a translation that calibrates distance and specificity. Instead, the goal of reaching justice in the translation of asylum demands and within the adjudication process as a whole should perhaps rest on establishing the space for what Maria Bo, following Vine Deloria Jr., calls the negotiation of "inequivalent equalities". "When translation is not simply the matching of one tongue to the idea of another," she writes in chapter 1 of this volume, "but rather the act of bringing linguistic fields together to reshape the idea itself, then translation become its own productive process." In translation theory, the power to estrange and unsettle the reader is generally granted to translations that maintain an element of foreignness and that ask the reader, and not the text, to bridge the distance between themselves and the story they are reading. Here, and in similar instances throughout the body of transcripts that I examined, this power of confusion and partial disorientation rests instead on domestication. The reader is not unsettled by the foreign, by an inaccessible element of culture that would require mediation. They are instead unsettled in their reading practice by the utterly domestic and familiar (*strade pedonali*) that diverts their understanding of the story and simultaneously weakens its coherence. For this reason, I chose to translate *strade pedonali*, a quintessentially urban phrase, as the English word *trails*, in an attempt to maintain the foreignness of the landscape throughout, to keep the reader "abroad" and therefore not disrupt the coherence of A. K.'s answer.

If one follows the steps of an asylum request—from the first intake forms to the preparatory meetings, the interview, and its transcript—we can see a general orientation toward dryness and concision, all aimed at enhancing intelligibility and truth through domesticating translation practices. But it would be wrong to consider this process a linear path toward *intelligibility*, with steps ordered chronologically. Although there is a chronological order, we see the biggest discrepancy between what is oral and what is written, between notes and official or fully redacted documents. From the complicated conversations and patchy acts of translation characterizing the meetings, we reach a dry and formally constricting document that presents information as empirical evidence, produced through a logic of translation as transparent equivalence. This results in the ultimate depersonalization of the narrative, which through indirect and reported speech and heavy-handed summaries is no longer more than a series of facts.

We now get a glimpse of how the seemingly neutral transparency of translation practices in asylum procedures conceals a process fraught with arbitrariness, during which the linearity of the narrative is constantly broken and remade by linguistic and cultural incommensurability. The format of the RSD interview pushes the practice of translation (and the role of the translator) to the margin of its economy. By operating under the principle of translation as a neutral act of semantic and information transmission, it conveniently compromises an otherwise complex process of negotiation within an uneven distribution of power. Consequently, it also confines the translator to a purportedly peripheral, vehicular, and therefore impactless role in the process of status determination while its asymmetrical multilingualism is loudly silenced in official transcripts. These efforts aim to make a contentious and opaque process look as transparent as possible. Translation as practiced in the RSD thus comes to resemble what Gayatri Spivak called the "wholesale translation of the Third World,"[42] which prompted her to demand that translation be recentered around the agency of the subject, rhetoricity, and intimacy of the translator with the source language. All the different textual (and procedural) steps of the current process are treated more as slight variations of the same act and moment and as different formats of the same story and identity. Consequently, their peculiarities and discrepancies are regarded as marginal differences, unimportant for the overall story, or they are simply overlooked.

Yet there is much understanding to gain in simultaneously acknowledging this deliberately instituted resemblance and all that is concealed and excluded from the documents in order for this resemblance to hold. And what is immediately visible in the layout of the official documents that form the asylum procedure is the stark contradiction between their content—seemingly pointing toward freedom of speech and of history ("Now, please elaborate *freely* on the reasons that led you to leave." "What would happen, *in your opinion*, if you had to return to your country?")—and the fact that the form and structure of the document already arrange this supposed freedom along a specific linearity of logic and temporality. What emerges from an analysis of the possibilities and impossibilities of the RSD format as it is currently practiced is the simultaneous erasure, through a systematic domestication of foreignness, of the contingent and contextual nature of asylum institutions and of the applicant's specificity.

NOTES

This study is the result of my experience as a nonparticipant observer in preparatory meetings at the legal clinic of Centro Servizi Intergrati per l'Immigrazione (CSII), a municipal office that provided legal counseling and immigration services to the population of Ferrara, Italy. In the summer and winter of 2018–2019, I attended several

THE ASYLUM TRIAL

preparatory meetings that took place before each asylum applicant's interview date. This chapter is thus indebted to all the men who allowed me to sit, listen, and take notes and to the CSII staff—in particular, Anna Lauricella, Stefano Marcolini, and Letizia Di Maglie.

1. Enshrined in the 1951 Convention on the Status of Refugees and Stateless Persons (1951 Convention) and in the 1967 Protocol, the protection of refugees and asylum seekers is incorporated into domestic law by each party after access and ratification—generally of both the 1951 Convention and the 1967 Protocol. These are also supplemented and expanded by regional instruments of protection, such as 1969 Organization of African Unity's Convention Governing the Specific Aspects of Refugee Problems in Africa and the Cartagena Declaration on Refugees, adopted in November 1984 by the Colloquium on the International Protection of Refugees in Central America, Mexico, and Panama, which took place in Cartagena de Indias, Colombia. All EU Member States have ratified the 1951 Convention and its 1967 Protocol, and asylum within the EU space is regulated by the Common European Asylum System, established in 1999. It is comprised of five legislative instruments, three directives and two regulations, as well as one agency, the European Union Agency for Asylum.
2. Following an *acquis* in EU human rights legislation, I include in this understanding of borders all agents of the state, whether mobile or fixed. This is particularly important in the context of sea crossing, because it allows for the legal extension of borders as far out as the state vessels are found to operate.
3. The interconnected questions of credibility and suspicion are central to the adjudication of asylum claims. Problems of credibility—and critical studies on the ways of assessing them—are raised at the institutional level, as described in several sets of official guidelines issued by both state and nonstate actors. Among the former are the Immigration and Refugee Board of Canada's guide on *Assessment and Credibility in Claims for Refugee Protection* (2020), available at https://irb.gc.ca/en/legal-policy/legal-concepts/Pages/Credib.aspx; and the *Guidelines on the Assessment of Credibility* (2017) published by the Migration and Refugee Division of Australia's Administrative Appeals Tribunal and available at https://www.aat.gov.au/AAT/media/AAT/Files/MRD%20documents/Legislation%20Policies%20Guidelines/Guidelines-on-Assessment-of-Credibility.pdf. The U.S. Citizenship and Immigration Services also has a multivolume *Policy Manual*, and section E of volume 1 is dedicated entirely to adjudications; it is available at https://www.uscis.gov/policy-manual/volume-1-part-e.

In Italy, the best examples of a comprehensive practitioner's guide to adjudication are the *Standard Procedures on the Identification and Referral of Victims of Gender-Based Violence Among Asylum Seekers* (2022), available at http://www.libertaciviliimmigrazione.dlci.interno.gov.it/sites/default/files/allegati/sops_gbv.pdf; and *Guidelines on the Identification of Victims of Human Trafficking among Asylum Seekers* (2017), available at http://www.libertaciviliimmigrazione.dlci.interno.gov.it/sites/default/files/allegati/lineeguida-edizione_aggiornata.pdf. Scholars around the world often base their research on national case studies. Some of the most relevant examples for this research include Nick Gill and Anthony Good, *Asylum Determination in Europe: Ethnographic Perspectives* (London: Palgrave Macmillan, 2019);

Bridget Haas and Amy Shuman, *Technologies of Suspicion and the Ethics of Obligation in Political Asylum* (Athens: Ohio University Press, 2019); C. Bohmer and A. Shuman, *Political Asylum Deceptions: The Culture of Suspicion* (London: Palgrave Macmillan, 2018); Juliet Cohen, "Questions of Credibility: Omissions, Discrepancies and Errors of Recall in the Testimony of Asylum Seekers," *International Journal of Refugee Law* 13, no. 3 (2001): 280–292; James A. Sweeney, "Credibility, Proof and Refugee Law," *International Journal of Refugee Law* 21, no. 4 (2009): 700–726; Robert Thomas, *Administrative Justice and Asylum Appeals: A Study of Tribunal Adjudication* (Oxford: Hart, 2011); and Erna Bordström, "Asylum Decisions as Performances: Intertextuality in Internal Credibility Assessment," *International Journal of Refugee Law* 32, no. 4 (2020) 623–644.

Italy has also been treated extensively as a case study. A few of the main sources for this research are Luca Minniti, "La valutazione di credibilità del richiedente asilo tra diritto internazionale, dell'UE e nazionale," *Diritti senza Confini*, January 21, 2020, https://www.asgi.it/notizie/la-valutazione-di-credibilita-richiedente-asilo-tra-diritto-internazionale-dellue-e-nazionale/; Barbara Sorgoni, "Storie dati e prove. Il ruolo della credibilità nelle narrazioni di richiesta di asilo," *Parolechiave* 2011, n. 2 (2011): 115–133, and "The Location of Truth: Bodies and Voices in the Italian Asylum Procedure," *PoLAR* 42, no. 1 (May 2019): 161–176; Tommaso Sbriccoli and Nicola Perugini, "Dai paesi di origine alle Corti Italiane. Campi, diritto e narrazioni nella costruzione della soggettività dei rifugiati," *AM. Rivista della Società italiana di antropologia medica* 14, no. 33–34 (October 2012): 95–128; and Simona Taliani, "Il passato credibile e il corpo impudico. Storia, violenza e trauma nelle biografie delle donne africane richiedenti asilo in Italia," *LARES* 77, no. 1 (2011): 135–158.

4. Article 12 of the EU Asylum Procedures Directive (2013/32/EU) states that Member States must ensure that all applicants:

> (a) . . . shall be informed in a language which they understand or are reasonably supposed to understand of the procedure to be followed and of their rights and obligations during the procedure and the possible consequences of not complying with their obligations and not cooperating with the authorities. . . .
>
> (b) . . . shall receive the services of an interpreter for submitting their case to the competent authorities whenever necessary. . . .
>
> (f) . . . shall be informed of the result of the decision by the determining authority in a language that they understand or are reasonably supposed to understand when they are not assisted or represented by a legal adviser or other counsellor. . . .

5. Guy Goodwin-Gill and Jane McAdam, *The Refugee in International Law*, 3rd ed. (Oxford: Oxford University Press, 2007), 7.
6. Article 1 of the 1951 Convention defines the refugee as "someone who is unable or unwilling to return to their own country owing to a well-founded fear of persecution for reasons of race, religion, nationality, membership of a particular social group, or political opinion." United Nations High Commissioner for Refugees, *Convention and Protocol Relating to the Status of Refugees* (Geneva: UNHCR, 2011), 2.

7. In chapter 1 of this volume, L. Maria Bo offers an extensive critical account of the history, implementation, and structural instabilities of linguistic rights within the post–World War II international human rights regime.
8. On assimilationist practices in human rights courts (including the European Court of Human Rights), see Moria Paz, "The Failed Promise of Language Rights: A Critique of the International Language Rights Regime," *Harvard International Law Journal* 54, no. 1 (2013): 157–218.
9. The 1967 Protocol was instrumental in creating contemporary international refugee law because it expanded the scope of the 1951 Convention beyond its originally intended historical and physical limits. Indeed, before the 1967 Protocol's adoption and ratification by Contracting States, the 1951 Convention was restricted to "persons fleeing events occurring before 1 January 1951 and within Europe." See UNHCR, "Introductory Note by the Office of the United Nations High Commissioner for Refugees," in *Convention and Protocol*, 2. On the interconnectedness of international and regional instruments of protection, see UNHCR, *Convention and Protocol*, ii.
10. The question of credibility is among the most central and debated issues in refugee law. Western states have striven to lay out guidelines to ensure a more transparent process, and calls for standardization across transnational spaces, such as the EU, have increased. See, for instance, the Migration and Refugee Division of Australia's Administrative Appeals Tribunal's *Guidelines on The Assessment of Credibility*, or the similar guidelines issued by the Immigration and Refugee Board of Canada under the title "Assessment of Credibility in Claims for Refugee Protection."
11. Linguistic justice in the context of illegalized migration calls for particular attention to institutional language, where terms function as more than just definitions: they are categories, status, and perceptions. A change in the terms—literally—can correspond to a dramatic change in someone's life routine, conditions, and outlook.
12. On this point, see, among others, Marco Jacquemet, "The Registration Interview: Restricting Refugees' Narrative Performances," in *Critical Readings in Translation Studies*, ed. Mona Baker (London: Routledge, 2010), 133–151; and Katrijn Maryns, *The Asylum Speaker: Language in the Belgian Asylum Procedure* (London: Routledge, 2006).
13. "Figures at a Glance," UNHCR, accessed September 13, 2021, https://www.unhcr.org/figures-at-a-glance.html.
14. *Subsidiary protection* is defined by Council Directive 2004/83/EC as "the protection given to a non-EU national or a stateless person who does not qualify as a refugee, but in respect of whom substantial grounds have been shown to believe that the person concerned, if returned to his or her country of origin or, in the case of a stateless person, to his or her country of former habitual residence, would face a real risk of suffering serious harm and who is unable or, owing to such risk, unwilling to avail himself or herself of the protection of that country." It is available on the European Commission website at https://ec.europa.eu/home-affairs/content/subsidiary-protection_en.
15. See the European Commission's "New Pact for Migration and Asylum," published September 23, 2020, and available in summary at https://commission.europa.eu/strategy-and-policy/priorities-2019-2024/promoting-our-european-way-life/new-pact-migration-and-asylum_en.

16. The original framework dates back to 2003. It has been altered throughout the years, but its core "first country" principle remains largely unaltered. Its latest iteration is Regulation (EU) No. 604/2013 (June 26, 2013), which establishes the criteria and mechanisms for determining the Member State responsible for examining an application for international protection lodged in one of the Member States by a third-country national or a stateless person. It is available at https://eur-lex.europa.eu/legal-content/EN/LSU/?uri=CELEX:32013R0604#:~:text=ACT-,Regulation%20(EU)%20No%20604%2F2013%20of%20the%20European%20Parliament,national%20or%20a%20stateless%20person.
17. In part due to the competing and opposing views on how the framework should be reformed, talks on a harmonized and EU-wide asylum policy to replace the Dublin regime have not yielded significant results. The most recent Pact for Migration and Asylum (2020), mentioned previously, focused primarily on making asylum less accessible by making it more difficult to file a claim in ways that at times include outsourcing some of the initial screening to third countries.
18. Ulrich Stege, "La normativa europea sul diritto d'asilo" (2017), quoted in Maurizio Veglio, "Uomini tradotti: prove di dialogo con richiedenti asilo," *Diritto, Immigrazione, Cittadinanza*, no. 2 (2017): 4.
19. For the official and precise numbers, see the website of the Interior Ministry, Department of Civil Liberties and Immigration, at http://www.libertaciviliimmigrazione.dlci.interno.gov.it/it/documentazione/statistica/i-numeri-dellasilo. For a more comprehensive picture of 2020 figures, see Fondazione Migrantes, *Diritto all'asilo—Report 2020* (Perugia: Tau, 2020), https://www.migrantes.it/il-diritto-dasilo-report-2020-costretti-a-fuggire-ancora-respinti/. For the breakdown of the state of the Italian asylum system pre-Minniti, I have drawn substantially from Veglio, "Uomini tradotti."
20. After the name of its *rapporteur*, then Minister of Interior Marco Minniti. Its full title is Legge 13 aprile 2017 n. 46 recante disposizioni urgenti per l'accelerazione dei procedimenti in materia di protezione internazionale, nonché per il contrasto dell'immigrazione illegale. Note, as a sign of the times, the seemingly natural coexistence of the phrases *international protection* and *illegal immigration* in the same sentence.
21. *Snellire e semplificare*, "to trim and simplify."
22. Following the Minniti law and, more recently, Salvini's amendments to it, this is what happens to an asylum request filed in Italy: A rejection by the commission can be appealed by the asylum seeker within thirty days of being notified. This is when the request for asylum enters the judiciary system, as it is heard by a judge at a specialized section of one of fourteen courthouses (*tribunali ordinari*) around the country (usually in the same region where the commission first interviewed the person). If the appeal is denied, the asylum seeker can petition the Corte di Cassazione to hear their case, something that is notoriously difficult. (Only certain attorneys are allowed to argue before the court, the procedure can be prohibitively expensive, etc.) Minniti's law took away one layer of appeal, that of the appeals court, which had existed until then.
23. Legge 1 Dicembre 2018, n. 132 recante disposizioni urgenti in materia di protezione internazionale, immigrazione e sicurezza pubblica, http://www.gazzettaufficiale.it/eli/id/2018/10/04/18G00140/sg.

24. Humanitarian protection status exists in several other EU countries, but the commissions' and courts' reliance on it varies largely from jurisdiction to jurisdiction. See Didier Fassin, *Humanitarian Reason: A Moral History of the Present* (Berkeley: University of California Press, 2012).
25. As in the language defining criteria for protection under the 1951 Convention.
26. As in the language defining criteria for protection under the 1984 Convention Against Torture, which defines torture as follows: "[f]or the purposes of this Convention, the term 'torture' means any act by which severe pain or suffering, whether physical or mental, is intentionally inflicted on a person for such purposes as obtaining from him or a third person information or a confession, punishing him for an act he or a third person has committed or is suspected of having committed, or intimidating or coercing him or a third person, or for any reason based on discrimination of any kind, when such pain or suffering is inflicted by or at the instigation of or with the consent or acquiescence of a public official or other person acting in an official capacity. It does not include pain or suffering arising only from, inherent in or incidental to lawful sanctions." CAT, Article 1, accessible at https://www.ohchr.org/en/instruments-mechanisms/instruments/convention-against-torture-and-other-cruel-inhuman-or-degrading.
27. D.L. 130/2020, October 31, 2020, accessible at https://www.gazzettaufficiale.it/eli/id/2020/12/19/20A07086/sg.
28. For other forms of implementation of (and resistance to) institutional processes of language hierarchization in multilingual contexts, see the chapters by Daniel Kaufman and Ross Perlin and by Madeleine Dobie in this volume.
29. UNHCR, *Aide-Memoire and Glossary of Case Processing Modalities, Terms and Concepts Applicable to Refugee Status Determination (RSD) Under UNHCR's Mandate (The Glossary)* (Geneva: UNHCR, 2017), https://www.refworld.org/docid/5a2657e44.html. The French translation is titled *Aide-mémoire et glossaire concernant les modalités de traitement des dossiers, termes et concepts applicables à la détermination du statut de réfugié relevant du mandat du HCR*.
30. On this point, see Emily Apter, *The Translation Zone: A New Comparative Literature* (Princeton, NJ: Princeton University Press, 2006).
31. Cristiana Giordano, *Migrants in Translation: Caring and the Logics of Difference in Contemporary Italy* (Berkeley: University of California Press, 2014), 16.
32. I refer to the concepts of testimonial and hermeneutical injustice developed by Miranda Fricker in *Epistemic Injustice: Power and the Ethics of Knowing* (Oxford: Oxford University Press, 2007).
33. Giordano, *Migrants in Translation*, 16.
34. The production of an asylum demand is, as we have seen, a process of layering. It starts in the tongue and mind of the applicant. The first layer is the C-3 intake form, which is completed with the assistance of an interpreter when the applicant and the police agent cannot communicate.
35. Defined by Katrijn Maryns as "the end product of the textual process" in "Procedures Without Borders: The Language-Ideological Anchorage of Administrative Procedures in Translocal Institutional Settings," *Language in Society* 42, no. 1 (2013): 76.
36. It is almost comically paradoxical that, in order to make sure that the translator is properly transferring information between the counsel and the applicant, the counsel must go through the translator. In other words, the counsel must ask through the translator whether *the translator* is making everything clear.

37. Often preceded by the uniquely and evenly loving and patronizing Italian expression *mi raccomando*.
38. The literal translation of the sentence is "My city *badarlan*." Every letter *a* in the word should be pronounced like the *a* in the Spanish word *agua*. Since A. K started his sentence in Italian, I am using an "Italian" transliteration, where *a* always sounds like *a*.
39. Gianfranco Rosi, dir., *Fuocoammare* (Rome: 01 Distribution, 2016), DVD.
40. The Italian version states: "Non c'è una strada principale, sono strade pedonali, non ci sono strade ben costruite." I discuss the implications of my choice to translate *strade pedonali* as "trails" shortly.
41. Marco Jacquemet, "Transcribing Refugees: The Entextualization of Asylum Seekers' Hearings in a Transidiomatic Environment," *Text & Talk* 29, no. 5 (2009): 525–546.
42. Gayatri Spivak, "The Politics of Translation," in *Outside in the Teaching Machine* (New York: Routledge, 1995), 182.

WORKS CITED

Apter, Emily. *The Translation Zone: A New Comparative Literature.* Princeton, NJ: Princeton University Press, 2006.

Bohmer, C., and A. Shuman. *Political Asylum Deceptions: The Culture of Suspicion.* London: Palgrave Macmillan, 2018.

Fassin, Didier. *Humanitarian Reason: A Moral History of the Present.* Berkeley: University of California Press, 2012.

Fondazione Migrantes. *Diritto all'asilo—Report 2020.* Perugia: Tau, 2020. https://www.migrantes.it/wp-content/uploads/sites/50/2020/11/DirittodAsilo2020-23-11.pdf.

Fricker, Miranda. *Epistemic Injustice: Power and the Ethics of Knowing.* Oxford: Oxford University Press, 2007.

Giordano, Cristina. *Migrants in Translation: Caring and the Logics of Difference in Contemporary Italy.* Berkeley: University of California Press, 2014.

Goodwin-Gill, G., and J. McAdam. *The Refugee in International Law.* 3rd ed. London: Oxford University Press, 2007.

Jacquemet, Marco. "The Registration Interview: Restricting Refugees' Narrative Performances." In *Critical Readings in Translation Studies*, ed. Mona Baker, 133–151. London: Routledge, 2010.

Jacquemet, Marco. "Transcribing Refugees: The Entextualization of Asylum Seekers' Hearings in a Transidiomatic Environment." *Text & Talk* 29, no. 5 (2009): 525–546.

Maryns, Katrijn. *The Asylum Speaker: Language in the Belgian Asylum Procedure.* London: Routledge, 2006.

Maryns, Katrijn. "Procedures Without Borders: The Language-Ideological Anchorage of Administrative Procedures in Translocal Institutional Settings." *Language in Society* 42, no. 1 (2013): 71–92.

Paz, Moria. "The Failed Promise of Language Rights: A Critique of the International Language Rights Regime." *Harvard International Law Journal* 54, no. 1 (2013): 157–218.

Rosi, Gianfranco, dir. *Fuocoammare.* Rome: 01 Distribution, 2016. DVD.

Spivak, Gayatri Chakravorty. "The Politics of Translation." In *Outside in the Teaching Machine*. New York: Routledge, 1995.

United Nations High Commissioner for Refugees (UNHCR). *Aide-Memoire and Glossary of Case Processing Modalities, Terms and Concepts Applicable to Refugee Status Determination (RSD) Under UNHCR's Mandate (The Glossary)*. Geneva: UNHCR, 2017. https://www.refworld.org/docid/5a2657e44.html.

United Nations High Commissioner for Refugees. *Convention and Protocol Relating to the Status of Refugees*. Geneva: UNHCR, 2011.

Veglio, Maurizio. "Uomini tradotti: prove di dialogo con richiedenti asilo." *Diritto, Immigrazione, Cittadinanza*, no. 2 (2017): 1–40.

I Am Not Your Data

ABHAY XAXA

I am not your data, nor am I your vote bank,
I am not your project, or any exotic museum project,
I am not the soul waiting to be harvested,
Nor am I the lab where your theories are tested.

I am not your cannon fodder, or the invisible worker,
Or your entertainment at India habitat center,
I am not your field, your crowd, your history,
your help, your guilt, medallions of your victory.

I refuse, reject, resist your labels,
your judgments, documents, definitions,
your models, leaders and patrons,
because they deny me my existence, my vision, my space.

Your words, maps, figures, indicators,
they all create illusions and put you on a pedestal
from where you look down upon me.

So I draw my own picture, and invent my own grammar,
I make my own tools to fight my own battle,
For me, my people, my world, and my Adivasi self!

Chapter Four

CHALLENGING "EXTINCTION" THROUGH MODERN MIAMI LANGUAGE PRACTICES

WESLEY Y. LEONARD

WHAT GETS NOTICED WITH INDIGENOUS LANGUAGES?

The most important part of this chapter is not its discussion of actual Miami language practices but rather the metaissue that the story needs to be told at all. It represents a series of findings that, although largely self-evident, challenge a common discourse in which American Indian cultures and languages are frozen in the past and are authentic only if unchanged relative to some perceived norm associated with their past. Because of this discourse, the present story becomes even more anomalous than it might otherwise be. Miami, an Algonquian language indigenous to Indiana and claimed by a contemporary population of several thousand people, has been termed "extinct" in widely consulted sources such as *Ethnologue*.[1] However, *myaamia* continues to exist in the linguistic repertoire of the Miami people.[2] A twelve-year-old participant at the conclusion of a 2007 Miami language and cultural youth camp addressed this paradox in her puzzlement by asking "If *myaamia* was a dead language, how would we be able to speak it?" Because of a robust language-reclamation effort that began during the 1990s, many Miami people, myself included, not only claim heritage to our language but also actually speak it to varying degrees, despite its supposed demise.[3]

It is for this reason that the story of Miami language use exemplifies the theme that Philip Deloria develops and deconstructs in *Indians in*

*Unexpected Places.*⁴ Deloria demonstrates how various patterns of colonialism have created a situation in which American Indians are expected to exist only in ways associated with perceived (and often incorrect) ideals of their pasts, in which the norms in question reflect patterns of colonialism, stem from domination, and often impose significant limitations to full participation in "modern" life. Behaviors that contradict these assumptions, even when they are common and normal to the people who perform them, get conceptualized as unexpected; they are anomalous in that they upset the status quo of what Indians are allowed to be. In doing so, they also challenge existing power structures by showing that Indians can and do participate in all aspects of life and will not accept an imposed narrative in which they live(d) only in the past.

For the story under discussion, this larger phenomenon is exemplified through the contemporary usage patterns of the Miami language—patterns that contradict common assumptions held within U.S. society regarding how Indian languages supposedly exist. This set of general assumptions, which I will refer to as the *dominant discourse*, starts with impositions of purism on the language structure and usage patterns of the American Indian language in question—in this case, *myaamia*. They also include the related idea that the speakers must be "pure" in their cultural identities and associated life practices, thus disallowing influence from other cultural or linguistic communities to which the members of the group may also belong.⁵

Within the Miami community, these themes are frequently discussed in terms of our language and certain recurring experiences several Miami people have had. Especially common are stories of individuals who have questioned our legitimacy, often without recognizing the strangeness of their inquiries when they ask if what we're speaking is really *myaamia*. Such themes are hardly unique to the Miami story but instead reflect a larger set of ideologies regarding American Indian languages and the people who claim them. As Anne Goodfellow concludes in her analysis of why Kwak'wala revitalization efforts are deemed to be failing despite an increase in younger speakers, "the greatest obstacle to keeping Native American languages thriving is a prevalent belief of linguists, language planners, teachers, and the general public that a language must somehow be maintained in its 'pure' form, which usually means the oldest form of the language now spoken by elderly people."⁶ Conversely, a widely held belief within the Miami community is that the language will be different in form with respect to any given point in the past and that this is fine. However—and this point is crucial—although there have been several outside (that is, non-Miami) scholars who have agreed with the sentiment behind this thinking, the dominant discourse still overwhelmingly imposes an expectation of purity on Miami. As with other Indigenous languages, regardless of what the heritage community may think or do, noncommunity members have ideas regarding what the language is supposed to be.

Clearly, the ideology underlying the dominant discourse creates and reinforces a situation in which Indigenous languages get constrained. Important to acknowledge, however, is that there usually does exist some idealized "legitimate" version of the target language, in terms of its form and its use. As such, it is not that the dominant discourse claims that Indian languages cannot exist or ever be used, but rather that it licenses their use only in certain forms, on certain topics, and in certain domains—generally ones that are considered "fully" Indian in that they are thought to lack (or at least minimize) Western influence. This discourse represents a challenge for Indigenous languages across the United States and elsewhere because it imposes significant restrictions on the recognition of their contemporary usage patterns, which often include practices that are shared with non-Indigenous groups. Therefore, even when the usage of these languages is increasing, this fact can easily be overlooked or dismissed because the specific uses at issue often fall outside of what the dominant discourse acknowledges to be legitimately Indian.

The story of the *myaamia* language takes this idea close to its logical extreme. This is because, in addition to its recent use in specific "unexpected" places—such as in contemporary songs, games, and computer-mediated communication—the "extinction" of Miami makes its use anomalous even in contexts that the dominant discourse otherwise recognizes as legitimately Indian, such as traditional ceremonies. Its active reclamation from historical documentation after a thirty-year period of dormancy reflects a scenario that most would acknowledge is technically possible, but that is anomalous because *extinct* means forever. Many people, experts and nonexperts alike, have not caught up to the reality that Miamis speak *myaamia* today and, moreover, that the ways in which we do so are, upon commonsense consideration, arguably expected in that they reflect the contemporary circumstances of being Miami.

CHALLENGING "EXTINCTION" THROUGH MODERN MIAMI LANGUAGE PRACTICES

This chapter has two major objectives. One is to exemplify several modern Miami language practices that the dominant discourse deems anomalous and to show why they are actually fully normal and expected, the expectations in this case being framed around the history and contemporary circumstances of the Miami people, along with general principles of language. The second is to critique and explore why this would even be an issue. The specific practices that I outline reflect that our *myaamia* language is important to us and that we Miamis are a diverse people, whose practices blend our *myaamia* background with the English language and elements of the various communities to which we belong.

I narrate this story from my own point of view as a Miami tribal member and linguist who specializes in Indigenous language reclamation as a social practice. The examples and arguments in this chapter come from approximately ten years of participant observation in Miami language programs—more recently, as chair of the Miami Tribe of Oklahoma Language Committee, a role that has fostered ongoing discussions about Miami language issues with a variety of audiences.[7] My goal is to tell the story as it is: we are Miami, we come from many backgrounds, and our ancestral heritage language underwent a period of dormancy, but we generally share a belief that it has contemporary value. The actions and language-usage patterns in light of these variables are relatively straightforward. Prior to telling this story, however, it is important to situate the context in which it becomes anomalous in the first place.

REGARDING THE SUCCESS OF MIAMI LANGUAGE RECLAMATION

> I give the revival of the Myaamia language a 1 percent chance of being successful and that is being optimistic.
>
> —THE LANGUAGE GUY, "REVIVING DEAD LANGUAGES"

It is not a shortcoming of organization that led me to share this particular prediction without having first provided sufficient information regarding the history or contemporary status of the Miami people and our language.[8] Rather, I do this intentionally; the lack of background information is what makes this example representative of a larger pattern that characterizes much of the Miami story. It reflects the ongoing problem of outside scholars and others making predictions about the "success" of Miami language reclamation without ever having asked the Miami people what our language goals are—and usually without fully understanding the larger context in which language shift has occurred in the Miami community. Jane Hill reminds us that academic work about endangered languages, even when well-intentioned and meant to evoke public awareness or concern, can also have damaging effects on these languages by reinforcing a norm by which experts gain or maintain the prerogative to determine their value.[9] There is an especially strong current focus on documenting these languages before they are "gone," their looming extinction framed primarily as a loss to universal (particularly scientific) knowledge, often with a secondary focus on the cultural implications for the communities that claim them.[10] In this frame, the vitality of an Indigenous language gets evaluated largely by its speaker population and transmission patterns, the stability of its grammatical structure relative to some perceived or actual historical norm, and the scope of its vocabulary—especially whether speakers command vocabulary domains that are deemed unique to their cultural group. From this common point of view, reclamation "success" probably would entail meeting targets in these areas and would be measured by the number of speakers and their linguistic fluency, along with the number and types of domains in which the language is used.

For these and related reasons, I am hypothesizing that *The Language Guy*'s statement above frames successful "revival" as something that would entail the full adoption of Miami—of its grammar and in terms of its usage—in a way that matches patterns for languages of personal familiarity to the author. Joseph Errington notes that linguistic analyses and their associated descriptions often share many similarities even when the languages under consideration are quite different and argues that this stems from a practice of conceptualizing analyses in terms of languages of familiarity to the researcher.[11] I have noticed a similar trend in several discussions I have had on Indigenous language learning and teaching efforts. Here, what I believe is the same underlying process gets manifested when the legitimacy, goals, and practices associated with Indigenous language efforts are unquestioningly framed in terms of norms for major world languages. An especially prevalent notion—one that is highly problematic for languages that have had a period of total dormancy—is that "genuine" language transmission is only that which occurs in the home unconsciously and completely, as with the common (though not universal) experience of children acquiring English in the United States.[12] By extension, if Miami isn't transmitted in this way, many quickly assume that its reclamation efforts are unsuccessful, even though languages that have had a period of dormancy can initially be learned only as second languages; intergenerational transmission is a later stage. Moreover, as Barbra Meek illustrates in her critique of the problematic ways in which success gets measured for Indigenous language efforts, general expectations for American Indians to fail can be augmented by discourses of failure specific to language efforts.[13] For all of these reasons, although it is not certain exactly how this blogger conceptualizes success, it's not surprising that he predicts a 99 percent chance of it not occurring. In this sense, "success" is clearly unexpected, if not almost impossible.

However, most Miami language programs are successful because they are framed around a series of attainable objectives that are informed by contemporary community needs and values. Goals include fostering a positive and informed *myaamia* identity, a connection to the larger Miami community, a cultural understanding of the language, and some linguistic proficiency. The goal is not full linguistic fluency by 100 percent of the Miami population. As tribal member and language leader Daryl Baldwin summed up in a keynote lecture for the 2004 Stabilizing Indigenous Languages Conference, "When we talk about language and cultural revitalization, we are in essence referring to the revitalization of belief, value and knowledge systems. It is through our language and culture that we express those ways of knowing. This all takes place as one interrelated process. So when I say, 'Is it really all about fluency?' the answer in my mind is 'no.' Fluency is an outcome of the collective effort."[14] A major goal—referenced in Baldwin's words and echoed by many other Miamis—is to achieve a certain level of what might be termed *cultural fluency*, in which proficiency in the language may ensue but in which this proficiency is not the immediate target. For this reason, an assessment of contemporary Miami language usage might most naturally be one that would consider cultural knowledge and the associated ways of expressing it through the language, not isolated measurements of linguistic competence (except insofar as a certain level of direct linguistic knowledge is necessary for some cultural practices).[15] Nevertheless, the reality is that the dominant discourse not only places the idea of Miami language reclamation into an unexpected category but also often unilaterally imposes its goals.

Furthermore, contemporary language efforts of the Miami people are motivated by a need to respond to our political and linguistic history. Our efforts are in some ways a healing process. They represent a way of responding to the past and contemporary circumstances that contributed to the shift away from *myaamia* and that were usually accompanied by the denigration of language and culture. As with American Indians of other nations, many Miamis went to Indian boarding schools where they were not allowed to speak *myaamia*, which in turn contributed to the nontransmission of the language in the home.[16] Other efforts to force-assimilate Miamis into "mainstream" culture, along with various economic struggles—especially those that contributed to migration away from centers of tribal population—also contributed to the shift away from the heritage language and toward (only) English. During the 1960s, *myaamia*, for the most part, went out of use altogether. At that time, living people held only very limited linguistic knowledge, and this is when the language became "extinct." However, there remained a very large corpus of written documentation spanning approximately three hundred years, and this is what eventually became the basis for learning and reintroducing the language into the community.[17]

Crucial to this story is that, through the lens of the dominant discourse, the passing of the "last" Miami speaker represents the end of the story. In most categorizations employed within the field of linguistics, this represents language extinction, and it is usually considered to be a key turning point in that the language is no longer thought to be able to contribute to linguistic theory (except in limited ways through new analysis of its historical documentation).[18] Looking at language "loss" from a more anthropological perspective, however, the pivotal turning point is the beginning of language shift—or, more accurately, the precursors to that process. This is what demonstrates that some sort of power imbalance has occurred, one that is frequently accompanied by a sense of shame in the language. For Miamis, this imbalance occurred at some point during the nineteenth century and likely reflected variables that include land loss, two removals, and formal education by the United States in which being Indian was said to be bad. What is important to recognize is that such factors do not automatically disappear when the language in question ceases to be known.

Rather, that second turning point commences a state in which the measurable symptom of declining language use is no longer overt but in which the underlying issues that led to language shift are usually still present.

Because Miami language efforts not only are focused on the language but also respond to these larger historical and contemporary series of events and ideologies, I have come to refer to what's happening in the Miami community as *language reclamation* instead of by the more commonly used term *language revitalization*. We certainly are breathing new life into the language—hence revitalizing it—and the outcomes of our efforts do include many of the common targets of revitalization, such as increasing the number of speakers, increasing the domains in which the language is used, and promoting intergenerational transmission of the language, which has begun in a few families.[19] However, these and other linguistically defined targets occur within a much larger social process of claiming—or reclaiming—the appropriate cultural context and sense of value that the language would likely have always had if not for colonization. Meeting language-specific targets represents part of the process, but it isn't the core. The fact that the members of a community assert their right to claim, learn, and speak their language is more fundamental.

Furthermore, the Miami people must also claim the prerogative to implement, talk about, and evaluate our language efforts in a way that reflects contemporary Miami people and our values, not through a dominant ideology that relegates success to a very narrow set of parameters while assuming that Indians are generally incompetent. Recognizing this prerogative also falls under the larger process that I call language reclamation.[20] In terms of language programs and their assessment, this entails that the goals of any program will stem from the community's values and needs and that evaluations of success will be based on these goals, not on somebody else's. Such examples of self-determination are also part of language reclamation.

In this respect, this chapter is an example of language reclamation in practice in that I am responding to the larger metaissue that clouds Miami language efforts. It's not that we aren't successfully learning *myaamia* and benefiting from doing so but rather that this process is impeded by a dominant discourse that doesn't establish a space in which it can occur. We Miamis challenge this discourse repeatedly and have what Paul Kroskrity calls "an awareness leading to the transformation of selves and systems."[21]

Our reclamation efforts include recognition and assertion of the agency that we, as Miami individuals and as a community, have in describing, adapting, and speaking our language. No longer do we accept the "e-word" (*extinct*) to describe *myaamia*; we instead use the term *sleeping* to refer to its status during its period of dormancy, noting that this term is not only more socially appropriate but also more accurate in that our language was never irretrievably lost.[22] No longer do we accept the ideology that our language cannot or should not change, and some of us have come to question why changes in Indigenous languages are often called *attrition* even when similar patterns in major languages are just called *change*. No longer do we evaluate our successes (and some failures) in terms of evaluation scales that don't reflect our own needs and values. No longer do we acquiesce to various related notions that stem from the colonialist idea that Indigenous cultures, languages, and identities are real only if they exist in a way that matches a perception of how they existed at some point in the past, the perception in question usually being one of "pure" peoples with relatively narrowly constrained cultural and linguistic practices.

In response to this issue, a recent theme in Miami cultural programs has been the promotion of the idea that tribal members are "100 percent *myaamia*" regardless of the specific history of a given tribal member's family. That is, our tribal citizenship cannot be reduced to smaller parts, in which, for example, some members would be one-fourth Miami and their children would be one-eighth. Though there are differences in any given tribal member's cultural knowledge (usually understood to refer to knowledge of traditional culture) and some tribal members more strongly identify with their Miami-ness than others, it is thought that demoting any tribal member's status as a full Miami citizen is always inappropriate. Nevertheless, the dominant discourse, in which many Miamis are called "part Miami," is still powerful.

Because the Miami people are phenotypically diverse, many tribal members must also confront a related line of thinking that claims they aren't really Indian because of how they look. Some Miamis do "look Indian," but many have blond hair, blue eyes, and other features that the dominant discourse indexes to a non-Indian (usually European) norm. Given patterns of intermarriage and some early adoption of Europeans into the tribe, this phenotypic variation is not surprising. However, what is striking is that people will sometimes say that they met a Miami person who didn't look

Miami—even when they, by virtue of not having had contact with many other Miamis, really would have no way of knowing what a prototypical Miami might look like or if there even is a norm. Such examples abound. Individuals without an appropriate frame of reference make unsubstantiated claims about the Miami people and do so in a way that would be likely recognized as ridiculous if the dominant discourse about American Indians, which includes what we look like in addition to how and what we speak (or don't speak), wasn't so pervasive.[23] Our reclamation efforts thus include discussions about how we are real Miamis, each with the full prerogative to participate in our nation and to speak *myaamia*, and how the notion of being "part Miami" was introduced through various policies by the United States.[24]

In general, this changed rhetoric in which Miamis are fully *myaamia* has led to positive outcomes in that it situates tribal members in a place of legitimacy and responsibility. That is, as people who are fully *myaamia*, we ought to care about Miami issues, perhaps more so than somebody who within the dominant discourse would be termed "part Miami" or a "Miami descendant." However, because bona fide Miami tribal citizenship is not limited by race, phenotype, religion, or blood quantum, the demographic outcome is that we who are legitimately *myaamia* comprise a diverse group of people, with significant cultural and linguistic influences from the various other groups and communities of practice to which we belong.[25] These include the "mainstream" social, cultural, and regional backgrounds that we come from and our occupational, religious, and political affiliations, which for any given Miami person will almost always incorporate at least some ways of being that differ from historical Miami norms. It ensues that our language practices would reflect this twenty-first-century multicultural reality. So-called unexpected uses of our language are surprising only when somebody is caught up in the notions that Indigenous languages cannot change and that their speakers exist in a cultural vacuum. The more straightforward expectation is that they would develop in ways that reflect their population of users and general developments in the world. The next section discusses several examples of this phenomenon, all of which I argue are legitimate and expected given the diverse nature of the Miami community. The more pressing question is not why these examples are legitimate and expected but rather why anybody would (continue to) question that this is so.

HOW DO CONTEMPORARY MIAMIS SPEAK *MYAAMIA*?

> The vocabulary of the Miamis was not very great, probably containing not over six hundred or eight hundred words, but it was all they needed in their savage life. They did not use all these words in ordinary conversation; they possibly used no more than one hundred in common conversation.
>
> —MARTHA UNA McCLURG, *MIAMI INDIAN STORIES*

Taken from the appendix to a 1961 publication of traditional Miami stories, this quotation is out of date, but I include it here because it isn't very different from the sorts of erroneous assumptions that people today have about Indigenous languages such as *myaamia*.[26] Like other languages, Miami has thousands and thousands of words, a fact that should have been patently obvious to McClurg just from a quick look at any number of historical word lists or dictionaries. What is more important about this statement is that many people today, including university students I have taught, often initially have no hesitation in believing that it is true.

As has been increasingly deconstructed in the academic literature, though far less so in everyday society, there exists within the dominant discourse an underlying belief that American Indian languages are limited, an assumption that likely reflects larger principles of colonization—particularly the idea that colonized peoples are themselves limited and inferior.[27] The corollary to this is the notion, my present focus, that these languages can or should be used in only very limited ways, as demonstrated in the preceding quotation. Such thinking partly reflects the more general misconception that American Indian cultures and languages are suitable only for old, "primitive" practices.

An additional and somewhat less obvious issue is that the dominant discourse prohibits certain counterexamples to this notion of limitedness to even come forward as counterexamples. This occurs when the discourse doesn't index those examples as "American Indian" even when they are practiced by American Indians in ways that incorporate elements of the Native language or culture in question. For example, borrowings from English, even when adapted in pronunciation to match the sound system of a given Indigenous language more closely and/or used in ways that differ from English, may not even be considered for evaluating the scope and size of that language's vocabulary. Responding to a similarly motivated issue, Anthony Webster relates a story of a Navajo author who prefers to use the plural form *sheeps* in his English instead of *sheep* and whose English is widely and easily assumed to be deficient because of his usage of this and other Navajo English forms.[28] In this case, it is the legitimacy of a Navajo dialect of English that is being questioned, and the assumption is couched within a larger expectation that American Indians cannot speak "correct" English.[29] Conversely for the Miami story, it is the *myaamia* forms that get questioned, especially if they appear to have English influence.[30] Regardless, all such examples reflect a shared underlying issue: the dominant discourse severely limits the possibilities of what can even be considered as a possible Native American word, grammatical pattern, or language variety. Cases that contradict those expectations simply get marked as non-Indian—and often also as incorrect. Beyond directly dealing with egregious ideas about our language such as the preceding example, part of Miami language reclamation has entailed associating a wide variety of practices—especially those that the dominant discourse is unlikely to recognize as Miami—as legitimately *myaamia*.

That noted, except insofar as any Miami use is anomalous because of the "extinction" factor, it's true that traditional practices and their associated language practices are comparatively accepted within the dominant discourse as legitimate. The more pressing issue thus becomes recognizing and legitimizing "newer" Miami practices, especially those that contain elements from the many other communities of practice to which Miami people belong.[31] Below I discuss several such examples, all of which involve some use of the *myaamia* language and which have been chosen for discussion because they include elements that the dominant discourse frames as non-Miami.

Though these examples come from a variety of sources, a significant portion occurred in the Miami Tribe of Oklahoma's *eewansaapita* language and cultural immersion camps for tribal youth, the design and scope of which have special relevance to the current discussion.[32] Happening annually since 2005, the *eewansaapita* program becomes an especially pertinent example for the current discussion for several reasons. It represents not only a gathering of people who happen to be Miami (as occurs naturally with most tribally sponsored events) but also one that was created specifically to be *myaamia* in every way that it could be and that includes teaching language and traditional cultural activities among its goals. These camps have twenty to thirty-five student participants ranging in age from nine to sixteen, along with several camp counselors, staff, and volunteers, all who have gathered to do *myaamia* things.[33] As a major event that tribal members from across the United States attend, the *eewansaapita* camp program is also representative of the demographics of the Miami Tribe of Oklahoma in a way that most locally oriented events are not. Although there are concentrations of Miamis in Oklahoma and Indiana, a majority of tribal members—including many camp staff and participants—live elsewhere. In this respect, the camps more accurately show the geographic diversity that characterizes the Miami people; some participants are local and others fly in for the program, and we thus bring different perspectives that reflect the regional diversity of the United States. Finally, language practices of the *eewansaapita* program are especially relevant for this chapter because the program is designed for youth, and even most staff are relatively young; most counselors, for example, are college students. I raise this last point not because Elder life isn't important—it very much is—but rather because the dominant discourse tends to be comparatively (though hardly fully) accepting of Indian Elders and their practices as "real," and one goal of this chapter is to show that Miami youth are real Miamis too.[34] For this reason, the following examples of song, play, and regular communication primarily come from younger Miamis.

ON SONG

Miami songs never had a true period of dormancy as with most of the language; certain song traditions have always been active. One Elder remembers and can sing a Miami lullaby that her grandmother sang to her when she was a child, and there are several other examples that are "only" *myaamia*. As traditional songs tend to fall within what the dominant discourse licenses as Indian, however, I am omitting them from the current discussion, though they are important to Miami life and worthy of discussion in their own right. My focus instead is on examples that more directly reflect the twenty-first-century multicultural, and increasingly multilingual, Miami community.

One such example occurs right at the beginning of *eewansaapita* camps, when Miami children learn a Miami number song. Knowledge of number vocabulary is necessary for many things—particularly for playing games. Games were especially prominent at the 2009 *eewansaapita* camp, where the theme was *weekihkaaminki-meehkintiinki*, or "ball games and games of chance," and where the games in question required counting and keeping track of points. Many participants come to programs already knowing such basic vocabulary; for them, the relevance of this song may be that it asserts their knowledge, similar to how a child who already knows the Latin alphabet may still sing the "ABC Song." Repetition of such songs also further establishes the camp as a place where Miami is spoken—or, in this case, sung.

Key to the current discussion is this song's tune. The lyrics are ones that the dominant discourse would likely recognize as fully *myaamia* because the number words have no similarity to their English counterparts. The tune for our number song, however, is that of "This Old Man," the English version of which is a counting song and already known to all Miami children. It was English-speaking Miamis (a redundant expression, as all Miamis minimally speak English, if not *myaamia* and other languages) who created this song in the first place by borrowing a familiar tune.[35] I have never heard a Miami person question the Miami-ness of this song, but I have encountered this question from non-Miamis.

Another song, one that was first widely introduced as part of the 2009 *eewansaapita* curriculum, further exemplifies the same mixture of influences. This is a song of greeting and thanks, the singing of which reflects core historical Miami practices of using song as one method of accomplishing these communicative goals. Its lyrics are as follows:

aya aya (× 2)	"Hello/hi"
neehaki-nko kiiyawi? (× 2)	"Are you well?"
neehaki niiyawi (× 2)	"I am well"
teepahki (× 2)	"It's good"

This was a song that the camp participants sang before meals to show appreciation to the camp cooks. As the motivation for singing this song falls into a more general and older Miami cultural practice of using song to show appreciation, the purpose of this song would probably not be considered unexpected. Its tune, however, is anomalous; the greeting song is sung to the tune of "Are You Sleeping?"—also known by its French title, "Frère Jacques." It is noteworthy that the borrowing of the song into

English from French—in this case, the tune and the content of the song—is rarely questioned; English borrows a lot from French, and this borrowing reflects contact. When Miami borrows the tune, however, the phenomenon is marked, even though Miami people today all speak English and likely all know this song. Moreover, as the first European language to come prominently to the Miami people, French has maintained a level of cultural and linguistic influence in Miami society that exceeds all other European languages aside from English. For example, French shows up frequently in Miami surnames, including my own. Given that French has special significance as part of the multicultural heritage that many Miamis have, incorporating elements of an originally French song becomes even more natural than it already would be by virtue of the status of French as a widely known language, not to mention the global popularity of this particular tune.

We also have short songs that are created on the fly, in which somebody notices something and starts singing about it in Miami, again following an old Miami practice. For example, I have observed this several times as a part of playful teasing—in which, for example, somebody might make up a simple tune to point out some negative attribute of somebody else, such as being stinky after strenuous activity. Similar to the previous examples, many of these fleeting songs are sung to well-known Western tunes, which is not surprising given that most Miamis grew up with these tunes. Unfortunately, the ephemeral nature of such examples makes them tricky to record for purposes of inclusion here, but it is important to note that they exist and should be expected. After all, why wouldn't Miami people use the full variety of language and music resources that we have to poke fun at each other?

ON GAMES

Many games at the 2009 *eewansaapita* camp were long-standing in Miami culture; in some cases, they were games that have always been played, but in other cases, they were games that had been newly learned from historical written descriptions and brought back into use. In the camp context, the point was not only to learn about those games as a part of Miami history but also to play them. In this way, this particular camp largely revolved around mixing older tradition with contemporary ways and then putting those mixtures into practice.

For example, *pakitahaminki*, or "lacrosse," is an old Miami game, likely originally learned from the Iroquois but well established as a Miami practice and currently played by many Miami people. It has not, to my knowledge, been questioned in terms of its Miami-ness, which is likely because early ethnographies of Miamis frequently refer to it and thus place it into the "expected"; expected practices can include borrowed games so long as they were borrowed before the Indian culture in question was initially described by the colonizers. Even practices that are authorized by the dominant discourse, however, usually have restrictions on the specific ways in which they occur. Let us consider the specifics of how lacrosse was played at this camp.

In the camp setting, participants normally play *pakitahaminki* using commercially produced lacrosse sticks with components made out of plastic or metal. However, at the 2009 camp, we also commissioned our artist-in-residence to make a traditional stick out of wood as a way of exploring and learning from this traditional practice. This is expected; cultural groups often adopt new technologies while maintaining a sense of value for older ones.[36] Participants used several common *myaamia* collocations while playing the game, such as *miililo*, or "give it to me," and *pemaahkiilo*, or "throw it." However, the more complicated directions for the game were largely explained in English. This is expected; we are in the early stages of language reclamation, and most Miamis have only limited proficiency in *myaamia*, so complex issues are often discussed in English.

Consider also the game of chess, which many Miami people already know by virtue of our other cultural backgrounds but which only recently started to be played in the *myaamia* language.[37] The pattern by which *myaamia* names were assigned to the pieces is important. The young Miami man who codified those names first considered how existing Miami roles might match those already established for chess pieces and then named them accordingly:

akima, or "chief" (king)
akimaahkwia, or "female chief" (queen)
kaapia, or "assistant to the chief" (bishop)
maamiikaahkia, or "warrior" (knight)[38]
niimihki, or "fort" (rook)
eetehsia, or "soldier" (pawn)

With its culturally informed "borrowings," chess becomes a very characteristic example of the ways in which multiculturalism plays out among contemporary Miami people. The pieces, although not traditionally Miami, have taken on Miami names—ones that reflect Miami roles. In this respect, the names are fully *myaamia*, and the game has become *myaamia*, but the original knowledge of what the pieces are supposed to represent likely stems from knowledge that Miami people held by virtue of membership in other cultural groups, not from historical Miami culture in a direct way. A similar example arises in Erin Debenport's discussion of the Tiwa soap opera *As the Rez Turns*.[39] Debenport notes that the creators of *As the Rez Turns* identified its genre as one whose origin was outside their own cultural group, but they nevertheless made it into a Tiwa soap opera—not only through language use but also by imbuing it with local features and themes. Likewise, beyond the culturally informed way in which the pieces were named, Miami chess also becomes *myaamia* in that there is an expectation that older people will guide and support younger ones, this being a tribal cultural norm. However, such guidance might occur in English, again reflecting how most Miami people grow up primarily as English speakers. For example, in chess games that I have observed being played by a Miami family, much communication does occur in *myaamia*, but as with the previous example of lacrosse, complicated rules are more likely to be explained in English. The following sentence, which comes from a young Miami man (then age twelve) from the family that explained the game to me, illustrates this pattern:

> The object of the game is *pakamaci akima*
>   you (sing.) strike him chief (king)
> "The object of the game is for you to strike the chief."

Beyond the historical norm, in which this sentence would likely have been entirely in the Miami language, the expected historical construction for the verb phrase is probably *pakamaaci akimali*, or "she/he strikes the king," as the logical subject of the second clause would be a third-person entity. "You" forms were never used as generic third-person references in Classical Miami, but it's not surprising that the English convention of using *you* as a generic third-person reference has been borrowed.[40] This is a common outcome of bilingualism. A similarly motivated example occurring in this and other games is *ayaalo*, an imperative that means "Go!" which historically likely occurred only as a command for the hearer to move away from a location, but now also means "Take your turn!"

Though it's true that most Miami lexical innovation (creation of new words) occurs with an awareness of historical cultural patterns and a desire to maintain them, many examples of lexical innovation occurring on the fly involve directly translating English proper nouns into a Miami form, a pattern that directly reflects multilingualism. For example, prior to one of the *eewansaapita* programs, some of the staff stayed at a place that they started calling *palaanikaani*, which literally means "eight building" and in this context referred to a Super 8 motel. By referring to things in *myaamia* that don't already have Miami names, we create a Miami space, which is a major component of our reclamation efforts and hence is not surprising; we want to do this. However, that English influences the forms expectedly reflects that the multicultural society in which we live is, for the most part, English speaking and that we are also English speakers.

As I have argued, the presence of these and similar examples is straightforward when one considers the variables at play. When the language in question is a major world language, this phenomenon is usually called language contact. When one of the languages is Indigenous, however, such changes can be accompanied by the idea that the Indigenous language is no longer authentic, even though there were likely similar contact-induced changes in the language before some variety of the language became established as "authentic."[41] It is essential that Miami people move beyond these ideas. If the language isn't allowed to change in order to reflect our contemporary circumstances as a multilingual and multicultural people, the reclamation sought by the Miami people truly might have only a 1 percent chance of occurring because we will have accepted the dominant discourse, which says our language is extinct and cannot change.[42]

ON REGULAR COMMUNICATION

Regular communication is the term I adopt here to refer to interactions characterized by the absence of rules or expectations that are marked to the extent that speakers are consciously aware that they are unusual. I make this distinction because specialized Indigenous language use of various kinds, particularly when associated with ritual, is often comparatively expected within the dominant discourse. For example, fixed expressions that occur during a ceremony in which the participants are dressed in traditional regalia are expected and accepted; this is one of the ways in which I personally have always been allowed to be an Indian. For the current discussion, I am referencing common situations in which, for example, Miami people might be communicating with each other about work, to plan activities, or to check in with each other as friends and relatives.

Throughout this chapter, I have been contending that the appropriate way to make a hypothesis or to frame an associated expectation is to consider the variables as they actually are, not as the dominant discourse assumes them to be. In this spirit, let us consider the variables at play in assessing the likely patterns of everyday communication by Miami people. All Miamis come from multicultural heritages and are dominant in English (at least in most domains—a few may be more proficient in *myaamia* in certain areas). Although we have varying levels of proficiency in *myaamia*, most of us share a belief that there's value in speaking it and make an effort to do so. The linguistic result is what one might expect. Many interactions among Miami people, whether in oral or written form, occur primarily in English but incorporate certain elements in *myaamia*. This trend shows up throughout our communicative practices, and the specific patterns of language mixing reflect our contemporary demographics.

For example, an increasing number of Miami families have adopted the convention of addressing each other with Miami kinship terms, a practice that had gone almost completely out of use prior to our reclamation efforts. Similarly, although naming traditions never ceased to be practiced, they did diminish. However, there has recently been a renewed interest in receiving Miami names, with many parents asking that the chief provide them for their children. It is perhaps to the point where Miami names, at least in certain circles, are again the norm. One telling example occurred several years ago when a series of friendly reprimands were directed to me for inadvertently bidding against other Miamis in a series of online auctions for Miami and Miami-related items such as books, art, or historically significant artifacts. My intent, which I later learned several other Miamis also shared, was that the items in question be in tribal hands, though it wasn't important that they be in mine specifically. The point of this anecdote is that I should have been aware that I was bidding against fellow tribal members, as this was supposed to be evident in that some of the other participants in the online auction had *myaamia* user IDs.[43]

That this last example involves computer-mediated interaction is also representative of a larger trend. Because the Miami people are scattered throughout the United States, and especially because tribal members in different cities usually coordinate language programs, our communication often occurs over a distance and employs *kiinteelintaakana*, or "computers" (literally "things that think fast"). Several Miamis involved with language efforts, myself included, work in academia; hence, we use email, instant messaging, and various networking sites as part of our professional lives and often also for personal purposes. Similarly, most of the counselors for the *eewansaapita* summer program are university students who use all of these technologies and others; based on a recent survey, the majority of the student participants report having and using the internet at home as well. A general trend that exists among youth in the United States, whether of Indigenous or other cultural affiliation, is the use of more and more internet-based communication and social networking. All of these variables predict that the Miami language will be used frequently in computer-mediated communication.

This prediction is borne out. Many Miamis use Facebook and similar social-networking sites. In doing so, it is common for us to intersperse *myaamia* within our English when communicating with other tribal members. As with the earlier example of online auction user IDs, the use of Miami names for email and social-networking user IDs is common. Similarly, for the main text of email and instant messages (or telephone texts), many Miamis incorporate quite a bit of *myaamia*, with some longer passages entirely in the language. Even for language learners whose linguistic knowledge is still relatively limited, one common pattern is to greet the interlocutor and to close the interaction in *myaamia*. As Jocelyn Ahlers argues, such uses of Indigenous languages allow an entire communicative event to be framed as an Indigenous one, even if most of the utterances within the event are in English.[44] Again, this is not surprising but rather reflects a strategy for asserting one's Miami-ness while reflecting the reality that most Miamis have limitations on what we know how to say in our language.

These general patterns noted, one practical issue is that computer-mediated communication in the United States is usually set up for the Latin alphabet and a few other commonly occurring characters and emoticons.

Although this is largely a nonissue for writing Miami because our orthography is for the most part based on the Latin alphabet, there is one character that is less straightforward to type. This is the *s*-wedge [š], which represents a voiceless postalveolar fricative—what in English orthography is usually written as *sh*. For example, in a conversation I was having with a fellow tribal member through an instant-messaging program, I had indicated that I was with our mutual friend and that we were about to leave for a previous engagement. He wrote:

> *neeyolaani kati . . . ii$i Leanne aya!*
> I see you FUTURE tell her Leanne hello
> "I'll see you later. Say 'hi' to Leanne [for me]!"[45]

In this example, a dollar sign is substituted for [š]. According to the dominant discourse, American Indian languages are not normally written—especially for computer-mediated communication—but given the contemporary needs of the Miami people, it stands to reason that *myaamia* would be used in such ways. Also, the reason for the orthographic substitution in this example is clear. Western keyboards are not created for modern Miami orthography, so when Miamis type in Miami (especially for "quick" communication such as instant messages), we have established a convention of using another symbol that can be typed in a more direct way. This is a straightforward example of a modern Indigenous nation using the resources of other communities—in this case, adapting existing keyboard conventions—in order to meet an everyday communicative need, a practice that is arguably expected by any reasoned consideration. What might be truly unexpected would be for Miami people to avoid typing words with that particular character.

Miami linguistic practices reflect the multicultural Miami people. We believe it is important to have access to *myaamia*, and we attempt to speak it when we can. However, we also speak English, and this shows up in our communicative practices. The only reason any of these examples seems anomalous is the pervasiveness of the existing—and too often unchallenged—dominant discourse that relegates Indigenous languages to tokens of the past, spoken by the "true" Indians and not by the "Indian descendants," which is what we tend to be called today. When framed within this damaging discourse, even contemporary language practices may be seen as evidence of loss or "extinction." I argue, on the contrary, that the ways in which the Miami language is spoken today show that the Miami people do still exist—as does our language—because the patterns in question demonstrate how we continue to adapt to our environment and to the evolving communicative and cultural needs of our population. Part of our reclamation process involves our recognition and legitimization of how we exist, which is as a diverse group of people who share a common history, language, and Miami cultural values.

Given these variables, the expectation regarding future use of the Miami language by current language learners appears relatively straightforward. Wider-scale linguistic proficiency or fluency will likely take time. Language reclamation is a multigenerational process, and the Miami community does not yet have the resources (for example, a large land base and tribally run schools) that may be necessary for later stages of the process. Nevertheless, most Miami children already know at least some *myaamia* and use it to varying degrees, and I see this continuing. I hope that all will quickly recognize the fallacy of statements regarding any inability of our language to be used for modern purposes, though changing the discourse of expectations regarding American Indians is a multifaceted process that will likely take ongoing efforts because the dominant discourse is so powerful.

That reality noted, one prediction—yet another challenge to that dominant discourse but again logically predicted upon more reasoned consideration—comes out of *eewansaapita* camp participants' own statements. At the end of the 2007 program, one of my roles was to create and administer a written questionnaire as part of a larger-scale assessment. One question read, "Do you plan to use the *myaamia* language at home after this camp?" and participants were asked to circle one of the following answers: *iihia* (yes), *moohci* (no), or *I'm not sure*. Two of the twenty participants indicated that they were unsure of their plans, but the other eighteen circled *iihia*. One young woman summed up a common sentiment in noting, "I think that it is important to be *myaamia* because when we get older and our elders pass away, we could be able to teach kids younger than us how to speak our language so then they can pass it down, generation to generation. I think it is very important to be *myaamia* and to be able to speak it!"

Having participated in Miami language efforts for more than a decade and having researched issues of minority languages for a good portion of that time, I was not surprised by these results. They corroborated what I have observed in the many efforts that I have been a part of, which is that children who have a positive association with any given aspect of their identity will normally want to claim and use specific things, such as language, that they associate with that aspect of their identity. However, I can still also hear challenges coming from wider society, questioning, for example, whether these children were really speaking *myaamia* and predicting that they certainly wouldn't do so once they got away from the language camp, or perhaps even suggesting that they had lied on the questionnaire because they felt pressure to give the "correct" answer.

Given the patterns in the dominant discourse discussed throughout this chapter, the first part of this challenge is not surprising; the legitimacy of modern Indigenous languages frequently gets called into question. This is something that we must continue to challenge and deconstruct. As for people predicting that these children would actually not continue speaking *myaamia*, it's true that this sometimes happens. However, the underlying assumption that people wouldn't want to speak their ancestral heritage language is a sociopolitically loaded one that needs to be deconstructed just as much as the norm of basing legitimacy on a perception of the past. This idea is situated within a long history of immigrant and Indigenous language shift in the United States, which in turn reflects a long history of restriction-oriented language policies and the associated dominance of English. Although very important for consideration as real variables, however, these patterns do not represent an inherent reality for American Indian languages. Rather, they represent a specific set of circumstances that can be changed. Having assessed the language-usage patterns of Miami children as part of my longitudinal research with Miami youth who participate in language and cultural programs, I can report that the actual norm is that they do use the language after events such as *eewansaapita* camps. Many of them make an explicit effort to share their language knowledge with their families and speak with pride of how they taught their parents and siblings some *myaamia*. This may not be what the dominant discourse expects, but it is the truth.

In closing, let us return to a major theme that underlies the Miami story: namely, that the reclamation of *myaamia* is multifaceted and occurs within and responds to a specific sociohistorical context. I introduced language reclamation as a process that includes not only language revitalization, but also requires feeling and asserting the prerogative to learn and transmit the language and to design, implement, and evaluate language programs in a way that reflects the community's needs and values. Miamis have done and continue to do these things. We refuse to acquiesce to outsiders' ideas that our heritage language does not have contemporary value; we know that we can learn it and use it and confront the ideology underlying the "e-word." Notably, this process has entailed a series of challenges to ideas that the dominant discourse classifies as anomalous, and this chapter attempts to reframe certain components of the reclamation process as the expected practices that they arguably are. In this broader sense, language reclamation might thus be said to include setting expectations that reflect the truth, a major one for the Miami case being *myaamiaatawiaanki noonki kaahkiihkwe*: "we speak Miami today."

ACKNOWLEDGMENTS

The ideas in this chapter have developed and evolved during many years of interactions, and I thank my fellow Miamis and the many non-Miami scholars who have been a part of this process. I offer a special *neewe* (thanks) to Leighton Peterson and Tony Webster for organizing the American Anthropological Association conference panel Indian Languages in Unexpected Places, for which this work was originally written. My appreciation extends to the audience and my fellow presenters on that panel for their contributions, to Paul Kroskrity for his insightful commentary, and to three reviewers for their critiques, all of which have benefited this chapter greatly. Any errors are my own.

NOTES

1. *Ethnologue: Languages of the World*, ed. Raymond J. Gordon Jr., 15th ed. (Dallas: SIL International, 2005), attempts to catalog all of the world's languages and to provide basic information about their speaker populations, language-family relationships, and alternate names as well as additional facts of potential interest to linguists and missionaries. I am referencing the 2005 edition of *Ethnologue* because most discussions within the Miami community about the term *extinct*, and our associated challenges to this label, have taken place in response to our language having been

categorized as such in this and earlier editions of *Ethnologue*. However, the most recent edition (*Ethnologue: Languages of the World*, ed. M. Paul Lewis, 16th ed. [Dallas: SIL International, 2009]) simply classifies Miami as "a language of the USA" and mentions that a revitalization program is in progress. The editors decided not to use the term *extinct* to describe languages with second-language speakers because they agreed with the Miami claim that this was inappropriate (M. Paul Lewis, personal communication, 2009).

2. *Myaamia* and Miami (pronounced *my-AM-ee* or *my-AM-uh*) are functionally equivalent, the former being the name of the language and people in that language (an endonym) and the latter being the exonym used in English and many other languages. As using an endonym has a certain sociopolitical impact in that it asserts a tribal identity, some tribal members make a point of using it. Moreover, as use of the language has become more common, the endonym has likely also become more common because we are more accustomed to saying and hearing it. However, particularly when speaking English, it is common for Miami people to alternate between both terms—perhaps with a general trend toward saying *myaamia* when referring to an identity or cultural frame, and I am following that convention here. This pattern exemplifies a theme of this chapter, which is that the Miami are a multicultural and multilingual people, and it thus makes sense that we would refer to ourselves and to our language in more than one language.

The spelling of *myaamia* words in this chapter, including the noncapitalization of the word *myaamia*, follows conventions that have developed in the Miami community. The phonetic values of the Miami orthography are described in Daryl Baldwin and David J. Costa, *myaamia neehi peewaalia kaloosioni mahsinaakani: A Miami-Peoria Dictionary* (Miami, OK: Miami Nation, 2005), and are close to those of the American Phonetic Alphabet.

3. Wesley Y. Leonard, "When Is an 'Extinct Language' Not Extinct? Miami, a Formerly Sleeping Language," in *Sustaining Linguistic Diversity: Endangered and Minority Languages and Language Varieties*, ed. Kendall A. King, Natalie Schilling-Estes, Lyn Fogle, Jia Jackie Lou, and Barbara Soukup (Washington, DC: Georgetown University Press, 2008), 23–33.

4. Philip J. Deloria, *Indians in Unexpected Places* (Lawrence: University Press of Kansas, 2004).

5. Because of space limitations, I am omitting a literature summary of the general principles of colonization and the associated expectations for Indigenous language purity, and, instead, I am detailing specific issues as they arise in the chapter. For a historical overview of this phenomenon, I suggest Richard Bauman and Charles L. Briggs, *Voices of Modernity: Language Ideologies and the Politics of Inequality* (Cambridge: Cambridge University Press, 2003), which details how ideologies of linguistic purity developed in Western scholarship. The essays in Paul V. Kroskrity and Margaret Field, eds., *Native American Language Ideologies: Beliefs, Practices, and Struggles in Indian Country* (Tucson: University of Arizona Press, 2009), illustrate how these ideologies affect Native American communities, as both outside forces and ideologies held by community members.

6. Anne Goodfellow, "The Development of 'New' Languages in Native American Communities," *American Indian Culture and Research Journal* 27, no. 2 (2003): 53. For discussion of Goodfellow's statement in terms of the Miami case, see Leonard, "When Is an 'Extinct Language' Not Extinct?," 28–30.

7. Because of the initial Miami Removal in 1846, which involved only part of the Miami community, there are two political entities called *Miami*—known officially as the Miami Tribe of Oklahoma (see http://www.miamination.com) and the Miami Nation of Indians of the State of Indiana (see http://www.miamiindians.org/) (both accessed March 4, 2011). For a detailed discussion of this removal and its effects, see Kate A. Berry and Melissa A. Rinehart, "A Legacy of Forced Migration: The Removal of the Miami Tribe in 1846," *International Journal of Population Geography* 9 (2003): 93–112. As a citizen of the Miami Tribe of Oklahoma whose experiences are primarily within the Oklahoma Miami political and cultural structure, I narrate this story with an Oklahoma Miami bent, and my examples come primarily from the Miami Tribe of Oklahoma members. However, I believe that the general discussions in this chapter hold for Miamis of any political affiliation—whether Oklahoma, Indiana, or, in some cases, no official tribal membership—as we all share our language and are thus challenged by the same dominant discourse.

8. *The Language Guy* (blog), "Reviving Dead Languages," February 24, 2007, http://thelanguageguy.blogspot.com/2007_02_01_archive.html. Many similar comments have been made about Miami language efforts, but I chose to include this one because it sparked some extended discussion by the Miami Tribe of Oklahoma Language Committee and other Miami language program leaders. We were struck because we saw that someone with a PhD in linguistics—hence an expert—wrote it, someone who had never asked us what we're trying to do in regard to "reviving" our language and yet made a dire prediction about our ability to do it.

9. Jane H. Hill, " 'Expert Rhetorics' in Advocacy for Endangered Languages: Who Is Listening, and What Do They Hear?," *Journal of Linguistic Anthropology* 12, no. 2 (2002): 119–133. See also Lise Dobrin, Peter K. Austin, and David Nathan, "Dying to Be Counted: The Commodification of Endangered Languages in Documentary Linguistics," in *Proceedings of Conference on Language Documentation and Linguistic Theory*, ed. Peter K. Austin, Oliver Bond, and David Nathan (London: SOAS, 2007), 59–68.

10. To be certain, the distinction is not so binary that the value placed on these languages resides either in their grammar/vocabulary or in their community/personal functions; rather, most of the literature explicitly recognizes the multiple values of language. Nevertheless, rhetoric of loss for general (scientific) knowledge has become especially common. Frequently cited examples include K. David Harrison's *When Languages Die: The Extinction of the World's Languages and the Erosion of Human Knowledge* (New York: Oxford University Press, 2007), and the documentary *The Linguists*, directed by Seth Kramer, Daniel A. Miller, and Jeremy Newberger (Garrison, NY: Ironbound Films, 2008).

11. Joseph Errington, *Linguistics in a Colonial World: A Story of Language, Meaning, and Power* (Malden, MA: Blackwell, 2008), 3; see also Michael Silverstein, "Contemporary Transformations of Local Linguistic Communities," *Annual Review of Anthropology* 27 (1998): 408.

12. I have observed this not only from non-Indigenous groups but also from Indigenous ones. See, e.g., Richard E. Littlebear's frequently cited analysis of why Indigenous languages "keep dying" in his preface to *Stabilizing Indigenous Languages*, ed. Gina Cantoni (Flagstaff, AZ: Center for Excellence in Education, 1996), xiii–xv. Littlebear argues that language transmission in the home is the most fundamental practice for revitalization. Many Miami people believe in the

importance of the home but also note that for a language with no speakers, the only way to bring it back into use is for a group of people first to learn it "unnaturally" as a second language.

13. Barbra A. Meek, "Failing American Indian Languages," *American Indian Culture and Research Journal* 35, no. 2 (2011): 51–54.
14. Quoted in Wesley Y. Leonard, "Miami Language Reclamation in the Home: A Case Study" (PhD diss., University of California, Berkeley, 2007), 36.
15. Following the convention in linguistics, I use the word *competence* to refer to the knowledge that allows a speaker of a given language to speak it in grammatically well-formed ways.
16. For an overview of Miami experiences in boarding schools, see Melissa A. Rinehart, "Miami Indian Language Shift and Recovery" (PhD diss., Michigan State University, 2006), 179–208. On U.S. educational policy toward Indigenous languages more generally, see Ofelia Zepeda and Jane H. Hill, "The Condition of Native American Languages in the United States," in *Endangered Languages*, ed. Robert H. Robins and Eugenius M. Uhlenbeck (New York: St. Martin's, 1991), 135–155; see also Paul V. Kroskrity and Margaret Field, "Introduction: Revealing Native American Language Ideologies," in Kroskrity and Field, *Native American Language Ideologies*, 3–30.
17. For discussion on the scope and usability of several main sources of Miami documentation, see David J. Costa, *The Miami-Illinois Language* (Lincoln: University of Nebraska Press, 2003), 10–33.
18. Due to length constraints, I am not listing the full set of endangerment frameworks in which this practice gets employed, but I have discussed and critiqued this practice in some detail in Leonard, "When Is an 'Extinct Language' Not Extinct?"
19. Leanne Hinton, "Sleeping Languages: Can They Be Awakened?," in *The Green Book of Language Revitalization in Practice*, ed. Leanne Hinton and Ken Hale (San Diego, CA: Academic, 2001), 416; Leonard, "Miami Language Reclamation in the Home."
20. Some scholars have adopted the term *reclamation* to refer specifically to bringing a language with no speakers back into use—also called *revival* (e.g., Nancy C. Dorian, "Purism vs. Compromise in Language Revitalization and Language Revival," *Language in Society* 23, no. 1 [1994]: 479–494)—and differentiate this process from *language revitalization*, which they in turn use to refer to a similar process for languages that have never ceased to be spoken. For example, Rob Amery adopts *reclamation* to describe recent efforts with the formerly sleeping Australian language Kaurna ("It's Ours to Keep and Call Our Own: Reclamation of the Nunga Languages in the Adelaide Region, South Australia," *International Journal of the Sociology of Language* 113 [1995]: 63–82), and Lenore A. Grenoble and Lindsay J. Whaley follow Amery's convention in *Saving Languages: An Introduction to Language Revitalization* (Cambridge: Cambridge University Press, 2006). Though the Miami example actually falls under *reclamation* per this other definition, I am adopting the term to refer to a widespread sociological process that I see occurring with endangered languages in general regardless of whether they have had a period of dormancy.
21. Paul V. Kroskrity, "Embodying the Reversal of Language Shift: Agency, Incorporation, and Language Ideological Change in the Western Mono Community of Central California," in Kroskrity and Field, *Native American Language Ideologies*, 192.

22. Leonard, "When Is an 'Extinct Language' Not Extinct?"
23. This "problem" of phenotypic variation and the associated racialization of American Indians is not unique to Miamis, as it stems from a wider experience that affects most Indigenous nations in the United States. See Circe Sturm, *Blood Politics: Race, Culture, and Identity in the Cherokee Nation of Oklahoma* (Berkeley: University of California Press, 2002), for an in-depth study of this issue.
24. Pauline Turner Strong and Barrik Van Winkle, "'Indian Blood': Reflections on the Reckoning and Refiguring of Native North American Identity," *Cultural Anthropology* 11, no. 4 (1996): 547–576.
25. Unlike many Indigenous nations of the United States, the Miami Tribe of Oklahoma has never had a blood-quantum requirement for official membership, though our eligibility for membership is biologically constrained under our current constitution. The basic rule is that one must be a biological descendant (however distant) of a person on a series of official rolls taken in the late nineteenth and early twentieth centuries. There have been discussions in the tribe that our constitution should be changed to grant membership to children adopted into Miami families, but this has not yet happened as of the writing of this chapter.
26. Martha Una McClurg, *Miami Indian Stories Told by Chief Clarence Godfroy Ka-pah-pwah (Great-Great-Grandson of Frances Slocum)* (Winona Lake, IN: Light and Life, 1961), 159.
27. I am assuming general familiarity with issues of language and social inequality and am leaving out significant discussion here for length considerations. Dell Hymes, *Ethnography, Linguistics, Narrative Inequality: Toward an Understanding of Voice* (Bristol, PA: Taylor and Francis, 1996), offers valuable insights on linguistic (in)equality, and I use it as a foundational source. Important discussions on this topic as it pertains to Indigenous languages include Nancy C. Dorian, "Western Language Ideologies and Small Language Prospects," in *Endangered Languages: Current Issues and Future Prospects*, ed. Lenore A. Grenoble and Lindsay J. Whaley (Cambridge: Cambridge University Press, 1998), 3–21; and Kroskrity and Field, "Introduction." I also offer the following principle that I created and have used as an epigraph for many course syllabi: "All languages are equal. But some languages are more equal than others."
28. Anthony K. Webster, "On Intimate Grammars: With Examples from Navajo English, Navlish, and Navajo," *Journal of Anthropological Research* 66 (2010): 191; see also Anthony K. Webster, "'Please Read Loose': Intimate Grammars and Unexpected Languages in Contemporary Navajo Literature," *American Indian Culture and Research Journal* 35, no. 2 (2011): 65.
29. See related discussions by Barbra A. Meek, "And the Injun Goes 'How!': Representations of American Indian English in White Public Space," *Language in Society* 35, no. 1 (2006): 93–128, and "Failing American Indian Languages."
30. Several linguistic anthropologists over the years have questioned whether the English of Miami people gets scrutinized or delegitimized in ways that are common for other Native American groups. Particularly given the recurring theme of "unexpected" American Indian Englishes developed in a collection of studies published in Anthony K. Webster and Leighton C. Peterson, eds., *American Indian Culture and Research Journal* 35, no 2 (2011), where I first published my piece, I will address the matter here.

To the best of my knowledge, this practice is relatively uncommon; it is only the *myaamia* of Miami people that gets questioned. Most Miamis speak forms of English that are associated with the regional and socioeconomic histories of their individual lives. For example, many in northeastern Oklahoma speak local (non-Indian) varieties of English. Only a few Miamis speak a form of English that would be widely indexed as "American Indian English." For discussion on what this name entails, see William L. Leap, *American Indian English* (Salt Lake City: University of Utah Press, 1993). It is interesting to note that recent trends in fields such as (linguistic) anthropology and Native American studies have fostered a prediction—perhaps even an expectation—that there would be a Miami form of English and that it would be nonstandard and stigmatized. However, there isn't a target English to denigrate (or valorize) because a distinct form doesn't widely exist for Miami people. This noted, given that more and more Miami people are learning the *myaamia* language and integrating elements of it into their English, a uniquely Miami form of English might be under development, and such a form could very well be met with the stigma that has been described for other American Indian Englishes.

31. It is important to note that these examples differ from the commonly discussed phenomenon of *globalization*, which often evokes a frame in which a given group of people has recently adopted a technology or practice to which the group did not previously have access. Although it's true that specific items and languages of European origin were introduced to Miami people historically, most "unexpected" practices by contemporary Miamis were not introduced recently but are instead things that Miami people were already using or doing. For example, it would be strange to talk about how the internet was introduced to the Miami, as the more accurate description would be that using the internet became common in the United States and Miami people were part of that process by virtue of being Americans, in addition to being Miami.

32. The word *eewansaapita* literally means "she/he rises" and is understood to mean "sunrise."

33. For detailed discussion on the history, changing goals, and outcomes of the *eewansaapita* and similar Miami language programs, see Wesley Y. Leonard and Scott M. Shoemaker, "'I Heart This Camp': Participant Perspectives on the Role of Miami Youth Camps," in *Papers of the 40th Annual Algonquian Conference*, ed. Karl S. Hele and J. Randolph Valentine (Albany: SUNY Press, 2012), 186–209.

34. Elder participation is actually crucial to the *eewansaapita* program and to all other programs for language and culture, as it is our Elders who provide the support for these efforts and in many cases provide direct language and culture knowledge. In most *eewansaapita* programs, for example, there have been Elder nights, during which the camp participants meet with tribal Elders over dinner. Some tribal Elders visit camp throughout the week. Unlike some other tribal programs that are specifically designed to be multigenerational, however, the *eewansaapita* program, in terms of its objectives, is for tribal youth and designed to be a place for them.

35. Some modern Miami songs don't borrow English tunes. For example, some tribal members sing what is called a community song, the music of which is distinctly American Indian. These, however, are not the focus of the current discussion, as they are "expected." The problem is that some see only those sorts of expected songs as truly Miami, thus reflecting and reinforcing a discourse in which being a real Miami Indian entails following an increasingly narrow set of parameters.

36. This practice could be seen as an example of Miamis clinging to the past, but my impression is that most Miamis view it as a way of respecting the past and incorporating our ancestors' wisdom into our own lives. Notable skill is involved with bending (without breaking) a piece of wood to be used for a lacrosse stick.
37. I have not seen chess played at the *eewansaapita* camps (where most games are more "active"), but it's possible that participants have played it there without my being aware of it. I first encountered Miami chess when spending time with another Miami family, in which two brothers were playing it with each other.
38. Over time, some Miami chess players have drifted away from this term and instead say *neekatikašia* (horse) for the knight piece, which is not surprising given that the horse that the knight rides often represents the knight figure.
39. Erin Debenport, "As the Rez Turns: Anomalies Within and Beyond the Boundaries of a Pueblo Community," *American Indian Culture and Research Journal* 35, no. 2 (2011): 100.
40. David Costa, personal communication, 2007.
41. E.g., Rosemary Henze and Kathryn A. Davis, "Authenticity and Identity: Lessons from Indigenous Language Education," *Anthropology and Education Quarterly* 30, no. 1 (1999): 3–21; Leanne Hinton and Jocelyn Ahlers, "The Issue of 'Authenticity' in California Language Restoration," *Anthropology and Education Quarterly* 30, no. 1 (1999): 56–67.
42. Several people, Miami and non-Miami, have mentioned to me that there are certain elements of their languages that they don't believe should change. The most common example referenced is certain prayers, which many people believe to have been bestowed onto their people in a certain form for specific purposes. My response is that I am referring to language for most everyday use; no good reason exists that traditions cannot or should not be maintained in a given form.
43. I was negligent in that I wasn't paying much attention to who was participating in the auction but instead was looking only at their bids.
44. Jocelyn C. Ahlers, "Framing Discourse: Creating Community Through Native Language Use," *Journal of Linguistic Anthropology* 16, no. 1 (2006): 58–75.
45. Following the convention in linguistics, the word *future* is in all capitals in order to indicate that *kati* is a grammatical particle that marks future tense.

WORKS CITED

Ahlers, Jocelyn C. "Framing Discourse: Creating Community Through Native Language Use." *Journal of Linguistic Anthropology* 16, no. 1 (2006): 58–75.

Amery, Rob. "It's Ours to Keep and Call Our Own: Reclamation of the Nunga Languages in the Adelaide Region, South Australia." *International Journal of the Sociology of Language* 113 (1995): 63–82.

Baldwin, Daryl, and David J. Costa. *myaamia neehi peewaalia kaloosioni mahsinaakani: A Miami-Peoria Dictionary*. Miami, OK: Miami Nation, 2005.

Bauman, Richard, and Charles L. Briggs. *Voices of Modernity: Language Ideologies and the Politics of Inequality*. Cambridge: Cambridge University Press, 2003.

Berry, Kate A., and Melissa A. Rinehart. "A Legacy of Forced Migration: The Removal of the Miami Tribe in 1846." *International Journal of Population Geography* 9 (2003): 93–112.

Costa, David J. *The Miami-Illinois Language.* Lincoln: University of Nebraska Press, 2003.
Debenport, Erin. "As the Rez Turns: Anomalies Within and Beyond the Boundaries of a Pueblo Community." *American Indian Culture and Research Journal* 35, no. 2 (2011): 87–110.
Deloria, Philip J. *Indians in Unexpected Places.* Lawrence: University Press of Kansas, 2004.
Dobrin, Lise, Peter K. Austin, and David Nathan. "Dying to Be Counted: The Commodification of Endangered Languages in Documentary Linguistics." In *Proceedings of Conference on Language Documentation and Linguistic Theory*, ed. Peter K. Austin, Oliver Bond, and David Nathan, 59–68. London: SOAS, 2007.
Dorian, Nancy C. "Purism vs. Compromise in Language Revitalization and Language Revival." *Language in Society* 23, no. 1 (1994): 479–494.
Dorian, Nancy C. "Western Language Ideologies and Small Language Prospects." In *Endangered Languages: Current Issues and Future Prospects*, ed. Lenore A. Grenoble and Lindsay J. Whaley, 3–21. Cambridge: Cambridge University Press, 1998.
Errington, Joseph. *Linguistics in a Colonial World: A Story of Language, Meaning, and Power.* Malden, MA: Blackwell, 2008.
Goodfellow, Anne. "The Development of 'New' Languages in Native American Communities." *American Indian Culture and Research Journal* 27, no. 2 (2003): 41–59.
Gordon, Raymond J., Jr., ed. *Ethnologue: Languages of the World.* 15th ed. Dallas: SIL International, 2005.
Grenoble, Lenore A., and Lindsay J. Whaley, eds. *Saving Languages: An Introduction to Language Revitalization.* Cambridge: Cambridge University Press, 2006.
Harrison, K. David. *When Languages Die: The Extinction of the World's Languages and the Erosion of Human Knowledge.* New York: Oxford University Press, 2007.
Henze, Rosemary, and Kathryn A. Davis. "Authenticity and Identity: Lessons from Indigenous Language Education." *Anthropology and Education Quarterly* 30, no. 1 (1999): 3–21.
Hill, Jane H. " 'Expert Rhetorics' in Advocacy for Endangered Languages: Who Is Listening, and What Do They Hear?" *Journal of Linguistic Anthropology* 12, no. 2 (2002): 119–133.
Hinton, Leanne. "Sleeping Languages: Can They Be Awakened?" In *The Green Book of Language Revitalization in Practice*, ed. Leanne Hinton and Ken Hale, 413–417. San Diego, CA: Academic, 2001.
Hinton, Leanne, and Jocelyn Ahlers. "The Issue of 'Authenticity' in California Language Restoration." *Anthropology and Education Quarterly* 30, no. 1 (1999): 56–67.
Hymes, Dell. *Ethnography, Linguistics, Narrative Inequality: Toward an Understanding of Voice.* Bristol, PA: Taylor and Francis, 1996.
Kramer, Seth, Daniel A. Miller, and Jeremy Newberger, dirs. *The Linguists.* Garrison, NY: Ironbound Films, 2008. 65 min.
Kroskrity, Paul V. "Embodying the Reversal of Language Shift: Agency, Incorporation, and Language Ideological Change in the Western Mono Community of Central California." In Kroskrity and Field, *Native American Language Ideologies*, 190–210.
Kroskrity, Paul V., and Margaret Field. "Introduction: Revealing Native American Language Ideologies." In Kroskrity and Field, *Native American Language Ideologies*, 3–30.

Kroskrity, Paul V., and Margaret Field, eds. *Native American Language Ideologies: Beliefs, Practices, and Struggles in Indian Country.* Tucson: University of Arizona Press, 2009.
The Language Guy (blog). "Reviving Dead Languages." February 24, 2007. http://thelanguageguy.blogspot.com/2007_02_01_archive.html.
Leap, William L. *American Indian English.* Salt Lake City: University of Utah Press, 1993.
Leonard, Wesley Y. "Miami Language Reclamation in the Home: A Case Study." PhD diss., University of California, Berkeley, 2007.
Leonard, Wesley Y. "When Is an 'Extinct Language' Not Extinct? Miami, a Formerly Sleeping Language." In *Sustaining Linguistic Diversity: Endangered and Minority Languages and Language Varieties,* ed. Kendall A. King, Natalie Schilling-Estes, Lyn Fogle, Jia Jackie Lou, and Barbara Soukup, 23–33. Washington, DC: Georgetown University Press, 2008.
Leonard, Wesley Y., and Scott M. Shoemaker, "'I Heart This Camp': Participant Perspectives on the Role of Miami Youth Camps." In *Papers of the 40th Annual Algonquian Conference,* ed. Karl S. Hele and J. Randolph Valentine, 186–209. Albany: SUNY Press, 2012.
Lewis, M. Paul, ed. *Ethnologue: Languages of the World.* 16th ed. Dallas: SIL International, 2009.
Littlebear, Richard E. Preface to *Stabilizing Indigenous Languages,* ed. Gina Cantoni, xiii–xv. Flagstaff, AZ: Center for Excellence in Education, 1996.
McClurg, Martha Una. *Miami Indian Stories Told by Chief Clarence Godfroy Ka-pahpwah (Great-Great-Grandson of Frances Slocum).* Winona Lake, IN: Light and Life, 1961.
Meek, Barbra A. "And the Injun Goes 'How!': Representations of American Indian English in White Public Space." *Language in Society* 35, no. 1 (2006): 93–128.
Meek, Barbra A. "Failing American Indian Languages." *American Indian Culture and Research Journal* 35, no. 2 (2011): 43–60.
Rinehart, Melissa A. "Miami Indian Language Shift and Recovery." PhD diss., Michigan State University, 2006.
Silverstein, Michael. "Contemporary Transformations of Local Linguistic Communities." *Annual Review of Anthropology* 27 (1998): 401–426.
Strong, Pauline Turner, and Barrik Van Winkle. "'Indian Blood': Reflections on the Reckoning and Refiguring of Native North American Identity." *Cultural Anthropology* 11, no. 4 (1996): 547–576.
Sturm, Circe. *Blood Politics: Race, Culture, and Identity in the Cherokee Nation of Oklahoma.* Berkeley: University of California Press, 2002.
Webster, Anthony K., and Leighton C. Peterson, eds. *American Indian Culture and Research Journal* 35, no 2 (2011).
Webster, Anthony K. "On Intimate Grammars: With Examples from Navajo English, Navlish, and Navajo." *Journal of Anthropological Research* 66 (2010): 187–208.
Webster, Anthony K. "'Please Read Loose': Intimate Grammars and Unexpected Languages in Contemporary Navajo Literature." *American Indian Culture and Research Journal* 35, no. 2 (2011): 61–86.
Zepeda, Ofelia, and Jane H. Hill. "The Condition of Native American Languages in the United States." In *Endangered Languages,* ed. Robert H. Robins and Eugenius M. Uhlenbeck, 135–155. New York: St. Martin's, 1991.

The *Vachanas*

MANU V. DEVADEVAN

In the latter half of the eleventh century, worshippers of Shiva in the Kannada-speaking region, known as *sharanas*, began to construct a new expressive aesthetic. It involved an approach to language and an understanding of human existence that was foundationally different from the dominant Jaina literary aesthetics that had appeared in the region in the ninth century in Sanskrit and in the tenth century in Kannada. The Shaiva transformation was pioneered by Madara Channayya, Dohara Kakkayya, and Devara Dasimayya, who belonged to the laboring classes and occupied lower positions of caste.

The *sharanas* came from all walks of life. There were renouncers and householders, brahmanas, merchants, soldiers, scribes, announcers, watchmen, and men and women who practiced a bewildering variety of professions that were organized into castes. There were people from castes of percussionists and performers, farmers, tanners, cane weavers, rope makers, ferrymen, washermen, betel bag bearers, toddy tappers, rice gatherers, yarn makers, paddy crushers, incense makers, and other such professions, in addition to a burglar and a sex worker. A number of them lent voice to their concerns through *vachanas*. The *vachanas* broke new grounds by the simplicity of their language, the depth of their moral and metaphysical ideas, their oral modes of transmission, and their greater inclusiveness in relation to caste, class, and gender. Over 90 percent of the 20,000 *vachanas* produced between 1000 and the present are from the twelfth century, and these are attributed to over 130 saint poets, including 33 women. Each *vachana* carried the *ankita* or signature of the composers, which consisted mostly of the names of the deities that they worshipped. In some instances—such as the *vachanas* of Chaudayya, the ferryman—the names of the composers themselves were used as signatures.

These poems are regarded by the Lingayats as their sacred texts. The production of *vachanas* has continued well into our times, although not with the spirit or sensibility found in those of the eleventh and twelfth centuries.

EDITORS' NOTE: Below are selected ancient vachanas translated by Devadevan. The name of each poet precedes the untitled verse in the English translation.

1. Chaudayya, the Ferryman

It's a debt to Brahma to say,
    "I've seen with the body."
It's a debt to Vishnu to say,
    "I've seen with life."
It's a debt to Rudra to say,
    "I've seen with knowledge."
It's debt to everyone in the land to say,
    "I saw everywhere that I see."
Chaudayya the Ferryman said no to them all,
    Held them, and saw.

2. Neelamma

Strength turned strength-less
In the legs that walk.
Word turned word-less
In the tongue that speaks.

Sound turned into silence,
Breath into transformation,
And when the sound wore off,
I wiped out the body's sign
To become "I,"
Sangayya.

1. Chaudayya, the Ferryman

ಕಾಯದಿಂದ ಕಂಡೆಹೆನೆಂದಡೆ ಬ್ರಹ್ಮನ ಹಂಗು,
ಜೀವದಿಂದ ಕಂಡೆಹೆನೆಂದಡೆ ವಿಷ್ಣುವಿನ ಹಂಗು,
ಅರಿವಿನಿಂದ ಕಂಡೆಹೆನೆಂದಡೆ ರುದ್ರನ ಹಂಗು,
ಕಾಬ ಕಾಬಲ್ಲಿ ಕಂಡೆಹೆನೆಂದಡೆ ನಾಡೆಲ್ಲರ ಹಂಗು.
ಇವನೆಲ್ಲವನಲ್ಲಾ ಎಂದು ನಿಲಿಕಿ ನೋಡಿ ಕಂಡ
ಅಂಬಿಗ ಚೌಡಯ್ಯ.

2. Neelamma

ನಡವ ಕಾಲಿಂಗೆ ಶಕ್ತಿ ನಿಃಶಕ್ತಿಯಾಯಿತ್ತು.
ನುಡಿವ ನಾಲಗೆಗೆ ವಚನ ನಿರ್ವಚನವಾಯಿತ್ತು.
ಶಬ್ದ ನಿಃಶಬ್ದವಾಗಿ ಪ್ರಾಣ ಪರಿಣಾಮವಾಗಿ
ಕಾಯದ ಕುರುಹನಳಿದು ಶಬ್ದನಂದಿಯಾನಾದೆನಯ್ಯ ಸಂಗಯ್ಯ.

3. Basava

When the lump of flesh becomes the beginning,
Knowledge turns into void,
The beginning and the end stand in the middle,
The hundred stands on the one,
The one as the hundred,
And the hundred and the one cease to be,
To make the word "Kudalasangamadeva" absent.

4. Channabasava

I'll say it's worldly to the core,
So long as doubts exist on the binary chain
Of the tendered and the untendered.

I'll call him imbued with linga to the core,
Who has the tendered
And the untendered spent.

I'll call him beyond word and mind
If he can tender the untendered
And accept the offering.

There is no tendered,
There is no untendered,
It is un-conceived,
Kudalachannasangamadeva.

3. Basava

ಪಿಂಡವೇ ಆದಿಯಾಗಿ,
ಜ್ಞಾನವೇ ಶೂನ್ಯವಾಗಿ,
ಆದಿ ಅಂತ್ಯಗಳೆರಡು ಮಧ್ಯದಲ್ಲಿ ನಿಲ್ಲಲು
ನೂರು ಒಂದರ ಮೇಲೆ ನಿಂದು
ಒಂದೇ ನೂರಾಗಿ ನಿಂದ ಮೇಲೆ
ನೂರೊಂದೆಂಬುದಿಲ್ಲವಾಗಿ
ಕೂಡಲಸಂಗಮದೇವನೆಂಬ ಸೊಲ್ಲು ಇಲ್ಲ.

4. Channabasava

ಅರ್ಪಿತ ಆನರ್ಪಿತವೆಂಬ ಉಭಯಕುಳದ
ಶಂಕೆವುಳ್ಳನ್ನಕ್ಕ ಅಚ್ಚಸಂಸಾರಿಯೆಂಬೆ.
ಅರ್ಪಿತ ಅನರ್ಪಿತವೆಂಬೆರಡ ಕಳೆದು ನಿಂದಾತನ
ಅಚ್ಚಲಿಂಗವಂತನೆಂಬೆ.
ಅರ್ಪಿತ ಅನರ್ಪಿತವನರ್ಪಿಸಿ
ಪ್ರಸಾದ ಸ್ವೀಕರಿಸಬಲ್ಲಡಾತನ ವಾಙ್ಮನಾತೀತನೆಂಬೆ.
ಅರ್ಪಿತವಿಲ್ಲ, ಅನರ್ಪಿತವಿಲ್ಲ,
ಅಕಲ್ಪಿತವಯ್ಯಾ, ಕೂಡಲಚೆನ್ನಸಂಗಮದೇವಾ.

5. Devara Dasimayya

He that has a body
Feels hunger.
He that has a body
Speaks falsehood.

Don't you ever speak a word
That belittles me
As the one with a body.

Take on a body like me
And see for yourself,
Ramanatha.

5. Devara Dasimayya

ಒಡಲುಗೊಂಡವ ಹಸಿವ;
ಒಡಲುಗೊಂಡವ ಹುಸಿವ.
ಒಡಲುಗೊಂಡವನೆಂದು
ನೀನೆನ್ನ ಜರಿದೊಮ್ಮೆ ನುಡಿಯದಿರಾ!
ನೀನೆನ್ನಂತೆ ಒಮ್ಮೆ ಒಡಲುಗೊಂಡು ನೋಡಾ!
ರಾಮನಾಥ.

Chapter Five

INDIGENOUS LANGUAGES BETWEEN ERASURE AND DISINVENTION

DANIEL KAUFMAN AND ROSS PERLIN

The New York metropolitan area is widely acknowledged to be one of the most linguistically diverse in the world, but there has never been a focused attempt to take full stock of that diversity. Before the arrival of European settlers, what may have been quite distinct varieties of the Indigenous Algonquian language known today as Lenape were spoken in dozens of independent settlements. The establishment of New Amsterdam in the seventeenth century resulted not in a Dutch colony but in an entrepôt consisting of Europeans, Africans, and Native Americans, where the Jesuit Father Isaac Jogues reported in 1646 that "there may well be four or five hundred men of different sects and nations . . . [including] men of eighteen different languages."[1] By the early twentieth century, New York had absorbed massive waves of immigration from every corner of Europe, with small but growing communities from the Caribbean, Latin America, and western and southern Asia. Now, in the early twenty-first century, New York City is "hyperdiverse," with communities from every corner of the globe, notably including newer arrivals from zones of deep linguistic diversity such as Mexico, Central America, and the Himalaya, in addition to West Africa, South Asia, China, and island Southeast Asia.

Until 1890, when the U.S. Census Bureau first asked about language, no information was collected systematically about the languages spoken in New York or any other American city. From then until 1970, various questions were asked about language use, typically about the "mother tongue" of non-English speakers or the foreign-born. Since the 1970 Census, a relatively stable set of questions has been asked—transferred in recent years from the decennial to the more detailed, sample-based, annual American Community Survey (ACS):

- Does this person speak a language other than English at home? (Yes/No)
- What is this language? _____ (For example: Korean, Italian, Spanish, Vietnamese)
- How well does this person speak English (very well, well, not well, not at all)?

This method of obtaining language data, despite the reach and resources of the Census Bureau, has consistently failed to do justice to the full breadth of linguistic diversity in the United States—and nowhere more so than in cities like New York. Indeed, any information gathered by the Census about linguistic diversity is perhaps best understood as almost incidental, with the main intent coded in the first and third parts of the question: to gauge segments of the population with low English proficiency. The five-year 2009–2013 ACS release, a particularly deep dive representing "the most comprehensive data ever released by the Census Bureau on languages," estimated "at least 192 languages" spoken at home in the New York metropolitan area. More typical in terms of granularity are the most recent five-year ACS data available (2015–2019), which break out and tabulate just over a hundred "languages." Of these, around one-fifth are groupings such as "Other Specified Native American," with no further information available.

As of 2021, mapping efforts at the Endangered Language Alliance (ELA), a New York–based nonprofit with a mission to document endangered languages and support linguistic diversity,[2] have confirmed at least three times that number: that is, over seven hundred languages spoken at least by one individual in the metro area, a sample of which can be seen in figure 5.1.[3]

In the majority of cases, these languages are spoken by substantial communities, though those communities vary enormously in terms of size, settlement patterns, and degree of organization. Moreover, cross comparison between ELA and census data suggests that the latter is consistently reliable and recognizable for only approximately sixty languages, almost all of which are major national languages.

FIGURE 5.1. ELA's *Languages of New York City* map. Ross Perlin and Daniel Kaufman, eds., *Languages of New York City*, map, 3rd ed. (New York: Endangered Language Alliance, 2020).

What is the significance of this gap between Census Bureau data and the kind of data collected by linguists and communities working in partnership? We argue that it is not just an issue of effort and focus; rather, Indigenous, minority, and primarily oral languages are systematically undercounted due to both historical reasons and aspects of the survey instrument itself, with major implications for those who speak them. Although the Census is supposed to enumerate every individual living in the country and the ACS is supposed to provide a reasonable sample of the same, there are many reasons why recent, undocumented, and non-English-speaking immigrants, in particular, might not be aware of or able or willing to take the Census. There is in fact significant overlap between areas of consistent undercount—in 2020, the response rate in New York City was approximately 62 percent—and areas of high ethnic and linguistic diversity, with ethnolinguistic communities in New York known to number in the thousands not taking the Census at all, not identifying themselves as such, or being lumped in with other groups.

INDIGENOUS LANGUAGES BETWEEN ERASURE AND DISINVENTION

An obvious factor is that the census instrument itself is available only in the languages with the most speakers. The 2020 Census, the best supported so far in terms of language access, was available in only thirteen major languages, though short guides were provided in fifty-nine languages. The question of how responses are collected is also significant. Whether online (advocated for strongly in 2020), by phone, by mail, or with an enumerator, the means at the Census Bureau's disposal have not inspired confidence among vulnerable and marginalized populations. During the lead-up to the 2020 Census, the Trump administration's attempt to insert a citizenship question, at a time of accelerating activity against undocumented immigrants, led to a further erosion of trust. It may be unsurprising that an instrument like the Census, with its roots in the political establishment, creates the appearance of a largely monoglot population speaking a set of official, national languages, so authority is thus creating diversity in its own image. Varied ideas in immigrant communities about what constitutes a *language* or a *dialect*, drawing on colonial and noncolonial ideologies, further complicate the picture. Perhaps most surprising is how academic critiques of such basic categories as *language* and *speaker*, though in some cases with a view toward social justice, also expose language communities to the consequences of invisibility.

What does it mean for a speech variety to be considered a language—in particular, for the surveyed? The first two language-related questions asked by the Census Bureau appear innocent enough: "Does this person speak a language other than English at home? What is this language?" Yet the word *language* itself and its various translations are loaded terms for many segments of the population. Though the terminology may vary, colonial notions of *language* (official, standardized, and written) versus *dialect* (no official status, unstandardized, primarily oral) are very much alive in many of New York's immigrant communities. While possibly finding some support in the way these terms are used in American contexts, these notions seem to draw most readily on distinctions made in immigrants' societies of origin: e.g., *lengua/lenguaje* versus *dialecto* in Mexico, *lingua* versus *dialetto* in Italy, 语言 *yǔyán* versus 方言 *fāngyán* (and sometimes 土话 *tǔhuà*) in China. The linguistic criterion of mutual intelligibility often plays little or no role in these distinctions. In Italian and Chinese cases, for instance, where language shift from one variety to another linguistically related variety may be taking place, such a distinction may be difficult to operationalize in the first place. In the Latin American context, the lack of mutual intelligibility is clear to any speaker but may not prevent them from using the term *dialecto* for what any linguist would term an Indigenous language.

In other cases, there may not be widespread use of dyadic terminology that can be mapped onto English language/dialect, but a fundamental diglossia may nonetheless drive language ideologies, similarly polarizing varieties into a "high" and a "low." In the Tibetan case, what is sometimes called "the Tibetan language" is now considered to be a family of at least some fifty distinct Tibetic languages descended from Old Tibetan, on the order of the Germanic or Romance subgroup within Indo-European.[4] In Tibetan itself, although there are terms for *language* and *dialect* (*skad rigs* and *yul skad*), individual speech varieties are usually named for a locality (of any size), such that the distinction between all of Tibet and the small Nyagchu River valley is at least somewhat obscured with the terms of *bod skad* (Tibet speech) and *nyag skad* (Nyagchu speech).[5] Nonetheless, the Tibetic languages are still often referred to in English, by both community members and non-specialist outsiders, as Tibetan dialects or simply as Tibetan because they share both an alphabet and Classical Tibetan as a literary/religious language.

For most speakers of distinct Tibetic languages whom we have interviewed, the power of the Standard Tibetan written tradition clearly outweighs concerns of mutual intelligibility in deciding what is a language and what is a dialect. In some ways parallel, the Italian-American case shows that home-region language ideologies were just as apt to come over with a different immigrant group half a century ago as they are now. The vast majority of Italian migrants to New York were speakers of the often very different Italo-Romance languages (*dialetti*) from Sicily, Naples, and elsewhere, sometimes with limited knowledge of Italian. Nevertheless, undergoing a process of "Italianization" both in Italy and in the Italian diaspora, "most individuals, regardless of regional origin or age, were in favor of continuing to cultivate Italian," as opposed to their own *dialetti*.[6] In particular, first-generation immigrants (born in Italy) were "more purist oriented, favoring Standard languages"—they "experienced the social stigmas of being deprived of a functional standard, and they are more willing to deemphasize the need for dialect." In contrast, "those born in America, by now fully fluent in English, feel no more the potential limitations of dialects, and in fact view dialectal speech and the hybrid variety as positive symbols of ethnicity, varieties which allow bonding between family members of different generations." Many support a tacit trilingualism: dialect at home, Italian for trips back to Italy, and English for the American context, but Herman Haller describes the emergence of a fourth variety, a "dialectal lingua franca" particular to contexts like New York (but not unlike the "regiolects" simultaneously developing back in Italy), where speakers from dialect backgrounds communicate with each other by aiming for Italian.[7] The result in the Italian case is that those New Yorkers who are most fluent in forms of Sicilian, Neapolitan, and other dialects are precisely those who might be the most motivated to disguise this fact in the ACS by claiming to only speak Italian. At the same time, those who might be most motivated to write in Sicilian, Neapolitan, or another dialect feel insufficiently fluent to do so.

In the most extreme cases, which we can exemplify with the Indigenous ethnolinguistic groups of Mexico, the divide between *lengua/lenguaje* and *dialecto* can be so strong as to dissuade speakers from considering their mother tongues within the same ontological category as the examples given by the Census Bureau (specifically, Korean, Italian, Spanish, and Vietnamese as of the most recent ACS). We have heard speakers of Indigenous Mexican languages tell us that, in contrast to Spanish, their language "has no rules" and cannot be written (despite having an orthography), thus reproducing colonial views of their languages. On this basis, and simply by virtue of being Indigenous, the label *dialecto* is applied, whereas *lengua/lenguaje* is applied to Spanish and state languages of other countries. Recently, the Mexican state has attempted to counter these notions with an ad campaign aimed at replacing *dialecto*, as a term of belittlement, with *lenguaje*, an effort amplified by intellectuals and public figures in various Indigenous communities as well.[8] Nonetheless, for the average speaker of a Mexican Indigenous language in New York who is not aware of these campaigns, the term *lenguaje* evokes national language, contributing further to the erasure of Mexican Indigenous languages not only in New York but also throughout the United States.

The linguistic erasure of Indigenous Latin Americans in the United States has real consequences for health and human rights, and, thus, we see it as far more pernicious than the epistemic violence of essentialization. A study on medical attention received by immigrants detained at the U.S.-Mexican border showed that Mexican migrants who were identified as speakers of Indigenous languages received care less often than did those who were identified as Spanish speakers: 24 percent of the former were given care versus 36 percent of the latter.[9] The study came in the wake of the 2018 death of seven-year-old Jakelin Caal, a Q'eq'chi Maya girl from Guatemala, who was denied medical attention and whose father was made to sign papers in a language he did not understand to absolve the authorities from responsibility.[10] The struggles do not abate for Indigenous migrants who have made it to safety; Rachel Nolan describes in detail the daunting obstacles faced by Mayan interpreters working in the courts to provide justice to asylum seekers.[11] It has only been through sustained advocacy on the part of groups like the Binational Front of Indigenous Organizations in California that city agencies, including the police, have begun to understand and address the linguistic realities of Indigenous Latin Americans.[12]

NAMED LANGUAGES: TO ENUMERATE OR DISINVENT?

Regardless of the perceived status of a speech variety within social hierarchies, there are well-known, deeper problems involved in treating languages as discrete, bounded entities—just as there are problems (detailed throughout this volume) with treating languages as individuated tools of communication divorced from interlocking political and social processes that put them in close and constant relation with other speech varieties. Some linguists adopt the view that discrete boundaries, in toto, are social constructions, typically imposed from above. Suzanne Romaine summarizes this position neatly: "The very concept of discrete languages is probably a European cultural artifact fostered by procedures such as literacy and standardization. Any attempt to count distinct languages will be an artifact of classificatory procedures rather than a reflection of communicative practices."[13] This stands in contrast to the more traditional position, in which speech varieties, despite contact effects, dialect differentiation, and other types of variation, can nonetheless be successfully categorized into discrete languages. In this latter view, truly mixed languages with multiple origins, such as Media Lingua, Michif, and Chavacano, are outliers, and varieties that blend seamlessly into each other are given a special treatment as "dialect continua."[14]

The understanding of *named* languages as individuated, describable entities that can be abstracted away from particular language contexts and users reflects a process of reification. One logical conclusion of this view, which is held by the majority of contemporary linguists, is that an individual's language can in theory be comprehensively described (or even generated algorithmically, as in Chomskyan approaches) and that, once described, any utterance can be objectively evaluated as being a possible or an impossible expression of its grammar. This view is clearly fundamental to any attempts toward standardization, and in practice, it underlies mainstream practices in language pedagogy and multilingual education as well. This approach, however, has come under critique from various angles. It is possible to summarize these critiques, some of which might be leveled not only against contemporary linguists but also against the design of most census instruments, as follows:

- The borders between named languages are often arbitrary;
- The names, descriptions, and borders of many languages have been imposed externally;
- The "standard language" represents but one register in a spectrum of language practices;
- There exists massive mixing and intermingling of codes in much actual language use; and
- Self-assessments of competency in a language are fluid and subjective.

In the purest instantiation of these critiques, what we can call *language skepticism* seeks to overcome the concept of language existing in the abstract altogether, instead opting for the position that each individual possesses a unique linguistic repertoire, constituted by features of potentially various origins.[15] Speakers, signers, and writers select linguistic features from their repertoire on the fly based on social context. In this view, the only scale at which language can be truly understood is the idiolect, the unique repertoire and usage of an individual; named languages are a cognitive illusion imposed by various institutions from above. This fluid, individual-oriented conception of language finds increasing support among scholars in the fields of multilingual education and language pedagogy under the rubric of *translanguaging*, a term coined by Cen Williams (originally in Welsh: *trawsieithu*) to describe multilingual practices in the Welsh classroom.[16] Translanguaging, as developed more recently, is defined as "the deployment of a speaker's full linguistic repertoire without regard for watchful adherence to the socially and politically defined boundaries of named (and usually national and state) languages."[17] The framework is envisioned first as a corrective to traditional practices in bilingual education, where bilingual children are still too often seen as an amalgamation of two deficient monolinguals.[18] Consequently, one of the main thrusts of translanguaging in education has been the recasting of bilingual learners as possessing a single repertoire of equal size and potential as their monolingual peers, an effort that requires reconceiving assessments without reliance on monoglot named languages.

Clearly, doing away with the concept of named languages has wider implications beyond the education of multilingual children. In Otheguy et al.'s view, the translanguaging framework "helps to disrupt the socially constructed language hierarchies that are responsible for the suppression of the languages of many minoritized peoples," a goal that they see as aligned with language maintenance and revitalization:[19]

> The concepts of translanguaging and idiolect allow us to more clearly connect our efforts on behalf of minoritized communities with the charge of essentialism that we have leveled against the notion of the named languages; for once we stop focusing on the task of preserving or strengthening an essentialist set of lexical and grammatical features that has been given the name Euskara or Māori or Hawaiian (or English, French, or Spanish, or whatever), we can more clearly see the object of our advocacy. The struggle is not to preserve a pure, well-bounded and essential collection of lexical and structural features, but rather a cultural-linguistic complex of multiple idiolects and translanguaging practices that the community finds valuable. It is toward the affirmation and preservation of these complexes, and not of named essentialist objects, that maintenance and revitalization efforts are properly directed.[20]

Sinfree Makoni and Alastair Pennycook stake out an even broader project—namely, the *disinvention* of languages rather than the mere transgression of their boundaries: "Unless we actively engage with the history of invention of languages, the processes by which these inventions are maintained, and the political imperative to work towards their disinvention, we will continue to do damage to speech communities and educational possibilities."[21] Together with Salikoko Mufwene, they view the promotion and revitalization of any named language as a naive and misguided enterprise.[22] In this view, the promotion of multilingualism, language rights, and linguistic diversity is also all inherently backward due to their reliance on the colonial language concept. Disinvention requires the abolition not only of language categories and fixed descriptions but also all that is contained by named languages, whose promotion now "constitutes a retrospective justification of colonial structures," as if such named languages cannot be liberated from their state-imposed definitions once they are contaminated by colonialism.[23]

We must emphasize here the critical distinction between languages that are named and promulgated by political fiat and those that are demarcated by linguistic criteria. The linguistic definition of language, which is based solely on mutual intelligibility, aims to free us from political considerations. Simply put, if two speech varieties can be understood mutually by their speakers, these varieties are considered to belong to the same language. If mutual intelligibility does not hold, they are considered independent languages. There are well-known caveats here that have long been recognized by linguists, principally having to do with the gradient nature of comprehension between related varieties, the asymmetrically wide dissemination of prestige varieties, and the interference of language attitudes. Despite these caveats, mutual intelligibility remains the bedrock of all linguistically grounded attempts to classify and enumerate languages and must be kept apart from state-engineered attempts to classify and enumerate languages based on political, ethnic, or other social criteria.

But let us put aside the fraught question of whether the languages of the world can be identified and enumerated objectively and scientifically. What is still sorely missing from this discourse is an account of Indigenous views on language identification. When we do expand our scope to include non-Western perspectives, we quickly encounter clear cases of language reification throughout the world. Northeast Amazonia, for instance, is well-known for the practice of linguistic exogamy, an entirely Indigenous institution in which spouses must be selected from outside the language group.[24] In this same area, code mixing is frowned on and in fact policed during child-rearing.[25] Luke Fleming further notes how Nheengatú speakers in this same region are viewed by neighboring Tukanoans as having lost their ethnicity because of their language mixing and borrowing, an attitude that has developed independent of the influence of any nation-state.[26] Jeffrey Heath describes a similar situation in Arnhem Land, Australia, where Aboriginal languages are "assigned by the dreamtime cult totems, and are inherited patrilineally as part of clan identity."[27] He goes on to explain that "among the Yuulngu groups, including the Ritharngu, this pattern was reinforced by a strong normative insistence that the child use his father's language as his principal medium of communications, at least after a certain age."[28]

Paul Kroskrity's extensive work on Tewa linguistic purism provides a Native American analogue from the Southwest.[29] After hundreds of years of intensive contact with Spanish, Hopi, and English, including long-standing Hopi-Tewa bilingualism, the Tewa language shows extremely few signs of that contact. Kroskrity attributes this to an emblematic extension of the ritual kiva space, where various types of purity are required, to the society as a whole. Regardless of the inferred cause, Kroskrity's description of Arizona Tewa language ideology provides a relatively straightforward example of Indigenous purism, which William Foley compares to the Herderian formula—Language = Culture = Nation.[30] Miki Makihara discusses a different type of scenario among the Polynesian Rapa Nui, the Indigenous people of Easter Island, who were colonized by the Chilean state.[31] While the colloquial language is a syncretic mix of native Rapa Nui and Spanish, a de-Hispanicized, purist register has come into existence and is deployed for political purposes to demarcate the border between the Rapa Nui and non-Indigenous Chileans. Makihara presents the example of a fully bilingual Rapa Nui leader who gives a speech to a visiting Chilean politician in the purist register with subsequent Spanish interpretation, the goal here being to assert autonomy by highlighting difference.

Even this brief review should make clear that the totalizing generalizations that lead us to posit purism, naming, and reification strictly as colonial artifacts do not withstand scrutiny once we look beyond state ideologies. By the same token, portraying language description and analysis as a colonial invention further obscures the pioneering contributions of non-Western linguists such as Sībawayhi, who described the intricacies of the Arabic language in the eighth century, and Pāṇini, who codified much of Sanskrit grammar using complex interacting rules, presaging generative grammar by over two thousand years.

We are in agreement with the translanguaging literature that the full embrace of a multilingualism that breaks the traditional boundaries of named languages is long overdue and goes hand in hand with undoing racist language ideologies and policies, especially as enacted in the education system.[32] At the same time, it seems the solution to the unilateral imposition of categories and labels cannot be the unilateral removal of these categories and labels, which at best amounts to a kind of postcolonial factory recall. Rather, an honest decolonization should demand that outsiders relinquish the power of naming *and* unnaming, invention *and* disinvention. As Gerald Roche points out, current critiques of language revitalization and language rights advocacy as hopelessly essentialist offer no alternative path to those fighting for what they envision as cultural continuity.[33] *Strategic essentialism*, to borrow Gayatri Chakravorty Spivak's term,[34] in fact continues to be recruited by disenfranchised groups in rebuilding solidarity, countering negative ideologies, and providing "stable ground for further social action."[35] Ironically, language disinvention, which takes an approach polemically opposed to that of the problematic normative ideology underlying the ACS, seems to march toward the same deleterious erasure of Indigenous languages by denying their historical unity as named entities, a unity that in some cases is the primary bond for a community of speakers or signers.

THE *LANGUAGES OF NEW YORK CITY* MAP

We have sought to overcome some of the theoretical dilemmas just discussed by producing a working model of New York City's linguistic diversity through iterative design. Our model began with ELA's Queens-focused contribution to Solnit and Jelly-Shapiro's *Nonstop Metropolis* (figure 5.2), developed into an all-city map[36] (figure 5.1), and now exists as a multilayered, interactive digital map (figure 5.3) that attempts to represent every distinct communalect in the city geographically.[37] The map is based on an effort beginning in 2010 to draw on all available sources, including thousands of interviews and sometimes in-depth discussions with community leaders, speakers, and other experts, to tell the continuing story of the city's many languages and cultures.

In particular, ELA is committed to representing the Indigenous, minority, and primarily oral language varieties that have neither public visibility nor official support. By design, "larger" languages are underrepresented in our map, applying to language mapping the spirit of *counter-mapping*, which

FIGURE 5.2. ELA's initial *Mother Tongues and Queens* map. Rebecca Solnit and Joshua Jelly-Shapiro, *Nonstop Metropolis: A New York City Atlas* (Berkeley: University of California Press, 2016), 194.

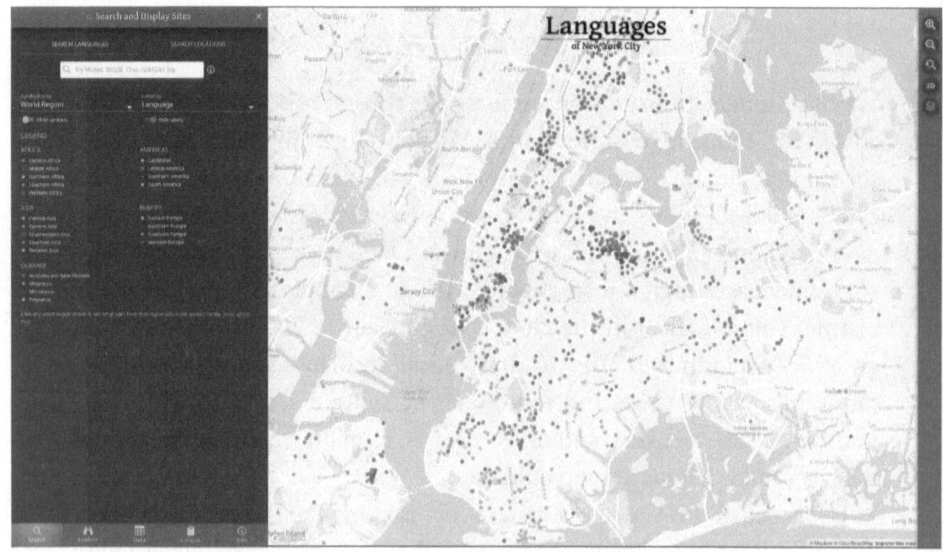

FIGURE 5.3. ELA's multilayered, interactive digital *Languages of New York* map. ELA, https://languagemap.nyc.

resists and inverts the cartographic practices of dominant cultures.[38] Instead of attempting to enumerate the number of speakers of major languages in every census tract, the ELA database maps significant sites, including residential clusters, community centers, religious institutions, restaurants, and other gathering places where community members affirm that their language is frequently spoken. Any private locations were "fuzzed" to protect speakers' privacy. In addition, community members posit an estimate for the size of the community as well as other information about its history, its present-day makeup, and its language practices—contributing to short descriptions that are included in the digital map for every language group, or at least for every macrolinguistic group.[39] Unlike the Census, the ELA database foregrounds endonyms, the names most commonly accepted by the speakers themselves (in the appropriate orthography) as well as English names, ISO codes, and glottocodes (https://glottolog.org) for the use of researchers and the public. This incidentally exposes an interesting diversity of names as well as clashing perceptions. A Hispanophone Puerto Rican hearing the ancestral language of the Sephardic Jews of the Balkans or Morocco would almost certainly recognize their language as Spanish, albeit with a few unfamiliar words and odd features. Yet the Balkan Jews would identify it as their own unique language called Ladino, while the Moroccan Jews would call their language Haketia, derived simply from the Arabic word for "talk." All three forms of speech—Caribbean Spanish, Ladino, and Haketia derive from a single source and are for the most part mutually intelligible. However, they correlate with vastly different identities and may be considered by their speakers as independent languages with unrelated names. Conversely, there are a multitude of languages in New York City referred to by their own speakers as some variation of the name *creole* or *patois*, both of which index a shared social history of these languages rather than a common origin. In this case, we find communities sharing a similar name for languages that are far from mutually intelligible. Differences in endonym and exonym may also reveal layers of history that many might consider long buried. In the case of many Indigenous Mexican languages, we find the exonyms still consistently reflect the Nahuatl names bestowed on them by their Aztec conquerors prior to European colonization. The (Hispanicized) Nahuatl language names Mixteco and Amuzgo, for instance, are referred to as Tu'un Savi (the language of the rain) and Ñomndaa (the language of water) by their own speakers. Yet the Nahuatl names are the ones with official currency and the only ones used by service providers, interpretation agencies, and others in the United States. While recognizing the problems inherent in language names and named languages, the map attempts to offer an enriched view that reveals these kinds of insights, among others.

As noted earlier, the disparity between ELA's mapping work and the census count, in nearly every respect, is too large to ignore, especially when the two data sets can be superimposed on each other in the digital version. A single category in the census data like Mande, referring to a large group of related languages spoken across West Africa with varying degrees of mutual intelligibility, is reflected when filtering the ELA data set as twenty distinct languages, including both widely spoken languages such as Bambara and Dyula and those with much more limited distribution such as Marka and Vai, which nonetheless have speakers or even substantial communities in New York. Census categories that speakers would hardly recognize, such as Niger-Congo (a language family with over fifty thousand "speakers" in New York), can be analyzed visually, by comparison with ELA data, as potentially involving dozens of languages but almost certainly featuring Akan, Igbo, Wolof, and Yoruba as major components.

In geographic terms, approximately 38 percent of the languages in the ELA database are from Asia, 24 percent from Africa, 19 percent from Europe, 16 percent from the Americas, and the rest from Oceania and the Pacific. Some of the patterns revealed—the dense clustering of West African languages in Harlem and the Bronx, the presence of Indigenous languages in areas usually just considered "Spanish-speaking," and the deep and multifaceted Asian language diversity of Queens, to name a few—at least hint at the complexity of the city's linguistic diversity in ways that Census Bureau data miss or distort. Communities undergoing language shift and likely to have large numbers of semispeakers, rememberers, etc. are shown as such, albeit with precedence given to the heritage language. The ELA database also contains information about over a dozen liturgical languages used by communities today (e.g., Latin, Coptic, and Ge'ez), several ongoing cases of (especially Indigenous) language revival such as Lenape and Taíno, and numerous ethnolects and dialects as well as a few dozen languages used historically by communities but never officially recorded as such. By no means does the map attempt to be comprehensive, and it, too, surely represents an undercount, a snapshot of Babel, and a crude reification of linguistic realities that are much more complex on the ground—though accompanying descriptions and media bring us closer to an accurate and representative understanding of the linguistic complexity of New York City.

The map makes visible not only hundreds of speech communities missed by the Census but also a whole range of settlement patterns and interaction zones that are integral to the city's linguistic ecology. Where residential concentrations exist, there may not be just one but several with important linguistic differences. Where the Census simply identifies Arabic-speaking tracts in Brooklyn, Queens, and the Bronx, the ELA map makes clear (as community members know) that those in Brooklyn are somewhat more likely to speak forms of Levantine Arabic, those in Queens speak more Moroccan and Egyptian Arabic, and those in the Bronx mostly speak forms of Yemeni Arabic. Coterritorial settlement patterns highlight the ways in which one group, for a variety of reasons, tends to settle (sometimes in a kind of succession pattern) with or near another one to which it has linguistic, historical, cultural, religious, or other connections. For example, throughout the city Albanian neighborhoods have formed in Italian areas in large part because many Albanians are proficient, for historical reasons, in Italian—which the New York settlement pattern only strengthens. In other cases, whole microcosms of world regions can form, as in the post-Soviet world of south Brooklyn, where Russophones from across the Soviet Union (especially central Asia) may find themselves using Russian more than either Uzbek (for instance) or English. In some cases, we find no pattern at all, with individuals simply settling where they can or wish for reasons of work, convenience, cost, etc. In others, communities that had initial nodes in the first generation experience dispersal, especially with suburbanization, and this may be associated with a shift to English and absorption into the wider society.

Patterns of language shift and change already under way in a home region often continue or accelerate with migration (itself often a multistop process that involves linguistic adjustments). Much depends on how movement and settlement bring speakers into contact with other groups, but the map makes clear that Indigenous Mexicans are within a Spanish-speaking matrix even in New York, just as Fujianese are within a Mandarin matrix and Mustangis are surrounded by Nepali and Tibetan, not to mention Urdu and Bengali. Far from a traditional model representing Americanization as a straightforward intergenerational shift from a mother language to English, we find a complex patchwork of multiple assimilations, based on differential settlement patterns in the city, often leading at least initially to high degrees of multilingualism and mixing.

A PLACE ON THE MAP, A PLACE IN THE CITY

Despite all the caveats applied, a professionally designed map, whether analog or digital, is an artifact that carries an apparently self-evident authority. Over several years of "road testing" the map, we have consistently found that people look for their language(s) where they think they should be. Overwhelmingly, the initial response from speakers of small languages is satisfaction at being represented, especially at seeing a name, particularly an endonym, which in many cases they have never seen printed (at least outside the community), put on the same plane as languages like English, Spanish, and Chinese. There is strong resonance here with Tommaso Manfredini's description (in this volume) of working with an asylum seeker to pinpoint the latter's hometown with Google Maps and being unable to do so—thus registering "absence of presence, absence of proof" that made his story "already a step removed from being entirely verifiable." We, too, have frequently had this experience and see the New York language map as a kind of response, providing proof of presence, albeit in the migrant's destination rather than their point of origin.

In some cases, visibility and recognition can come almost as something of a shock. While displaying a blown-up version of the map at a festival in Prospect Park, Brooklyn, we were approached by a young Senegalese-French man who had recently moved to the area and was visibly astonished to find his heritage language, Baïnounk, shown in the very first place on the map he looked, among the Senegalese languages spoken in the Bronx. He eagerly called over his wife, telling us that she was a speaker of Monokutuba from the Republic of Congo-Brazzaville—a language not then on the map but one that both were happy to see added, even if she was the only speaker they knew of in the city. There was no small irony in it being a speaker of Baïnounk who searched for and found his language community on the map that day, as Baïnounk has been held up as a particularly thorny case of sociolinguistic complexity, where defining the language itself is a challenge due to the extreme multilingualism and language contact found in Casamance, Senegal (as can be noted from the very title of Freiderike Lüpke's "Language and Identity in Flux: In Search of Baïnounk"[40]). But this betrays an important truth: while linguists and other specialists have been anxiously pondering the definition, demarcation, invention, and disinvention of languages, the labels in question, whatever their provenance, gain significant traction "on the ground" in the meantime. Both the linguist and the speaker are in search of Baïnounk in their own ways. Linguists may try to document and describe a language by sorting through layers of multilingualism, while native speakers may be more concerned with locating themselves in the multilingual diaspora city.[41]

In another public exposition of the map, this time on a street corner in the South Bronx, a child, roughly ten years old, approached and began scanning the language names intently. He was trying to remember the name of his parents' language, he told us. "It begins with a *G*," he said, starting to look in the section of the map representing where we stood (a major center for Garifuna people) and coming upon the name with the force of discovery: "Garifuna!" In this case, the map had unexpectedly served as both reminder and validation of a buried heritage language.

These are not outliers. A group of Indigenous Latin American language activists, lacking any census data about their communities, asserts that the map will be the most powerful tool at their disposal for lobbying for recognition and resources from city government. An Armenian New Yorker is delighted to find not just that Armenian is displayed but also that someone outside the community has noted and made clear the distinctions among Western Armenian (endangered), Eastern Armenian (the national language), and Classical Armenian (the liturgical language). An activist supporting the West African script N'ko proudly notes the correct use, production, and encoding of the script in the endonym for the Mandinka language. No community or individual has asked for their language to be removed from the map, though eyebrows have been raised about ethnolects included such as Jewish English and Mexican Spanish, reflecting sensitivity that these may somehow be nonstandard or insufficiently distinctive variants.

For policy makers at the city level—our most extensive experience has been with the city's 2020 Census outreach team and the Department of Health—the map can be a desperately needed guide to known blind spots.

In these environments, resources simply cannot be allocated to communities without some justification drawing on a published source, ideally statistical. The map at least provides a starting point, a validation from a linguistic point of view of what community leaders and organizers already know, something to which they can point.

For journalists, whose work often takes the positive side of visibility as a given but who have also evolved safeguards to protect individual identities, the map is serving as a reference that leads them to ask the right questions and discover that their sources are Indigenous. Major news stories, from immigration to Covid-19, have vital Indigenous dimensions that have been consistently overlooked because of invisibility. Amanda Holpuch's article on Covid-19, for example, cited the map and centered Indigenous voices in Corona, Queens, one of the neighborhoods hardest hit by the pandemic in the country,[42] while similar and otherwise exemplary pieces discussed the struggles of Indigenous Latin Americans in New York City without acknowledging their identities beyond Guatemalan and Mexican.

Social justice in a representative democracy is presumed to depend on the visibility of its constituent communities, and, thus, every group in the United States with a shared sense of identity and the means to mobilize has fought for increased "visibility" for the betterment of its people. We have seen how the presence of certain migrants has been occluded as their languages easily slip through the sieve of the ACS and similar surveys due in part to the terms *language*, *speaker*, and *spoken at home*. Clearly, the underlying liberal ideology that there exists a straight line from visibility to justice cannot be assumed lightly. There are also communities that could be harmed by visibility, and visibility does not ensure that society will be moved to action; neither does it protect against empty gestures of recognition.[43] Censuses, maps, and other tools of visibility have furthermore long been deployed by states and missionary organizations to place populations under their control. The reduction of complex ecologies of speech to named languages has also played a role in colonial projects of categorization, racialization, and subjugation.[44] But while such exploitation has been largely a colonial European affair over the last several centuries, we must also recognize the agency of Indigenous and other marginalized peoples in implementing their own regimes of naming and categorization, both as traditional practice and as acts of resistance.

Despite the spotted history of language naming and enumeration, we have argued here that the erasure of ethnolinguistic groups through policy and practice can be more pernicious than the hazards of categorization and identification. Just as Isabelle Zaugg (in this volume) argues for a sensitive three-pronged approach that recognizes the "double-edged sword" of digital visibility and usability for all languages, we see linguistic countermapping as involving a balance between pursuing greater equity and attending to those hazards. Our argument draws largely on experience with Indigenous immigrants in New York City who face inherent barriers to visibility, rendering them doubly minoritized within their respective national communities and as minorities themselves within American society and without access to basic services. Our answer to this, the *Languages of New York City* digital map, attempts to bring light to myriad hidden language communities that have until recently gone unnoticed by the city at large. While acknowledging the thorny problems of linguistic essentialization, the mapping project gives named languages a fair shake as a representation of urban multilingualism. While we are seeing success in the former goal as language communities themselves begin to use the map as official validation of their presence in the city, we continue to work toward an equally tangible but truer representation of all those communicative practices that exist between named languages.

ACKNOWLEDGMENTS

We are indebted to Mark Turin, Sienna Craig, and Maya Daurio for comments on an earlier draft, none of whom should be held responsible for any views expressed herein. The chapter arose as part of the language mapping efforts at the Endangered Language Alliance under a Peter Wall Institute Wall Solutions Grant (University of British Columbia).

NOTES

Certain sections of this chapter overlap with Ross Perlin, D. Kaufman, M. Turin, M. Daurio, S. Craig, and J. Lampel, "Mapping Urban Linguistic Diversity in New York City: Motives, Methods, Tools and Outcomes," *Language Documentation and Conservation* 15 (2021): 458–490. The focus there, however, is on the development of the *Languages of New York City* digital map. Here we focus less on the technical aspects and more on the ontological ones in relation to the recent literature on translanguaging and language disinvention.

1. Father Isaac Jogues, "Novum Belgium," in *Narratives of New Netherland, 1609–1664*, ed. J. Franklin Jameson (New York: Barnes & Noble, 1953), 259.
2. Daniel Kaufman and Ross Perlin. "Language Documentation in Diaspora Communities," in *The Oxford Handbook of Endangered Languages*, ed. Kenneth L. Rehg and Lyle Campbell, 399–418 (Oxford: Oxford University Press, 2018).
3. This effort began as our contribution to a cultural atlas of New York City. See Rebecca Solnit and Joshua Jelly-Schapiro, *Nonstop Metropolis: A New York City Atlas* (Berkeley: University of California Press, 2016), map 24.
4. Nicolas Tournadre, "The Tibetic Languages and Their Classification," in *Trans-Himalayan Linguistics: Historical and Descriptive Linguistics of the Himalayan Area*, ed. Thomas Owen-Smith and Nathan W. Hill (Berlin: De Gruyter Mouton, 2014), 105–130.
5. Gerald Roche and Hiroyuki Suzuki, "Tibet's Minority Languages: Diversity and Endangerment," *Modern Asian Studies* 52, no. 4 (2018): 1227–1278.
6. Herman W. Haller, "Between Standard Italian and Creole: An Interim Report on Language Patterns in an Italian-American Community," *Word* 32, no. 3 (1981): 186.
7. Herman Haller, "Italian in New York," in *The Multilingual Apple: Languages in New York City*, ed. Ofelia García and Joshua A. Fishman (Berlin-New York: Mouton De Gruyter, 1997), 133.
8. Among other popular efforts, the Mixteco rapper Una Isu (Miguel Villegas Ventura) tackles the colonial dichotomy directly in a trilingual song entitled "Mixteco es un lenguaje" (Mixteco is a language).
9. Jeremy Slack, Daniel E. Martínez, and Josiah Heyman, "Immigration Authorities Systematically Deny Medical Care for Migrants Who Speak Indigenous Languages," Center for Migration Studies, December 21, 2018, https://cmsny.org/publications/slackmartinezheyman-medical-care-denial/.
10. Greg Grandin and Elizabeth Oglesby, "Who Killed Jakelin Caal Maquín at the US Border?," *The Nation*, December 17, 2018.
11. Rachel Nolan, "A Translation Crisis at the Border," *New Yorker*, January 6, 2020.
12. Leila Miller, "Nine Years After Guatemalan Man's Shooting, LAPD Officers Get Help to Identify Indigenous languages," *Los Angeles Times*, December 12, 2019.
13. Suzanne Romaine, *Language in Society: An Introduction to Sociolinguistics* (Oxford: Oxford University Press, 1994), 12.
14. For discussion, see Sarah Grey Thomason and Terrence Kaufman, *Language Contact, Creolization and Genetic Linguistics* (Berkeley: University of California Press, 1988); and Yaron Matras, *Language Contact* (Cambridge: Cambridge University Press, 2015).
15. Earlier expressions of these ideas can be found in Peter Mühlhäusler, "Language Planning and Language Ecology," *Current Issues in Language Planning* 1, no. 3 (2000): 367; and Timothy Reagan, "Objectification, Positivism and Language Studies: A Reconsideration," *Critical Inquiry in Language Studies* 1, no. 1 (2004), 41–60, among many others.

> The notion of a "language" is a recent culture-specific notion associated with the rise of European nation states and the Enlightenment. The notion of "a language" makes little sense in most traditional societies. (Mühlhäusler, "Language Planning," 358.)
>
> There is, or at least there may well be, no such thing as English. Indeed, my claim is even a bit stronger than this—not only is there no such thing as English, but there is arguably no such thing as Russian, French, Spanish, Chinese, Hindi, or any other language. . . . [Languages are] ultimately a collection of idiolects which have been determined to belong together for what are ultimately non- and extra-linguistic reasons. (Reagan, "Objectification," 42, 56.)

16. C. Williams, "Arfarniad o Ddulliau Dysgu ac Addysgu yng Nghyd-destun Addysg Uwchradd Ddwyieithog [An evaluation of teaching and learning methods in the context of bilingual secondary education]" (unpublished doctoral thesis, University of Wales, Bangor, 1994).
17. See Ricardo Otheguy, Ofelia García, and Wallis Reid, "Clarifying Translanguaging and Deconstructing Named Languages: A Perspective from Linguistics," *Applied Linguistics Review* 6 (2015): 283.
18. Francois Grosjean, "Neurolinguists, Beware! The Bilingual Is Not Two Monolinguals in One Person," *Brain and Language* 36 (1989): 3–15.
19. Otheguy et al., "Clarifying Translanguaging," 282–283. See Wesley Y. Leonard, "Producing Language Reclamation by Decolonising 'Language,'" *Language Documentation and Description* 14 (2017): 15–36, and "Framing Language Reclamation Programmes for Everybody's Empowerment," *Gender and Language* 6, no. 2 (2012): 339–367. Leonard usefully teases apart traditional language revitalization, with its focus on reviving a named language, from what he terms *language reclamation*, "a larger effort by a community to claim its right to speak a language and to set associated goals in response to community needs and perspectives" (Leonard, "Framing Language Reclamation Programs," 359), activities that grapple directly with the essentialization decried by Otheguy et al., "Clarifying Translanguaging." See also Leonard's chapter in this volume.
20. Otheguy et al., "Clarifying Translanguaging," 299.
21. Sinfree Makoni and Alastair Pennycook, "Disinventing and Reconstituting Languages," in *Disinventing and Reconstituting Languages*, ed. Sinfree Makoni and Alastair Pennycook (Clevedon, England: Multilingual Matters, 2007): 21.
22. Salikoko Mufwene, *Language Evolution: Contact, Competition and Change* (London: Continuum Press, 2008).
23. Makoni and Pennycook, "Disinventing and Reconstituting Languages," 26.
24. Jean Jackson, *The Fish People: Linguistic Exogamy and Tukanoan Identity in Northwest Amazonia* (Cambridge: Cambridge University Press, 1983).
25. Alexandra Aikhenvald, "Language Awareness and Correct Speech Among the Tariana," *Anthropological Linguistics* 43, no. 4 (2001): 411–430.
26. Luke Fleming, "From Patrilects to Performatives: Linguistic Exogamy and Language Shift in the Northwest Amazon" (PhD diss., University of Pennsylvania, 2010), 12.
27. Jeffrey Heath, *Linguistic Diffusion in Arnhem Land* (Canberra: Australian Institute of Aboriginal Studies, 1978), 15.
28. Heath, *Linguistic Diffusion*, 19.

29. See Paul Kroskrity, "Arizona Tewa Kiva Speech as a Manifestation of a Dominant Language Ideology," in *Linguistic Anthropology: A Reader*, ed. A. Duranti (Oxford: Blackwell, 2001), 402–419; "Language Ideologies in the Expression and Representation of Arizona Tewa Ethnic Identity," in *Regimes of Language*, ed. Paul Kroskrity (Santa Fe, NM: School of American Research, 2000), 329–359; and *Language, History and Identity: Ethnolinguistic Studies of the Arizona Tewa* (Tucson: University of Arizona Press, 1993).
30. William A. Foley, "Personhood and Linguistic Identity, Purism and Variation," *Language Documentation and Description* 3 (2005): 157–180. Foley named the formula after the eighteenth-century philosopher Johann Gottfried von Herder, who identified a correlation between the language of a community and that community's mind or spirit.
31. Miki Makihara, "Linguistic Purism in Rapa Nui Political Discourse," in *Consequences of Contact: Language Ideologies and Sociocultural Transformations in Pacific Societies*, ed. Miki Makihara and Bambi B. Schieffelin (Oxford: Oxford Univeristy Press, 2007), 49–69.
32. See Ofelia García, *Bilingual Education in the 21st Century: A Global Perspective* (Malden, MA: Wiley-Blackwell, 2009).
33. Gerald Roche, "Abandoning Endangered Languages: Ethical Loneliness, Language Oppression, and Social Justice," *American Anthropologist* 122 (2020): 164–169.
34. Gayatri Chakravorty Spivak, "Subaltern Studies: Deconstructing Historiography," in *Selected Subaltern Studies*, eds. Ranajit Guha and Gayatri Chakravorty Spivak (London: Oxford University Press, 1988), 3–32.
35. M. Bucholtz, "Sociolinguistic Nostalgia and the Authentication of Identity," *Journal of Sociolinguistics* 7 (2003): 401.
36. Ross Perlin and Daniel Kaufman. eds., *Languages of New York City*, map, 3rd ed. (New York: Endangered Language Alliance, 2020).
37. Perlin et al., "Mapping Urban Linguistic Diversity."
38. N. Peluso, "Whose Woods Are These? Counter-Mapping Forest Territories in Kalimantan, Indonesia," *Antipode* 27, no. 4 (1995): 383–406.
39. Perlin et al., "Mapping Urban Linguistic Diversity."
40. Freiderike Lüpke, "Language and Identity in Flux: In Search of Baïnounk," *Journal of Language Contact* 3 (2010): 155–174.
41. Baïnounk is not even among the languages in the greatly expanded coding scheme of the U.S. Census, so his elation at finding Baïnounk in the map's alternative representation seems well justified.
42. Amanda Holpuch, "Corona in Corona: Deadly Toll in a New York Neighborhood Tells a Story of Race, Poverty and Inequality," *The Guardian*, June 15, 2020.
43. Glen Sean Coulthard, *Red Skin White Masks: Rejecting the Colonial Politics of Recognition* (Minneapolis: University of Minnesota Press, 2014).
44. J. J. Errington, *Linguistics in a Colonial World: A Story of Language, Meaning and Power* (New York: Blackwell, 2007).

WORKS CITED

Aikhenvald, Alexandra. "Language Awareness and Correct Speech Among the Tariana." *Anthropological Linguistics* 43, no. 4 (2001): 411–430.

Bucholtz, M. "Sociolinguistic Nostalgia and the Authentication of Identity." *Journal of Sociolinguistics* 7 (2003): 398–416.
Coulthard, Glen Sean. *Red Skin White Masks: Rejecting the Colonial Politics of Recognition*. Minneapolis: University of Minnesota Press, 2014.
Errington, J. J. *Linguistics in a Colonial World: A Story of Language, Meaning and Power*. New York: Blackwell, 2007.
Fleming, Luke. "From Patrilects to Performatives: Linguistic Exogamy and Language Shift in the Northwest Amazon." PhD diss., University of Pennsylvania, 2010.
Foley, William A. "Personhood and Linguistic Identity, Purism and Variation." *Language Documentation and Description* 3 (2005): 157–180.
García, Ofelia. *Bilingual Education in the 21st Century: A Global Perspective*. Malden, MA: Wiley-Blackwell, 2009.
García, Ofelia, and Li Wei. *Translanguaging: Language, Bilingualism and Education*. London: Palgrave Macmillan, 2014.
Grandin, Greg, and Elizabeth Oglesby. "Who Killed Jakelin Caal Maquín at the US Border?" *The Nation*, December 17, 2018.
Grosjean, Francois. "Neurolinguists, Beware! The Bilingual Is Not Two Monolinguals in One Person." *Brain and Language* 36 (1989): 3–15.
Haller, Herman W. "Between Standard Italian and Creole: An Interim Report on Language Patterns in an Italian-American Community." *Word* 32, no. 3 (1981): 181–191.
Haller, Herman. "Italian in New York." In *The Multilingual Apple: Languages in New York City*, ed. Ofelia García and Joshua A. Fishman, 119-142. Berlin-New York: Mouton De Gruyter, 1997.
Haller, Herman. "Italian Speech Varieties in the United States and the Italian-American Lingua Franca." *Italica* 64 (1987): 393–409.
Harris, Roy. "The Role of the Language Myth in the Western Cultural Tradition." In *The Language Myth in Western Culture*, ed. Roy Harris, 1–24. London: Curson, 2002.
Heath, Jeffrey. *Linguistic Diffusion in Arnhem Land*. Canberra: Australian Institute of Aboriginal Studies, 1978.
Holpuch, Amanda. "Corona in Corona: Deadly Toll in a New York Neighborhood Tells a Story of Race, Poverty and Inequality." *Guardian*, June 15, 2020.
Jackson, Jean. *The Fish People: Linguistic Exogamy and Tukanoan Identity in Northwest Amazonia*. Cambridge: Cambridge University Press, 1983.
Jogues, Father Isaac. "Novum Belgium." In *Narratives of New Netherland, 1609-1664*, ed. J. Franklin Jameson. New York: Barnes & Noble, 1953.
Kaufman, Daniel, and Ross Perlin. "Language Documentation in Diaspora Communities." In *The Oxford Handbook of Endangered Languages*, eds. Kenneth L. Rehg and Lyle Campbell, 399–418. Oxford: Oxford University Press, 2018.
Kroskrity, Paul. "Arizona Tewa Kiva Speech as a Manifestation of a Dominant Language Ideology." In *Linguistic Anthropology: A Reader*, ed. A. Duranti, 402–419. Oxford: Blackwell, 2001.
Kroskrity, Paul. *Language, History and Identity: Ethnolinguistic Studies of the Arizona Tewa*. Tucson: University of Arizona Press, 1993.
Kroskrity, Paul. "Language Ideologies in the Expression and Representation of Arizona Tewa Ethnic Identity." In *Regimes of Language*, ed. Paul Kroskrity, 329–359. Santa Fe, NM: School of American Research, 2000.
Leonard, Wesley Y. "Framing Language Reclamation Programmes for Everybody's Empowerment." *Gender and Language* 6, no. 2 (2012): 339–367.

Leonard, Wesley Y. "Producing Language Reclamation by Decolonising 'Language.'" *Language Documentation and Description* 14 (2017): 15–36. http://www.elpublishing.org/PID/150.

Lüpke, Friederike. "Language and Identity in Flux: In Search of Baïnounk." *Journal of Language Contact* 3, no. 1 (2010): 155–174.

Makihara, Miki. "Linguistic Purism in Rapa Nui Political Discourse." In *Consequences of Contact: Language Ideologies and Sociocultural Transformations in Pacific Societies*, ed. Miki Makihara and Bambi B. Schieffelin, 49–69. Oxford: Oxford University Press, 2007.

Makoni, Sinfree, and Alastair Pennycook. *Disinventing and Reconstituting languages*. Clevedon, England: Multilingual Matters, 2007.

Matras, Yaron. *Language Contact*. Cambridge: Cambridge University Press. 2015.

Miller, Leila. "Nine Years After Guatemalan Man's Shooting, LAPD Officers Get Help to Identify Indigenous Languages." *Los Angeles Times*, December 12, 2019.

Mufwene, Salikoko. *Language Evolution: Contact, Competition and Change*. London: Continuum, 2008.

Mühlhäusler, Peter. "Language Planning and Language Ecology." *Current Issues in Language Planning* 1, no. 3 (2000): 306–367.

Nolan, Rachel. "A Translation Crisis at the Border." *New Yorker*, January 6, 2020.

Otheguy, Ricardo, Ofelia García, and Wallis Reid. "Clarifying Translanguaging and Deconstructing Named Languages: A Perspective from Linguistics." *Applied Linguistics Review* 6 (2015): 281–307.

Peluso, N. "Whose Woods Are These? Counter-Mapping Forest Territories in Kalimantan, Indonesia." *Antipode* 27, no. 4 (1995): 383–406.

Perlin, Ross, and Daniel Kaufman, eds. *Languages of New York City*. Map. 3rd ed. New York: Endangered Language Alliance, 2020.

Perlin, Ross, D. Kaufman, M. Turin, M. Daurio, S. Craig, and J. Lampel. "Mapping Urban Linguistic Diversity in New York City: Motives, Methods, Tools and Outcomes." *Language Documentation and Conservation* 15 (2021): 458–490.

Reagan, Timothy. "Objectification, Positivism and Language Studies: A Reconsideration." *Critical Inquiry in Language Studies* 1, no. 1 (2004): 41–60.

Roche, Gerald. "Abandoning Endangered Languages: Ethical Loneliness, Language Oppression, and Social Justice." *American Anthropologist* 122 (2020): 164–169.

Roche, Gerald. "Articulating Language Oppression: Colonialism, Coloniality and the Erasure of Tibet's Minority Languages." *Patterns of Prejudice* 53, no. 5 (2019): 487–514.

Roche, Gerald, and Hiroyuki Suzuki. "Tibet's Minority Languages: Diversity and Endangerment." *Modern Asian Studies* 52, no. 4 (2018): 1227–1278.

Romaine, Suzanne. *Language in Society: An Introduction to Sociolinguistics*. Oxford: Oxford University Press, 1994.

Rosa, Jonathan, and Nelson Flores. "Unsettling Language and Race: Toward a Raciolinguistic Perspective." *Language in Society* 46 (2017): 621–647.

Sabino, Robin. *Languaging Without Languages: Beyond Metro-, Multi-, Poly-, Pluri- and Translanguaging*. Leiden, Netherlands: Brill, 2018.

Slack, Jeremy, Daniel E. Martínez, and Josiah Heyman. "Immigration Authorities Systematically Deny Medical Care for Migrants Who Speak Indigenous Languages." Center for Migration Studies, December 21, 2018. https://cmsny.org/publications/slackmartinezheyman-medical-care-denial/.

Solnit, Rebecca, and Joshua Jelly-Schapiro. *Nonstop Metropolis: A New York City Atlas.* Berkeley: University of California Press, 2016.
Spivak, Gayatri Chakravorty. "Subaltern Studies: Deconstructing Historiography." In *Selected Subaltern Studies*, eds. Ranajit Guha and Gayatri Chakravorty Spivak, 3–32. London: Oxford University Press, 1988.
Thomason, Sarah Grey, and Terrence Kaufman. *Language Contact, Creolization and Genetic Linguistics.* Berkeley: University of California Press, 1988.
Tournadre, Nicolas. "The Tibetic Languages and Their Classification." In *Trans-Himalayan Linguistics: Historical and Descriptive Linguistics of the Himalayan Area*, eds. Thomas Owen-Smith and Nathan W. Hill, 105–130. Berlin: De Gruyter Mouton, 2014.
U.S. Census Bureau. "Detailed Languages Spoken at Home and Ability to Speak English for the Population 5 Years and Over: 2009–2013 [American Community Survey]." October 2015. https://www.census.gov/data/tables/2013/demo/2009-2013-lang-tables.html.
Williams, C. "Arfarniad o Ddulliau Dysgu ac Addysgu yng Nghyd-destun Addysg Uwchradd Ddwyieithog [An evaluation of teaching and learning methods in the context of bilingual secondary education]." Unpublished doctoral thesis, University of Wales, Bangor, 1994.

Words
MOHAMMED BENNIS

Words hewn
breath
not flushed
Words burning the origin of their desires in me
with a rush of passages threatening

Words gathering union
wandering
Words rising behind a screen of words

The shadows carried their clouds to my hands
Tomorrow they will leave
through
vaults open
to their butterflies

The silence there is busy
multiplying in
the flames
of the ghombaz
drawing near the dead
who cross over
from the memory of words

Translated by Camilo Gomez-Rivas

كلمَات

محمد بنيــس

كلماتٌ ينْحَتُها
نفَسٌ
منْ غيْرِ شُحُوبْ
كلماتٌ
توقظُ فيّ سُلالةَ شهْوتهَا
بهُجوم مَجازاتٍ تتهَدّدُني
كلماتٌ تحْشُدُ
وحْدَتَها
وَتتُوهْ
كَلماتٌ تُشرقُ خلفَ ستائرَ منْ كلمات

ليَدي يرْفعُ هذا الظلُّ سحَابتهَا
وغداً ستُهَاجرُ
بيْنَ
سَراديبَ انكشفتْ
لفراشَتهَا

والصّمتُ هنالكَ مُنشغلٌ
يتضَاعفُ في
شُعَلِ
الغُنْبَازِ
يقرّبُ منّي أمواتاً
عَبرُوا منْ ذاكرةِ الكلمَاتْ

Chapter Six

LINGUISTIC DEMOCRACY AND THE ALGERIAN HIRAK

MADELEINE DOBIE

LANGUAGE RIGHTS AND DELIBERATIVE DEMOCRACY

Calls for language justice can rest on a number of different foundations. As Lydia Liu and Anupama Rao write in their introduction to this volume, they are sometimes predicated on arguments in favor of *diversity*: i.e., the view that language is an essential medium of culture and that the variety of human cultures is inherently worthy of preservation. In other instances, the defining issue is *equality*: i.e., the potential for speakers of minority languages to suffer marginalization and discrimination. A spectrum of models of language justice stretching from ecology (the defense of endangered languages) to equality (the elimination of the exclusion faced by those who don't speak the dominant language) and from the attachment of rights to languages to the claim that languages are essential to the delivery of human rights has taken shape within a growing philosophical debate. As Liu and Rao write, "Clarifying the difference between ideas of linguistic diversity, which privilege discourses of protection . . . and the democratic commitment to equal rights is a useful first step" toward articulating the claims and objectives of advocates of language justice.

Theorists of liberalism such as Charles Taylor and Will Kymlicka argue that language rights—which might encompass the right to bilingual education, to the publication of official documents in multiple languages, or to the provision of resources for cultural conservation—should be regarded as human rights because people's values and identity are formed within cultural and linguistic groups.[1] As L. Maria Bo explains in her chapter in this volume, this perspective underpins the efforts of international bodies such as UNESCO and PEN International to champion the rights of minority languages as essential vehicles of cultural heritage.[2] Yet these claims and their supporting arguments have been challenged from other quarters. Some political philosophers express the concern that placing the protection of languages on a par with freedom from violence or hunger dilutes the notion of human rights, which is troubling given the historically weak enforcement of even the most basic protections.[3] Bo cites the work of Michael Walzer, who cautions that multiplying rights is more likely to engender conflict about social goods than to promote a holistic model of justice.[4] Other thinkers question the ascription of rights to collectivities rather than individuals, seeing this as a recipe for coerced conformity or dangerous identitarianism.[5]

Scholars who focus specifically on language rights have questioned the idea that protecting languages means—or should mean—defending *cultures*; indeed, they challenge the notion that there are discrete cultures organized around languages. Though calls for language rights are often predicated on the recognition of ethnic groups, these identities should not go unquestioned, not least because—as I develop here with respect to the Amazigh and Kabyle movements in Algeria—they are often rooted in colonial categories. A related set of concerns is that language rights promote linguistic conservatism, generating purist conceptions of language that stigmatize loanwords, neologisms, and other forms of fluidity and hybridization. With this problem in mind, the sociolinguist Lionel Wee suggests that rather than approaching language as a "fully-formed cognitive system that happens to be realized in actual behavior," we should construe it as a practice: i.e., "a social activity whose regularity is the outcome of temporarily conventionalized patterns of usage."[6] Taking a different approach to what language is, Wee argues, carries important implications for how we think about language justice, favoring a political model that emphasizes process—i.e., the continuous democratic negotiation of different interests—rather than the establishment and defense of entrenched rights. This perspective correlates broadly with the approach of this volume, which apprehends languages as components of constantly evolving *lifeworlds* and explores the meaning of language justice in inherently fluid contexts such as migration (in the chapter by Tommaso Manfredini) and urban diasporas (in the chapter by Daniel Kaufman and Ross Perlin).

Acknowledging fluidity and relationality does not, however, mean abandoning the notion of language justice. Wee himself looks to theories of deliberative or reflexive democracy as possible foundations, drawing on the ideas of Seyla Benhabib and John Dryzek, among others.[7] These thinkers reject liberal models of cultural rights because carving out cultural and other group rights contributes to the entrenchment of religious, racial, ethnic, and linguistic subcommunities whose interests may appear to be in competition with each other. The search for identity, Benhabib writes, entails the process of "differentiating oneself from what one is not . . . [;] identity politics is always and necessarily a politics of the creation of difference."[8] Given the many contexts around the world in which democracies are struggling to navigate explosive questions of identity and difference, this concern is far from academic. A second prong of their critique questions the role of the state as the fixed center of political life. Benhabib, Dryzek, and Walzer all argue that while liberal-constitutional theory provides crucial foundations for basic justice, it also extends the state's role in adjudicating among societal interests far beyond these necessary provisions. They advocate instead for the central role of the citizen-actor, arguing that democracy should rest on what Benhabib, harking back to a Rousseauian tradition of political thought, calls the "public use of reason jointly exercised by autonomous citizens."[9] According to this model, rather than being anchored by mechanisms designed to ensure their permanence, rights are understood to be subject to constant renegotiation and, as Benjamin Barber puts it, "dependent for their normative force on the engagement and commitment of an active citizen body."[10]

Theories of deliberative/procedural democracy can take many different forms, with some thinkers—e.g., Chantal Mouffe and Ernesto Laclau— identifying dissent and struggle as essential components of democracy.[11] Yet there is a broad consensus on the importance of open public debate. For Benhabib, deliberative democracy rests on a discourse model of ethics: i.e., on "the idea that rules of action and institutional arrangements would only be agreed to if they were achieved by open and symmetrical discussion."[12] Building on this foundation, she argues that regular collective deliberation conducted rationally and fairly among equal individuals can determine what is in the common interest more flexibly and with greater nuance than a dispensation by which the state is charged with interpreting and enforcing a corpus of rights. In addition, rather than steering people toward the defense of their rights, open public discussion informs them about other points of view and makes room for changes of opinion.

Like all political philosophies, deliberative democracy raises its own set of questions, not least of which is how to achieve the conditions of free, fair, and rational discussion. It nonetheless offers the framework of a constructive approach to contemporary political blockages that are interwoven with increasingly entrenched levels of inequality and cultural polarization. As such, deliberative democracy has been a valuable point of reference for several recent citizen movements that have created forums for the open exchange of ideas. In the case of language rights, theories of deliberative democracy provide a compelling alternative to liberal theories of cultural rights because they accommodate an understanding of languages as forms of social practice rather than as fixed ontological categories.[13] The emphasis that theorists place on the continuous reexamination and negotiation of interests helpfully aligns with what Jan Blommaert describes as "the actual and densely contextualized forms in which language occurs in society."[14] Since language use is both highly context specific and constantly in flux, it makes sense to approach language justice in ways that reflect and adapt to practice.

I next consider how the principles of deliberative democracy elucidate a specific contemporary context: the prodemocracy protests that since 2019 have challenged the political status quo in Algeria. The interpretation that I lay out has affinities with other arguments for the reframing of language justice presented in this volume, notably the chapter by Bo. Though Bo focuses on the difficulties associated with the notion of equality rather than on theories of cultural rights, we both affirm the open-ended negotiation of political interests by actors in addition to the state and highlight the fact that language is not a neutral vehicle of political concepts but rather the ground of their encounter, translation, and comparison.

LANGUAGE AND IDENTITY POLITICS IN ALGERIA

Defenses of the prerogatives of various languages in Algeria stretch back to the French colonial era, but they have been reframed in the context of the antigovernment, prodemocracy protest movement known as the *hirak*. Since February 2019, millions of Algerians have taken to the streets to challenge the corrupt, military-backed regime that has ruled the country since it won its independence from France in 1962, expressing their dissatisfaction with the deep social and economic inequalities that have accompanied this monopoly on power. The hirak garnered support from Algerians from many regions and social backgrounds, unexpectedly unifying previously divided groups in a common demand for radical political change. For over a year, protesters voiced their opposition at weekly Friday marches through the streets of Algiers and other cities. The marches were suspended in March 2020 due to the Covid-19 pandemic. Since they resumed in February 2021, they have been met with vigorous government crackdowns, including the arrest of several leading figures. While it seems fair to say that the hirak has suffered a loss of momentum as a result, the spirit of the movement persists in a number of political parties and citizen movements as well as in the work of journalists, artists, and intellectuals, and it would be a mistake to conclude that it has simply run its course.

Throughout the protests of 2019 and 2020, language was an important object of attention. A wide array of slogans—single words or phrases in various languages, including many with multilingual or translational dimensions—circulated on handmade signs, T-shirts, and graffiti and in songs, street chants, and online forums, channeling the spirit of dissent in pithy, often humorous rallying cries. The hirak indeed generated so many catchphrases that scholars have compiled glossaries that tease out their meaning and origins.[15] This attentiveness to language continues a long tradition of language politics in Algeria. Yet whereas in previous political conflicts the claims made for one of the country's principal languages—Modern Standard Arabic (*fusha*), the regional Arabic dialect (*darija*), the main Amazigh or Berber dialect (Tamazight), and French—were frequently advanced at the expense of another—perpetuating what Benhabib might characterize as a politics of rights resting on the presumption of difference—the hirak protesters for the most part embraced linguistic diversity as a foundation for unified dissent.

In this chapter, I explore possible conceptual framings within which to understand the linguistic and political dynamics of the hirak. I suggest that long-standing demands for linguistic rights that have been interwoven with the view that the population is divided into two different ethnic and cultural groups were replaced by a new form of activism that privileges collective political engagement over demands for the rights of specific groups. Further, I point to affinities between this new practice of dissent and theories of deliberative democracy as they intersect with thinking about language justice.

What I am characterizing as the linguistic pluralism of the hirak is striking given Algeria's long history of deeply polarizing discourses about language. Since the colonial period, languages have coexisted in shifting patterns of power and prestige. Attitudes toward Arabic, French, and Tamazight have been tightly interwoven with perspectives on colonialism, nationalism, and regional identity. From the late nineteenth to the mid-twentieth century, the colonial authorities enshrined French as the language of administration and education while essentially suppressing Arabic as a medium of cultural and intellectual life.[16] This policy was rooted both in the ideology of the French "civilizing mission" and in the fear that Arabic might become a medium of political resistance. At the same time, the colonial authorities encouraged Tamazight speakers and especially the population of Kabylia, the region to the south and east of Algiers, to think of themselves as a distinct people with social and religious traditions that were markedly different from those of "Arabs."[17] In the twentieth century, when France remedied its domestic labor shortage by importing factory and mine workers from its overseas colonies, these ethnic distinctions played an important role in the selection process. Considered to be more tractable than Arabs, Kabyles were the group most heavily recruited as immigrant workers. One long-term effect of this selection has been that Tamazight speakers are disproportionately represented in the Algerian diaspora in France.[18] Another related repercussion is that they have sometimes been considered—or have considered themselves—to be closer to France than to fellow Algerians.

The Algerian nationalist movement, the Front de libération nationale (FLN), reacted to the colonial promotion of French by embracing a slogan invented by Abdelhamid Ibn Badis, a leading Muslim reformer of the 1930s: "Islam is our religion, Algeria is our homeland and Arabic is our language." After independence, they set about reversing colonial policy and making Arabic rather than French the language of government and culture. This transition was, however, slow and uneven, since very few Algerians had received any formal education in Arabic.[19] Yet if French was never fully eliminated as a language of culture and business, it was often deployed as a political lever. In the 1980s, a time of growing disenchantment with government authoritarianism and corruption, the FLN regime doubled down on its official policy of Arabicization in an effort to shore up its legitimacy. In these years, the Arabic expression "حزب فرانس" (*hizb frança* or "the party of France") was used to suggest that anyone who used French was subject to foreign influence.[20] Over time, *Hizb frança* became a free-floating detraction that could be deployed from various quarters against perceived political enemies.

In the immediate aftermath of independence, Arabicization was celebrated as an important decolonial ideal. Several of Algeria's most accomplished writers valiantly attempted to make the transition from French, the language in which they had been educated, to Arabic and in some cases opted to abandon writing altogether rather than authoring books in the colonizer's tongue.[21] Yet disenchantment with official nationalism has gradually changed perceptions of French, which has been reclaimed not only in literature but also in popular music as a potential medium of dissent and as a valuable component of Algeria's cultural pluralism. A similar set of forces has prompted a backlash against Modern Standard Arabic, strongly associated with the state and with figures of Islamic religious authority, and in favor of local Maghrebi Arabic. The journalist and novelist Kamel Daoud, one of Algeria's leading intellectual provocateurs, has gone so far as to suggest that *fusha* is as foreign to Algeria as French and that its adoption as the national language is a mark of self-hatred. Paraphrasing Frantz Fanon, Daoud (who publishes in French) evoked a destructive dichotomy of "Langue algérienne, masques arabes" (Algerian language, Arab(ic) Masks).[22]

From the standpoint of calls for language rights, the most sustained struggle has involved the relationship between Arabic and Tamazight. These tensions crystallized during the Berber Spring of 1980, when the cancellation of a lecture by a leading scholar of Amazigh culture provoked weeks of demonstrations and school strikes. Two decades later the Black Spring of 2001 saw even more violent clashes over language, culture, and policing. In the wake of this flare-up, the government agreed to officially recognize Tamazight, which was enshrined in 2002 as a national language by a constitutional amendment and elevated in 2016 to the status of an official language on the same symbolic footing as Arabic.[23] Though there is no likelihood that Tamazight will one day occupy the same position as Arabic, the teaching of Berber languages in secondary and higher education has expanded and improved in quality, and road signs in the Tifnagh alphabet have become common in Kabylia.

To recount this story as a case of linguistic oppression that has been redressed by the constitutional recognition of rights would, however, be to omit some key dimensions. The campaign *for* Amazigh linguistic and cultural rights has frequently been interwoven with discourses directed *against* not only the Algerian state but also, to some extent, the Arabic language.[24] The objective of some Amazigh activists—notably, the supporters of the Mouvement pour l'autodétermination de la Kabylie, or MAK—is indeed not just language equality but also autonomy or even independence for the region. A second important consideration is the transnational basis of Amazigh activism, which the large Kabyle diaspora in France has helped to frame and fund. Though it would be unfair to see this French-Algerian transnationalism as a simple continuation of colonial dynamics, it has undoubtedly shaped the depiction of the Amazigh and Kabyle movements as cosmopolitan and secular and the countervailing depiction of the Algerian state, and to some extent the Arabic language, as provincial and Islamic.[25]

While it could perhaps be said that the campaign for Amazigh language rights was ultimately successful, it also reinforced divisions between so-called Arabs and Berbers that were inherited from colonial ideology, and its actual impact on linguistic practice remains somewhat limited. It is also worth noting the deeply ironic position occupied by French in this contest for linguistic recognition. French is not mentioned at all in the Algerian Constitution, even though this document has always been promulgated in French as well as Arabic, a linguistic practice that attests to the fact that despite the official rhetoric of decolonization, it remains an essential medium of administration and public culture.[26]

The perception of linguistic practices as expressions of underlying ethnic and cultural identities reflects a broader tendency toward what can be described as the culturalization of politics in Algeria. As Walid Benkhaled and Natalya Vince have observed, even before independence, when prominent thinkers such as Frantz Fanon set about defining a new cultural identity for Algeria, the quest was framed in the language of personal and collective identity.[27] For these scholars, the perennial focus on the Algerian personality (*shaksiyya/haouiya*) and the question "Who are we?" has too often usurped the place of the question "Who do we want to be?"

and its translation into institutions and policies. Citing the historian Malika Rahal, Benkhaled and Vince argue that basic political questions have been obscured by the recurrent sorting of Algerians into three competing identity groups: nationalists, who identify with the foundational role of the FLN and its Arab and socialist rhetoric; pluralists, who embrace a cosmopolitan vision of Algeria that includes the legacy of French; and Islamists, who oppose both the state and the Francophones and who aspire to a theocratic polity (in this schema, Amazigh activists, or Berberists, historically associated with France, somewhat ironically fall into the pluralist camp).[28] Though these types fail to offer an accurate picture of Algerians' cultural and political perspectives, different versions of these categories have often served as surrogates for social and political analysis, helping to catalyze and entrench conflict. Benkhaled and Vince's goal in highlighting the overemphasis on identity and cultural politics isn't to suggest that Tamazight shouldn't enjoy official status or that education shouldn't be provided primarily in Arabic. The takeaway with respect to language politics is rather that campaigns for the rights of Amazigh speakers or on behalf of Arabic are embedded in social, political, and economic dynamics that, until now, these demands have tended to obscure. The hirak marked an important departure by centering these political and economic issues while treating cultural diversity less as a site of conflict than as a wellspring of collective pride.

ACTIVISM AND MULTILINGUALITY IN THE HIRAK

The hirak was launched in February 2019 following the announcement that President Abdelaziz Bouteflika planned to seek a fifth term in office. In the early years of his presidency, Bouteflika enjoyed considerable popular support as the man who brokered an end to the decade-long struggle known variously as the Algerian Civil War, *décennie noire* (Black Decade), or *snin el-irhab* (years of terrorism), during which the state battled and ultimately defeated an array of Islamist militias.[29] This murky conflict, which claimed as many as 150,000 lives, made it possible for the regime to fend off a democratic challenge that had taken shape in 1988, when mass protests brought an end to the one-party system that had been in place since independence. However, in later years Bouteflika's political image became increasingly tarnished. In 2013, he suffered a debilitating stroke that left him virtually paralyzed and unable to speak. Rarely appearing in public, he came to be known as the *momie* (the mummy) or the *poupiya* (*la poupée* or "the doll or puppet"). Algerians were left to wonder who was really in charge in the already opaque leadership structure often designated as *le pouvoir*. The announcement of a fifth term was at first greeted with outraged demands for Bouteflika's resignation. But as the protest movement gained momentum, demonstrators began to call for extensive democratic reforms and an end to the army's influence over politics. The name conferred on the protests—*Al-hirak* (الحراك), which means simply "the movement"— was significant in its avoidance of any reference to the political parties formed after the opening of the party system in 1988. It is also a term that accommodates a spectrum of opinion, making room for coalitional politics. It conveys the idea that change is an open-ended process, not the fulfillment of a single goal, and alludes to the specific form that the protests have taken: i.e., regular weekly marches through the streets of Algiers and other cities.

The hirak achieved a first major success in March 2019, when Bouteflika, abandoned by his long-time ally General Ahmed Gaïd Sālaḥ, the army's chief of staff, was forced to step down. Sālaḥ ordered the arrest of other leading members of the ruling *aissaba* (عصابة or "gang") on charges of corruption and conspiring against the state, claiming that these purges cleared the way for a free presidential election. The protesters, however, saw this shake-up as just another chapter in a long history of in-fighting among the country's political and military "clans" and continued to demand more far-reaching changes. Though a presidential election was held in December 2019, the turnout was extremely low. Rather than accepting its outcome, the protesters called for the creation of a constituent assembly that would completely overhaul Algeria's political institutions. A few days after presiding over the presidential election, Gaïd Sālaḥ died suddenly of a heart attack, becoming a vivid symbol of a regime that was as gerontocratic as it was autocratic.[30] In a further confirmation of this decline, the newly installed president, Abdelmadjid Tebboune, almost immediately contracted Covid-19 and spent the next several months convalescing in a German hospital. The global pandemic, however, also represented a major setback for the hirak, since the weekly marches had to be suspended for several months. Its reprise in March 2021 was met by a government crackdown: several prominent militants and journalists were arrested, and a new requirement for official permits was announced. The government also redoubled its efforts to foment division within the movement. Within the ranks of the protesters, the questions of how to sustain the revolutionary momentum and when and how to make the transition from opposition movement to political program now loom very large.

The hirak's successes were in large part due to its achievement in channeling widespread anger and frustration into a collective sense of opposition. A crucial factor in sustaining this energy and unity was the array of creative and humorous slogans, memes, and songs in various languages that helped to crystallize the movement's spirit while also showing that unity can be reconciled with diversity. Posters, memes, and other insider jokes gesture to a shared lifeworld, referencing the multilingualism of a society in which people routinely navigate between *fusha* and *darija*, Tamazight and French.[31] The catchphrases and memes of the hirak in fact redirected old language conflicts and competitions toward a new set of goals.

Consider, for example, the slogan that perhaps most powerfully captured the spirit of the protest: *Yetnahaw gaâ!* (يتنحاو قاع), which means "They must all go!" First spoken by a young resident of Algiers named Sofiane Bakir Turki during a television interview with Sky News Arabia, these words subsequently acquired a hashtag and came to be featured in songs and on buttons and T-shirts.[32] This happened not just because they voiced a widely shared view that all those who have held power, and not just Bouteflika and his closest allies, should step down but also because Turki dismissed the Sky News reporter's request that he speak in Modern Standard Arabic, stating that he didn't know *fusha* and would therefore express himself in *darija*. The point of this brush-off, however, probably wasn't to make an ideological statement against Modern Standard Arabic but rather to signal suspicion of a foreign media company whose relationship to the state is subject to question. In the background of this exchange are changes to the Algerian media landscape made in response to the unrest sweeping the region during the Arab Spring of 2011. The government made cosmetic gestures toward opening up the state-controlled television sector, but the channels that were added were owned by foreign companies based in the Persian Gulf. Sky News Arabia, for example, is an Abu Dhabi–based rival of Al-Jazeera. In Turki's response to the reporter, we can thus read irritation with the promotion of *fusha* mixed with suspicion of the political allegiances of Sky News Arabia.

In the widely reproduced image that recaptures this exchange,[33] the slogan *Yetnahaw gaâ!* signifies on multiple levels. In addition to the literal demand for the departure of the entire political class, it conveys local pride that includes but is not driven by an affirming relationship to *darija*. The image also captures Turki's body language—notably, the decisive sweep of the arm by which he evokes the exit of the political leadership, indexing and celebrating a political practice that is communicative, embodied, and enlanguaged.

A different kind of linguistic encounter can be heard in the hirak's most emblematic song, Soolking's "La Liberté."[34] Soolking, who has family roots in Kabylia, sings primarily in French, but the song's melody and *darija* chorus are borrowed from a football chant, "La Casa del Mouradia," the anthem of the Algiers club Ouled al-Bahja, which anticipated the hirak's criticisms of the political system. The chant's title alludes to the presidential palace, El Mouradia, and indirectly to the globally popular Spanish TV show *La Casa de Papel*, which is about an audacious hold-up at the national mint, the implication being that Algeria's political leaders have perpetrated a decades-long heist of the country's revenues. When incorporated into a soulful French song, the neighborhood- and city-oriented politics of the football chant merge with a French history of revolution and calls for liberty. It is not by chance that the accompanying video features Soolking writing the song's lyrics in a letter to the government using a quill rather than a pen.[35]

One gauge of the disruptive potential of such multi- and translingual forms of protest was the government's effort to counter the movement by stirring up linguistic and ethnic conflicts. The claim that *la main de l'étranger* (a foreign hand—i.e., French meddling) was behind the unrest became a recurrent refrain. Following Bouteflika's departure in April 2019, the newly installed leadership tried to use the relationship between Arabic and French as a political lever. The minister of higher education Tayeb Bouzid ordered universities to use only Arabic and English in correspondence and official documents as a first step to finally replacing French with English in the sphere of education. He justified this directive with the claim that English is more useful for conducting scientific research and connecting to international networks.[36] Hirak protesters, however, responded to government attacks on the French language with skepticism. A message expressed on many street signs in French was that if there's a *main de l'étranger*, it's guiding the government, not the people. In a cartoon by Ali Dilem (one of Algeria's leading caricaturists), President Tebboune denounced international solidarity with the detained journalist Khaled Drareni as further evidence of the *main de l'étranger*.[37]

Though the protesters have made it perfectly clear that they don't want French intervention, relations between Algerians and French citizens of Algerian descent became warmer than they had previously been.[38] As noted earlier, Francophone Algerian writers and intellectuals had in the past tended to approach the question of language apologetically, characterizing the French language as a *butin de guerre* (war booty) wrested from the colonizer. These kinds of justifications were strikingly absent from the hirak marches, in which French was used widely, often in combination with *fusha* and *darija*. Protesters indeed essentially rejected the equation of French with France, along with government insinuations about the *main de l'étranger*.

The regime also sought to reopen old questions about the loyalties of Berbers, going so far as to spread the rumor that the hirak has been infiltrated by the MAK. These tactics harken back to the Black Spring of 2001, when the regime claimed that protesters in Kabylia were being manipulated by a foreign hand while the local police, who were aligned with the government, thanked *les Algérois*—i.e., people from the capital—for saving them from a foreign invasion![39] In June 2019, following the death of an Amazigh rights activist and hunger striker while in custody, Gaïd Sālaḥ banned the Amazigh flag from street protests, where it had been well represented.[40] This prohibition may have reflected genuine government sensitivity to displays of Berber identity, but it was certainly also calculated to remind the protestors of their different interests. The bait was, however, not taken. Instead, at the following Friday march, large numbers of protesters waived the Amazigh flag in defiance. As Muriam Haleh Davis, Hiyem Cheurfi, and Thomas Serres explain, the marchers in fact dispelled the idea of an Arab-Berber divide by incorporating the idea that Kabyles and Arabs are brothers into a street chant. This chant, *Jīsh sh'ab . . . khawa* (the Army, the People are brothers, brothers), began its life as a way of discouraging repression of the demonstrations by the armed forces.[41] It was later modified to communicate the idea that Gaïd Sālaḥ was not a brother but *ma' lkhawana* (among/with the traitors). After the order to seize the Amazigh flag was given, the chant evolved again to become *Qbāyel, 'rab .. Khawa, Khawa w l'Gaïd Sālaḥ ma' l'Khawana* (Kabyles, Arabs are brothers, brothers, but Gaïd Sālah is with the traitors). Signs that communicated the will to build a just Algeria in three different languages and scripts—Tamazight, written in the Tifnagh alphabet; Arabic; and French—were not uncommon.[42]

REFRAMING LINGUISTIC JUSTICE

The hirak's Friday marches, sometimes designated by the French coinage *vendredires* (Friday speak-outs), enacted not only a right to speak but also what Henri Lefebvre called a "droit de la ville" (right to the city): i.e., the right to public spaces that are not subjected to repressive policing and surveillance or coopted by private interests.[43] In this regard, the hirak built not only on the strategies of the Occupy movement and the Arab Spring but also on previous grassroots political and cultural activism in Algeria, including initiatives with a strong spatial orientation. The establishment of film and street-arts festivals, literary cafés, and new publishing houses—and, by extension, the circulation of new literary and cinematic images of Algerian society—have slowly nurtured a new relationship to the built and natural environment, helping to establish the conditions for a street-level citizen movement. The scale, duration, and civility of the protests took observers in and beyond Algeria by surprise. This is largely because when uprisings broke out in other North African and Middle Eastern nations in 2011 and 2012, Algeria remained relatively quiet, and commentators speculated that since calls for democratic reforms in 1988–1991 had been the prelude to a decade of horrific violence, Algerians had grown wary of political activism. Yet this analysis reflects a simplified and teleological understanding of the Arab Spring that underestimates long-standing dissent in the region and ignores the variety of channels through which opposition has been expressed. In reality, the years since 2012 have seen a steady rise in citizen action in Algeria, particularly in the social and cultural spheres.

The association of substantive political change and a new relationship to space is exemplified by Raja Meziane's viral rap, "Allô le système."[44] In this popular song, Meziane denounces government corruption and its impact on the Algerian economy and the prospects of young people and, in the anthemic chorus, calls for "a people's democracy, not a monarchy." The accompanying video depicts Meziane descending into a subway tunnel and trying to use an old pay phone to call a *système* that won't listen to the people. This scene is intercut with footage of the hirak showing protesters occupying the city streets, much of it captured on cell phones. The video in fact unfolds as a series of contrasts: people are no longer underground but out occupying the streets, where new telecommunications have replaced the obsolete pay phone. Knowing that "the system" doesn't hear them, they have stopped calling and are establishing other lines of communication. The medium of the song is also part of its message: Meziane sings in *darija* but channels a musical form that is globally popular with the generation that has come of age since the 1990s.

DEMOCRACY AND REPRESENTATION

As a political form, massive popular demonstrations express the unity of a people against a regime and can also reflect a commitment to popular participation in political decision-making. This was certainly the case for the hirak, which rejected the state's proposals for constitutional reforms and instead demanded the radical reinvention of Algeria's political institutions along lines to be determined by the people. This model of political agency has obvious affinities with the principles of deliberative democracy, which, in addition to according a central decision-making role to citizens, prescribe "collective deliberation conducted rationally and fairly among free and equal individuals."[45] Thus far, the hirak has shown a rather strong level of commitment to political inclusiveness. For the first time in several decades, people with different gender, religious, and linguistic identities marched side by side, accepting each other's involvement in a common project.

But the hirak also raises many of the questions that accompany theories of deliberative democracy. How can the democratic process conducted on the street translate into political institutions? Since its inception, hirak protesters have rejected measures that promise to reform the system from within. Unsatisfied by Ahmed Gaïd Sālaḥ's purge of the senior leadership, they also greeted proposals for constitutional reforms with skepticism. Following his election to the presidency, Abdelmadjid Tebboune attempted to establish his legitimacy by presiding over a revision of the constitution. Though these reforms were voted through, the extremely low voter turnout (the official estimate of 24 percent is certainly too high) reflected deep distrust of a political mechanism that had been used in the past to confer rights but not to constrain executive power.[46] The most substantial political coalition to have emerged thus far from the hirak, the Pacte de l'Alternative démocratique (Pact for a Democratic Alternative, or PAD), called in January 2020 for the annulment of Tebboune's constitutional reforms (and indeed his election), advocating instead for the creation of a new "social republic" by a constituent assembly with no membership from anyone with significant ties to the regime.[47] It's not clear, however, whether a body such as the PAD might ultimately represent the hirak or whether a constituent assembly will in the end be formed. What is clear is that for months the protestors deferred the question of representation in a political transition and instead placed a premium on the mass mobilization of citizens in weekly marches.

Political models that privilege discourse over the attribution of rights also raise other questions—notably, whether the views of a vocal majority can be prevented from silencing other voices. One of the most divisive moments experienced by the hirak occurred when a group of feminist protesters calling for full legal equality for women, which is not currently guaranteed under Algeria's Family Code, were verbally assaulted and told that it was not the right time to advocate for the rights of a specific group.[48] While it is hard to say whether this harassment was a manifestation of sexism or antifeminism or simply a misguided affirmation of the need for unity, this incident reveals the potential for the wishes of a specific group to be suppressed in the name of a greater good. If the hirak movement survives, it will have to negotiate demands of the kind formulated by protesters of the *carré féministe*, whether by establishing gender-specific rights or by insisting on the full and equal citizenship of all citizens.

And if the ruling regime were somehow dismantled as a result of popular protest, decisions would have to be made about the status of Algeria's languages and the contexts in which they can or must be used. This could potentially entail a constitutional/rights-based approach that maintains continuity with the past, or it could yield temporally limited compromises and working agreements that reflect, as Wee puts it, an understanding of languages as forms of social practice rather than as permanent, quasi-ontological categories and that align more closely with the principles of deliberative democracy.[49] The hirak certainly laid foundations for this second kind of approach by downplaying associations between languages and ethnic and cultural identities while celebrating multilingualism and linguistic hybridity. The translation of this grassroots practice into concrete policies in spheres such as education and official communication, however, remains to be theorized and implemented.

NOTES

1. Will Kymlicka, *Multicultural Citizenship: A Liberal Theory of Minority Rights* (Oxford: Oxford University Press, 1996); Charles Taylor, "The Politics of Recognition," in *Multiculturalism: Examining the Politics of Recognition*, ed. Amy Guttman (Princeton, NJ: Princeton University Press, 1994), 25–74.
2. Bo discusses the European Charter for Regional or Minority Languages (1992) and the International Declaration of Language Rights, which was prepared with support from PEN International. A further example is UNESCO's Convention on the Promotion and Protection of the Diversity of Cultural Expression (2005).
3. Michele Moody-Adams, "Towards a Philosophy of Linguistic Diversity and Rights," Columbia University, New York, filmed on May 6, 2019, YouTube video, 1:14:19, https://www.youtube.com/watch?v=VI-y9YnVaz4.
4. Michael Walzer, "Beyond Humanitarian Intervention. Human Rights in a Global Society," in *Thinking Politically: Essays in Political Theory*, ed. David Miller (New Haven, CT: Yale University Press, 2007), 151–161.
5. Kymlicka, *Multicultural Citizenship*, 36–48; William E. Connolly, *Identity/Difference: Democratic Negotiations of Political Paradox* (Ithaca, NY: Cornell University Press, 1991).
6. Lionel Wee, *Language Without Rights* (Oxford: Oxford University Press, 2011).
7. Seyla Benhabib, "The Democratic Moment and the Politics of Difference," in *Democracy and Difference: Contesting the Boundaries of the Political*, ed. Seyla Benhabib (Princeton, NJ: Princeton University Press, 1996), 3–18; John S. Dryzek, *Deliberative Democracy and Beyond: Liberals, Critics, Contestations* (New York: Oxford University Press, 2000).
8. Benhabib, "Toward a Deliberative Model of Democratic Legitimacy," 3.
9. Benhabib, "Toward a Deliberative Model of Democratic Legitimacy," 6.
10. Benjamin Barber, "Foundationalism and Democracy," in *Democracy and Difference: Contesting the Boundaries of the Political*, ed. Seyla Benhabib (Princeton, NJ: Princeton University Press, 1996), 354.
11. Ernesto Laclau and Chantal Mouffe, *Hegemony and Socialist Strategy: Towards a Radical Democratic Politics* (London: Verso, 1985).
12. Benhabib, "Toward a Deliberative Model of Democratic Legitimacy," 70.
13. See Wee, *Language Without Rights*, 18.
14. Jan Blommaert, *Discourse: A Critical Introduction* (Cambridge: Cambridge University Press, 2005), quoted in Wee, 5.
15. Muriam Haleh Davis, Hiyem Cheurfa, and Thomas Serres, "A Hirak Glossary: Terms from Algeria and Morocco," *Jadaliyya*, June 13, 2019, https://www.jadaliyya.com/Details/38734; Rafik Lebdjaoui, "Le lexique du *hirak*: la bataille des mots," in *Hirak en Algérie—L'invention d'un soulèvement*, ed. Omar Benderra, François Gèze, and Rafik Lebdjaoui (Paris: La Fabrique, 2020), 263–267.

16. Mohamed Benrabah, *Language Conflict in Algeria: From Colonialism to Post-independence* (Bristol, England: Multilingual Matters, 2013).
17. Patricia Bins Lorcin, *Imperial Identities: Stereotyping, Prejudice and Race in Colonial Algeria* (London: Tauris, 1995).
18. As Patricia Bins Lorcin observes, French praise for the Berber lifestyle didn't confer any special rights or privileges on Berbers, and Kabylia as a region suffered acute poverty as a result of the encroachments of colonial agriculture. Lorcin, *Imperial Identities*.
19. Given this knowledge gap, teachers had to be imported from Egypt and other Arabic-speaking countries. Some Algerians report negative experiences with the heavy-handed pedagogy of these educators, while others remember their foreign teachers more fondly. On the myths and realities of Arabic pedagogy in postindependence Algeria, see Erin Twohig, *Contesting the Classroom: Reimagining Education in Moroccan and Algerian Literatures* (Liverpool: Liverpool University Press, 2019).
20. In 1990, it was ruled that only Arabic should be used in state institutions and public service, establishing imprisonment as a penalty for violating this law.
21. Algeria's most emblematic writer, Kateb Yacine, gave up writing for oral theater in *darija*, Tamazight, and French. Assia Djebar turned from literature to film for the best part of a decade, and Malek Haddad, who served in the late 1960s as minister of culture, stopped producing literature.
22. Kamel Daoud, "Le manifeste de ma langue," *Chroniques régulières*, September 9, 2013, https://www.lacauselitteraire.fr/le-manifeste-de-ma-langue.
23. This second amendment was widely seen as an effort to distract government critics when the country was experiencing an economic downturn and when the political future of President Bouteflika was increasingly in doubt. For a good analysis of the political calculations and debates surrounding changes to the status of Tamazight, see Hisham Aidi, "Algeria's Berbers Cautiously Optimistic About Reforms," Al Jazeera, February 16, 2016, https://www.aljazeera.com/opinions/2016/2/16/algerias-berbers-cautiously-optimistic-about-reforms.
24. For a detailed history of Berberist movements, see Ali Guenoun, *Chronologie Du Mouvement Berbère, 1945–1990: Un Combat et Des Hommes* (Algiers: Casbah Éditions, 1999).
25. With encouragement from the MAK, Kabyle activists have made a point of eating in public during Ramadan. While their goal is ostensibly to demonstrate freedom of conscience, this gesture is also calculated to provoke a reaction, thus generating newsworthy images of courageous secularists defying Islamic orthodoxy. For an example, see "Algérie: contre l'" islamisation, "un pique-nique géant en plein ramadan," *Le Figaro International*, August 4, 2013, https://www.lefigaro.fr/international/2013/08/04/01003-20130804ARTFIG00119-algerie-contre-l-islamisation-un-pique-nique-geant-en-plein-ramadan.php.
26. On the political and ideological underpinnings of the rhetoric of decolonization in the French and Algerian contexts, see Todd Shepard, *The Invention of Decolonization: The Algerian War and the Remaking of France* (Ithaca, NY: Cornell University Press, 2006).
27. Walid Benkhaled and Natalya Vince, "Performing Algerianness: The National and Transnational Construction of Algeria's Culture Wars," in *Algeria: Nation, Culture and Transnationalism, 1988–2015*, ed. Patrick Crowley (Liverpool: Liverpool University Press, 2017), 243–269.

28. Malika Rahal, "Fused Together and Torn Apart: Stories and Violence in Contemporary Algeria," *History and Memory* 24, no. 1 (Spring/Summer 2012): 118–151.
29. The labeling of this conflict as a civil war has been questioned on the grounds that this suggests an ideological fracture within the population rather than more segmented fighting between security forces and Islamist militias.
30. Jean-Pierre Filiu, *Algérie, La Nouvelle Indépendance* (Paris: Éditions du Seuil, 2019).
31. This sense of complicity extends to signs and slogans that tap into transnational and global issues. For example, signs in French referred to the protesters as *les gilets gentils*, linking them to but also contrasting them with the disruptive French working-class movement *les gilets jaunes*, while English signs bearing the slogan "Not my President" implicitly compared Bouteflika and Tebboune to Donald Trump.
32. See the interview at https://www.youtube.com/watch?v=kYT-O4glR54&t=2s; see the images at: https://www.google.com/search?sxsrf=APwXEdezECXXM0dj6tBydhad p9H64cVp6Q:1684154030757&q=Yetnahaw+ga3!&tbm=isch.
33. See the image at: https://maghrebfacts.com/2019/11/07/yetnahaw-ga3-ils-doivent-tous-degager/.
34. Soolking, "La Liberté," filmed on March 14, 2019, YouTube video, 4:50, https://www.youtube.com/watch?v=CTAH-AqYm48.
35. Both "Casa del Mouradia" and "La Liberté" were sung or hummed by protesters throughout 2019. On Algerian football culture and the hirak, see Filiu, *Algérie*, 117–129.
36. See "Le Monde Is Angry with Algeria's New Language Policy," Echorouk (English ed.), August 27, 2019, https://www.echoroukonline.com/french-le-monde-is-angry-with-algerias-new-language-policy/; Adlène Meddi, "Algérie—Anglais contre français: la guerre des langues bientôt ravivée?," *Le Point-Afrique*, July 24, 2019, https://www.lepoint.fr/afrique/algerie-anglais-contre-francais-la-guerre-des-langues-bientot-ravivee-24-07-2019-2326512_3826.php. This was not the first time that the government had announced plans to replace French with English: the idea that English should be the first foreign language taught in schools was indeed a topic of government posturing throughout the 1990s.
37. See the cartoon at: https://information.tv5monde.com/dilem/2020-09-15.
38. In the summer of 2019, the Algerian national football team won the Coupe d'Afrique des nations for the first time since 1990, largely due to the contributions of a coach and several key players who were Franco-Algerians. Following their victory, the team signaled its solidarity with the hirak, further boosting its popularity; Filiu, *Algérie*, 127–129.
39. The regime has used social media to try to stir up ethnic conflict and division: e.g., by using the term *Zouaves* (i.e., Indigenous colonial troops) to designate Kabyles, implying that they are loyal to France.
40. Kamel Eddine Fekhar had long advocated for Amazigh cultural, linguistic, and political rights in the Algerian south.
41. Davis, Cheurfa, and Serres, "A Hirak Glossary."
42. See, for example, https://www.francetvinfo.fr/monde/afrique/societe-africaine/pourquoi-le-mouvement-citoyen-en-algerie-pourrait-pretendre-au-prixnobel-delapaix_3905235.html.
43. Henri Lefebvre, *Le Droit à la ville* (Paris: Anthropos, 1968).

44. Raja Meziane, "Allo le système," Filmed March 4, 2019, YouTube video, 3:37, https://www.youtube.com/watch?v=0-ajCGiDlrg.
45. Benhabib, "Toward a Deliberative Model of Democratic Legitimacy," 69.
46. Algeria's constitution has been amended with some frequency and in self-serving ways. It was modified in 2008 to allow Abdelaziz Bouteflika to run for a third term and then changed back in 2016 to prevent future presidents from serving more than two terms—which, of course, did not prevent Bouteflika from seeking a fifth term in 2019. Given this history, it would be surprising if Algerians showed much faith in constitutional amendments.
47. On the PAD's January 2020 platform, see Hacène Ouali, "Le Mouvement a tenu ses assises hier à Alger: le PAD tient à la transition démocratique," *El-Watan*, January 26, 2020, https://www.elwatan.com/edition/actualite/le-mouvement-a-tenu-ses-assises-hier-a-alger-le-pad-tient-a-la-transition-democratique-26-01-2020.
48. This incident was widely reported and discussed. See, for example, Mustapha Benfodil, "Vague d'indignation après l'agression du 'carré féministe,'" *El-Watan*, May 21, 2020, https://web.archive.org/web/20191216132515/https://www.elwatan.com/edition/actualite/vague-dindignation-apres-lagression-du-carre-feministe-ce-vendredi-la-democratie-se-fera-avec-les-femmes-ou-ne-se-fera-pas-31-03-2019. The Family Code of 1984 made women dependent on or subordinate to male relatives in areas such as marriage and inheritance.
49. Wee, *Language Without Rights*, 18.

WORKS CITED

Aidi, Hisham. "Algeria's Berbers Cautiously Optimistic About Reforms." Al Jazeera, February 16, 2016. https://www.aljazeera.com/opinions/2016/2/16/algerias-berbers-cautiously-optimistic-about-reforms/#:~:text=Official%20status&text=As%20the%20new%20constitution%20states,official%20language%20of%20the%20state.%E2%80%9D&text=An%20Algerian%20Academy%20of%20the,the%20president%20of%20the%20republic.%E2%80%9D.

Barber, Benjamin. "Foundationalism and Democracy." In *Democracy and Difference: Contesting the Boundaries of the Political*, ed. Seyla Benhabib, 348–360. Princeton, NJ: Princeton University Press, 1996.

Benfodil, Mustapha. "Vague d'indignation après l'agression du 'carré féministe.'" *El-Watan*, May 21, 2020. https://www.elwatan.com/edition/actualite/vague-dindignation-apres-lagression-du-carre-feministe-ce-vendredi-la-democratie-se-fera-avec-les-femmes-ou-ne-se-fera-pas-31-03-2019.

Benhabib, Seyla. "The Democratic Moment and the Politics of Difference." In *Democracy and Difference: Contesting the Boundaries of the Political*, ed. Seyla Benhabib, 3–18. Princeton, NJ: Princeton University Press, 1996.

Benkhaled, Walid, and Natalya Vince. "Performing Algerianness: The National and Transnational Construction of Algeria's Culture Wars." In *Algeria: Nation, Culture and Transnationalism, 1988–2015*, ed. Patrick Crowley, 243–269. Liverpool: Liverpool University Press, 2017.

Benrabah, Mohamed. *Language Conflict in Algeria: From Colonialism to Post-independence*. Bristol, England: Multilingual Matters, 2013.

Blommaert, Jan. *Discourse: A Critical Introduction*. Cambridge: Cambridge University Press, 2005.
Connolly, William E. *Identity/Difference: Democratic Negotiations of Political Paradox*. Ithaca, NY: Cornell University Press, 1991.
Daoud, Kamel. "Le manifeste de ma langue," *Chroniques régulières*, September 9, 2013. https://www.lacauselitteraire.fr/le-manifeste-de-ma-langue.
Davis, Muriam Haleh, Hiyem Cheurfa, and Thomas Serres. "A Hirak Glossary: Terms from Algeria and Morocco." *Jadaliyya*, June 13, 2019. https://www.jadaliyya.com/Details/38734.
Dryzek, John S. *Deliberative Democracy and Beyond: Liberals, Critics, Contestations*. New York: Oxford University Press, 2000.
Echorouk (English ed.). "Le Monde Is Angry with Algeria's New Language Policy." August 27, 2019. https://www.echoroukonline.com/french-le-monde-is-angry-with-algerias-new-language-policy/.
Le Figaro International. "Algérie: contre l'"islamisation," un pique-nique géant en plein ramadan." August 4, 2013. https://www.lefigaro.fr/international/2013/08/04/01003-20130804ARTFIG00119-algerie-contre-l-islamisation-un-pique-nique-geant-en-plein-ramadan.php.
Filiu, Jean-Pierre. *Algérie, La Nouvelle Indépendance*. Paris: Éditions du Seuil, 2019.
Guenoun, Ali. *Chronologie Du Mouvement Berbère, 1945–1990: Un Combat et Des Hommes*. Algiers: Casbah Éditions, 1999.
Kymlicka, Will. *Multicultural Citizenship: A Liberal Theory of Minority Rights*. Oxford: Oxford University Press, 1996.
Laclau, Ernesto, and Chantal Mouffe. *Hegemony and Socialist Strategy: Towards a Radical Democratic Politics*. London: Verso, 1985.
Lebdjaoui, Rafik. "Le lexique du *hirak*: la bataille des mots." In *Hirak en Algérie—L'invention d'un soulèvement*, ed. Omar Benderra, François Gèze, and Rafik Lebdjaoui, 263–267. Paris: La Fabrique, 2020.
Lefebvre, Henri. *Le Droit à la ville*. Paris: Anthropos, 1968.
Lorcin, Patricia Bins. *Imperial Identities: Stereotyping, Prejudice and Race in Colonial Algeria*. London: Tauris, 1995.
Meddi, Adlène. "Algérie—Anglais contre français: la guerre des langues bientôt ravivée?" *Le Point-Afrique*, July 24, 2019. https://www.lepoint.fr/afrique/algerie-anglais-contre-francais-la-guerre-des-langues-bientot-ravivee-24-07-2019-2326512_3826.php.
Meziane, Raja. "Allo le système." Filmed March 4, 2019. YouTube video, 3:37. https://www.youtube.com/watch?v=o-ajCGiDlrg.
Moody-Adams, Michele. "Towards a Philosophy of Linguistic Diversity and Rights." Columbia University, New York. Filmed on May 6, 2019. YouTube video, 1:14:19. https://www.youtube.com/watch?v=VI-y9YnVaz4.
Ouali, Hacène. "Le Mouvement a tenu ses assises hier à Alger: le PAD tient à la transition démocratique." *El-Watan*, January 26, 2020. https://www.elwatan.com/edition/actualite/le-mouvement-a-tenu-ses-assises-hier-a-alger-le-pad-tient-a-la-transition-democratique-26-01-2020.
Rahal, Malika. "Fused Together and Torn Apart: Stories and Violence in Contemporary Algeria." *History and Memory* 24, no. 1 (Spring/Summer 2012): 118–151.
Saward, Michael, ed. *Democratic Innovation: Deliberation, Representation and Association*. London: Routledge, 2000.

Shepard, Todd. *The Invention of Decolonization: The Algerian War and the Remaking of France*. Ithaca, NY: Cornell University Press, 2006.
Soolking. "La Liberté." Filmed on March 14, 2019. YouTube video, 4:50. https://www.youtube.com/watch?v=CTAH-AqYm48.
Taylor, Charles. "The Politics of Recognition." In *Multiculturalism: Examining the Politics of Recognition*, ed. Amy Guttman, 25–74. Princeton, NJ: Princeton University Press, 1994.
Twohig, Erin. *Contesting the Classroom: Reimagining Education in Moroccan and Algerian Literatures*. Liverpool: Liverpool University Press, 2019.
Walzer, Michael. "Beyond Humanitarian Intervention: Human Rights in a Global Society." In *Thinking Politically: Essays in Political Theory*, ed. David Miller, 151–161. New Haven, CT: Yale University Press, 2007.
Wee, Lionel. *Language Without Rights*. Oxford: Oxford University Press, 2011.

Between English and Chinese
OUYANG JIANGHE

I live in square blocks of Chinese writing,
casting my glances here and there amidst images.
They're separate but contiguous, with uncertain limbs
and a rhythm uniform as gunfire.
The dust settles: the characters are simplified.
Off tumble legs, arms, eyes.
But my language still runs, still reaches, sees.
These mysteries give birth to hunger pangs.
And there are plenty of suns and moons left
to linger over with my comrades-in-tongue.
In this vast crystal aggregate of accents and dialects,
this murky admixture of ancient and new,
my mouth is a circular ruin,
teeth plunging into space,
never hitting bone.
Such vistas, such meat: Chinese is a banquet for all.
I eat up my suns and moons, and the ancients' too, till

one evening I walk through the English corner, and see
a bunch of Chinese mobbing an American kid: it seems
they want to make their homes in English.
Alas, English has no sovereign turf in China.
It's a class, a test, a TV show,
a way of speaking, words on paper.
On paper, we behold our penciled nature.
A sketch, a life of worn erasers.
After centuries of inkwells, spectacles, typewriters,
after years of accumulated lead,
how could English be so light, folded and tucked in our corner?
Now we speak diplospeak, acronyms,
muffins, aspirin, forks and knives.
But these changes do not affect the nose, the skin:
like the toothbrush you pick up in the morning, English

汉英之间

欧阳江河

我居住在汉字的块垒里,

在这些和那些形象的顾盼之间。

它们孤立而贯穿,肢体摇晃不定,

节奏单一如连续的枪。

一片响声之后,汉字变得简单。

掉下了一些胳膊,腿,眼睛。

但语言依然在行走,伸出,以及看见。

那样一种神秘养育了饥饿。

并且,省下很多好吃的日子,

让我和同一种族的人分食,挑剔。

在本地口音中,在团结如一个晶体的方言

在古代和现代汉语的混为一谈中,

我的嘴唇像是圆形废墟,

牙齿陷入空旷

没碰到一根骨头。

如此风景,如此肉,汉语盛宴天下。

我吃完我那份日子,又吃古人的,直到

一天傍晚,我去英语角散步,看见

一群中国人围住一个美国佬,我猜他们

想迁居到英语里面。但英语在中国没有领地。

它只是一门课,一种会话方式,电视节目,

大学的一个系,考试和纸。

在纸上我感到中国人和铅笔的酷似。

轻描淡写,磨损橡皮的一生。

经历了太多的墨水,眼镜,打字机

以及铅的沉重之后,

英语已经轻松自如,卷起在中国的一角。

它使我们习惯了缩写和外交辞令,

还有西餐,刀叉,阿司匹林。

这样的变化不涉及鼻子

和皮肤,像每天早晨的牙刷

glides lightly over the teeth, whitening language.
With so much ink caked in my gums, I'd better
brush every day: this requires water, a cleaning agent, and perspective.
It gives rise to theories of taste, and countless
disparities in everyday usage.
It also requires a hand, reaching into English,
two fingers apart, a letter, a triumph,
a Nazi experiment upon the self.
A cigarette falls to the ground still burning
like history, which after all
is what happens when nations stammer through their wars
One step backward, you've got the Third Reich, Hitler.
I don't know if that madman gunned down English,
massacred Shakespeare and Keats.
But I do know that English comes in two flavors:
the aristocratic, alphabetized English of OED,
and the English of Churchill and Roosevelt, armed to the teeth.
Its metaphors, its materials its obliterating aesthetics
landed on Hiroshima and Nagasaki.
I saw piles of Chinese characters fall like corpses into Japanese—
but outside of language, we were allies with the British and Americans
I've read this history, and I'm suspicious.
I don't know which is crazier, history or me.

What's happened, this past hundred years, between Chinese and English?
Why are so many Chinese streaming into English,
trying hard as they can to blanche their own skin?
Why do they treat their language like an estranged wife,
a home in a broken mirror?
I live alone amid my stacked bricks, conversing
with paper dolls, dreaming in English, while all around me
Chinese mount the steps to English, turning
from people of images to people of sound.

Translated by Austin Woerner

英语在牙齿上走着,使汉语变白。

从前吃书吃死人,因此

我天天刷牙,这关系到水,卫生和比较。

由此产生了口感,滋味说

以及日常用语的种种差异。

还关系到一只手,它伸进英语

中指和食指分开,模拟

一个字母,一次胜利,一种

对自我的纳粹式体验。

一支烟落地,只燃到一半就熄灭了

像一段历史。历史就是苦于口吃的

战争,再往前是第三帝国,是希特勒。

我不知道这个狂人是否枪杀过英语,枪杀过

莎士比亚和济慈。

但我知道,有牛津辞典里的、贵族的英语,

也有武装到牙齿的、邱吉尔或罗斯福的英语。

它的隐喻,它的物质,它的破坏的美学

在广岛和长崎爆炸。

我看见一堆堆汉字在日语中变成尸首——

但在语言之外,中国和英美结盟。

我读过这段历史,感到极为可疑。

我不知道历史和我谁更荒谬。

一百多年了,汉英之间,究竟发生了什么?

为什么如此多的中国人移居英语,

努力成为黄种白人,而把汉语

看作离婚的前妻,看作破镜里的家园?究竟

发生了什么?我独自一人在汉语中幽居

与众多纸人对话,空想着英语。

并看着更多的中国人跻身其间

从一个象形的人变为一个拼音的人。

Chapter Seven

DIGITAL VITALITY FOR LINGUISTIC DIVERSITY

The Script Encoding Initiative

DEBORAH ANDERSON

The representation of diverse languages in the digital sphere—a central concern of global language justice—depends on their support in the Unicode® Standard (Unicode[1]). This is the international standard that underlies searching, texting on phones, sending email, posting social media messages, displaying web pages, and typing documents with a word processor. Unicode provides the critical infrastructure necessary for text to be transmitted across devices and programs in a universally legible form. Because Unicode is widely supported by computer companies around the world, text sent from a Samsung device should be accurately received on an Apple or Huawei device. Similarly, text should be able to be sent and received without error whether it was typed with Microsoft Word or other word-processing software. Unicode also makes it possible for text to be copied and pasted across documents, email, and web pages without the text being garbled.

Not all languages, however, are supported in Unicode. Some technology users cannot fully participate in the digital world because they cannot type or receive text in their languages on a computer or other device. These languages may be used in the home, the community, or a liturgical setting, or they may be studied at school or contained in literary, religious, or historical documents that are important to communities. To incorporate these languages into Unicode, the focus is necessarily on their *written* versions—specifically, the *script* used to write the languages (such as Latin or Cyrillic). The reason to focus on *script*, rather than language, is that a script can be used to write many different languages: the Latin script, for example, is used to write French, English, Swahili, Finnish, Hungarian, and Hawaiian. As a result, there are fewer scripts than there are languages in the world. The basic set of characters for French and for English are the same because they both use the Latin script.

The infrastructure necessary to represent scripts in the digital sphere extends beyond the technical; it also involves networks among language communities and persons fluent in technological, bureaucratic, and corporate lingo necessary to encode a script and ensure its accessibility. Through this convergence of fluencies, a language can be made legible across programs and devices and gain representation in the digital sphere. The fact that the voice of some language communities was not regularly being represented in standards groups' meetings (and relayed to companies implementing scripts) prompted the creation of the Script Encoding Initiative (SEI) project, which I founded in 2002 in the Department of Linguistics at the University of California, Berkeley.[2] SEI works with user communities to help shepherd proposals through the opaque character-approval process and into Unicode. SEI generally prepares proposals for new scripts based on requests that have come from the language communities themselves. It also assists with the other steps necessary to make the script and language accessible on computers and devices, such as creating fonts and keyboards.

THE SIGNIFICANCE OF SCRIPTS

The goal of Unicode is to make it possible for text typed in a language to be received on a computer, phone, or tablet with the very same characters, without question marks, boxes, or nonsense characters appearing (see figures 7.1 and 7.2). For many major languages that use a Latin-based system, typing, sending, receiving, and copying and pasting text generally work well. For example, text in Sango, a creole language written with Latin characters and used in the Central African Republic, Chad, and the Democratic Republic of the Congo, can be copied and pasted without getting garbled text (see figure 7.3).

FIGURE 7.1. Mongolian script working correctly with characters in Unicode and supported on devices and in fonts.

FIGURE 7.2. Mongolian script not working correctly. Text is being received as "tofu" (boxes) or question marks.

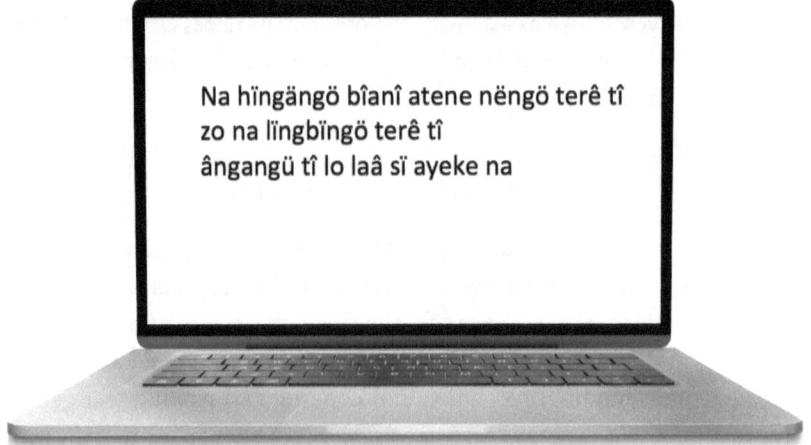

FIGURE 7.3. Unicode-based text from the Universal Declaration of Human Rights in Sango, copied and pasted without errors from the UDHR in Unicode project. UDHR in Unicode, Unicode Consortium, accessed April 15, 2023, https://www.unicode.org/udhr/d/udhr_sag.html.

DIGITAL VITALITY FOR LINGUISTIC DIVERSITY

FIGURE 7.4. What users might see on their computers or devices if they receive text written in a script not in Unicode.

Text written in less dominant scripts that are not in Unicode, in contrast, is at risk of being garbled. Such text does not transfer accurately when it is sent from one computer or device to another. Often what users see is boxes, question marks, or nonsense characters (see figure 7.4). From the perspective of linguistic diversity and global language justice, including all scripts in Unicode is important because those scripts that are missing are the ones used to write either minority or historical languages. By depriving such communities of access to their language, we restrict their access to education in their first language, which brings with it serious political, ecological, and economic consequences, as Suzanne Romaine describes in her contribution to this volume.

For many smaller minority-language communities, a script is often closely tied to the community members' identity and is a special source of self-respect and pride, even if many people cannot read it. In many cases, the script was created by a member of the community rather than being imposed by missionaries or colonial empires; as such, it often may spark pride that reflects the community's cultural and linguistic autonomy and uniqueness. For example, the Santali language of India and surrounding countries can be written in several scripts: Bangla, Devanagari, Latin, Odia, and Ol Chiki. The Latin script was used by Christian missionaries to write Santali. The language has also been written in scripts of the various states of India, such as Bangla in West Bengal and Odia in Orissa. However, only the Ol Chiki script was created specifically for Santali by a member of the community, Raghunath Murmu, and, hence, Ol Chiki represents a special symbol of identity and dignity.[3]

Getting the script into the global standard Unicode is considered an important step in raising awareness of the script and its user community within the global community and in obtaining political recognition. When the Hanifi Rohingya script was approved and published in Unicode 11.0, Tun Khin, president of the Burmese Rohingya Organization in the UK, said that "[now] our identity and culture will be preserved for the future"—a critical step, he explained, since "the government has denied our existence for many decades."[4] Having a script in Unicode also allows users to communicate on computers and devices in their preferred script.[5] After the Hanifi Rohingya script was included in Unicode, users could, for example, choose to write messages in this script instead of the Bangla or Myanmar (Burmese) script.

As an example of the importance of a script to its community, consider the Bamum script, created by Sultan Njoya and used between 1896 and the 1930s in western Cameroon. In the 2000s, the script was on the verge of extinction, though it appeared in art and display. In 2005, the Bamum Scripts and Archives Project, a joint venture of the Bamum Palace Archives and the Endangered Archives Programme, was established to digitize the hundreds of manuscripts written in Bamum, including texts covering history, traditional medicine, local cartography, personal correspondence, and folktales. According to the project codirectors, Nji Oumarou Nchare and Konrad Tuchscherer, this digitization effort helped to revitalize the script. It is now being taught in small clubs and appears in signage (see figure 7.5), but it is not the primary means of written communication.[6] Instead, French is the main language of written communication, while Bamum is the primary language of oral communication. Although most of the Bamum community cannot read the Bamum script, Konrad Tuchscherer reports that the script is regarded as "an important trademark of Bamum cultural and artistic identity . . . [and] a remarkable cultural achievement."[7]

However, the process to get such "missing" scripts into Unicode and ultimately onto computers and devices is not simple or quick. The Bamum

DIGITAL VITALITY FOR LINGUISTIC DIVERSITY

FIGURE 7.5. A sign with Bamum script from a workshop in Foumban, Cameroon, June 2018. The Bamum text was created with the Noto Sans Bamum font. Konrad Tuchscherer.

script was published in Unicode in 2009,[8] and the older, historical form of the script was published in 2010.[9] Eight years later, in 2017, a freely available font was released, thanks to the Noto font project of Google.[10] In 2019, a freely available mobile keyboard for the script became available from Gboard, a virtual keyboard app for Android and iOS.[11] Though the basic components are present for Bamum to be used in the digital world—the script is in Unicode and has a font and keyboard—the script is still not widely used on mobile phones.[12] Without access to the script—particularly on mobile phones—the script may not be adopted by the younger generation, which can threaten the vitality and future of the script and the language, as Isabelle Zaugg notes in this volume. It also means that content in the script on the web and in print publications may be limited. Bamum exemplifies the issues faced by users of scripts of modern minority languages who still cannot fully participate in the digital world and who are faced with infrastructural obstacles to the representation of scripts that extend beyond incorporation into Unicode.

There are, however, examples where incorporating scripts into Unicode has led to increased representation of languages in the digital realm and even to their revitalization. While it is not possible to predict the exact outcome of getting a script into Unicode and completing the other steps needed to make it accessible on devices, the effort can pay off. One success story is the ADLaM script, which was created by the brothers Abdoulaye and Ibrahima Barry to write the Pular language of Guinea and surrounding countries (figure 7.6). The brothers were inspired to create a script for

FIGURE 7.6. A sign with ADLaM script, alongside French (in the Latin script). Abdoulaye and Ibrahima Barry.

their language because Arabic, which was the script they had been using to write Pular, was not able to represent the sounds of the language well. They also wanted a script that could be used among all Pular speakers, who were spread across several countries, with different official languages and scripts. Both brothers have acted as strong advocates for the script, engaging with the Unicode Consortium and companies for the years it took for a script to be approved and implemented. The script is available today on Microsoft Office, iPhone, Android,[13] and the social media platforms Facebook, WhatsApp, and Telegram. ADLaM may also be able to make inroads in improving literacy, especially among women and children.[14]

Modern-day scripts are not the only ones of interest to communities today. Through the SEI, work is under way to help get Mayan hieroglyphs into Unicode. To many modern-day Mayan speakers, the Mayan hieroglyphs are an important symbol of their heritage. As part of the current work, a virtual workshop was held with Mayan speakers in Guatemala to introduce them to hieroglyphic texts and provide them with some basic tools for deciphering them, since they may eventually decide to write their own language using the hieroglyphic script rather than the Latin alphabet. Such efforts to revive older scripts can be successful. In the country of Mongolia, where Cyrillic has been employed since the early 1940s to write the Mongolian language, the government is requiring that the historical Mongolian script be used for official documents by 2025[15] and be taught in the schools.[16]

Occasionally, a new script can help to revitalize a language. The last person who spoke the Osage language from childhood died in 2012. The Osage Nation established the Osage Language Program in 2004. As part of the program, a new script was created, since the language had only ad hoc Latin-based orthographies before then. The newly created Osage script has been in use since 2006 and underwent a reform in 2014 (figure 7.7). Osage was published in Unicode in 2016 and has a font and keyboard. Thanks to ongoing efforts by the community, there are perhaps as many as a thousand users who can read the script.[17] Such efforts resonate with the work of *myaamia* communities discussed by Wesley Leonard in this volume.

The first version of Unicode, published in 1993, contained 23 scripts; Unicode 15.0, published in September 2022, contained 161,[18] so considerable progress had been made. However, today over 140 scripts are still not in Unicode.[19] When Unicode was established, it allocated space for over one million characters. Unicode 15.0 includes 149,186 characters,[20] so there

FIGURE 7.7. Osage script shown on the exterior of the Osage Nation Language Department. Michael Everson, Herman Mongrain Lookout, and Cameron Pratt, "Final Proposal to Encode the Osage Script in the UCS," Unicode Consortium, September 21, 2014, 10, https://www.unicode.org/L2/L2014/14214-n4619-osage.pdf.

is ample space for more characters and scripts. Theoretically, Unicode has the structure in place to be able to include all the various scripts of the world. Still, a number of hurdles need to be overcome in order for a script to be approved and to become usable on computers and devices, particularly for minority language users.

INCORPORATING A SCRIPT INTO UNICODE AND CHALLENGES FOR SMALLER COMMUNITIES

Increasing the representation of minority scripts in the digital sphere extends far beyond technical aspects of character encoding. It also involves building networks between minority language communities and those fluent in the technical and bureaucratic languages necessary to develop a script proposal that is legible across the digital divide. While the steps needed to get a script into Unicode and onto devices can be identified,[21] many additional hurdles exist for smaller minority-language communities, particularly when dealing with companies and standards groups.

Minority communities often experience great difficulty trying to navigate the networks necessary to draft a script proposal and have that script incorporated into Unicode, as it requires specialized language and technological

DIGITAL VITALITY FOR LINGUISTIC DIVERSITY

expertise and fluency in English, the language of the standards. Adoption of a script by companies once it is in Unicode takes years, and the process is especially difficult for minority language users, who don't often have direct contacts at tech companies. The N'Ko script used to write the Mande languages of West Africa was approved and published in Unicode in 2006 but had the expected character-joining behavior only in 2012 with Windows 8. It was supported in iOS9 in 2015[22] and in Android around 2016, a decade after it was published in Unicode. These delays are at least partially attributable to the difficulties of building connections between local language communities and specialists across the digital divide.

The process of getting a new script into Unicode and supported on devices involves several steps (see figure 7.8), each with its own complexities.

Once a community determines that a script needs to be on computers and devices and recognizes that Unicode inclusion is the first step, a Unicode proposal must be written. The proposal includes details about the script, such as its history, where it is used and for which languages, and the number of users. It must include a list of characters used in the script with proposed names and additional information, including whether the character is a number or a letter and, if it is a letter, whether it has casing (i.e., if it has upper- and lowercase forms).[23] Writing a proposal poses challenges for smaller communities. Some of these challenges may arise from collecting all the technical details of the scripts themselves, while others are due to difficulties connecting language communities with the networks necessary to produce a script proposal. Funding can help overcome such

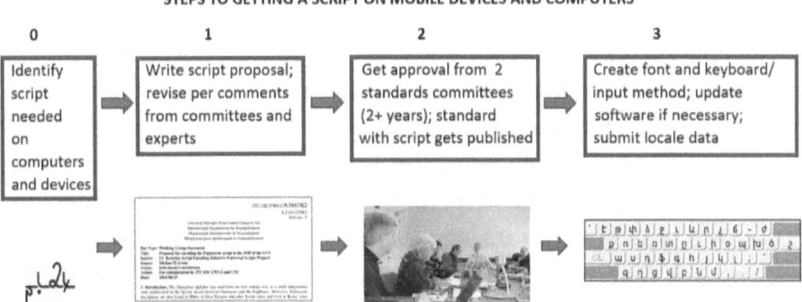

FIGURE 7.8. The steps needed to get a script into Unicode and on devices and computers.

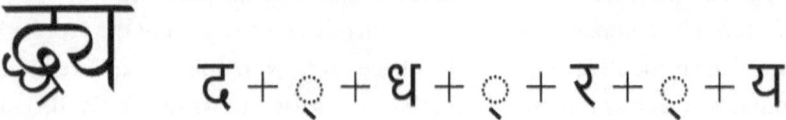

FIGURE 7.9. An example of a complex script. The Devanagari ligature on the left represents *ddhrya* and is made up of the sequence of characters shown on the right. Being able to support the correct drawing (or rendering) of the glyphs into the shape on the left requires font and software technology support. "Complex Text Layout," Wikipedia, last edited November 1, 2021, https://en.wikipedia.org/wiki/Complex_text_layout.

barriers, but finding money can be difficult for small user communities. In addition, the proposal should be written in English, a further burden for those without such fluency.

Certain scripts present additional hurdles in the encoding process. Scripts with characters that have special behavior—especially complex scripts, typical of those from India and surrounding countries (figure 7.9)—should be tested in implementations using a web browser such as on Firefox or Chrome, preferably as part of the script-writing process.[24] Such testing can ensure the script works on computers and meets user expectations. However, implementation testing puts a high burden on proposal authors, since it typically involves areas outside the expertise of many of them. As a result, additional funding may be required for testing.

In other instances, it is difficult to determine the necessary details of scripts due to a scarcity of print materials, which are needed for the proposal. The Kpelle script of Liberia and Guinea was created in the 1930s, but most written materials appear to have been destroyed during the Liberian civil wars. What remains is a handful of texts, including records of taxes (figure 7.10), debts, and a recipe book. An analysis of the script was done in the 1950s and 1960s and includes a list of characters and their phonetic values; this information provides the basis of a preliminary script proposal.[25] However, additional examples of the script are needed in order to have enough information for the script to work on computers: a recipe book and tax records typically won't show how text wraps around lines in sentences. Still, there is reportedly interest amongst the community in reviving the script.[26] Although no one uses the script today, if the script was revived, educational primers developed, and texts created, there would be adequate

DIGITAL VITALITY FOR LINGUISTIC DIVERSITY

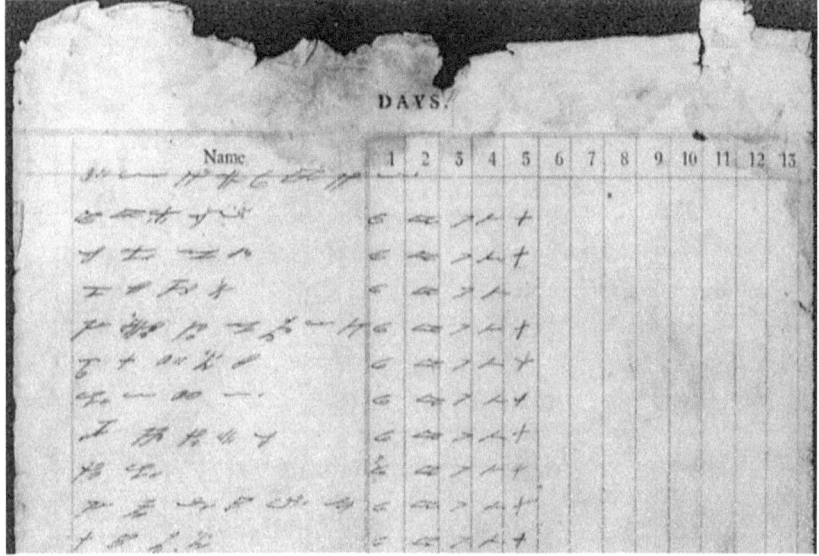

FIGURE 7.10. A Kpelle tax table. Michael Everson and Charles Riley, "Preliminary Proposal for Encoding the Kpelle Script in the SMP of the UCS," Unicode Consortium, February 23, 2010, 7, http://www.unicode.org/L2/L2010/10063-n3762-kpelle.pdf.

information for a full Unicode proposal. Funding would likely be needed to bring users and encoding experts together to create an agreed-on set of characters and to develop and publish texts.

Communication between language communities and proposal authors, navigating both geographic distance and linguistic differences, can be a further hurdle. Proposals involve consultation and involvement of members of the user community, who may be difficult to reach. Travel by the proposal author or a contact may be required, sometimes to remote geographical locations where internet connections may not be available or reliable. For example, the users of the Bété script of Côte d'Ivoire (figure 7.11) live in a small village. To get information, the Bété contact who assisted on the proposal traveled to the village to meet with users and then relayed information on the script upon return to his home elsewhere in the country. Interaction with the user community usually necessitates explaining the basics of Unicode in an easy-to-understand way, preferably in the users' native language, so translators may be needed, which may require funding.

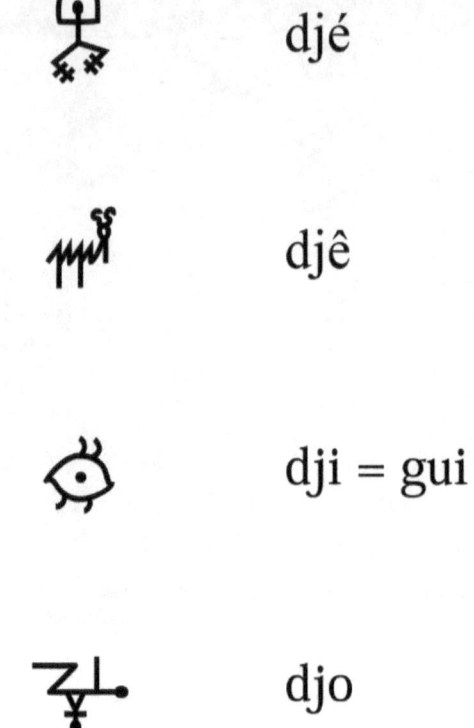

FIGURE 7.11. An example of characters in the Bété script of Côte d'Ivoire with phonetic values. Deborah Anderson, "Bété Script Working Documents," Unicode Consortium, January 10, 2019, 6, https://www.unicode.org/L2/L2019/19044-bete-script.pdf.

Finally, proposal preparation requires that not only sufficient knowledge about a script but also detailed technical information be provided in English. Such information involves familiarity with Unicode and its related technical specifications—a formidable obstacle for new proposal authors. To aid user communities whose members don't have the time or availability to learn the finer details of Unicode, a veteran Unicode proposal author can be enlisted to help write a proposal. However, seasoned proposal authors often need funding to support their work, a further burden on communities with limited resources.

The proposal process may be further complicated by disagreements among experts or users. Such was the case for Old Hungarian (figure 7.12),

DIGITAL VITALITY FOR LINGUISTIC DIVERSITY

FIGURE 7.12. A text sample of Old Hungarian. Michael Everson and André Szabolcs Szelp, "Consolidated Proposal for Encoding the Old Hungarian Script in the UCS," Unicode Consortium, October 2, 2012, 25, http://www.unicode.org/L2/L2012/12168r-n4268r-oldhungarian.pdf.

a runic script studied by academics and used today by groups of enthusiasts. The main disagreement was over the name of the script and a handful of characters. The conflict divided the Hungarian national standards body during balloting in one of the standards committees. Finally, the script was approved, but the process took seventeen years from the first draft proposal until publication. In other cases, politics has impacted the process: the Tai Tham script got caught up in a debate in the standards committees over its name, since it is used in Thailand, China, and Myanmar and is known in those countries by different names. The final agreed-on name, Tai Tham, isn't the typical name used for this script in any of the countries but was considered acceptable to all groups involved.

Once a proposal is approved and a script has been incorporated into Unicode, a number of other infrastructural components are necessary in order to ensure that the language can be widely represented in the digital sphere. A font based on Unicode code points (i.e., the numbers assigned by Unicode to the letters and symbols of a script) is needed. Using a non-Unicode-based font will affect language support on computers and digital devices because the data created with nonstandard fonts will not be easily transmitted to others; will be less stable, since it is not supported by an international standard; and may not be recoverable, since most text interchanged today is encoded with Unicode code points. In short, it may result in garbled text or a return to "tofu" (empty boxes) when this text is exchanged on devices.

The Google Noto project is presently committed to creating a free font for all the scripts in Unicode, subject to funding.[27] However, there is frequently a lag time between when a script is published in Unicode and when its font is released by Noto, which can be very frustrating for users who are anxious to use the script. The Noto fonts can be used on all platforms and are open-source under the SIL Open Font License, Version 1.1, so they can be modified.[28] The Noto Fonts project encourages users to review the glyphs and provide feedback to improve the fonts.[29] Another option is to encourage type design students to create a font as part of their studies, as happened in the master's program in typeface design at England's University of Reading[30] and the Missing Scripts project at the Atelier National de Recherche Typographique in Nancy, France.[31] If a font is for a complex script, then a font designer whose skill set is more advanced than that of a student may be necessary and again requires funding.

But even when a font is available, getting it onto a device such as a phone is not always easy. Ideally, the font should be preloaded onto the device or computer. However, users may need to lobby the device manufacturer to include the font on a device, another potential stumbling block for smaller, less politically powerful communities. Alternatively, bundling a font with an app or relying on a web page to supply the font (as a web font) is one approach, especially for deploying to older devices. However, fonts downloaded via an app typically will work only in that application. As a result, having fonts preloaded on devices is the best approach. Having at least one Unicode-based font is critical, but ideally several fonts should be available, fulfilling different uses, such as for public signage, newspaper publications, and formal and informal documents.

A keyboard or other input mechanism is also very useful, since it can speed up typing over other methods, such as inserting each character individually through the "insert symbol" option or a character picker. There is software available for users to create their own keyboards, such as Keyman[32] and Microsoft Keyboard Layout Creator.[33] Keyboards can be installed on most platforms. Google currently makes keyboards for over eight hundred languages and seventy scripts for mobile devices in its Gboard app, which works on Android phones and, to a lesser extent, on iPhones. Keyboards created with Keyman are now freely available in over two thousand languages.[34] Another option is a virtual keyboard for use on browsers.[35]

Developing the necessary digital infrastructure requires attention not only to the characteristics of a script but also to language-specific data. New scripts need to have at least one language associated with the script, with a language code from the ISO 639-3 standard.[36] While keyboards and fonts will allow users to create digital content, additional information is needed if they want to interact with their language in a manner similar to how predominant scripts and their languages work on devices and computers. Such information is called locale data and includes language-specific data, such as the names of the days of the week and the accepted time and date format. These locale data need to be submitted to the Unicode Common Locale Data Repository (CLDR),[37] a source from which tech companies and developers draw. A problem with CLDR is that the website can be difficult to navigate, making it hard for nonengineers to submit data. However, work is under way to make it easier for nonengineers to participate in data submission.[38] As of April 2023, CLDR had data on 319 languages,[39] meaning the rest of the approximately 7,000 languages are not included. For example, only fifteen Indigenous languages from the Americas are present.

Other language-specific information is needed to build spellcheckers and other tools, if required by the community. Such information includes machine-readable dictionaries and rules about spaces and punctuation, which affect line breaking and word selection. However, many minority languages may not yet be standardized, so spellcheckers may still be premature. Some languages—such as historical ones—may not need all the features provided for modern major languages, such as predictive text.

The functioning of such digital infrastructure may require updates to software, especially if the script characters have special combining behaviors, as well as support for the script in specific applications. New scripts generally require the latest operating system, so they may not work on older mobile devices. Upgrading to the latest operating system may require buying a new device—a cost that may be prohibitive for language communities with fewer financial resources.

Furthermore, many users have requested that their script and language be accessible in social media apps, such as Facebook Messenger and WhatsApp. If the script and language are not supported by these social media platforms,[40] a case may need to be made to Facebook and WhatsApp to support them. As a result, vibrant language communities may have a stronger case than less active or smaller communities.

Given the complications of ensuring the digital representation of scripts, even when a script is in Unicode, as was the case for Bamum—a language with approximately 420,000 speakers[41]—there is no assurance it will quickly be available for use on computers or devices. This is dependent on the particular obstacles encountered when developing the necessary digital infrastructure for the representation of a script—as well as the value accorded to the script both within and beyond the digital sphere.

LINGUISTIC VALUES AND DIGITAL REPRESENTATION

Adding a language and script onto computers and devices necessarily involves tech company employees developing, implementing, and maintaining the data. However, some companies question the importance of supporting all the world's languages. They may require information sufficient to indicate a market potential that justifies supporting additional languages and scripts. For most of the scripts not in Unicode, however, providing such information is often difficult for a number of reasons. As such, linguistic hierarchies—including the differential values placed on scripts—are reproduced within the digital realm, as market forces further the reach of already dominant scripts at the expense of scripts of minority language communities.

Determining whether there is a viable market to support a script depends on the number of users—as well as their degrees of literacy. Though the number of speakers of a minority language can usually be identified, the number of minority-language *script* users is hard to calculate. The number of speakers may be very small (for Medefaidrin, for example, there are about twenty adult speakers) or relatively small compared to English, Spanish, or Chinese. Chakma, for example, is spoken by 378,000 people, which still pales in comparison to 1.4 billion English speakers worldwide.[42] Minority language users often are from areas where literacy rates may be low. If this is the case, the adoption of the script will likely take time and be hard to track. (One approach taken by the creators of ADLaM script to address the literacy issue has been to make a special effort to teach the script to women and children, whose rate of literacy can be low.[43])

The return on investment for a company may also be compromised by minority language communities' restricted access to technological resources. The number of printed publications in a script not in Unicode is often low, since access to fonts for printing materials, as well as historical access to printing presses, typewriters in a minority script, etc., may be limited. A recent proposal for the Tangsa script of Lakhum Mossang, for example, states that the script has been in use for twenty-one years, but no books had been published in the script before December 2020.[44] Minority language communities often lack monetary resources, so even if their populations are large, tech companies may not see much market return by supporting their script and language needs. Understanding the importance of supporting *all* the world's languages as a fact of human existence and livelihood is needed, despite the low number of users (consumers). Certainly support from noncorporate entities would be welcome.

Despite these challenges, it is crucial to improve the representation of minority languages in the digital sphere. The market values of languages and scripts do not correspond to their cultural values. Numbers of users and their degrees of access to technology do not accurately reflect how vital a script and the language that uses it are to a community and the world. Given the growth and importance of digital presence today, if a language and its script are *not* in Unicode, it can be a death knell for the language: the younger generation will not use it, and written materials will not be easily typed, searched, and sent electronically. In addition, literary or historical works will not be preserved in a stable format. If a script is not in Unicode, then nonstandard approaches to its digital use (such as the use of a nonstandard, or "hacked," font) may be used, which makes materials difficult to search, find, and transmit to others, thus limiting what users can accomplish on digital devices in their language.

LOOKING FORWARD

Ensuring the representation of minority scripts and languages in the digital sphere is dependent not only on the persistence of language communities to get their script into Unicode but also on wider networks of support traversing the digital divide. It is critical to continue to relay the importance of digitally supporting minority scripts and languages to companies, governments, NGOs, and other entities. Support on computers and devices can create lifelines for scripts and languages that are struggling and, more importantly, for the speakers of the languages themselves. With digital support, users can communicate in email and text messages among themselves and with the outside world and not be drowned out by large, predominant languages. It also makes it possible to preserve languages and their literary and cultural contributions for posterity. Companies, governments, NGOs, and other groups should try to provide financial means to support Unicode proposal work as well as to support work on fonts, keyboards, and locale data, recognizing not only the market value of languages but also their cultural significance.

NOTES

1. *Unicode* will be used henceforth in this chapter to refer to the Unicode® Standard itself. Note that the Unicode Consortium, which oversees the development and maintenance of the Unicode® Standard, also oversees other projects.
2. Deborah Anderson, "Script Encoding Initiative," University of California, Berkeley, accessed April 15, 2023, https://linguistics.berkeley.edu/sei/index.html. The project is moving to Stanford University in late 2023.
3. See Deborah Anderson, "Ol Chiki Correspondence Summary," Unicode Consortium, February 23, 2003, http://www.unicode.org/L2/L2003/03062-olchiki-summary.pdf, and "Comments on Ol Chiki/Summary of Report from West Bengal," Unicode Consortium, December 9, 2002, https://www.unicode.org/L2/L2002/02456-ol-chiki-comment.pdf.
4. Quoted in Aamna Mohdin, "The Language of the Persecuted Minority Rohingya Will Be Digitized," *Quartz*, December 20, 2017, https://qz.com/1161582/the-language-of-myanmars-persecuted-minority-rohingya-will-be-digitized/.
5. There are, of course, languages for which no writing system has yet been developed. In general, however, when a writing system is developed, a script already in Unicode (i.e., Latin, Cyrillic, Arabic, etc.) could be used, though it may not be the preferred script.
6. Konrad Tuchscherer, email message to author, August 22, 2019.
7. Konrad Tuchscherer, "Recording, Communicating and Making Visible: A History of Writing and Systems of Graphic Symbolism in Africa," in *Inscribing Meaning: Writing and Graphic Systems in African Art*, ed. Christine Mullen Kreamer, Mary Nooter Roberts, Elizabeth Harney, and Allyson Purpura (Milan: Five Continents Editions, 2007), 49.
8. "Unicode 5.2.0," Unicode Consortium, last modified June 24, 2015, https://www.unicode.org/versions/Unicode5.2.0/.
9. "Unicode 6.0.0," Unicode Consortium, last modified September 14, 2016, https://www.unicode.org/versions/Unicode6.0.0/. (The historical additions are in the "Bamum Supplement" block.)
10. "Noto: A Typeface for the World," Google Fonts, accessed April 15, 2023, https://www.google.com/get/noto/; "Noto fonts," GitHub, accessed April 15, 2023, https://github.com/notofonts.
11. Shivam, "Gboard for Android Updated with Support for Horizontal Emoji Scrolling and 100+ New Languages," NokiaPowerUser, September 25, 2019, https://nokiapoweruser.com/gboard-for-android-updated-with-support-for-horizontal-emoji-scrolling-and-100-new-languages/.
12. Charles Riley, catalog librarian for African languages at Yale University, reports that Bamum is supported at the system level in Windows as of March 2022 and that Noto fonts have been enabled on Macs and iOS for some time. However, diacritic placement needs work. Charles Riley, "Update on Implementation Status of African Scripts," Unicode Consortium, March 3, 2022, https://www.unicode.org/L2/L2022/22073-african-script-status.pdf. Tuchscherer writes: "If a Bamum were technically instructed in [using Bamum script on phones], it would be HUGE in the Bamum Kingdom. Everyone would want it. It would then encourage literacy." He also adds that the new Bamum king, King Njoya, who was crowned in October 2021,

can read and write in the Bamum script. Konrad Tuchscherer, email message to author, August 3, 2022. In April 2023 Konrad Tuchscherer reported that the difficulty in getting Bamum on phones involves needing someone on the ground to demonstrate how to install the font and keyboard.

13. The font may, however, be removed by mobile vendors: i.e., the vendor Samsung may decide not to include ADLaM in phones that are sold in Korea, as an example.
14. Neil Patel, email message to author, January 24, 2020. Patel's company, Jamra Patel, produces an ADLaM keyboard app. Images provided to the author by Patel in August 2021 show ADLaM being taught in classrooms in Mali and Cameroon with male and female children and a female teacher.
15. "President Orders Use of Mongolian Script in Official Work," news.mn, July 8, 2010, https://news.mn/en/19924/; Unurzul.M, "Official Documents to Be Recorded in Both Scripts from 2025," Montsame, March 18, 2020, https://montsame.mn/en/read/219358.
16. The script has been taught in schools since 1987. Badamsuran B., email message to author, April 16, 2023. Note that the situation in Inner Mongolia, an autonomous region of China, differs from that in the country of Mongolia, since in Inner Mongolia the script has been in continuous use.
17. Mark Pearson, email message to author, January 28, 2020.
18. "Supported Scripts," Unicode Consortium, accessed April 15, 2023, https://www.unicode.org/standard/supported.html.
19. Deborah Anderson, "Alphabetical List of Scripts Not Yet Encoded," Script Encoding Initiative, University of California, Berkeley, last updated March 2023, http://linguistics.berkeley.edu/sei/scripts-not-encoded.html.
20. "Unicode Statistics," Unicode Consortium, last modified February 11, 2022, https://www.unicode.org/versions/stats/.
21. A project to create a guide for Indigenous language users has been initiated by Translation Commons for UNESCO's International Year of Indigenous Languages, 2019: "Indigenous Languages: Zero to Digital," December 2019, https://drive.google.com/file/d/1JB6nXz6kpqcXfKaZR3VEYvrC9M2x7qOj/view?usp=sharing.
22. Ned Holbrook (typographic engineer at Apple), email message to author, August 9, 2022.
23. See "Submitting Character Proposals," Unicode Consortium, last modified April 1, 2016, https://www.unicode.org/pending/proposals.html.
24. A complex script is one that has combining characters (as in figure 7.9), bidirectional text (such as Arabic or Hebrew), has characters that change shape based on their location or surrounding characters, or requires characters to be displayed in a different order from that in which the characters are stored.
25. Michael Everson and Charles Riley, "Preliminary Proposal for Encoding the Kpelle Script in the SMP of the UCS," Unicode Consortium, February 23, 2010, http://www.unicode.org/L2/L2010/10063-n3762-kpelle.pdf.
26. As reported by Maria Konoshenko in an email message to the author, August 26, 2021. She says there is some interest among those few Guineans who know about the script, but most are not aware of it.
27. The most up-to-date Noto font website is https://github.com/notofonts. Another website with links to guidelines and installation instructions is https://fonts.google.com/noto.

28. Nicolas Spalinger and Victor Gaultney, "SIL Open Font License (OFL)," SIL International, February 26, 2007, http://scripts.sil.org/OFL.
29. "Noto Dashboard: Report an issue in a Noto font," Google Fonts, accessed April 15, 2023, https://notofonts.github.io/reporter.html.
30. The home page of the Department of Typography and Graphic Communication at the University of Reading is located at http://www.reading.ac.uk/typography/.
31. The home page of the Atelier National de Recherche Typographique is located at https://anrt-nancy.fr/fr/presentation/.
32. The home page of Keyman is located at https://keyman.com/.
33. The Microsoft Download Center page with Microsoft Keyboard Layout Creator 1.4 is located at https://www.microsoft.com/en-us/download/details.aspx?id=102134. MKLC 1.4 is recommended only for simple orthographies, such as alphabets. For complex scripts, Keyman is recommended.
34. This figure is cited on the Keyman home page, https://keyman.com/, which also provides access to the keyboards.
35. For example, Google Input Tools (https://www.google.com/inputtools/) is a Chrome extension implementing over 130 virtual keyboards for the Chrome browser on computers (but not mobile devices).
36. "ISO 639 Code Tables," SIL International, accessed April 15, 2023, https://iso639-3.sil.org/code_tables/639/data.
37. "Unicode CLDR Project," Unicode CDLR, accessed April 15, 2023, http://cldr.unicode.org/.
38. "Information Hub for Linguists," Unicode CLDR, accessed April 15, 2023, http://cldr.unicode.org/translation.
39. "CLDR Charts: Locale Coverage," Unicode Consortium, last modified April 11, 2023, https://www.unicode.org/cldr/charts/43/supplemental/locale_coverage.html. Languages written in more than one script are counted only once in the 319 figure. For basic information on coverage levels, see the Unicode CLDR Project page located at http://cldr.unicode.org/index/survey-tool/coverage.
40. Both social media platforms get fonts and keyboards from preloaded selections on a device, or if the platform allows it, a font can be downloaded from an app.
41. David M. Eberhard, Gary F. Simons, and Charles D. Fennig, eds., *Ethnologue: Languages of the World*, 26th ed. (Dallas: SIL International, 2023), "Bamun," https://www.ethnologue.com/language/bax (subscription required).
42. Eberhard et al., *Ethnologue*, "Chakma," https://www.ethnologue.com/language/ccp (subscription required), and "English," https://www.ethnologue.com/language/eng (subscription required).
43. Neil Patel, email message to author, January 24, 2020.
44. Stephen Morey, "Proposal to Add the Tangsa Script in the SMP of the UCS," Unicode Consortium, January 29, 2021, http://www.unicode.org/L2/L2021/21027r-tangsa.pdf.

WORKS CITED

Anderson, Deborah. "Alphabetical List of Scripts Not Yet Encoded." Script Encoding Initiative, University of California, Berkeley. Last updated March 2023. http://linguistics.berkeley.edu/sei/scripts-not-encoded.html.

Anderson, Deborah. "Bété Script Working Documents." Unicode Consortium, January 10, 2019. https://www.unicode.org/L2/L2019/19044-bete-script.pdf.

Anderson, Deborah. "Comments on Ol Chiki/Summary of Report from West Bengal." Unicode Consortium, December 9, 2002. https://www.unicode.org/L2/L2002/02456-ol-chiki-comment.pdf.

Anderson, Deborah. "Ol Chiki Correspondence Summary." Unicode Consortium, February 23, 2003. http://www.unicode.org/L2/L2003/03062-olchiki-summary.pdf.

Anderson, Deborah. "Script Encoding Initiative." University of California, Berkeley. Accessed April 15, 2023. http://linguistics.berkeley.edu/sei/index.html.

Eberhard, David M., Gary F. Simons, and Charles D. Fennig, eds. *Ethnologue: Languages of the World*. 26th ed. Dallas: SIL International, 2023. See "Bamun," https://www.ethnologue.com/language/bax (subscription required); "Chakma," https://www.ethnologue.com/language/ccp (subscription required); and "English," https://www.ethnologue.com/language/eng (subscription required).

Everson, Michael, Herman Mongrain Lookout, and Cameron Pratt. "Final Proposal to Encode the Osage Script in the UCS." Unicode Consortium, September 21, 2014. https://www.unicode.org/L2/L2014/14214-n4619-osage.pdf.

Everson, Michael, and Charles Riley. "Preliminary Proposal for Encoding the Kpelle Script in the SMP of the UCS." Unicode Consortium, February 23, 2010. http://www.unicode.org/L2/L2010/10063-n3762-kpelle.pdf.

Everson, Michael, and André Szabolcs Szelp. "Consolidated Proposal for Encoding the Old Hungarian Script in the UCS." Unicode Consortium, October 2, 2012. http://www.unicode.org/L2/L2012/12168r-n4268r-oldhungarian.pdf.

GitHub. "Noto Fonts." Accessed April 15, 2023. https://github.com/notofonts.

Google Fonts. "Noto Dashboard: Report an issue in a Noto font." Accessed April 15, 2023. https://notofonts.github.io/reporter.html.

Google Fonts. "Noto: A Typeface for the World." Accessed April 15, 2023. https://fonts.google.com/noto.

Mohdin, Aamna. "The Language of the Persecuted Minority Rohingya Will Be Digitized." *Quartz*, December 20, 2017. https://qz.com/1161582/the-language-of-myanmars-persecuted-minority-rohingya-will-be-digitized/.

Morey, Stephen. "Proposal to Add the Tangsa Script in the SMP of the UCS." Unicode Consortium, January 29, 2021. http://www.unicode.org/L2/L2021/21027r-tangsa.pdf.

News.mn. "President Orders Use of Mongolian Script in Official Work." July 8, 2010. https://news.mn/en/19924/.

Riley, Charles. "Update on Implementation Status of African Scripts." Unicode Consortium, March 3, 2022. https://www.unicode.org/L2/L2022/22073-african-script-status.pdf.

Shivam. "Gboard for Android Updated with Support for Horizontal Emoji Scrolling and 100+ New Languages." NokiaPowerUser, September 25, 2019. https://nokiapoweruser.com/gboard-for-android-updated-with-support-for-horizontal-emoji-scrolling-and-100-new-languages/.

SIL International. "ISO 639 Code Tables." Accessed April 15, 2023. https://iso639-3.sil.org/code_tables/639/data.

Spalinger, Nicolas, and Victor Gaultney. "SIL Open Font License (OFL)." SIL International, February 26, 2007. http://scripts.sil.org/OFL.

Translation Commons. "Indigenous Languages: Zero to Digital." December 2019. https://drive.google.com/file/d/1JB6nXz6kpqcXfKaZR3VEYvrC9M2x7qOj/view?usp=sharing.

Tuchscherer, Konrad. "Recording, Communicating and Making Visible: A History of Writing and Systems of Graphic Symbolism in Africa." In *Inscribing Meaning: Writing and Graphic Systems in African Art*, ed. Christine Mullen Kreamer, Mary Nooter Roberts, Elizabeth Harney, and Allyson Purpura, 37–53. Milan: Five Continents Editions, 2007.

UDHR in Unicode Project. "Universal Declaration of Human Rights—Sango." Unicode Consortium. Accessed April 15, 2023. www.unicode.org/udhr/d/udhr_sag.html.

Unicode CLDR. "Information Hub for Linguists." Accessed April 15, 2023. http://cldr.unicode.org/translation.

Unicode CLDR. "Unicode CLDR Project." Accessed April 15, 2023. http://cldr.unicode.org/.

Unicode Consortium. "CLDR Charts: Locale Coverage." Last modified April 11, 2023. https://www.unicode.org/cldr/charts/43/supplemental/locale_coverage.html.

Unicode CLDR. "Submitting Character Proposals." Last modified April 1, 2016. https://www.unicode.org/pending/proposals.html.

Unicode CLDR. "Supported Scripts." Accessed April 15, 2023. https://www.unicode.org/standard/supported.html.

Unicode CLDR. "Unicode 5.2.0." Last modified June 24, 2015. https://www.unicode.org/versions/Unicode5.2.0/.

Unicode CLDR. "Unicode 6.0.0." Last modified September 14, 2016. https://www.unicode.org/versions/Unicode6.0.0/.

Unicode CLDR. "Unicode 15.0.0." Last modified September 13, 2022. https://www.unicode.org/versions/Unicode15.0.0/

Unicode CLDR. "Unicode Statistics." Last modified February 11, 2022. https://www.unicode.org/versions/stats/.

Unurzul, M. "Official Documents to Be Recorded in Both Scripts from 2025." *Montsame*, March 18, 2020. https://montsame.mn/en/read/219358.

Wikipedia. "Complex Text Layout" entry. Last edited November 1, 2021. https://en.wikipedia.org/wiki/Complex_text_layout.

Square Word Calligraphy

XU BING

The Square Word Calligraphy (SWC) is an alphabetic script designed by Xu Bing to write non-linear words in English. An English text can be written using the radicals that make up Chinese characters. This quote from Henry Wadsworth Longfellow's poem "Elegiac Verse"—to be read vertically from left to right—is not a Chinese translation of the English verse but the original English text written in SWC.

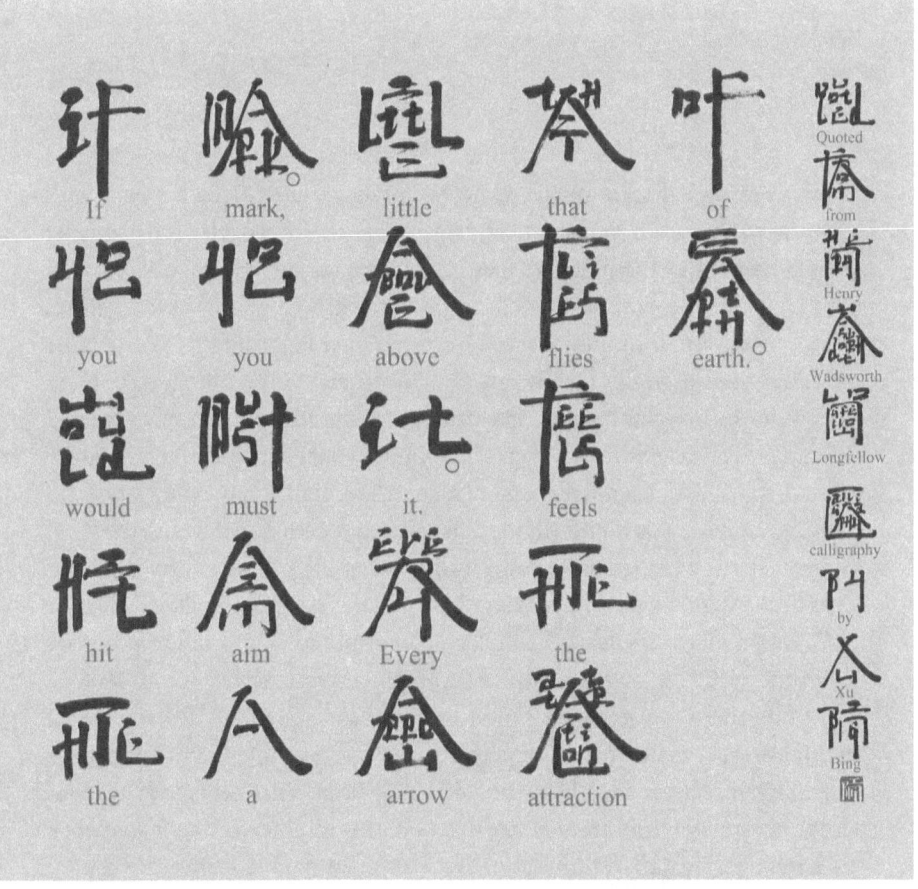

Xu Bing, *Square Word Calligraphy*. Quotation from Henry Wadsworth Longfellow's "Elegiac Verse" in calligraphy, 2016, 177–192 cm.

Chapter Eight

LANGUAGE JUSTICE IN THE DIGITAL SPHERE

ISABELLE A. ZAUGG

How does digital technology relate to language justice? In a world with approximately seven thousand languages, digital technologies fully support only a handful of them. Languages of former and current imperial powers and high-income nations are well supported, while languages of Indigenous and minoritized communities and even national languages of low-income countries are digitally disadvantaged. In other words, the global power dynamics of marginalization, exclusion, and oppression that have created hierarchies among human beings and their languages are fully present in the digital sphere. As such, language justice in the digital sphere goes beyond closing the linguistic digital divide; it is rather a redefining of whose lives and languages truly matter online and in the cascading offline effects triggered within the digital sphere. Realizing this vision will require multistakeholder efforts that follow the lead of language communities. This chapter proposes a vision for digital language justice through a three-pronged approach.

While there is a growing canon that elucidates ways that digital technologies exacerbate social inequalities, the specific interplay of language diversity has been mostly neglected. It is important to rectify this, as language-power hierarchies are part of the intersectional framework of privileges and discrimination that has been mapped onto the digital sphere. Because digital technologies mediate communication, their ability to support, exchange, or exclude particular languages and scripts makes them a particularly important site for language justice. I draw here on my extended research on the Ethiopic script and the languages that use it, with a particular focus on Ethiopia's national language Amharic,[1] to address this gap by providing a window into global trends affecting digitally disadvantaged languages as a class.

Why should gaps in digital support for languages, as well as for many written scripts, concern us? Linguists posit that youth play an outsize role in determining whether or not a language will be transmitted to the next generation. As youth build language skills in the digital sphere, they also develop opinions regarding which languages are "cool" and "practical" based on which languages their peers are using (or are able to use) in this context. If their mother tongue is not digitally supported, this sends a clear message of exclusion and low status and pushes youth to use a more dominant language or script that is digitally supported while online. Language choices made online can also impact the language youth feel most comfortable using offline. If this pattern persists, youth can lose fluency in their mother tongue and/or literacy in their native script, reducing the likelihood that they will pass these on to the next generation. In short, lack of digital support for a language can suppress its use online, in turn contributing to its real-world extinction.[2]

Language extinction brings loss of identity, culture, intergenerational cohesion, and embedded wisdom needed to address both personal and global challenges.[3] As Suzanne Romaine highlights in her contribution to this volume, linguistic diversity's linkage to ecological diversity indicates that its decline may lead to negative impacts on our world's ecosystem. Shifts in language decline are taking place rapidly; scholars estimate between 50 and 90 percent of languages risk extinction this century.[4] In the digital sphere, at least 95 percent of languages are digitally disadvantaged,[5] with gaps in digital support likely contributing to declines in the use of some languages and even potentially to language extinction. So does language justice in the digital sphere equate to digital support for all languages?

In many cases, yes. Many language advocates and speaker communities are working to expand digital supports for their language. Other communities do not want linguistic digital support or do not want corporate platforms to engage with their language. This hints at the complexity of inclusion as a path toward language justice in the digital sphere. It must not only take into account each speaker community's unique (and nonuniform) aspirations but also confront the fact that digital inclusion is a double-edged sword. On the one hand, digital inclusion presents promise to many language communities that have been historically marginalized, excluded, or oppressed. Yet, on the other, digital tools designed to support a language can also be used to surveil and coerce its speaker communities. This reality is particularly fraught for communities facing displacement, state-sanctioned violence, criminalization, and ongoing infringements on sovereignty. Language justice therefore includes advocating for and developing new digital supports, as well as economic and governance structures in the digital sphere, that not only foster the use of disadvantaged languages (to the degree desired) but also further their speakers' broader interests.

I propose a three-pronged approach to language justice in the digital sphere: (1) equitable access to digital tools in one's primary language, which requires that digital supports be developed for all languages and scripts where there is community desire; (2) maintenance of languages' script(s), orthography, and diction within digital tools,[6] lest digital support sap them of the integrity and intricate knowledge they contain; and (3) justice for speakers who may face harmful digital surveillance or undermoderation of language content, once their language gains a foothold in the digital sphere. Across these domains, the stakes are high for multistakeholder action regarding language justice in the digital sphere.

Note that I propose a *justice* rather than a *rights* approach to advocacy, for two reasons. First, as L. Maria Bo explicates in her contribution to this volume, a rights-based approach to language is limited by its reliance on a culturally specific vision of *equality* that resists other perspectives on how we can respectfully live in harmony despite our diversity. Second, as Bo elucidates, a rights approach leans heavily on government enforcement, yet language rights have not developed a track record of defensibility in the courts. I utilize the term *justice* to encompass a space in which we can collectively develop a vision for a richly multilingual global internet while acknowledging that this effort will require the support of not only governments but also corporate, nonprofit, and community actors.

EQUITABLE ACCESS

Techno-optimism and Under-resourced Languages

Our digital sphere is marked by the techno-optimistic value that its technologies are "for everyone." This view is reinforced by the mission statements and ad campaigns of companies like Facebook (rebranded at a corporate level as Meta), Google, and Microsoft; by governmental rhetoric; and by international development initiatives focused on tech solutions to persistent problems. In turn, global infrastructure such as undersea cables[7] and internet governance institutions like the Internet Corporation for Assigned Names and Numbers[8] sustain an integrated internet that engages over 60 percent of the world's population.[9] The global reach of the digital project carves out a logical imperative to support language diversity; yet there are both technical and financial challenges involved in supporting "everyone's" language and script. Despite the rhetoric, the profit imperative of most tech firms has meant, with few exceptions, that only languages with major "markets" have garnered significant support.

Among technologists, languages are classified by their level of digital resources. High-resource languages enjoy *full stack* support, which includes fonts, keyboards, software and platform support, and natural language processing (NLP) tools such as spellcheck, predictive typing, voice recognition, and optical character recognition.[10] Given the market incentives that drive most digital development, only a few languages are high-resource; these are primarily the languages of high-income countries, many with colonial and imperial histories. Developing NLP tools for high-resource languages is straightforward thanks to the hundreds of millions of online documents and large labeled data sets available. It is a formidable challenge, however, to develop NLP tools for low-resource languages because they lack robust digital corpora due to limited digital use, while digital use is limited by lack of digital support, creating a vicious cycle. While a number of European languages and a few other large official languages are classified as medium-resource languages, the vast majority of the world's languages are low-resource—i.e., digitally disadvantaged. Patterns in the digital sphere contribute to what Romaine in her contribution calls "a vicious circle of intersecting disadvantages [that] pushes language minorities into [the] bottom billion."

Speakers of low-resource languages face burdensome choices in the digital sphere: whether to (1) struggle to use their mother tongue despite lack of supports, (2) switch to a second language that is well supported (if they have fluency in a high-resource language like English), or (3) in the case of languages written in non-Latin scripts, haphazardly transliterate their language into Latin characters against the grain of tools such as English autocorrect that constantly rewrite their communications. Even widely used non-Latin scripts are frequently transliterated into Latin characters in digital communication due to QWERTY keyboards and other Latin-based defaults; for example, Arabic, a high-resource language that enjoys robust digital support, is commonly typed in Latin character–based "Arabizi."

Origin Stories and Digital Standards

Language bias in the digital sphere stems from its origins. While early innovations, including non-Latin character support, took place in western Europe, Russia, Asia, and elsewhere, the digital revolution initially began in the English-speaking contexts of the United States and the UK. The earliest computers were designed to calculate, and therefore supported only numerical text. As a need for written notations grew, computers were adapted to support Latin characters used to write English.

The 1964 U.S. encoding standard ASCII assigned each character a numerical identifier (figure 8.1). It quickly became a default international

USASCII code chart

b_7 b_6 b_5					0 0 0	0 0 1	0 1 0	0 1 1	1 0 0	1 0 1	1 1 0	1 1 1
Bits	b_4	b_3	b_2	b_1 Column Row	0	1	2	3	4	5	6	7
	0	0	0	0 0	NUL	DLE	SP	0	@	P	`	p
	0	0	0	1 1	SOH	DC1	!	1	A	Q	a	q
	0	0	1	0 2	STX	DC2	"	2	B	R	b	r
	0	0	1	1 3	ETX	DC3	#	3	C	S	c	s
	0	1	0	0 4	EOT	DC4	$	4	D	T	d	t
	0	1	0	1 5	ENQ	NAK	%	5	E	U	e	u
	0	1	1	0 6	ACK	SYN	&	6	F	V	f	v
	0	1	1	1 7	BEL	ETB	'	7	G	W	g	w
	1	0	0	0 8	BS	CAN	(	8	H	X	h	x
	1	0	0	1 9	HT	EM	)	9	I	Y	i	y
	1	0	1	0 10	LF	SUB	*	:	J	Z	j	z
	1	0	1	1 11	VT	ESC	+	;	K	[	k	{
	1	1	0	0 12	FF	FS	,	<	L	\	l		
	1	1	0	1 13	CR	GS	-	=	M	]	m	}
	1	1	1	0 14	SO	RS	.	>	N	^	n	~
	1	1	1	1 15	SI	US	/	?	O	_	o	DEL

FIGURE 8.1. US-ASCII Code Chart. Scanned from the material delivered with a TermiNet 300 impact-type printer with keyboard, February 1972. General Electric Data Communication Product Department, Waynesboro, VA. (https://commons.wikimedia.org/wiki/File:USASCII_code_chart.png)

standard, allowing devices to interoperably exchange text written in the 128 most common characters in American English. While over time other scripts and languages have gained a foothold within digital infrastructure, the ASCII and QWERTY foundations for digital tools remain consequential. As Lydia H. Liu and Anupama Rao aptly point out in this book's introduction, "Global English would not be what it is today without the support of an elaborate infrastructure of information technology that enables it to do what it does with efficiency while denying the same privilege to most other languages."

Over time. digital supports expanded for Latin-based writing systems like Spanish and German that utilize diacritics or additional Latin characters. National standards were also developed for scripts such as Hanzi (used to write Mandarin Chinese, Cantonese, and many other languages of China, as well as Japanese and historically Korea and Vietnamese), Devanagari (used to write over 120 languages, including Sanskrit, Prākrit, Hindi, Marathi, and Nepali), Arabic (used to write Persian, Pashto, Kurdish, and Urdu, among others), and Hebrew (used to write Hebrew, Yiddish, Ladino, Judeo-Arabic, and Judeo-Persian). These scripts benefited from strong financial support for digital infrastructure from one or more national governments.

The desire to support all languages' writing systems through a single interoperable standard culminated in the synchronized "universal" standards of Unicode and ISO 10646 in the early 1990s.[11] More than thirty years later, Unicode 15.0 supports a total of 149,186 characters and 161 scripts. The Script Encoding Initiative at the University of California, Berkeley, led by contributing author Deborah Anderson, is at the forefront of efforts to encode approximately 150 additional modern and historical scripts that still fall outside this foundational level of support.

As Anderson explains, this ongoing effort enjoys no guarantee of completion, considering the time and expense involved in encoding each new script. Just as contributors Daniel Kaufman and Ross Perlin document the pride New Yorkers feel when identifying their language on the Endangered Language Alliance (ELA) map, many script communities' push for Unicode inclusion is driven by equal measures of pride and practicality. Unicode's influence extends beyond its role as a foundational step in interchanging readable text in a script. In the same way that language communities of New York City instrumentalize the ELA map to lobby for official recognition, Anderson states that "getting the script into the global standard Unicode is considered an important step in raising awareness of the script and its user community within the global community"—and often by national governments, in particular. This also speaks to the import of the digital sphere (and particularly projects like Unicode with a goal of universal completeness) in terms of "legitimizing" one's script, language, homeland, or even worthiness as a human being. The stakes of digital inclusion can be high, as contributor Tommaso Manfredini so poignantly demonstrates through asylum seeker Applicant K's inability to locate on Google Maps his hometown in the contested borderland between Pakistan and India.

Measuring Digital Vitality

While different approaches have been taken to measure the prevalence of language diversity in the digital sphere, the findings concur. Despite content diversification and growing numbers of non-English-speaking internet users,[12] English remains atop the digital heap among a handful of high-resource languages. In a stark prediction, the computational linguist András Kornai estimates in "Digital Language Death" that at most 5 percent of languages will achieve vitality in the digital sphere and that lack of digital support and use of the remaining 95 percent will contribute to their "digital extinction."[13]

Expanding on the methodology of Kornai and colleagues in their 2017 follow-up study,[14] I assessed the digital vitality of Ethiopian languages and the Eritrean languages that utilize the Ethiopic script (see table 8.1).[15] *Digital vitality* is defined as a combination of digital support and digital use. In this methodology, twenty-three digital supports are identified that, to a great extent, determine whether a language is supported or technically excluded from the digital sphere. These language supports include a Keyman keyboard; support on major operating systems such as Windows, Mac, and Ubuntu; support on leading platforms such as Google Search, Google Translate, Twitter, and Facebook; and support from widely used software such as Microsoft Office, Adobe Acrobat, and Firefox. Digital use is evaluated based on language presence on Wikipedia,[16] *Indigenous Tweets*,[17] the Open Language Archives Community,[18] and the Crúbadán Project.[19]

LANGUAGE JUSTICE IN THE DIGITAL SPHERE

TABLE 8.1
Digital vitality of Ethiopian languages and Ethiopic-based languages of Eritrea

Thriving	None
Vital	*Ethiopic*: Amharic
	Latin: Somali
Emergent	*Ethiopic*: Tigre, Tigrinya, Ge'ez, Blin, Awngi, Basketo, Bench, Dirasha, Dizin, Sebat Bet Gurage, Suri, Gumuz, Harari, Konso, Me'en, Mursi, Zayse-Zergulla
	Ethiopic/Latin: Afar
	Latin: Oromo, Sidamo, Wolaytta, Nuer
Latent/Static	*Ethiopic*: Aari, Alaba-K'abeena, Borna, Gedeo, Hamer-Banna, Hozo, Kistane/Sodo, Male, Silt'e, Xamtanga
	Ethiopic/Latin: Dawro, Kafa, Kambaata, Koorete, Majang
	Latin: Argobba, Bambasi, Daasanach, Kacipo-Balesi, Komo, Kunama, Kwama, Libido, Nara, Nyangatom, Opuuo, Borana-Arsi-Guji Oromo, Oromo Eastern, Oyda, Shekkacho, Sheko, Yemsa
Absent	Ethiopian Sign Language
	Ethiopic: Anuak, Burji, Qimant
	Ethiopic/Latin: Haddiya, Saho
	Unwritten: Anfillo, Arbore, Baiso, Busaa, Chara, Daats'iin, Dahalik, Dime, Dorze, Ganza, Gawwada, Gayil, Inor, Kachama-Ganjule, Karo, Kwegu, Melo, Mesmes, Mesqan, Nayi, Ongota, Rer Bare, Seze, Shabo, Tsamai, Wolane, Zay

The fact that Amharic, Ethiopia's most widely spoken national language, is deemed digitally "vital" is heartening. This classification puts it in a privileged class as one of a very few Indigenous African languages—particularly those written in a non-Latin script—to achieve this level. That eighteen other Ethiopic-based languages are digitally "emergent" underscores the impact of early work to support Ethiopic characters through Unicode encoding, font design, etc., described later. Of great concern are the large majority of languages that remain digitally "latent/static" or "absent." That none of the languages studied is digitally "thriving" reflects the ongoing global digital dominance of only a few languages.[20]

Creative Resistance and Multistakeholder Efforts

The advances in digital vitality for some Ethiopian and Eritrean languages are the result of multistakeholder efforts. While Silicon Valley companies, the Ethiopian government, and international governance organizations have all played a role, my extended research on Ethiopic digital history underscores the major—and often volunteer—efforts by native speakers and advocates to encourage the development of foundational supports. The very abbreviated history included here allows only limited acknowledgment of the many individuals who have contributed to this work over the years.

Ethiopians and Eritreans in the diaspora, who embraced digital tech as a path to maintain community, were among the first to develop supports for Ethiopic-based languages. Fesseha Atlaw, an engineer in California who loved to write poetry in Amharic, was one such pioneer. The companies manufacturing Ethiopic typewriters had exclusive contracts with the Ethiopian government, and he was unable to smuggle one out of Ethiopia.[21] Inspired by the new affordances of personal computers, by the mid-1980s he had succeeded in developing the Dashen Ethiopic word processor (figure 8.2), which he distributed to clients including Ethiopian Airlines. The entry of other Ethiopic word processors into the market, such as Aberra Molla's ModEth, EthioWord, and GeezEdit offerings, expanded access but raised problems of interoperability, as files prepared using one software program could not automatically be opened in another.[22]

FIGURE 8.2. Dashen Engineering logo. Used with permission from Fesseha Atlaw.

Consensus arose among a few key Ethiopic digital pioneers that the solution was encoding the Ethiopic script in Unicode. Atlaw—with the help of other Ethiopic digital pioneers, including Abass Alemnehe and Yitna Firdyiwek (who among other projects developed the EthTex and GohaTibeb fonts, respectively), as well as Terrefe Ras-Work (who invented the Amharic telex)—provided expertise on the Ethiopic script to Unicode starting in 1992. The Ethiopic encoding was also informed by Joseph Becker, a Unicode founder who as a Xerox employee developed an Ethiopic word-processing system for Voice of America in 1986, where broadcast materials in Amharic were previously handwritten.[23]

These collaborative efforts culminated in the encoding of a core set of Ethiopic characters in Unicode 3.0 in 1999, making Ethiopic the first African script in Unicode. The encoding included all the characters used to write Amharic, Oromo (now predominantly written in the Latin script), and Tigrigna as well as the classical language Ge'ez. Building on this milestone, Daniel Yacob, a technologist who has worked on many fronts to support digital Ethiopic, spearheaded a massive cross-community effort in Ethiopia and Eritrea to document the additional Ethiopic characters used to write Awngi, Blin, Me'en, Mursi, Suri, Sebetbeit, and Xamtanga.[24] Thanks to this effort, Ethiopic characters essential to these languages were added to Unicode 4.1 in 2004. A third set of characters supporting Basketo, Gamo-Gofa-Daro, and Gumuz was encoded in Unicode 6.0 in 2009. In 2021, additional Ethiopic characters for Gurage were encoded in Unicode 14.0, thanks to further work by Yacob and colleagues.[25] See figure 8.3 to view the Ethiopic characters supported and their Unicode code points.

The Persistence of Language and Script Bias in the Digital Sphere

Ethiopic's inclusion in Unicode has paved the way for Amharic support within Facebook, Google Translate, and Google Search and partial support within Microsoft Office 2019, Windows 10, and some Apple applications. These are all promising steps toward full stack support; however, roadblocks to Amharic's digital use persist. For example, default QWERTY keyboards, a widespread lack of know-how regarding how to download Ethiopic keyboards and fonts, and nonstandard and nonoptimized Ethiopic keyboards are ongoing barriers that Amharic speakers face.

LANGUAGE JUSTICE IN THE DIGITAL SPHERE

Ethiopic[1][2]
Official Unicode Consortium code chart (PDF)

	0	1	2	3	4	5	6	7	8	9	A	B	C	D	E	F
U+120x	ሀ	ሁ	ሂ	ሃ	ሄ	ህ	ሆ	ሇ	ለ	ሉ	ሊ	ላ	ሌ	ል	ሎ	ሏ
U+121x	ሐ	ሑ	ሒ	ሓ	ሔ	ሕ	ሖ	ሗ	መ	ሙ	ሚ	ማ	ሜ	ም	ሞ	ሟ
U+122x	ሠ	ሡ	ሢ	ሣ	ሤ	ሥ	ሦ	ሧ	ረ	ሩ	ሪ	ራ	ሬ	ር	ሮ	ሯ
U+123x	ሰ	ሱ	ሲ	ሳ	ሴ	ስ	ሶ	ሷ	ሸ	ሹ	ሺ	ሻ	ሼ	ሽ	ሾ	ሿ
U+124x	ቀ	ቁ	ቂ	ቃ	ቄ	ቅ	ቆ	ቇ	ቈ		ቊ	ቋ	ቌ	ቍ		
U+125x	ቐ	ቑ	ቒ	ቓ	ቔ	ቕ	ቖ		ቘ		ቚ	ቛ	ቜ	ቝ		
U+126x	በ	ቡ	ቢ	ባ	ቤ	ብ	ቦ	ቧ	ቨ	ቩ	ቪ	ቫ	ቬ	ቭ	ቮ	ቯ
U+127x	ተ	ቱ	ቲ	ታ	ቴ	ት	ቶ	ቷ	ቸ	ቹ	ቺ	ቻ	ቼ	ች	ቾ	ቿ
U+128x	ኀ	ኁ	ኂ	ኃ	ኄ	ኅ	ኆ	ኇ	ኈ		ኊ	ኋ	ኌ	ኍ		
U+129x	ነ	ኑ	ኒ	ና	ኔ	ን	ኖ	ኗ	ኘ	ኙ	ኚ	ኛ	ኜ	ኝ	ኞ	ኟ
U+12Ax	አ	ኡ	ኢ	ኣ	ኤ	እ	ኦ	ኧ	ከ	ኩ	ኪ	ካ	ኬ	ክ	ኮ	ኯ

FIGURE 8.3. A portion of the Unicode code blocks for Ethiopic. "Ethiopic (Unicode Block)," Wikipedia, last edited August 27, 2021, https://en.wikipedia.org/w/index.php?title=Ethiopic_(Unicode_block)&oldid=1040842710.

A nontraditional content analysis I conducted in 2017 focused on language and script choices in one thousand public comments on the five Facebook pages most popular among Ethiopians.[26] Facebook has historically been the most popular social media platform in Ethiopia,[27] and Amharic is among the 111 languages[28] the platform officially supports. The analysis revealed that just under half of the comments were written in Amharic, with English a close second (table 8.2).

When adding a consideration of script choice to the analysis, a concerning trend appears. More than 50 percent of Amharic comments were written in the Latin script rather than the Ethiopic (figure 8.4), a clear indication that gaps in or low awareness of how to access digital supports, even in seemingly well-supported languages, is impacting script shift. Furthermore, these gaps incentivize language shift; many bilingual/multilingual Ethiopians understandably prefer to type in English rather than haphazardly type Amharic with Latin characters or struggle with a nonoptimized Ethiopic keyboard.

LANGUAGE JUSTICE IN THE DIGITAL SPHERE

TABLE 8.2
Language choices within Facebook comments

Language choice	Number of comments (2011–2017)	Percentage
Amharic	458	45.8%
Tigrigna	1	0.1%
Oromo	9	0.9%
English	328	32.8%
English and Amharic	58	5.8%
Empty	47	4.7%
Other	82	8.2%
Unclear, no agreement	17	1.7%
Total	1,000	100%

There are a number of downloadable Ethiopic keyboards that have been developed by language advocates and digital pioneers as well as a few Ethiopic Gboard (Google) offerings, including one for Amharic. The Ethiopic characters used for Amharic number more than two hundred, presenting a challenge for keyboard designers using the QWERTY setup as a base (figures 8.5 and 8.6). But lest we fall back on the faulty assumption that the

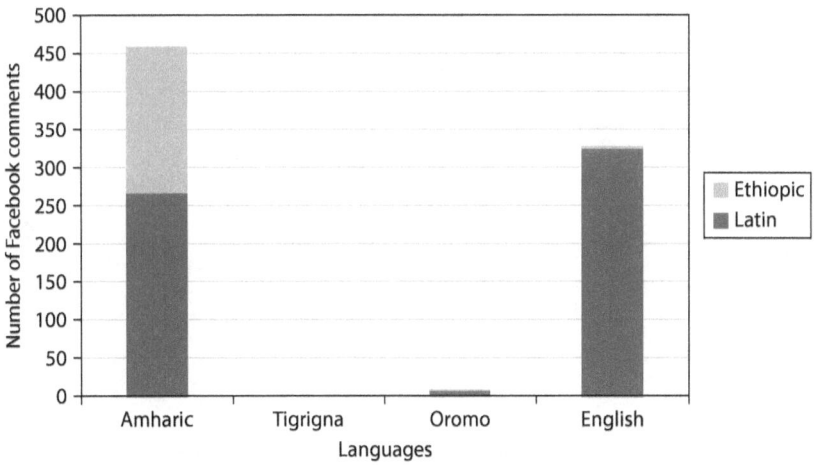

FIGURE 8.4. Script choice within language choices.

FIGURE 8.5. GFF Amharic Classic, v2.0 for iPhone, 2020. In this early keyboard (updated in 2020), Ethiopic characters are mapped phonetically onto a QWERTY layout, demonstrating the influence of Latin digital support defaults within other digital-linguistic realms. Ge'ez Frontier Foundation.

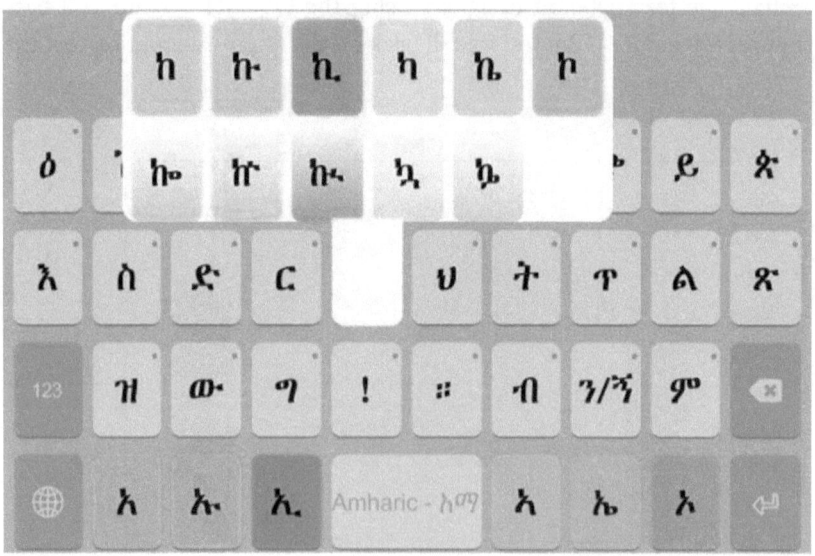

FIGURE 8.6. GFF Amharic, v2.2 for iPhone, 2021. Here Ethiopic characters are arranged in a new formation meant to be intuitive to Amharic speakers who may not be familiar with QWERTY keyboards. Users hover to choose a character from within its family of characters. Ge'ez Frontier Foundation.

twenty-six-character basic Latin alphabet is naturally more suited to digital tech, it's worth noting that thanks to predictive typing and five-stroke input systems, it is now faster to type in Mandarin Chinese's Hanzi characters than in English.[29] If standardized Ethiopic keyboards eventually become ubiquitous and include predictive typing, we will likely see more Amharic in the digital sphere—and nearly all of it written in the Ethiopic script. Be it at the level of keyboards, platform support, or NLP, language justice in the digital sphere challenges us to adapt digital tools to fit the linguistic needs of humans rather than expecting humans to bend to the limitations of digital tools.

LANGUAGE AND SCRIPT INTEGRITY

Recognizing the importance of digital use to the enduring vitality of a language and its script, advocates often seek to develop and encourage the use of first-language digital supports by youth for social media, text messaging, and the like. But what does digital support actually entail? And what are the consequences of superficial supports that fail to take into account the complexity of a language and its script?

As detailed in the introduction and Anderson's contribution, languages and scripts do not have a one-to-one or static relationship. Latin script is used to write approximately one hundred languages, including English, German, Turkish, Swahili, Igbo, and Tagalog. Hanzi characters are not unique to Chinese languages, having been adapted for writing Japanese, Korean, and Vietnamese, among others. Some languages have passed through multiple script shifts; for example, Azerbaijani has been written in Arabic, Cyrillic, and Latin scripts at different, sometimes overlapping points over the last century. Other languages, such as Mongolian, are written in multiple scripts simultaneously. In some cases, largely identical languages, such as Hindi and Urdu, are differentiated by use of different scripts. Moreover, approximately 43 percent of languages are oral, meaning they do not currently have a written form.[30]

Writing systems and the scripts they employ are frequently developed in the service of empires and political rule.[31] As one group attempts to wield power over great distances and populations, written communication facilitates governance. In turn, the ebb and flow of empires and allegiances, including religious affiliations, often leave script shift in their wake. For example, Azerbaijani officially switched from Cyrillic to Latin script in 1991 after the fall of the USSR, making a symbolic break from Communist rule and signaling allegiances with neighboring Turkey and Western Europe.[32] Such decisions at the political level can have costly personal impact, rendering people illiterate or making historical documents inaccessible to current-day scholars.

Romanization and Digital Tech

The West's victory in the Cold War is only one facet in the spread of the Latin script, known as romanization. Colonization transplanted Latin-based European languages onto American, African, and Asian soils while promoting Latin-based writing systems for Indigenous languages. Long-standing and ongoing Protestant proselytization has included Bible translation in which oral languages are transcribed using the Latin script, creating Latin-based writing systems in the process. Western assumptions of cultural and script superiority—specifically, the idea that an alphabetic script represents the pinnacle of linguistic and civilizational evolution—have fueled romanization even in societies with extensive, ancient literary traditions, such as China, Ethiopia, and Turkey.[33]

Arguments favoring the Latin script were bolstered by wide adoption of Western-designed communication technologies such as the telegraph and the typewriter, making "obvious" the superiority of a small set of alphabetic characters—as opposed to a large set of ideographic or syllabic characters. This, of course, belied the fact that these technologies were designed with the Latin alphabet in mind. Digital technologies often spring from these same linguistic and design legacies, with default QWERTY keyboards on devices the world over being the most obvious example. As described previously in relation to Amharic Facebook comments, privileging the Latin script in the digital sphere has major consequences for script use, both online and in the wider world. Script bias in the digital sphere creates a "logic" that expands into many other arenas, to the detriment of digitally disadvantaged scripts. For example, under the ethnic federalist system that replaced the socialist Derg regime in Ethiopia in 1991, the regional government of Oromia shifted from Ethiopic to Latin script for written Oromo. Though widely recognized as a political move to distance ethnic Oromos from other Ethiopic language communities, one justification given was that Latin characters are better supported by digital technologies.[34]

Understanding and Encoding Rich Script Traditions

Scripts are a complex topic deserving greater scholarly attention. Liu notes that the assumption that alphabetic scripts, by theoretically capturing the phonetic quality of words with a small character set, comprise the most elegant and advanced solution to written language has largely blinded us to the amazingly rich communication modes encoded within other writing systems.[35] For example, the ideographic Hanzi script, while requiring fluency in thousands of characters, made it possible to read in all languages using these characters, whether or not one could converse in them or understand them as speech. To borrow from technology lingo, this lent an incredible amount of *interoperability* to a single script throughout East Asia, a feature that the Latin script cannot replicate.

The common practice of transliterating Amharic and other Ethiopic-based languages into Latin in the digital sphere, while an ingenious workaround facilitating communication via Latin-based digital tools, also fundamentally degrades the integrity and depth of the language. The Ethiopic script is known in English and European literature as a syllabic script,[36] in which each character represents the pronunciation of a syllable, but in fact each character captures and represents multiple levels of meaning.[37] Well-documented in both literary and oral traditions is the fact that beyond its phonetic value, each Ethiopic character has a religious meaning as well as a numerical value within the millennia-old Ethiopian Orthodox Tewahedo Church.[38] Therefore, an Ethiopic text carries manifold levels of meaning. Taking these layers of meaning into account clarifies how depleted an Amharic word truly is when transliterated into Latin characters because of technological deficiencies.

Furthermore, several Ethiopic characters sound identical in modern Amharic pronunciation. However, orthographic tradition dictates the use of particular characters for reverential words associated with religion or royalty. A parallel in English would be the capitalization of titles and proper nouns to signal respect. During Ethiopia's socialist Derg regime from 1974 to 1991, characters associated with religious or royal fealty were characterized as redundant, and their use was discouraged in education and excluded from government publications. While these orthographic changes were justified under the guise of modernizing and streamlining the script, they changed the meanings of words on multiple levels. One telling example is the word አግዚአብሐር, the name of the Holy Trinity. According to Ethiopian Orthodox Tewahedo Christian belief, there is no separation between the name and the presence of the Creator. Therefore, using correct characters to spell the Creator's name is paramount, and these characters are not interchangeable with homophonous characters, let alone with characters from the Latin script. Yet we now see instances where platforms like Google Translate treat homophonous characters interchangeably (substituting ኂ for ሒ, for example), contributing to the depletion of centuries-long orthographic traditions and the multiple meanings they contain.

Features such as spellcheck, autocorrect, and predictive typing will be a boon for Amharic speakers only if they are designed with in-depth understanding and appreciation that goes beyond the script's misportrayal in Western literature as simply syllabic. Conceptions of the power of both language and script in the Ethiopian context point to challenges inherent in maintaining the integrity of all languages and scripts within digital platforms largely designed with little or no input from those most knowledgeable about the language. Language justice in the digital sphere requires linguistic integrity, including a deep attention to script. The way forward is through multistakeholder design built upon a foundation of participatory research:[39] deep engagement among technologists; scholars immersed in the literature, history, and culture of the languages in question; and language community members who are most able to shed light on integral features that may escape outsider understandings.[40]

DIGITAL JUSTICE

Once full stack support for a language exists, including tools that respect the language's script and orthographic integrity, we might hope that the battle for language justice is won. While making the benefits of digital tools accessible to language speakers is an important step toward digital equity, it in turn opens up new questions of justice. In examples such as the Algerian hirak, described in Madeleine Dobie's contribution to this volume, multilingual memes, hashtags, and online music videos utilize digital technology as a tool for (and symbol of) a democratic revolution; yet simultaneously "the regime has used social media to try to stir up ethnic conflict and division: e.g., by using the term *Zouaves* (i.e., Indigenous colonial troops), to designate Kabyles, implying that they are loyal to France." In various ways, digital linguistic support can be turned against communities, making these tools a double-edged sword for digitally disadvantaged languages.

Data collection and surveillance are the bedrock on which the digital ecosystem is built; digital support for a language makes the communications of its speakers far more intelligible within this surveillance framework. Since many minoritized and Indigenous language communities exist in politically, socially, and economically precarious positions, we must consider not only the benefits of digital inclusion but also the unique vulnerabilities that it may expose.[41] This section investigates the unwanted exposure digital inclusion may bring through corporate, state, and humanitarian surveillance as well as the harms that gaps in prudent content moderation can bring.

Corporate Surveillance

While surveillance has traditionally been associated with governments, the digital ecosystem provides surveillance opportunities to any actor that can pay. *Surveillance capitalism*[42] is a system in which human experience, mediated by digital technologies, is translated into behavioral data that are typically extracted without real consent or awareness about downstream uses. Fed into machine learning systems, these data are used to predict future behaviors; these predictions are valuable to marketers, insurance providers, potential employers, criminal justice decision makers, lenders, etc. While data mining funds valuable "free" services such as search, email, and social media platforms, the perils of these systems tend to be felt most acutely by the least privileged.

In a U.S. context, examples are myriad: Google search results for predominantly African-American names were found to disproportionately include AdSense links suggesting possible criminal records;[43] automated hiring systems promoted as "objective" reinforce historical biases by sifting for racial and status markers, such as "lacrosse," that replicate qualities of existing employees;[44] users of government food assistance who shop for groceries online are likely to become targets for unhealthy food ads and inferences about their economic or health status that negatively affect downstream decisions regarding employment, health insurance, housing, credit, etc.[45] We have every reason to expect that such data-fueled predictive practices will become increasingly common globally, perpetuating cycles in which both advantage and disadvantage are magnified. Digitally disadvantaged language communities, once brought more fully into the digital fold, are likely to be on the losing side of these predictive systems.

Many advocates for digitally disadvantaged languages share digital content in their languages to build community, share knowledge, and keep their language vital. YouTube is a commonly embraced platform, thanks in part to the fact that video hosting does not require as much language-specific support as primarily text-based platforms. Consequently, there is amazing linguistic and cultural diversity on the site, including poetry, music, and information sharing in thousands of languages. While this holds rich potential to promote language vitality and bring language communities together, troubling issues remain. Many "free" online platforms like YouTube and Facebook are designed to be addictive, using strategies like infinite scroll, recommended content, and autoplay to maximize user engagement—and thus exposure to advertising and data extraction. Such profit models encourage consumption patterns that may pull young language speakers into addictive online usage and away from essential face-to-face language immersion experiences within their families or language communities.

Furthermore, platforms like YouTube promote sensational content, making them breeding grounds for actors seeking to politically divide communities[46] or push youth toward allegiance with extremist and violent groups.[47] Language justice entails not only developing the digital supports that allow all language communities to "join" these digital spaces but also taking the more radical steps needed to dismantle the dangerous aspects of these systems. A first step in this direction is increased inclusion of diverse language speakers in positions of power where they can help shape these sites into digital spaces that honor and enrich their languages, lives, and communities.

State-Sponsored Surveillance

Digital surveillance by state actors may also run counter to the well-being of digitally disadvantaged language speakers. State-sponsored digital surveillance can take a number of forms from the forced collection of biometric data and CCTV systems that monitor the behavior of a city's or country's residents to automated inspection of verbal and written communications that relies on the legibility of a language to automated systems. The more advanced the digital supports and NLP systems for a language are, the more transparent the community using that language becomes to state surveillance. This is of particular import because the speakers of the minoritized and Indigenous languages that are least supported digitally are also disproportionately at odds with national governments. Conflictual relations with governments span the histories and ongoing realities of land dispossession, the removal of youth from families, forced residential or boarding school education, and the growing numbers of climate refugees seeking to cross borders without permission.[48] Increasing their reliance on digital tools, and therefore their surveillance vulnerability, is the fact that many of these language communities are also spread in diasporic patterns spurred by involuntary displacement.

Tools to surveil digitally disadvantaged language groups who represent a potential national security threat are often developed by resource-rich countries that make large investments in military intelligence.[49] While this form of surveillance is typically justified on the grounds of peacekeeping, these tools have the potential to serve authoritarian governments or other third-party entities whose interests are at odds with the language community in question. Thus, it is naive to think that "language tech for all" is a simple good, untainted by the same power structures that have disadvantaged these language communities in the first place.

Humanitarian Surveillance

Concern for the unintended long-term consequences of technologies developed for vulnerable language communities applies to humanitarian efforts as well. A push for digital language support often takes on more urgency during humanitarian crises, as digital technologies can help connect displaced communities and spread life-saving information during disasters. While digital innovation and data collection practices are increasingly core to humanitarian response efforts, they tend to further entrench discrimination and power asymmetries over the long run.[50] For example, data collected to identify, serve, and give voice to refugees can later, through "function creep," be used to monitor their activities and limit their movements as their status in neighboring countries shifts from targets of sympathy to threatening intruders.[51]

Sensitive data are often collected through partnerships among humanitarian organizations, tech companies, and governments with whom the UN works hand in glove. Such multifaceted partnerships raise questions about who owns, profits from, and can access data over the long term. For example, Rohingya refugees have expressed grave concerns that personal data collected by humanitarian organizations may be shared with the Myanmar government, the same actor that has perpetrated atrocities against them.[52] Corporate partners may neglect the long-term interests of vulnerable populations when their data can be put to other uses, such as bolstering facial recognition systems that can be sold to governments seeking to keep refugees out. Language justice efforts must not lose sight of the fact that improving digital support for the languages of humanitarian aid recipients has the potential to open them to harm when humanitarian, state, and corporate data collection enables surveillance.

Content Moderation

Surveillance can also have a positive role to play in achieving language justice in the digital sphere. Community-oriented surveillance, such as content moderation, is necessary to keep language communities safe. Unfortunately, social media content written in digitally disadvantaged languages suffers from a severe lack of moderation. Facebook serves around a third of the global population, with more and more language communities represented each year; yet content moderation is close to nonexistent for all but the most globally dominant languages.[53] Gaps in oversight create vacuums in which fake news, calls to violence, and hate speech can go viral. Incidents of violence stemming from such posts in Myanmar,[54] Nigeria,[55] Ethiopia,[56] and elsewhere demonstrate that gaps in content moderation have life-and-death consequences.

Platforms like Facebook are ill-equipped to combat trends of violence-inducing communication in digitally disadvantaged languages, as they have not invested sufficient resources in language-specific AI systems, have not provided linguistically diverse information regarding the communal need to flag bad content, and have not hired sufficient personnel who speak, and understand the political context of, these languages. To be fair, it is a difficult task to serve all the world's language communities, yet the company's global customer base demands this responsibility.

There are a number of possible advocacy approaches to reversing these troubling trends in the under-moderation of digitally disadvantaged languages. These include public pressure on social media companies to fulfill their corporate social responsibility and potentially legislation and criminal charges. Unfortunately, monetary incentives are currently insufficient, considering that the data of users in high-income countries are far more monetizable than the data generated by the growing user base in the linguistically diverse developing world—and in fact reprehensible content in many cases increases customer engagement and corporate profits. Alternatively, the failures of Big Tech to adequately support language diversity and protect speaker communities may create increasing incentives for communities to seek out alternate platforms that can preserve data sovereignty while fostering their own communication norms and well-being.

Digitally disadvantaged language communities have struggled for survival, respect, and autonomy under colonial and imperial conquest, within extractive capitalist practices or homogenizing socialist ideologies, and within nation-building projects that sought to assimilate, exclude, or exterminate them. The fact that their languages are digitally underresourced is a continuation of these power dynamics and their resulting hierarchies of language. As such, language justice in the digital sphere is not just a matter of bridging the digital divide by playing catch-up to provide full stack support. It also calls for a redefinition of whose languages and lives truly matter online and offline.

While there are many factors that contribute to the vitality or death of languages, with digital support perhaps a minor one, it is likely to play a growing role as communities across the world increasingly rely on digital communication. Minoritized and Indigenous language speakers stand to lose the most from language extinction, but loss of language diversity impacts us all. Language is intertwined with human knowledge; when we lose one, we lose the other. K. David Harrison states that "the extinction of ideas we now face has no parallel in human history."[57] Like biodiversity, language diversity holds unique ways of knowing that may solve problems we cannot even predict. Coexisting patterns of language diversity and ecological diversity on our planet, described in Romaine's chapter and Laura Kurgan's interview with Charlotte Silverman, also indicate that these language communities are custodians of robust knowledge regarding how to coexist with and cultivate diverse ecosystems. This knowledge is more critical than ever for our world, and language justice in the digital sphere is one small step toward fostering its continuation and application to a resilient and biodiverse planet.

Building language justice in the digital sphere requires efforts on multiple fronts—efforts by government, the private sector, and NGOs to support education, provide legal protections, and encourage the adoption of more nuanced ways of understanding and supporting multilingual realities. Multistakeholder efforts are key, but a delicate balance is required. On the one hand, this work should follow the lead of the language communities in question: "Nothing about us without us."[58] On the other, support from outside a language community may be needed during the development of digital supports for a language and its script. This may entail technical support on a Unicode proposal, keyboard and font development, or NLP tools. Without such collaboration, linguistic inaccessibility of digital tools may make it impossible for speakers of minoritized and Indigenous languages to develop the expertise to build digital supports for their language communities—a vicious cycle.

While examples of creative resistance within the realm of digital innovation abound in Ethiopia and many other contexts, institutions such as the Script Encoding Initiative, described by Anderson in her contribution, offer a model for balancing language-community interest and expertise with technical know-how and corporate interests. Ideally, collaborations between language experts and technologists will extend to fonts, keyboards, and NLP tools that maintain a language's complexity, integrity, and inherited knowledge. We must also honor a politics of "refusal"[59] as a legitimate response to digital tools that were developed without community permission,[60] detract from communal communication practices, or promote unwanted surveillance.[61]

Finally, scholarship on the disparate impacts of digital surveillance on ethnically and economically marginalized communities globally must be informed by a focus on how digital support for their languages increases their legibility to surveilling actors. I hope that the three-pronged approach offered here will be useful to these efforts and that an assessment of the potential for harm to the most digitally disadvantaged language communities will push us to reassess digital impacts on us all. Just as language is at the heart of our humanity, let us place language at the heart of a push for digital justice broadly.

NOTES

1. In 2020, the Ethiopian government introduced four additional official languages alongside Amharic, which alone had held this designation since the reign of Emperor Haile Selassie. The four languages incorporated as working languages of government are Afan Oromo, Afar, Somali, and Tigrigna, although the extent to which this will be a symbolic versus a substantial gesture remains to be seen.
2. András Kornai, "Digital Language Death," *PLoS ONE* 8, no. 10 (October 22, 2013): e77056, https://doi.org/10.1371/journal.pone.0077056.
3. K. David Harrison, *When Languages Die: The Extinction of the World's Languages and the Erosion of Human Knowledge* (Oxford: Oxford University Press, 2007); Nicholas Evans, *Dying Words: Endangered Languages and What They Have to Tell Us* (Chichester, England: Wiley-Blackwell, 2010).
4. Suzanne Romaine, "The Global Extinction of Languages and Its Consequences for Cultural Diversity," in *Cultural and Linguistic Minorities in the Russian Federation and the European Union*, ed. H. F. Marten, M. Rießler, J. Saarikivi, and R. Toivanenet (Cham, Switzerland: Springer, 2015), 31–46.
5. Kornai, "Digital Language Death."
6. While not a focus of this chapter, designing voice-activated tools that understand oral languages and audio tools that mirror the diction of "accented" speakers of dominant languages, as well as speakers of digitally disadvantaged languages and dialects, is an important step toward language justice in the digital sphere.
7. Undersea cables have been the site of fierce geopolitical battles, as they carry close to 99 percent of the world's data traffic and are vulnerable to data collection through submarine espionage, disruptions in service due to accidental or malicious cuts, and cyberattacks against secure computer systems. Also prevalent have been concerns about state- and corporate-owned cables being sites of mass surveillance conducted by their owners. The implications of surveillance of digitally disadvantaged language communities are central to this chapter.
8. The Internet Corporation for Assigned Names and Numbers (ICANN) makes a unified, global internet possible by overseeing the interconnected network of unique identifiers that allow devices on the internet to consistently find one another. For example, ICANN helps to coordinate the Domain Name System, known as "the phone book of the internet" because it matches domain names with IP address numbers. The internationalization of domain names, meaning the inclusion of non-Latin characters in web addresses, is one contested arena of language justice in the digital sphere.
9. International Telecommunication Union, "Statistics," ITU, accessed April 13, 2020, https://www.itu.int/en/ITU-D/Statistics/Pages/stat/default.aspx.

10. Steven R. Loomis, Anshuman Pandey, and Isabelle Zaugg, "Full Stack Language Enablement," *Steven R. Loomis* (blog), June 6, 2017, https://srl295.github.io/2017/06/06/full-stack-enablement/.
11. Isabelle Zaugg, "Digitizing Ethiopic: Coding for Linguistic Continuity in the Face of Digital Extinction" (PhD diss., American University, 2017).
12. "Internet World Users by Language: Top 10 Languages," Internet World Stats, March 21, 2020, https://www.internetworldstats.com/stats7.htm.
13. Kornai, "Digital Language Death."
14. Gary F. Simons, Abbey Thomas, Maik Gibson, and András Kornai. "A Scale for Assessing Digital Language Vitality," in *An Extended Abstract Submitted to ComputEL-2: A Workshop on Computational Methods for Endangered Languages* (Honolulu, 2017).
15. For further methodological details, see Zaugg, "Digitizing Ethiopic."
16. "List of Wikipedias," Wikimedia, accessed August 28, 2021, https://meta.wikimedia.org/wiki/List_of_Wikipedias.
17. Kevin Scannell, *Indigenous Tweets*, accessed August 28, 2021, http://Indigenoustweets.com/.
18. "OLAC: Open Language Archives Community," Open Language Archives Community, accessed August 28, 2021, http://www.language-archives.org/.
19. Kevin Scannell, "The Crúbadán Project: Corpus Building for Under-Resourced Languages," Louvain-la-Neuve, Belgium, 2007, http://borel.slu.edu/pub/wac3slides.pdf.
20. Kornai classifies sixteen languages as digitally thriving: English, Japanese, French, German, Spanish, Italian, Portuguese (both Brazilian and European), Dutch, Swedish, Norwegian (Bokmål), Danish, Finnish, Russian, Polish, Chinese, and Korean. Kornai, "Digital Language Death," 6.
21. Fesseha Atlaw, interview by Isabelle Zaugg, May 7, 2015.
22. See Deborah Anderson's contribution to this volume for an in-depth description of the challenges posed when software and devices do not share a common character encoding standard.
23. Joe Becker, "Proposal for Ethiopian Encoding in Unicode/10646," October 30, 1992.
24. Daniel Yacob, interview by Isabelle Zaugg, November 22, 2014.
25. Daniel Yacob, email message to author, March 13, 2021.
26. Zaugg, "Digitizing Ethiopic."
27. Sileshie Semahagne Kumlachew, "Challenges and Opportunities of Facebook as a Media Platform in Ethiopia," *Journal of Media and Communication Studies* 6, no. 7 (July 2014): 99–110.
28. Maggie Fick and Paresh Dave, "Facebook's Flood of Languages Leave It Struggling to Monitor Content," Reuters, April 23, 2019, https://www.reuters.com/article/us-facebook-languages-insight-idUSKCN1RZ0DW.
29. Sarah Zhang, "Chinese Characters Are Futuristic and the Alphabet Is Old News," *The Atlantic*, November 1, 2016.
30. David M. Eberhard, Gary F. Simons, and Charles D. Fennig, eds., *Ethnologue: Languages of the World*, 24th ed. (Dallas: SIL International, 2021).
31. Lydia H. Liu, "Scripts in Motion: Writing as Imperial Technology, Past and Present," *Theories and Methodologies* 130, no. 2 (2015): 375–383.
32. Toby Lester, "New-Alphabet Disease?," *The Atlantic*, July 1997.
33. Liu, "Scripts in Motion." See also Nergis Ertürk, *Grammatology and Literary Modernity in Turkey* (New York: Oxford University Press, 2011); Yurou Zhong, *Chinese*

Grammatology: Script Revolution and Literary Modernity, 1916–1958 (New York: Columbia University Press, 2019).
34. Baye Yimam, "(Ethiopian) Writing System," trans. Samuel Kinde and Minga Negash, Addis Ababa University, 1992, http://www.ethiopians.com/bayeyima.html.
35. Liu, "Scripts in Motion."
36. Getatchew Haile, "Ethiopic Writing," in *The World's Writing Systems*, ed. Peter T. Daniels and William Bright (New York: Oxford University Press, 1996).
37. Isabelle A. Zaugg, "Digital Inequality and Language Diversity: An Ethiopic Case Study." In *Digital Inequalities in the Global South*, ed. Massimo Ragnedda and Anna Gladkova (Cham, Switzerland: Palgrave Macmillan, 2020), 247–267.
38. Asires Yineysew Zebihere Gojjam, የካም መተሰቢያ [Ye Kam Metesebiya] (Asemera Bekokeb Tsibahi Matemiya Bet, Hemahabere Hawariyat Fre Haymanot Tateme, 1951); Nuhamin WaqiGira, *Mahatote Tibeb Zelisane Ge'ez*, vol. 2 (Addis Ababa: B'Etiopia Ortodox Tewahedo Bete Kristiyan Timertebetotoch Maderaja Memariya Mahabere Qidusan, 2016); Asteraye Tsigie, interview by Isabelle Zaugg, March 21, 2017; Seyoum Muluneh, interview by Isabelle Zaugg, April 1, 2017.
39. Wilhelmina Nekoto et al. "Participatory Research for Low-Resourced Machine Translation: A Case Study in African Languages," ArXiv:2010.02353 [Cs], November 6, 2020, https://doi.org/10.48550/arXiv.2010.02353.
40. As important as it is that digital tools integrate rich historical understandings of scripts and languages into their design, from the translanguaging perspective explicated by Kaufman and Perlin in their contribution, there is also a need for tools to support (rather than autocorrect) the code switching common within many multilingual communities. These goals may be contradictory in nature, making it all the more necessary that the user community have input into the context-specific preferred outcomes of digital tools.
41. Zaugg, Isabelle A. "Digital Surveillance and Digitally-Disadvantaged Language Communities," *Proceedings of the International Conference on Language Technologies for All* (Paris: UNESCO, 2019), https://lt4all.elra.info/media/papers/O8/188.pdf.
42. Shoshana Zuboff, *The Age of Surveillance Capitalism: The Fight for a Human Future at the New Frontier of Power* (New York: PublicAffairs, 2019).
43. Latanya Sweeney, "Discrimination in Online Ad Delivery," Social Science Research Network, January 28, 2013, https://doi.org/10.2139/ssrn.2208240.
44. Ifeoma Ajunwa, "The Auditing Imperative for Automated Hiring," *Harvard Journal of Law and Technology* 34, no. 2 (2021): 621–699, https://doi.org/10.2139/ssrn.3437631.
45. Jeff Chester, Katharina Kopp, and Kathryn C. Montgomery, "Does Buying Groceries Online Put SNAP Participants at Risk?," Center for Digital Democracy, July 16, 2020, https://www.democraticmedia.org/article/does-buying-groceries-online-put-snap-participants-risk.
46. danah boyd, "The Fragmentation of Truth," *Data & Society: Points* (blog), April 24, 2019, https://points.datasociety.net/the-fragmentation-of-truth-3c766ebb74cf.
47. Max Fisher and Amanda Taub, "We Wanted to Know How Online Radicalization Was Changing the World. We Started with Brazil," *New York Times*, August 11, 2019.
48. United Nations, Department of Economic and Social Affairs, Division for Social Policy and Development, Secretariat of the Permanent Forum on Indigenous Issues, *State of the World's Indigenous Peoples* (New York: United Nations, 2009), https://www.un.org/esa/socdev/unpfii/documents/SOWIP/en/SOWIP_web.pdf.

49. Amandalynne Paullada, "Machine Translation Shifts Power," The Gradient, July 31, 2021, https://thegradient.pub/machine-translation-shifts-power/.
50. Mirca Madianou, "Technocolonialism: Digital Innovation and Data Practices in the Humanitarian Response to Refugee Crises," Social Media + Society 5, no. 3 (July 1, 2019), https://doi.org/10.1177/2056305119863146.
51. Btihaj Ajana, Governing Through Biometrics: The Biopolitics of Identity (Basingstoke, England: Palgrave Macmillan, 2013).
52. Madianou, "Technocolonialism."
53. Jason Koebler and Joseph Cox, "The Impossible Job: Inside Facebook's Struggle to Moderate Two Billion People," Vice News, August 23, 2018, https://www.vice.com/en_us/article/xwk9zd/how-facebook-content-moderation-works.
54. Oren Samet, "Assessing Facebook's Role in the Violence Against the Rohingya," Pacific Standard, April 20, 2018, https://psmag.com/news/assessing-facebooks-role-in-myanmar-violence.
55. Yemisi Adegoke and BBC Africa Eye, "Like. Share. Kill. Nigerian Police Say 'Fake News' on Facebook Is Killing People," BBC News, November 13, 2018, https://www.bbc.co.uk/news/resources/idt-sh/nigeria_fake_news.
56. David Gilbert, "Hate Speech on Facebook Is Pushing Ethiopia Dangerously Close to a Genocide," Vice News, September 14, 2020, https://www.vice.com/en/article/xg897a/hate-speech-on-facebook-is-pushing-ethiopia-dangerously-close-to-a-genocide.
57. Harrison, When Languages Die, viii. See also Evans, Dying Words.
58. Jessa Rogers, "Redfern Statement: Nothing About Us Without Us." Woroni, June 24, 2016, https://www.woroni.com.au/words/redfern-statement-nothing-about-us-without-us/.
59. Carole McGranahan, "Theorizing Refusal: An Introduction," Cultural Anthropology 31 (August 17, 2016): 319–325; Audra Simpson, "The Ruse of Consent and the Anatomy of 'Refusal': Cases from Indigenous North America and Australia," Postcolonial Studies 20, no. 1 (January 2, 2017): 18–33.
60. "Mapuche Indians to Bill Gates: Hands off Our Language," Sydney Morning Herald, November 24, 2006, http://www.smh.com.au/news/biztech/mapuche-indians-to-bill-gates-hands-off-our-language/2006/11/24/1163871586715.html.
61. Donavyn Coffey, "Māori Are Trying to Save Their Language from Big Tech," Wired UK, April 28, 2021, https://www.wired.co.uk/article/maori-language-tech.

WORKS CITED

Adegoke, Yemisi, and BBC Africa Eye. "Like. Share. Kill. Nigerian Police Say 'Fake News' on Facebook Is Killing People." BBC News, November 13, 2018. https://www.bbc.co.uk/news/resources/idt-sh/nigeria_fake_news.
Ajana, Btihaj. Governing Through Biometrics: The Biopolitics of Identity. Basingstoke, England: Palgrave Macmillan, 2013.
Ajunwa, Ifeoma. "The Auditing Imperative for Automated Hiring." Harvard Journal of Law and Technology 34, no. 2 (2021): 621–699. https://doi.org/10.2139/ssrn.3437631.
Atlaw, Fesseha. Interview by Isabelle Zaugg, May 7, 2015.
Becker, Joe. "Proposal for Ethiopian Encoding in Unicode/10646," October 30, 1992.

boyd, danah. "The Fragmentation of Truth." *Data & Society: Points* (blog), April 24, 2019. https://points.datasociety.net/the-fragmentation-of-truth-3c766ebb74cf.
Chester, Jeff, Katharina Kopp, and Kathryn C. Montgomery. "Does Buying Groceries Online Put SNAP Participants at Risk?" Center for Digital Democracy, July 16, 2020. https://www.democraticmedia.org/article/does-buying-groceries-online-put-snap-participants-risk.
Coffey, Donavyn. "Māori Are Trying to Save Their Language from Big Tech." Wired UK, April 28, 2021. https://www.wired.co.uk/article/maori-language-tech.
Eberhard, David M., Gary F. Simons, and Charles D. Fennig, eds., *Ethnologue: Languages of the World*, 24th ed. Dallas: SIL International, 2021.
Ertürk, Nergis. *Grammatology and Literary Modernity in Turkey*. New York: Oxford University Press, 2011.
Evans, Nicholas. *Dying Words: Endangered Languages and What They Have to Tell Us*. Chichester, England: Wiley-Blackwell, 2010.
Fick, Maggie, and Paresh Dave. "Facebook's Flood of Languages Leave It Struggling to Monitor Content." Reuters, April 23, 2019. https://www.reuters.com/article/us-facebook-languages-insight-idUSKCN1RZ0DW.
Fisher, Max, and Amanda Taub. "We Wanted to Know How Online Radicalization Was Changing the World. We Started With Brazil." *New York Times*, August 11, 2019. https://www.nytimes.com/2019/08/11/reader-center/brazil-youtube-radicalization.html.
Gilbert, David. "Hate Speech on Facebook Is Pushing Ethiopia Dangerously Close to a Genocide." Vice News, September 14, 2020. https://www.vice.com/en/article/xg897a/hate-speech-on-facebook-is-pushing-ethiopia-dangerously-close-to-a-genocide.
Haile, Getatchew. "Ethiopic Writing." In *The World's Writing Systems*, ed. Peter T. Daniels and William Bright. New York: Oxford University Press, 1996.
Harrison, K. David. *When Languages Die: The Extinction of the World's Languages and the Erosion of Human Knowledge*. Oxford: Oxford University Press, 2007.
International Telecommunication Union. "Statistics." ITU. Accessed April 13, 2020. https://www.itu.int/en/ITU-D/Statistics/Pages/stat/default.aspx.
Internet World Stats. "Internet World Users by Language: Top 10 Languages," March 31, 2020. https://www.internetworldstats.com/stats7.htm.
Koebler, Jason, and Joseph Cox. "The Impossible Job: Inside Facebook's Struggle to Moderate Two Billion People." Vice News, August 23, 2018. https://www.vice.com/en_us/article/xwk9zd/how-facebook-content-moderation-works.
Kornai, András. "Digital Language Death." *PLoS ONE* 8, no. 10 (October 22, 2013): e77056. https://doi.org/10.1371/journal.pone.0077056.
Lester, Toby. "New-Alphabet Disease?" *The Atlantic*, July 1997. http://www.theatlantic.com/magazine/archive/1997/07/new-alphabet-disease/306207/.
Liu, Lydia H. "Scripts in Motion: Writing as Imperial Technology, Past and Present." *Theories and Methodologies* 130, no. 2 (2015): 375–383.
Loomis, Steven R., Anshuman Pandey, and Isabelle Zaugg. "Full Stack Language Enablement." *Steven R. Loomis* (blog), June 6, 2017. https://srl295.github.io/2017/06/06/full-stack-enablement/.
Madianou, Mirca. "Technocolonialism: Digital Innovation and Data Practices in the Humanitarian Response to Refugee Crises." *Social Media + Society* 5, no. 3 (July 1, 2019). https://doi.org/10.1177/2056305119863146.

McGranahan, Carole. "Theorizing Refusal: An Introduction." *Cultural Anthropology* 31 (August 17, 2016): 319–325. https://doi.org/10.14506/ca31.3.01.

Muluneh, Seyoum. Interview by Isabelle Zaugg, April 1, 2017.

Nekoto, Wilhelmina, Vukosi Marivate, Tshinondiwa Matsila, Timi Fasubaa, Tajudeen Kolawole, Taiwo Fagbohungbe, Solomon Oluwole Akinola, et al. "Participatory Research for Low-Resourced Machine Translation: A Case Study in African Languages." *ArXiv:2010.02353 [Cs]*, November 6, 2020. https://doi.org/10.48550/arXiv.2010.02353.

Open Language Archives Community. "OLAC: Open Language Archives Community." Accessed August 28, 2021. http://www.language-archives.org/.

Paullada, Amandalynne. "Machine Translation Shifts Power." *The Gradient*, July 31, 2021. https://thegradient.pub/machine-translation-shifts-power/.

Rogers, Jessa. "Redfern Statement: Nothing About Us Without Us." *Woroni*, June 24, 2016. https://www.woroni.com.au/words/redfern-statement-nothing-about-us-without-us/.

Romaine, Suzanne. "The Global Extinction of Languages and Its Consequences for Cultural Diversity." In *Cultural and Linguistic Minorities in the Russian Federation and the European Union*, ed. H. F. Marten, M. Rießler, J. Saarikivi, and R. Toivanen, 31–46. Cham, Switzerland: Springer, 2015.

Samet, Oren. "Assessing Facebook's Role in the Violence Against the Rohingya." *Pacific Standard*, April 20, 2018. https://psmag.com/news/assessing-facebooks-role-in-myanmar-violence.

Scannell, Kevin. "The Crúbadán Project: Corpus Building for Under-Resourced Languages." Louvain-la-Neuve, Belgium, 2007. https://cs.slu.edu/~scannell/pub/wac3.pdf.

Scannell, Kevin. *Indigenous Tweets*. Accessed August 28, 2021. http://indigenoustweets.com/.

Semahagne Kumlachew, Sileshie. "Challenges and Opportunities of Facebook as a Media Platform in Ethiopia." *Journal of Media and Communication Studies* 6, no. 7 (July 2014): 99–110.

Simons, Gary F., Abbey Thomas, Maik Gibson, and András Kornai. "A Scale for Assessing Digital Language Vitality." In *An Extended Abstract Submitted to ComputEL-2: A Workshop on Computational Methods for Endangered Languages*. Honolulu, 2017.

Simpson, Audra. "The Ruse of Consent and the Anatomy of 'Refusal': Cases from Indigenous North America and Australia." *Postcolonial Studies* 20, no. 1 (January 2, 2017): 18–33. https://doi.org/10.1080/13688790.2017.1334283.

Sweeney, Latanya. "Discrimination in Online Ad Delivery." *Social Science Research Network*, January 28, 2013. https://doi.org/10.2139/ssrn.2208240.

Sydney Morning Herald. "Mapuche Indians to Bill Gates: Hands off Our Language." November 24, 2006. http://www.smh.com.au/news/biztech/mapuche-indians-to-bill-gates-hands-off-our-language/2006/11/24/1163871586715.html.

Tsigie, Asteraye. Interview by Isabelle Zaugg, March 21, 2017.

United Nations, Department of Economic and Social Affairs, Division for Social Policy and Development, Secretariat of the Permanent Forum on Indigenous Issues. *State of the World's Indigenous Peoples*. New York: United Nations, 2009. https://www.un.org/esa/socdev/unpfii/documents/SOWIP/en/SOWIP_web.pdf.

WaqiGira, Nuhamin. *Mahatote Tibeb Zelisane Ge'ez*. Vol. 2. Addis Ababa: B'Etiopia Ortodox Tewahedo Bete Kristiyan Timertebetotoch Maderaja Memariya Mahabere Qidusan, 2016.

Wikimedia. "List of Wikipedias." Accessed August 28, 2021. https://meta.wikimedia.org/wiki/List_of_Wikipedias.
Yacob, Daniel. Email message to author. March 13, 2021.
———. Interview by Isabelle Zaugg, November 22, 2014.
Yimam, Baye. "(Ethiopian) Writing System." Trans. Samuel Kinde and Minga Negash. Addis Ababa University, 1992. http://www.ethiopians.com/bayeyima.html.
Yineysew Zebihere Gojjam, Asires. የካም መታሰቢያ [Ye Kam Metesebiya]. Asemera Bekokeb Tsibahi Matemiya Bet, Hemahabere Hawariyat Fre Haymanot Tateme, 1951.
Zaugg, Isabelle. "Digital Inequality and Language Diversity: An Ethiopic Case Study." In *Digital Inequalities in the Global South*. ed. Massimo Ragnedda and Anna Gladkova, 247–267. Cham, Switzerland: Palgrave Macmillan, 2020.
———. "Digital Surveillance and Digitally-Disadvantaged Language Communities." *Proceedings of the International Conference on Language Technologies for All*. Paris: UNESCO, 2019. https://lt4all.elra.info/media/papers/O8/188.pdf.
———. "Digitizing Ethiopic: Coding for Linguistic Continuity in the Face of Digital Extinction." PhD diss., American University, 2017. https://eric.ed.gov/?id=ED579672.
Zhang, Z. "Chinese Characters Are Futuristic and the Alphabet Is Old News," *The Atlantic*, November 1, 2016.
Zhong, Yurou. *Chinese Grammatology: Script Revolution and Literary Modernity, 1916–1958*. New York: Columbia University Press, 2019.
Zuboff, Shoshana. *The Age of Surveillance Capitalism: The Fight for a Human Future at the New Frontier of Power*. New York: PublicAffairs, 2019.

FIGURE 9.1. First Scene *EXIT*: Population Shifts: Cities. Diller Scofidio + Renfro, Mark Hansen, Laura Kurgan and Ben Rubin, in collaboration with Robert Gerard Pietrusko and Stewart Smith, *EXIT*, 2008–2015. Immersive audiovisual installation based on an idea by Paul Virilio (45 min.). View of the installation at the Palais de Tokyo, Paris, 2015. Collection Fondation Cartier pour l'art contemporain, Paris. Photo by Luc Boegley.

Chapter Nine

EXIT

An Interview

LAURA KURGAN AND CHARLOTTE A. SILVERMAN

A globe circulates around an audience. It prints geographic data visualizations and constructs a narrative. The text, written in capital letters in French and English, is stark white on a black screen. Its angular letters are composed of pixels. As the globe begins its travels across the screen, the sound of voices melds with the sound of mechanized typing: "The world's population is in motion. Current levels of political, economic and environmental forces have led to levels of migration never before seen in history. Our understanding of the extent of this migration is limited to the data made available by various organizations. Data 1990–2014." The audience of the artwork at once seems removed from the Earth, as if viewing it from outer space, and at the same time at the center of its orbit, as the Earth and its text scroll around them. Thus unfolds *EXIT*—and the audience's entrance into a planetary perspective on global migration.

EXIT was first exhibited in Paris in 2008 as part of *Native Land, Stop Eject*, a show prompted by Paul Virilio and commissioned by the Cartier Foundation. It was produced by Diller Scofidio + Renfo, Mark Hansen, Laura Kurgan, and Ben Rubin in collaboration with Robert Gerard Pietrusko and Stewart Smith. The artwork made its debut together with *Hear Them Speak*, an exhibition by photographer Raymond Depardon and film director Claudine Nougaret, which filled the museum's upstairs space. *EXIT* was exhibited on the floor below, in a circular room with a panoramic screen wrapping around its perimeter. In 2009, it was supplemented with the final section, "Speechless Deforestation," which was exhibited for the first time at the Kunsthal Charlottenborg in Copenhagen during the fifteenth session of the Conference of the Parties (COP 15) to the United Nations Framework Convention on Climate Change. In 2010, it was the inaugural exhibit at the Alhondiga in Bilbao. The data were updated one more time in 2015 for an exhibition at the Palais De Tokyo in Paris during COP 21. The production of *EXIT* was followed by a collaboration on another exhibition, *In Plain Sight*, in 2018. Both exhibitions have continued to travel, their depictions of the circulating globe performing their own global circulation.

Both *EXIT* and *In Plain Sight* raise questions critical to conversations about global language justice. *EXIT* is concerned with the linkages between linguistic and ecological diversity and with the movements of both languages and people across the globe. There are also analytical affinities, including attention to the power of data in the construction of narratives and to colonial and imperial histories imbricated in technologies of representation. The intersections between *EXIT*—particularly its final section, "Speechless Deforestation"—and the Global Language Justice initiative sparked innovative exchanges and collaborations between the Institute for Comparative Literature and Society (ICLS) and the Center for Spatial Research (CSR) at Columbia University. This interview between Laura Kurgan, one of the exhibition's authors and the Director of CSR, and Charlotte Silverman, a Graduate Fellow for the Mellon-Sawyer Seminar on Global Language Justice at ICLS, took place near the seminar's conclusion, following four years of collective dialogue about languages and their lifeworlds.

CHARLOTTE SILVERMAN: Thank you so much, Professor Kurgan, for your willingness to discuss both *EXIT* and *In Plain Sight*. There are so many points of intersection between the exhibitions and conversations about global language justice, but let's begin with the most immediate. Can you tell us about "Speechless Deforestation," the section of *EXIT* that explores the relation between linguistic diversity and biodiversity?

LAURA KURGAN: Yes, this is the section of the exhibition that immediately came to mind when I learned about the Global Language Justice initiative. I cotaught a seminar with Lydia Liu on language justice because of the exhibition—and particularly because of this section.

EXIT

CHARLOTTE SILVERMAN: There are two different data sets operating together, one addressing deforestation and another addressing language endangerment. Both of these issues are central to Suzanne Romaine's piece in the volume—as well as, of course, the Global Language Justice initiative as a whole. How did you go about determining representative data sets for both?

LAURA KURGAN: In working with data, the best narratives or arguments often result from the overlap of data of different kinds. In this case, I had a hunch that endangered language and endangered ecology must be related to one another. I knew about a data set called The Last of the Wilds, which is now called The Anthropogenic Biomes of the World. The other was UNESCO's Endangered Languages of the World data set. We overlaid the two data sets on one another. What became clear was that endangered languages and endangered biodiversity were twins. They go hand-in-hand. And they were correlated with the places where a lot of Indigenous peoples live.

CHARLOTTE SILVERMAN: How was each of the sets sourced?

FIGURE 9.2. Sixth Scene *EXIT*: Speechless Deforestation. Diller Scofidio + Renfro, Mark Hansen, Laura Kurgan, and Ben Rubin, in collaboration with Robert Gerard Pietrusko and Stewart Smith, *EXIT*, 2008–2015. Immersive audiovisual installation based on an idea by Paul Virilio (45 min.). View of the installation at the Palais de Tokyo, Paris, 2015. Collection Fondation Cartier pour l'art contemporain, Paris. Photo by Luc Boegley.

LAURA KURGAN: The Anthropogenic Biomes of the World is produced by the Center for International Earth Science Information Network (CIESIN) at Columbia. They collect incredibly detailed data about the underlying causes of climate change. This is a publicly available data set, so we didn't need to ask for permission. The second data set, Endangered Languages of the World, was assembled by UNESCO. It is not publicly available, but we received special permission to map it. There were many other data sets included in this scenario, but it was these first two that formed the core of the argument we were narrating and visualizing.

CHARLOTTE SILVERMAN: The "Speechless Deforestation" section presents a global view of deforestation through the depiction of particular examples. There's a focus on deforestation in Brazil as well as in Indonesia and Cameroon. How was each of these countries chosen?

LAURA KURGAN: First off, the overlay of the two data sets guided us to these rain forests as locations to look at more closely. But the choices involved a lot of conversation. We were collaborating with Bruce Albert, who began by focusing us on the Amazon in Brazil, which he knows intimately from decades of work there. Since the rest of the scenes (we called each of the six segments of *EXIT* a scene) were planetary pictures, we decided to emphasize the Amazon as rain forest and introduce some comparative cases, which led us to these other two countries, Cameroon and Indonesia, where forest loss happened for very different reasons. Then we had to gather the data resources and imagery for each. I worked with people at the Global Forest Watch, part of the World Resources Institute, on the data sources and imagery for Cameroon and Indonesia, and Bruce knew the anthropologists who had been doing long-time work in Cameroon and Indonesia, similar to the work he does in Brazil. In Cameroon, the picture was very stark—forest loss is the result of legal and illegal road construction, and many Indigenous people had relocated along roads in order to survive economically. So economic structures were also contributing to the demise of their culture and language. In Indonesia, a primary culprit was the clearing of land for palm oil plantations, which is decimating the rain forest. But we didn't only focus on these three locations and their endangered languages and biomes. We also visualized the endangered language data set itself to show the phenomenon globally.

CHARLOTTE SILVERMAN: That visualization was particularly interesting. It was not only visual but also sonic. The audience at once reads the names of the languages, in latinized script, and also hears them spoken. It's two very different renditions coming together. Where were the recordings from? And what about the data used for that segment—what was the source?

LAURA KURGAN: The recordings were gathered by our team wherever we could find them. As far as we could determine, recordings of language have not been assembled systematically as a data set. The other part of that visualization showed the Endangered Languages database by naming and organizing each language by its classification. The classifications are really interesting because first and foremost they are not about quantification. The five gradations of language endangerment are based on who speaks the language—specifically, which generations and how many of them. It's very qualitative. One classification, for example, is if a grandchild speaks the language. Then it's considered alive. If only the great-great-grandmother speaks the language, on the other hand, it's about to die, and it's considered critically endangered.

CHARLOTTE SILVERMAN: In the artwork itself, these categories seem quite definite. But you're suggesting a much more complicated picture.

FIGURE 9.3. Sixth Scene *EXIT*: Speechless Deforestation: Visualization of Language Data Set. Diller Scofidio + Renfro, Mark Hansen, Laura Kurgan, and Ben Rubin, in collaboration with Robert Gerard Pietrusko and Stewart Smith, *EXIT*, 2008-2015. Immersive audiovisual installation based on an idea by Paul Virilio (45 min.). View of the installation at the Palais de Tokyo, Paris, 2015. Collection Fondation Cartier pour l'art contemporain, Paris. Photo by Luc Boegley.

LAURA KURGAN: Yes. It is often the case that data categories are more complex than they are presented on a legend—and especially this one. There are many complications, conflicts actually, about how and why endangered language data are collected and categorized. The most "complete" endangered language data set is collected in a project called Ethnologue. It is produced by missionaries with the intent of translating the Bible into every language in the world. They have become the keepers of a vast trove of knowledge about human languages. The fact that this group was responsible for these data gave rise to a conflict on our team. I was able to download that data set, but the team, including me, thought we should not use it and should find a better source for the data. This is also the reason that we didn't produce "Speechless Deforestation" in time for the 2008 show. The consensus was that we should obtain that data from UNESCO rather than use Ethnologue's. We knew it would be a complicated and lengthy process to obtain permission from UNESCO to acquire and map their data set in our own way. Some of the data sets in the show are easily downloadable. They're public resources. Some of the data sets were not. This was one of the sets that was not. It took a really long time to get. And then when we got the data—

CHARLOTTE SILVERMAN: Was it from Ethnologue?

LAURA KURGAN: You guessed it. When I looked at the sources in the UNESCO data set, they were not always but very often listed as "Ethnologue," "Ethnologue," . . . . There were so many languages with data attributed to Ethnologue. Maybe we shouldn't have, but we did use the UNESCO data in the end. It's a complex question, and this is just a good example of something that in a certain sense we confront and acknowledge with every data set: Where does it come from? Why was it collected? What sort of project am I piggybacking on? Are there some data sets that you just have to forgo using? Of course, in our exhibition, the data were used very differently than by Ethnologue, even if it was a source. Mapping the data about endangered languages in direct relation to endangered biodiversity told a distinct story about the vulnerability of the planet. Still, the situation highlighted the fact that obtaining pure or neutral data is an impossibility; there are just degrees of "contamination," and it's a fundamental ethical and political decision about how much and what sort of contaminated data you'll tolerate. And we face it at a very basic level—not just when we decide about this or that data set but in the deepest preconditions of the sort of mapping work we tend to do. The very language of most of our cartographic representation, longitude and latitude, in itself has problematic origins and assumptions built into it.

CHARLOTTE SILVERMAN: Maria Bo's discussion of the framework of linguistic rights raises similar questions, as does Madeleine Dobie's contribution to the volume. It discusses the ways that protestors in the hirak have incorporated French into signage and slogans despite its history as a colonial language. Your own work has navigated this not only in terms of language but also in terms of mapping. Can you tell us a little about this?

LAURA KURGAN: I try to embrace and critique these technologies at the same time. I've been doing that since my first projects on the Global Positioning System. Should you insist that longitude and latitude can't go together with Indigenous mapping systems and that Indigenous systems should defy the very codification of colonization? There are powerful reasons to do that. But it's not an absolute rule. When you think about mapping and the question of decolonization, there's no easy answer. There are examples in which Indigenous activists and advocates use GPS to make the maps that help them reclaim stolen land. There are also reasons that Indigenous people should *not* map the sacred sites, or at least not publicly, even when they are trying to protect these sites in courts of law. We just have to keep finding ways to respond to these realities. My work has always taken on the political nature of mapping, and today this also means the political nature of representations of spatial data.

CHARLOTTE SILVERMAN: This seems to speak to Daniel Kaufman's and Ross Perlin's contribution to the volume. It discusses the ways in which categorizing and mapping languages can increase their visibility in important ways—even if the technologies employed may have colonial underpinnings.

LAURA KURGAN: Right, right. They do the beautiful work of bringing the topic of endangered language to the map of New York City. The Endangered Language Alliance, which is founded and run by Kaufman and Perlin, faces a different set of ethical concerns that were amplified during the Trump administration but that they had always been aware of. They ask themselves whether, when they put an endangered language in New York City onto a map, it might expose—by making them more easily identified—undocumented people who happened to be speakers of that language and are living there. Being acutely aware of this problem, the map that they publish is intentionally made blurry so that you cannot identify specific addresses or even microneighborhoods. That way the map tries not to put anybody in danger. But it's a recurring problem of mapping—the question of when something should not be put on a map.

CHARLOTTE SILVERMAN: Let's turn to the movement of migrants, some of whom may speak languages that are represented on Kaufman's and Perlin's maps of New York. One of the contributions to the volume—Tommaso Manfredini's—describes a scenario in which an asylum seeker wants to locate his home on a map and is unable to do so. The piece is concerned with the representation of refugees and the narratives of their flight. *EXIT*, too, crafts narratives of migration, especially in the section about refugees and those who are internally displaced. In the artwork, one means of representing refugees is the citation of definitions from the UN. Another is their representation on a map through pixels. There are also sound effects that accompany these pixelated flows. How are these different forms of representation envisioned to work together?

LAURA KURGAN: In each scene in *EXIT*, we were trying to find a data set that could be represented at the planetary scale. The United Nations High Commissioner for Refugees (UNHCR) data set we used to map refugee flow is not perfect. It's impossible to count every refugee, in any conflict, large or small. So they have established a guiding rule: every time five thousand people cross a border because of a political conflict, the UNHCR deems them a refugee population and starts counting the number of people crossing that border in their data set. They document it with the name of the country of departure, the name of the country of arrival, and the number of people crossing that border. So it's pretty crude. We tried a lot of different ways of representing this. Trained as we were on hi-res data sets, we thought at first that we could map the physical routes people were taking. We actually tried at the time to get a road map of the whole world and to represent refugees moving along those roads. But that was in 2008, and we couldn't do it. Ultimately, we had to settle on staying true to the UNHCR data set, so we chose, like many others mapping these data, to map the flow as if it went from the center of one country to the center of the other. That's the only way that made sense for our particular visualization.

CHARLOTTE SILVERMAN: So these data come from the UNHCR data set?

LAURA KURGAN: Absolutely. And we were very aware of its limitations. During the height of the multisided civil conflict in Colombia, the data set documented 3 million internally displaced people. You know that that's an estimation because it can't be exactly 3 million and not 3 million and one or

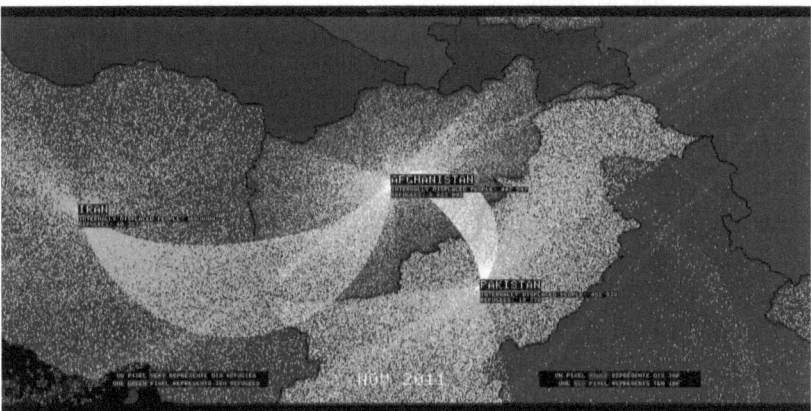

FIGURE 9.4. Fourth Scene *EXIT*: Political Refugees and Forced Migration: Visualization of Refugee Flows, Afghanistan, 2011. Diller Scofidio + Renfro, Mark Hansen, Laura Kurgan, and Ben Rubin, in collaboration with Robert Gerard Pietrusko and Stewart Smith, *EXIT*, 2008–2015. Immersive audiovisual installation based on an idea by Paul Virilio (45 min.). View of the installation at the Palais de Tokyo, Paris, 2015. Collection Fondation Cartier pour l'art contemporain, Paris. Photo by Luc Boegley.

3 million and two. So it's limited in that way. But on the other hand, it is the data set that allows you to say that in 2008, there were 16 million refugees (when you include Palestinians), and in 2015, the year of the updated version of *EXIT*, there were 60 million and more refugees. And that number, the change in those numbers, is of massive political significance. It allows you to say all kinds of things about the state of the world. A lot of data sets are very flawed, but that doesn't mean that you shouldn't work with them. Rather, you have to commit to representing the flaws and the uncertainties while you tell the stories that you *can* tell despite the limitations. That's how I think about these things.

CHARLOTTE SILVERMAN: How does this relate to your more current work? Do you find that it is also animated by these concerns?

LAURA KURGAN: Yes, the limitations and uncertainties of data are something we work with daily at the Center for Spatial Research. I'll give you one example. That three million number that was so glaringly estimated in Colombia propelled one of our first projects for a multiyear research initiative on conflict urbanism, funded by the Architecture, Urbanism, and the Humanities program of the Mellon Foundation. Juan Saldarriaga, a research associate at the center, obtained a very detailed version of the Victims Register, which was being collected by the Colombian government as part of the peace process just established as we were beginning our work in 2015. This registry records victims' accounts of the kinds of violence they encountered during the conflict, where they were living when the event happened, and where they are living now. Again, the uncertainty of this data set is clear. People are self-reporting, and many people have not wanted to come forward with their stories. However, millions of people *have* reported, and the data are worth looking at. Without going into too much detail, since the project is well-documented on our website, what this data set allowed us to do was to map rural-urban migration due to the conflict as well many other forms of internal migration. In general, when one hears statistics such as "66 percent of the world's population will live in cities by the year 2030," there are very few maps that show these particular trajectories from rural to urban. This data set allowed us to show details of displacement from village X and displacement to city Y for millions of people. It showed stark patterns about the extended conflict and the intensity of internal displacement from 1999 to 2005. Bogota and Medellin, the two largest cities in the country, were obvious destinations, but many other patterns of movement from and to small towns are visible over time.

CHARLOTTE SILVERMAN: It's interesting to think about this approach to the representation of data in relation to *EXIT*, which focuses on the depiction of planetary-wide migration but also utilizes more specific examples to portray this perspective. What sort of connections or causalities do you think were made apparent through the visualization of both global and country-specific data in *EXIT*?

LAURA KURGAN: It allows for different types of comparisons. In the section on population growth, for example, you see the swarm of pixels assembling the world, and you immediately see that China and India are much brighter than the United States. You can understand very quickly that there are more people in those countries because there are more pixels on those spots. Or in the section on floods, in which we compared floods of the same magnitude in different places, you can see that far fewer people are displaced by the same size flood in Australia than in Pakistan. That's very easy to see at a planetary scale. But then you also want to see the specific numbers. This is why we zoomed in—so that the audience could learn from specific examples. It was very didactic. There was a lot of statistical analysis, but we wanted to present the analysis in a narrative form for a nonscientific audience, on the

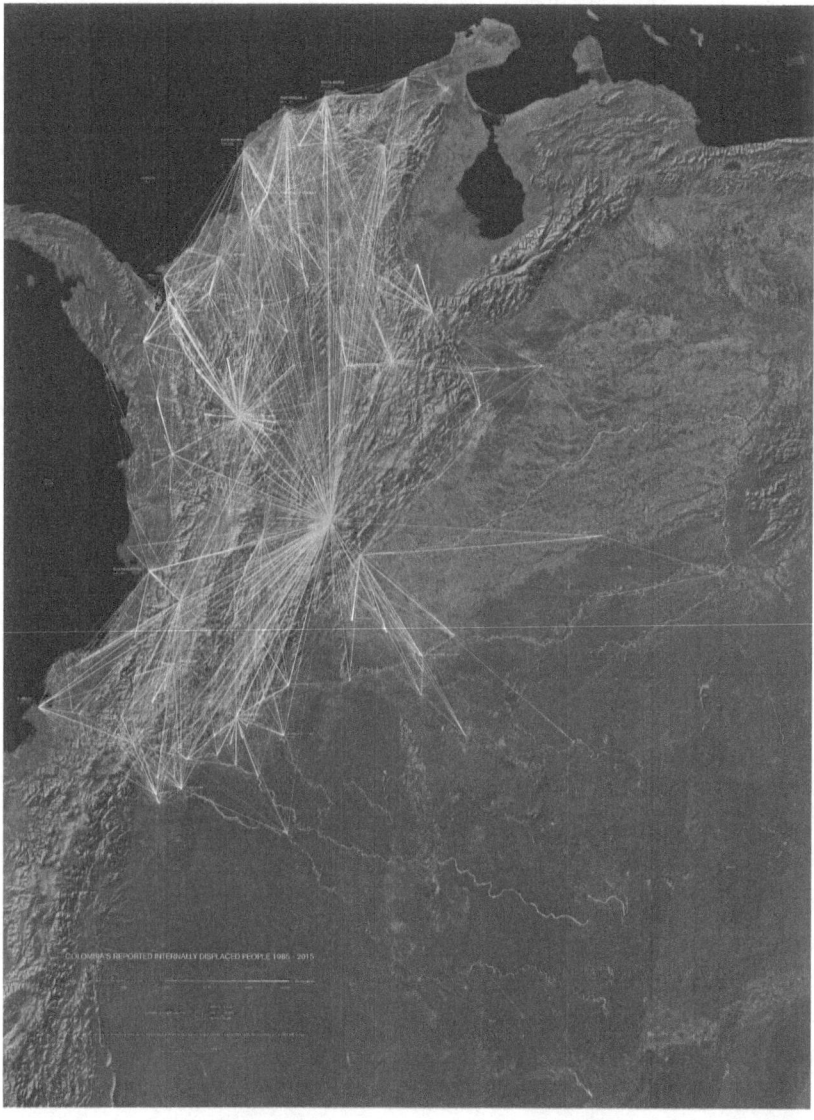

FIGURE 9.5. Colombia's Reported Internally Displaced People. *Conflict Urbanism: Colombia*, Center for Spatial Research, Columbia University, 2016.

one hand, while still making an argument with the data. The aim was to depict a specific point of view with the map and take ownership of that point of view. Too many maps claim objectivity through numbers. We claim that maps and statistics have a point of view and make an argument, and admitting that there is a point of view doesn't stop you from making an argument.

CHARLOTTE SILVERMAN: *In Plain Sight* seems to take a similar approach. It also moves between satellite images of the entire globe and particular cases, and it also seems to have a pedagogical impulse. The argument it constructs, meanwhile, focuses on extractive economies and their infrastructures. In this sense, it overlaps particularly closely with the "Speechless Deforestation" scene of *EXIT*. What was the relation between the two exhibitions?

LAURA KURGAN: We considered *In Plain Sight* as a sort of update to *EXIT*. It was created for the Venice Biennale and included members of the same team. In a sentence, what we did was compare the blue marble with the black marble. The blue and black marbles are images taken by the same NASA MODIS satellite at different times of the day. They're satellite images—but at

FIGURE 9.6. Fourth Scene *EXIT*: Natural Disasters: Visualization of Floods. Diller Scofidio + Renfro, Mark Hansen, Laura Kurgan, and Ben Rubin, in collaboration with Robert Gerard Pietrusko and Stewart Smith, *EXIT*, 2008-2015. Immersive audiovisual installation based on an idea by Paul Virilio (45 min.). View of the installation at the Palais de Tokyo, Paris, 2015. Collection Fondation Cartier pour l'art contemporain, Paris. Photo by Luc Boegley.

a very low resolution, one kilometer per pixel. The black marble is an image of the night-lights view of the world. It shows the Earth, which means the light visible to the satellite, at 1:00 a.m., which is to say in the pitch black of the night, so there's only infrastructural light and almost no residential light. The blue marble image is taken every day at 1:00 p.m. in the afternoon, which is to say in full daylight. Both the day and the night images are composite views. Many images are assembled digitally to compose a visible planet with no clouds.

CHARLOTTE SILVERMAN: So the result is a sense of consistency, but that very sense of consistency is generated through difference. The images are not taken at a single time—or at least not at a single moment—even if they appear to be.

LAURA KURGAN: They're taken at different points in time—but always at the same time of day. And then the cloudless version is multiple views and time frames embedded in a single image, but each time it encapsulates a split-second view taken from a satellite. I've written a lot about the composite image of the blue marble in my book *Close Up at a Distance: Mapping, Technology, and Politics*.

CHARLOTTE SILVERMAN: What did you hope to make visible through this composite view—especially the night-lights view of the world?

LAURA KURGAN: What you see at night is the light of infrastructure. We found ourselves being fascinated by the discrepancies between places in the world where there were lights but no people and places in the world where there were many people but no lights. When we looked at the most extreme discrepancies, a common feature emerged: they were spaces of inequality and conflict, and particularly they were landscapes of extraction. Places where there are mines showed lots of night light—many lights, very few people. However, there are also populations living quite close by with little visible infrastructural electricity—many people, very few lights. The same turned out to be true for sites of mass tourism. We showed places with huge hotels and very bright light in the Dominican Republic, while just two kilometers away were towns and villages with very unstable electricity. The stable lights of the hotel are powered by private generators and the shaky lights of the nearby towns by public utilities.

CHARLOTTE SILVERMAN: What data set underlaid the work?

LAURA KURGAN: We used a data set that we also used in *EXIT*, the Gridded Population of the World, and compared the night lights against this data set.

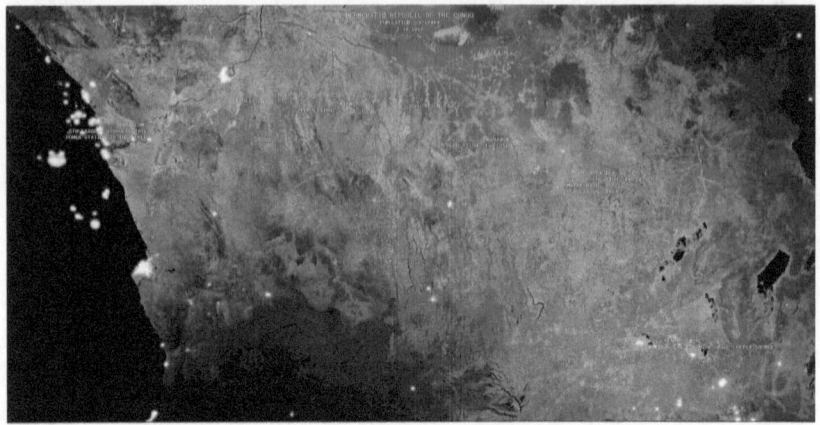

FIGURE 9.7. *In Plain Sight*: Still from the Cameroon scene. Diller Scofidio + Renfro, Laura Kurgan, and Robert Gerard Pietrusko with the Center for Spatial Research. The installation was conceived and designed for Dimensions of Citizenship, the U.S. Pavilion at the Sixteenth International Architecture Exhibition of La Biennale di Venezia, 2018. Commissioned by the School of the Art Institute of Chicago and the University of Chicago.

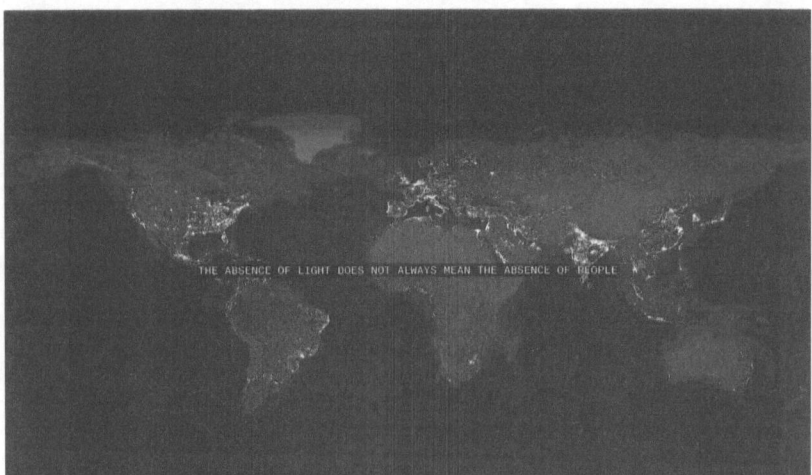

FIGURE 9.8. *In Plain Sight*: Still from the introduction. Diller Scofidio + Renfro, Laura Kurgan, and Robert Gerard Pietrusko with the Center for Spatial Research. The installation was conceived and designed for Dimensions of Citizenship, the U.S. Pavilion at the Sixteenth International Architecture Exhibition of La Biennale di Venezia, 2018. Commissioned by the School of the Art Institute of Chicago and the University of Chicago.

FIGURE 9.9. *In Plain Sight*: Still from the introduction. Diller Scofidio + Renfro, Laura Kurgan, and Robert Gerard Pietrusko with the Center for Spatial Research. The installation was conceived and designed for Dimensions of Citizenship, the U.S. Pavilion at the Sixteenth International Architecture Exhibition of La Biennale di Venezia, 2018. Commissioned by the School of the Art Institute of Chicago and the University of Chicago.

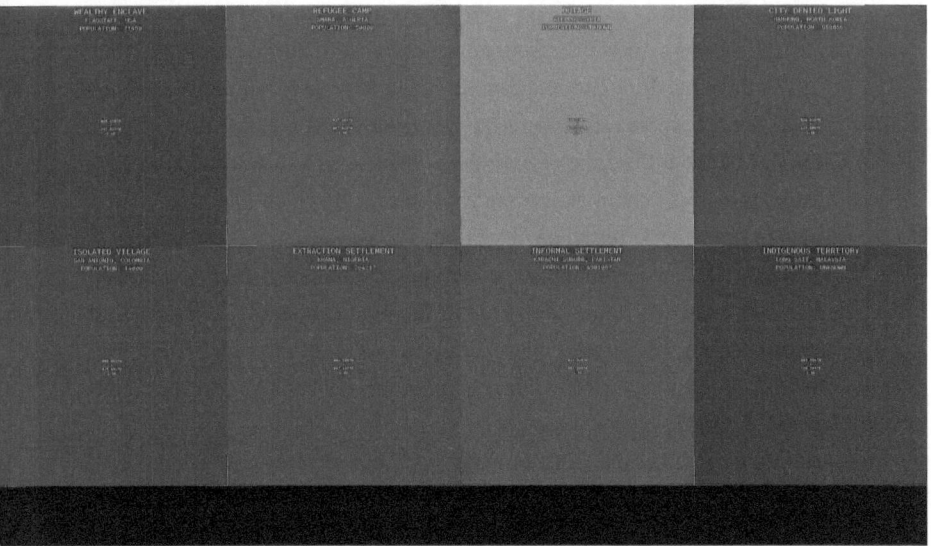

FIGURE 9.10. *In Plain Sight*: Still from the introduction. Diller Scofidio + Renfro, Laura Kurgan, and Robert Gerard Pietrusko with the Center for Spatial Research. The installation was conceived and designed for Dimensions of Citizenship, the U.S. Pavilion at the Sixteenth International Architecture Exhibition of La Biennale di Venezia, 2018. Commissioned by the School of the Art Institute of Chicago and the University of Chicago.

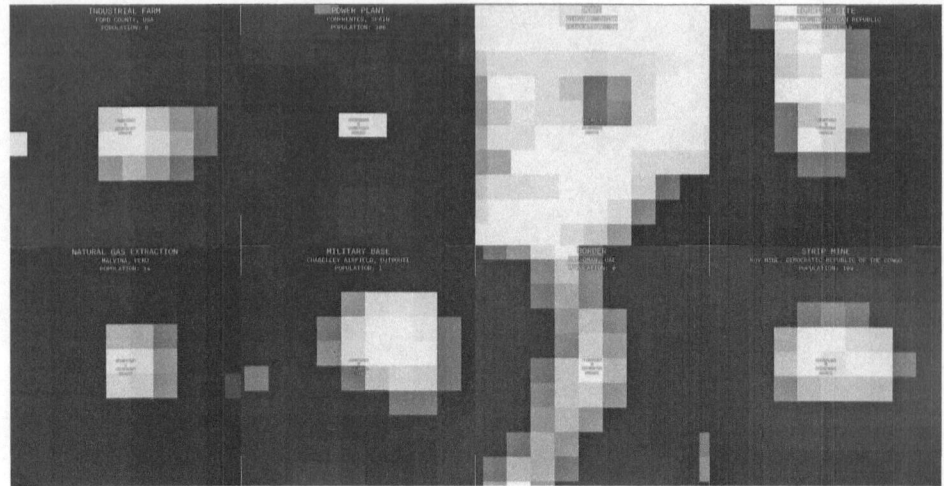

FIGURE 9.11. *In Plain Sight*: BrightGrid. Diller Scofidio + Renfro, Laura Kurgan, and Robert Gerard Pietrusko with the Center for Spatial Research. The installation was conceived and designed for Dimensions of Citizenship, the U.S. Pavilion at the Sixteenth International Architecture Exhibition of La Biennale di Venezia, 2018. Commissioned by the School of the Art Institute of Chicago and the University of Chicago.

CIESIN collects census data from governments around the world and then gathers them together into one data set. Then they turn that into a pixelated image. By a process called rasterization, the map of the world becomes a series of pixels at the scale of one square kilometer, and embedded in each pixel is the census count of how many people are living on that pixel. (These data are in the background of a lot of popular visualizations and statistics—especially the new commonplace that more than half the world's population now lives in cities.) We're very aware of the political pitfalls of that data set because some governments collect census information in more detailed ways than others. But, nevertheless, it is a good approximation of where people are in the world.

CHARLOTTE SILVERMAN: Both *In Plain Sight* and *EXIT* appear grounded in numerical data sets and spatial arrangements, yet language also plays such an important role in the representation of data in both works. Take the play in the titles, for instance. *In Plain Sight* reveals things that might not actually seem to be "in plain sight." *EXIT* seems at once to be an exit away from the Earth and also an entrance into it. And then there's the scene in *EXIT* that we've discussed—it's titled "Speechless Deforestation" but flooded with speech. What was the impetus for these particular titles—and for their seemingly paradoxical formulations?

LAURA KURGAN: To get you to think hard about the implications of the data and not to take anything for granted. It was really designed to have you think about both sides of the problem and not to just give everything one interpretation. That's what we mean when we say no data set is neutral. There's no such thing as an objective data set. As a team, we were always looking for the politics behind the data set and what it means to use it, bearing in mind the incomplete nature of so many of them. As far as *EXIT*, the title also really drew from Virilio, who did challenge us with the idea that our only choice was to try to exit the planet, though our team stayed firmly and representationally on the Earth.

CHARLOTTE SILVERMAN: Much of *EXIT* involves overlaying one data set onto another, as we see in "Speechless Deforestation." How does this enable the audience to see things differently?

LAURA KURGAN: One way to tell a powerful story is often to put two or more data sets together. None of the data presented in *EXIT* are real-time data. The bulk of the work we did in making this piece was assembling data sets that talk to each other. We were interested, for instance, in showing the unequal ways that the phenomena we were mapping are manifested globally. The people who are least responsible for climate change are also the most affected by it. There are lots of maps and visualizations of climate change. There are also lots of visualizations about population growth and sea-level rise as well as refugee maps. We tried to put some of these together in a narrative because none of them happens in a vacuum. And that was the prompt from Virilio that we responded to with such passion: to show not just *that* but *how* these three things—politics, environment, and economics—are intertwined.

CHARLOTTE SILVERMAN: Have you carried this approach to data visualization forward into more recent projects, especially work related to climate change?

LAURA KURGAN: I'm interested in the ways projects like these might allow an imagination of what can be done to reverse, solve, or at least mitigate this crisis or to reimagine ways forward. My current work is involved in thinking about alternative tools, counter-mapping, new forms of collaboration and direct action. I'll never completely shy away from the planetary view because the patterns of that spatial imagination are deeply ingrained in so much of our culture and its multiplicity of infrastructures. In response, I often work, like we do in *EXIT* and in other projects, with examples—local conditions, policies—to address the variety of patterns that arise from climate and its increasingly rapid pace of change. That is to say, at microscales in the context of macroscales. Going back to my earlier example, Pakistan is repeatedly flooded. The overarching theme of the exhibit—those responsible for climate events are the least affected by them—was a large part of our narrative in 2008 and in 2015. Today, the call for accountability is louder, especially in light of the severity of events such as the 2022 flood in Pakistan. Who should pay for the loss and damage? Is payment even the right turn of phrase? And if not, what are the right kinds of reparations for these immeasurable losses?

CHARLOTTE SILVERMAN: It's clear that numbers are important in these discussions but also not enough. There's also a need for narratives and for dialogue—in a multitude of languages. Calls for climate justice are inseparable from calls for language justice, in this way and others. *EXIT* illustrates this with such lucidity. Thank you so much for your willingness to share some of the deliberations and conversations that shaped both this project and more recent ones—and your thoughts on their resonance in the present.

CONTRIBUTORS

Deborah Anderson is a researcher in the Department of Linguistics at the University of California, Berkeley, where she runs the Script Encoding Initiative. She is also chair of the Unicode Consortium's Script Ad Hoc Group and a representative for the U.S. National Body on the ISO/IEC Subcommittee on Character Sets. She holds a PhD in Indo-European studies (linguistics emphasis) from the University of California, Los Angeles. She authors quarterly recommendations to the Unicode Technical Committee on new characters and scripts.

Bei Dao is one of the most influential writers in China. He is the author of many books of poetry, essays, and fiction, including *The Rose of Time, Unlock, At the Sky's Edge, Landscape Over Zero, Old Snow,* and *The August Sleepwalker*. His works have been translated into over thirty languages. He has received numerous awards and honors, including the Aragana Poetry Prize in Casablanca, the PEN/Barbara Goldsmith Freedom to Write Award, and a Guggenheim Fellowship. He was elected an honorary member of the American Academy of Arts and Letters and was awarded an honorary doctor of letters degree by Brown University. He lives in Hong Kong and Beijing.

Mohammed Bennis is a Moroccan poet. He was born in 1948 in Fez, Morocco. In 1974, he founded the magazine *Al Thaqâfa Al Jadida* (The new culture). He was primarily responsible for the establishment of the International Day of Poetry by UNESCO in 2000. He has published sixteen poetry collections and more than forty titles of poetry, prose, studies, essays, and translations. His translation of Stéphane Mallarmé's poem "Throw of the Dice" is the first in Arabic. He has received several awards, and his poetry has been translated into numerous languages, including French, German, Spanish, English, Italian, Turkish, Chinese, and Japanese.

L. Maria Bo is assistant professor at California State University, Fullerton. She has published in *Comparative Literature* and *Arizona Quarterly* and at present serves on a committee for the Circle of Asian American Literary Studies. She is currently working on a monograph on translation's effects on literary propaganda between the United States and China during the Cold War.

Manu V. Devadevan is associate professor of history at the School of Humanities and Social Sciences at the Indian Institute of Technology–Mandi. He has published two poetry collections in Kannada and routinely translates from English, Kannada, and Malayalam. His recent publications include *The Early Medieval Origins of India* (2020); *God Is Dead, There Is No God: Vachanas of Allama Prabhu; Translations of Allama Prabhu from Kannada* (2019); and *A Pre-history of Hinduism*, an original and wide-ranging work on premodern India, which won the Infosys Prize in 2019.

Madeleine Dobie is professor of French and comparative literature at Columbia University. She is the author of *Foreign Bodies: Gender, Language, and Culture in French Orientalism* (2001), *Trading Places: Colonization and Slavery in Eighteenth-Century French Culture* (2010), and, with Myriam Cottias, *Relire Mayotte Capécia: une femme des Antilles dans l'espace colonial français, 1916–1955* (2012), She is the editor of the forthcoming *A Comparative Literary History of Slavery*, Vol. 1, *Slavery, Literature and the Emotions*. She has published widely on the literature and cinema of the Maghreb and is currently working on a book titled *After Violence: Society, Politics and the Algerian New Wave*.

Daniel Kaufman is associate professor of linguistics at Queens College and the Graduate Center, City University of New York, and codirector of the Endangered Language Alliance (www.elalliance.org), a nonprofit organization based in New York City that collaborates with Indigenous and immigrant New Yorkers on various aspects of language documentation and conservation. He received his PhD from Cornell University in 2010 and specializes in the Austronesian language family of Island Southeast Asia. In this connection, he serves as coeditor of *Oceanic Linguistics*, the foremost journal in the field of Austronesian languages.

Laura Kurgan is a professor at the Graduate School of Architecture Planning and Preservation at Columbia University, where she directs the Master of Science in

CONTRIBUTORS

Computational Design Practices program and the Center for Spatial Research. She is the author of *Close Up at a Distance: Mapping, Technology, and Politics* (2013) and the coeditor of *Ways of Knowing Cities* (Columbia University Press, 2019). Kurgan's work explores the ethics and politics of digital mapping and its technologies; the art, science, and visualization of big and small data; and design environments for public engagement with maps and data.

Wesley Y. Leonard is a citizen of the Miami Tribe of Oklahoma and associate professor of ethnic studies at the University of California, Riverside. Drawing from his training in linguistics and experience in community-based language programs, he works to build capacity for Native American language reclamation in ways that support tribal sovereignty and wellness. A project that he codeveloped, Natives4Linguistics, broadens Indigenous participation in language sciences. His articles have appeared in a variety of edited volumes and journals such as *Gender and Language, Language Documentation and Conservation, Language Documentation and Description,* and *Journal of Linguistic Anthropology.*

Lydia H. Liu is the Wun Tsun Tam Professor in the Humanities at Columbia University and teaches in the Department of East Asian Languages and Cultures and at the Institute for Comparative Literature and Society. Her books include *The Freudian Robot: Digital Media and the Future of the Unconscious* (2010), *The Clash of Empires: The Invention of China in Modern World Making* (2004), and *Translingual Practice: Literature, National Culture and Translated Modernity* (1995). As a bilingual writer and translator, she has published widely in Chinese, including creative writing such as *The Nesbit Code* (2013).

Tommaso Manfredini is a lecturer in the Department of French and the Institute for Comparative Literature and Society at Columbia University. His research investigates the construction of the "illegality" of migration around the borders of the West and in the central Mediterranean in particular. He is also a volunteer translator and interpreter for immigrant justice organizations in New York City.

Ouyang Jianghe is an acclaimed avant-garde poet, calligrapher, and critic in China. He has published fifteen books of poetry, including *Through the Glass of Words, Tears of Things,* and *Who Departs and Who Stays* as well as essay collections such as *Standing on This Side of Fiction*. His poems have been translated into German, French, Spanish, Arabic, and English, including *Phoenix* and *Doubled Shadows*. The celebrated long poem *Phoenix* is a companion piece to Xu Bing's art installation of the same name. He is the recipient of the Chinese Literature Media Award in Poetry and the Xu Zhimo Poetry Prize.

CONTRIBUTORS

Ross Perlin is a linguist, writer, and translator focused on exploring and supporting linguistic diversity. Since 2013, he has been codirector of the Endangered Language Alliance, managing research projects on language mapping, documentation, policy, and public programming for urban linguistic diversity. He also teaches linguistics at Columbia University. He is the author of a book on unpaid work (*Intern Nation: How to Earn Nothing and Learn Little in the Brave New Economy*, 2012) and a forthcoming book about endangered languages in New York City.

Anupama Rao is professor of history (Barnard College) and Middle Eastern, South Asian, and African studies (Columbia University); director of the Institute for Comparative Literature and Society at Columbia University; and convener of the Ambedkar Initiative. She is the author of numerous works on caste, gender, and global histories of democracy, including the groundbreaking *Caste Question: Dalits and the Politics of Modern India* (2009) as well as *Gender, Caste, and the Imagination of Equality* (2018) and *Memoirs of a Dalit Communist: The Many Worlds of R. B. More* (2019).

Suzanne Romaine is professor emerita, University of Oxford and fellow of both the Finnish Academy of Science and Letters and the Norwegian Academy of Science and Letters. Her book *Vanishing Voices: The Extinction of the World's Languages*, coauthored with Daniel Nettle, situates the loss of linguistic diversity within the near-total collapse of the global ecosystem. In collaboration with Conservation International, she coauthored *Linguistic Diversity in High Biodiversity Regions*, focusing on the cooccurrence of languages and species in thirty-four hotspots and five high biodiversity wilderness areas. Her most recent research examines the interface of biodiversity, linguistic diversity, and poverty.

Charlotte Silverman is a doctoral candidate in the Department of Anthropology and the Institute for Comparative Literature and Society at Columbia University and has taught at a range of educational institutions in Laos. She works at the intersections of anthropology, comparative literature, and education, with a focus on Southeast Asia. Her dissertation examines the role of literacy in the transformation of values underwriting processes of globalization, bringing analyses of contemporary dance, popular music, and film together with ethnographic techniques.

Orlando White is Diné from Sweetwater, Arizona. He holds a BFA from the Institute of American Indian Arts and an MFA from Brown University. He is the author of *Bone Light* (2009) and *LETTERRS* (2015), which won the San Francisco Poetry Center Book Award. He is the recipient of a Truman Capote Creative Writing Fellowship, a Lannan Foundation Residency, and a Bread Loaf John Ciardi Fellowship. He has taught at the Art Center Design College and

CONTRIBUTORS

Brown University. Currently, he teaches at Diné College in Tsaile, Arizona, and in the low-residency MFA program at the Institute of American Indian Arts.

Abhay Xaxa was trained in law and sociology. Before his untimely death in 2020, Xaxa played a critical role in agitating for Adivasi land in India and environmental rights and challenging the erasure of Adivasi histories. In addition to authoring a rich body of poetry and other writings, including the coedited volume *Being Adivasi: Existence, Entitlements, Exclusion*, he worked as a research fellow at the Indian Institute of Dalit Studies in Delhi, was a program coordinator with the National Campaign for Dalit Human Rights from 2012 to 2019, and served as convener of the National Campaign for Adivasi Rights and coconvener of the Tribal Intellectual Collective.

Xu Bing is one of the most important contemporary artists working today. Known for his printmaking and installation art, including *Book from the Sky*, *Square Word Calligraphy*, *Tobacco Project*, *Background Story*, *Book from the Ground*, and *Phoenix Project*, he has exhibited at the Museum of Modern Art, Metropolitan Museum of Art, Guggenheim Museum, Arthur M. Sackler Gallery of the National Museum of Asian Art, and numerous venues around the world. Among his awards and honors, he has received the MacArthur Genius Award (1999), the Medal of Arts from the U.S. Department of State's Office of Art in Embassies (2015), and an honorary doctorate in humane letters from Columbia University (2010).

Isabelle A. Zaugg is a lecturer at Columbia University's Institute for Comparative Literature and Society, where she was a Mellon postdoctoral fellow with the Sawyer Seminar on Global Language Justice from 2017 to 2019. She also holds a program manager position at Columbia's Data Science Institute. Her recent publications include "Imagining a Multilingual Cyberspace" in the online anthology *Finding ctrl: Visions for the Future Internet* (2019) and "Digital Inequality and Language Diversity: An Ethiopic Case Study" in *Digital Inequalities in the Global South* (2020).

Zhai Yongming is a prominent poet, essayist, and critic in China and founder of the renowned White Night art and literary salon in Chengdu. Among her many poetry collections are *Woman*, *Above All Roses*, *Collected Poems of Zhai Yongming*, *Call It All*, *Fourteen Plain Songs*, and *Interlinear Spaces*. She has also published six collections of essays and literary criticism. Her poetry has been translated into English, French, Dutch, Italian, Spanish, and German, including *The Changing Room*. She is the recipient of many awards, including the Italian Ceppo Pistoia International Literary Prize, the 31st Annual Northern California Book Award for Poetry, and the Chinese Media Award.

INDEX

Page numbers in *italics* indicate figures.

aboriginal languages, Australian dreamtime and, 176
absolutism, of individual rights, 43–44
abstract language, rights in society and, 44
access, English lessons, 21, 52
accurate messaging, Unicode and, 220–221
ACS. *See* American Community Survey
activism, for endangered languages, 2–3, 201, 212n40, 281
addictive design, of online platforms, 262
ADLaM script, 226, *226*–227, 236, 239nn13–14
adult illiteracy, 75–76
Afghan refugee example, 6
Africa: development landscape of, 73; exclusion from global flow of information of, 74; HIV risks of women in, 76; ineffectiveness of English language information in, 77; language policy in postcolonial, 79–80; languages in New York of, 180; pathways contrasted with outcomes of, 83; primary school completion in, 79–80; South Africa, 79; southern Asia and, 68. *See Also* sub-Saharan Africa
African women, HIV risks of, 76

agency, of Indigenous people, 5, 47–50, 133–134, 184–185
Ahlers, Jocelyn, 145
Aide-Mémoire and Glossary, of Case Processing Modalities (EU document), 107–108
AJK. *See* Azad Jammu and Kashmir, Pakistan
Albanian neighborhoods, in Italian areas of New York, 181
Albert, Bruce, 278
Alemnehe, Abass, 253
Alexander, Neville, 79
Algeria: dialects of Arabic in, 18–19, 49, 198–199; Dobie on, 194–210, 260–261; identity groups of, 202; language politics in, 197–198; revision of constitution in, 208–209, 213n46; Transition of Arabic to language of, 199–200, 211n19
Algerian Civil War, 202–203
Algerian media landscape, changes in, 204
Algerians and French, relationship between, 206
Alhondiga museum, Bilbao, 276
Al-Jazeera (news network), 204
"Allô le système" (song), 207–208

INDEX

alphabetic script, bias toward, 259
Amazigh activism, transnational basis of, 201, 212n40
Amazigh flag, at protests, 206
Amazigh linguistic and cultural rights, campaign for, 201
Amazon rain forest, 278
American Community Survey (ACS), 13, 167, 171, 184
American context, of human rights, 43
American Declaration of Independence, 37–38
American Empire, 25–26
American Indian English, 153n30
American Indians, perceived ideals of, 127
Amery, Rob, 152n20
Amharic, exclusion of religious characters from, 259–260
Amharic language, 244–245, 251, 251–252, 253, 254; keyboards for, 256, 257; in Latin script, 254–255, 255, 259; as official language, 244–245, 267n11; reverential words in, 259–260
Amuzgo (Ñomndaa) language, 179–180
ancestral habitat loss, language loss and, 7
Anderson, Deborah, 23, 24, 26, 74, 220–221; on Unicode digital inclusion and, 250, 266; on writing systems scripts and, 257
ankita (signature of composers), 159
"The Anthropogenic Biomes of the World" (data set), 277–278
appearance differences, in Miami people, 134–135, 153n23
Applicant K, 110–111; attachment to home of, 113–114; difficulty in finding birthplace of, 112–113, 122n35, 122n40, 182, 282
Arabic, 18–19, 206; in Algeria, 18–19, 49, 198–199; campaign for Amazigh linguistic rights and, 201; distinctions in dialects of in New York, 181; French and, 205–206; Latin-based scripts and, 248; Pular language and, 226–227; suppression in Algeria of, 199; Tamazight and, 200–201; transition to official language of Algeria of, 199–200, 211n19
Arabicization, in Algeria, 200, 211n21
Arabic version, of *Aide-Mémoire*, 108

Arabizi script, 248
Arabs, Berbers and, 18–19, 49, 201, 206
Arab Spring, of 2011, 204, 207
arbitrariness, of asylum interview process, 116
Architecture, Urbanism, and the Humanities program, of Mellon Foundation, 283–284
Arendt, Hannah, 60n14
"Are You Sleeping?" ("Frère Jacques.") (song), 139–140
Armenian speaker, response to ELA map of, 183
"the Army, the People are brothers, brothers" chant *(Jīsh sh'ab . . . khawa)*, 206–207
Arnhem Land, Australia, 176
ASCII Code Chart, 248, 248–249
assimilation, treatment of English and French versions of ULDR in, 56–58
assimilationist force, during asylum process, 100–101
As the Rez Turns (soap opera), 142
asylum: commission appearance, 106, 110–117; European Union (EU) and, 99, 102–104, 117nn1–2, 118n4; requests in Italy after 2013, 105, 120n19
Asylum Procedures Directive, of EU, 99, 118n4
asylum process: arbitrariness of, 116; assimilationist force during, 100–101; attempted streamlining of, 105, 120n21; credible narrative and, 12, 98–117, 117n3, 119n10; ease of participation in, 110, 121n34, 122n36; European union and, 102–103; interpreter in, 111, 122n36; of Italian state, 104–117, 117n3; linguistic justice during, 100; procedure for, 101–102; textual steps of, 116; translation during, 99
asylum requests in Italy, after 2013, 105, 120n19
asylum seekers: language loss and, 12, 27–28, 98–99; limited rights of, 100; Mayan interpreters and, 172; translation for, 98–99
asymmetrical power relationship, between applicant and reviewing commission, 108–109, 116

INDEX

Atelier National de Recherche Typographique, of Nancy, France, 234
Atlaw, Fesseha, 252
"Ats'íísts'in" (poem), 35
attempted citizenship question, of Trump administration, 169, 281–282
aunt, of Bird, 52–53
Australia: Aboriginal languages dreamtime and, 176; Arnhem Land, 176
ayaalo ("Go!") game, 143
Azad Jammu and Kashmir, Pakistan (AJK), 112
Azerbaijani language, scripts used for, 257–258

badarlan (borderland), 112, 122n35
Baïnounk speaker, at festival, 182–183, 188n41
Baldwin, Daryl, 131
Balibar, Etienne, 62n31
ball games and games of chance (*weekihkaaminki-meehkintiinki*), 139
Bamum Palace Archives, 224–225
Bamum script, 224–225, 225, 238n12
Bangladeshi neighborhoods of New York, accurate information in, 77
Barber, Benjamin, 196
Barry, Abdoulaye, 226–227
Barry, Ibrahima, 226–227
"Basava" (poem), 163, 164
"Becoming a Child" (poem), 96–97; Yongming, Zhai, 96
Bei Dao, 66; "February" (poem), 66–67
Benedict, Ruth, 30n21
Benhabib, Seyla, 16–17, 196
Benkhaled, Walid, 201–202
Bennis, Mohammed, 192; "Words" (poem), 192–193
Berbers, Arabs and, 18–19, 49, 201, 206
Berber Spring, 200
Bété script, 231–232, 232
"Between English and Chinese" (poem), 216–219
Big Tech, lack of support for linguistic diversity of, 265
Bilbao, Spain, 276
bilingual education: in Senegal, 80–81; translanguaging and, 173–174

biodiversity, linguistic diversity and, 8, 69–70, 265–266, 280
biometric data, digital collection of, 262–263
biophysical footprints, economic growth and, 86
Bird, Gloria, 52–54
birthplace of Applicant K, difficulty finding, 112–113, 122n35, 122n40, 182, 282
Black Power movement, 47–48
Black Spring, of 2001, 200, 206
Blommaert, Jan, 197
blood quantum requirement, for tribal citizenship, 134–135, 153n25
Bo, L. Maria, 15, 19, 36–37, 98–99, 195; on differing ideas of "equality," 246; on minority language activism, 210n2, 281
Boas, Franz, 30n21
Bogota, Colombia, 284
borderland *(badarlan)*, 112, 122n35
borders, of Europe, 104, 117n2
borrowing: from English in Indigenous languages, 136–137; from French into English acceptability of, 140
bottom billion, of Collier, 69, 71, 87, 247
Bouteflika, Abdelaziz, 211n23, 212n31, 213n46; response to fifth term of, 202–203; stroke of, 203–204
Bouzid, Tayeb, 205–206, 212n36
Brazil, deforestation in, 278
Brigham and Women's Hospital, English skills of patients in, 77–78
British Empire, 20
Brooklyn, Russian speakers in, 181
brotherhood theory, of V. Deloria, 50
Brundtland Commission, 87
Butler, Judith, 62n31

C-3 form. *See* intake form, for refugees to Italy
Caal, Jakelin, 172
cake metaphor, 85, 86
Cambodia, 10
Cameroon: Bamum script in, 224; deforestation in, 278; road construction in, 278
capitalist agendas, dominant language theory and, 10

INDEX

carré féministe group, 209
Cartier Foundation, 275–276
"La Casa del Mouradia" (football chant), 205, 212n38
La Casa de Papel (TV show), 205
castes, of *sharanas*, 159
Census Bureau: disparity between work of (ELA) and, 179–180; language information of, 166–169, *168*; mistrust of, 169; success of in 2020, 169–170; use of map for blind spots of, 183–184
Census of 2020, 169
Center for International Earth Science Information Network (CIESIN), 278, 290
Center for Spatial Research (CSR), 276–277, 283–284
Central Immigration Service (Centro Servizi Intergrati per l'Immigrazione), 109, 117
Chakma language, 236
Chakrabarty, Dipesh, 29n7
challenging of state, language rights and, 45
"Channabasava," 163, 164
"Chaudayya, the Ferryman" (poem), 161, 162
chess: Miami names for pieces of, 141–142, 155n38; use of *myaamia* in game of, 142–143, 155n37
Cheurfi, Hiyem, 206–207
Chilean state, Rapa Nui people and, 176
China, 20, 55, 56
Chinese version, of UDLR, 56, 58, 63n46
CIESIN. *See* Center for International Earth Science Information Network
"Citizenship and Social Class" (Marshall), 15
city residents, digital surveillance of, 262–263
Clayton, Stephen, 10
CLDR. *See* Unicode Common Locale Data Repository
climate change, inequality and, 70, 86, 290–292
Close Up at a Distance (Kurgan), 287
collective, rights of, 15, 41, 46–47; individual rights and, 43–44, 56, 60n14, 61n21, 101–102

collective action, Hobbes on, 42
collective deliberation, 16–17
collective identity, American culture and, 47, 60n14
collective political engagement, 198–199
collective sense of opposition, hirak and, 204
Collier, Paul, 69; bottom billion, of, 71, 87, 247
Colloquium on the International Protection of Refugees in Central America, 117n1
Colombia, 282–284; Reported Internally Displaced People of, *285*
colonialism/colonization: in Algeria, 199; Latin script and, 258–259; named languages and, 175, 184–185; perceptions on Indigenous languages and, 136, 153n27; politics of, 18
colonial languages, problems with education in, 79
common property, private property and, 45–46
communication, during Ebola outbreak, 76–77, 89n36
communicative justice, 89n36
communicative subject, 17
comparative orientation, of rights activists, 49
completely consistent participation (*vishi*), 56
complex equality, simple equivalences and, 46–47
complex scripts, 230, *230*, 239n24
complicated government relationships, digital tools and, 263, 266
computer-mediated interaction, in *myaamia*, 144–146
computers (*kiinteelintaakana*), use of by Miami people, 145
Conference of the Parties (COP 15), 276
consciousness (*yishi*), 58
constituent assembly in Algeria, public call for, 203, 209
constitution, revision of in Algeria, 208–209, 213n46
content moderation, 264–265
Convention Against Torture, 121n26
Convention Relating to the Status of Refugees, 101–102, 105–106, 117n1, 119n6; expansion of, 119n9

INDEX

COP 15. *See* Conference of the Parties
"correct" English, Indigenous dialects and, 137, 153n30
Corte di Cassazione (Italian Supreme Court), 105
counsel, in asylum interview, 111
counter-mapping, 177, *178*, 179
counting, in *myaamia*, 139
courthouses *(tribunali ordinari)*, 120n22
covenantal model, 50
Covid-19: Americans during, 43; communication during, 77; education and, 84; hirak in Algeria and, 203–204; Indigenous Latin Americans in New York and, 184
creative resistance, multistakeholder efforts and, 251–252
Creator, Ethiopian Orthodox Tewahedo Church beliefs on name of, 260
credible narrative, asylum process and, 12, 98–102, 98–117, 117n3, 119n10
creole languages in New York, wide differences between, 179
CSR. *See* Center for Spatial Research
cultural assimilation, different ideas of, 58
cultural fluency, 131–133
cultural identity: of Algeria forming of, 201–202; purity, flawed assumptions about, 127–128, 134, 150n5
Cyrillic script, 227

Dakar Framework for Action, 75–76
Dakota Grammar (Boas and E. Deloria), 30n21
Daoud, Kamel, 200
darija dialect, of Arabic, 198, 204–205
Dashen Ethiopic word processor, 252, *252*
data collection, surveillance and, 261–262
data-fueled predictive practices, 262
data mining, 261–262
data sets, complications of, 279–281, 290–291
Davis, Muriam Haleh, 206–207
Debenport, Erin, 142
deconstruction, of script systems, 25
defense of language, defense of cultures and, 195
deforestation, 278
deliberate choice *(délibéré)*, use of term in UDLR of, 56–57, 58

deliberative democracy, 57, 196–197
délibéré (deliberate choice), use of term in UDLR of, 56–57, 58
Deloria, Ella Cara, 30n21
Deloria, Philip, 126–127
Deloria, Vine, Jr., 19, 30n21, 40–41, 47–52
democracy: deliberative, 57, 196–197; representation and, 208
democratic theory, deliberative turn in, 57
Depardon, Raymond, 275–276
Department of Typography and Graphic Communication, University of Reading, 234, 240n30
Derg regime, 258–260
Derrida, Jacques, 25
details of scripts, difficulty in finding, 230
Devadevan, Manu, 19, 159; "The Vachanas," 159–164
"Devara Dasimayya" (poem), 165
device manufacturers, lobbying for font inclusion of, 234
dialect, distinction between language and, 169–171, *178*, 179, 186n15
dialectal lingua franca, among Italian immigrants, 171
dialetti (Italo-Romance languages), 170
diction, within digital tools, 246, 267n7
digital inclusion, 23–26, 220–221, 222, 223, 223–237; Amharic and, 253–254; language justice and, 246–267; language loss and, 27, 29n9, 245–246; level of support of languages of, 247, 250
digital infrastructure, for Unicode inclusion, 233–235
digital justice, 260–261
"Digital Language Death" (Kornai), 250
digitally disadvantaged language group: social media lack of moderation of, 254–265; tools development by military intelligence of, 263
digital pioneers, in Ethiopic skills, 252, 252–253
digital presence, 23–25, 185
digital representation, linguistic values and, 236
digital sphere: language bias in, 248–249; language justice in, 265–266
digital surveillance, state-sponsored, 262, 266–267

INDEX

digital tech, romanization and, 258
digital vitality, 19–20, 220–221, 250–252, *251*
Dilem, Ali, 206
discrete language boundaries, as social constructs, 172
disinvention, of languages, 174–177
diversity, equality and, 19, 194–195
Djebar, Assia, 211n21
Dobie, Madeleine, 15, 16–17, 18–19, 49, 98–99; on Algeria, 194–210, 260–261
Doctors without Borders (Médecins Sans Frontières), 77
documentation of Indigenous languages, overemphasis on, 130
dollar sign, use of for s-wedge, 146, 155n45
dominance of English, undoing of, 20
dominant discourse, on Indigenous languages, 127–135, 146–149; difficulty with counterexamples to, 136–137
dominant economic world order, inequality of, 85
domination, historical relations of, 14
Dorian, Nancy C., 7, 10
doughnut economics, 9, 68–72, *72*, 83–86
downloadable Ethiopic keyboards, 255, *256*, 257
Draren, Khaled, 206
"*droit de la ville*" (right to the city), 207
dropout rates, mother tongue education and, 80–81
Dryzek, John, 196
D'Souza, Radha, 43
Dublin Regulation, 104, 120n17

eagle and cow example, of Sitting Bull, 49–50, *51*
East Asia, lingua franca in, 22–23
Ebola outbreak, 76, 89n36; ineffectiveness of untranslated posters during, 77
eco-, from etymon *oikos*, 9
ecological ceiling, 71
ecological devastation, language loss and, 1–2, 6, 27–28, 30n17, 276–292
Ecological diversity, language diversity and, 245, 266, 276–292
ecological responsibility, 51
ecology, of languages, 6–7
ecology-based covenant theory, of V. Deloria, 50–51, 55

economic growth: at expense of environment, 71, 86–87; inequality and, 85–86; literacy and, 75–76, 84–85
economy, language loss and, 11, 14–15
education, in international languages, 9–10, 79–81
Education 2030 Framework for Action, 70
Education for All (EFA), 68, 69
eewansaapita language and cultural immersion camp, for Miami youth, 137–141, 145–147, 152n32
EFA. *See* Education for All
efficacy, of language, 7, 10
ELA. *See* Endangered Language Alliance
Elder life, in Miami community, 138, 154n34
electoral participation, newspaper readership and, 80–81
embodied identity, 18
Endangered Archives Programme, 224–225
Endangered Language Alliance (ELA) map, 167–168, 177, 183–185; disparity between work of Census Bureau and, 179–182, 281; endonyms on, *178*, 179; response of Indigenous communities to, 182, 249–250
endangered languages: activism for, 2–3, 201, 212n40, 281; classifications of, 279, 279; number of, 2. *See Also* Endangered Language Alliance (ELA) map
"Endangered Languages of the World" (UNESCO), 277–280, *279*
endonyms, on New York City language map, *178*, 179
England, University of Reading in, 234, 240n30
English: attempted replacement of Arabic by, 205–206, 212n36; borrowings from French into, 140; borrowings from in Indigenous languages, 136, 153n30; Global English, 21–26, 27–27, 249; information in West Africa ineffectiveness of, 77; lessons access to, 21, 52; skills foreign aid in Cambodia and, 10; status in world of, 20–22; technical knowledge needed for Unicode in, 232; version of *Aide-Mémoire* deference to, 108–109

INDEX

English-language education, cost of multilingual education contrasted with, 21

English-language learning: native language literacy and, 10, 79–80; promotion of, 10, 20, 30n22, 52; UDLR translation of, 55–56

The Enlightenment, 42

environmental degradation, poverty and, 70

equality: problems with American idea of, 43, 48–49, 60n14; Western idea of, 40–41, 60n14

equal rights, linguistic justice and, 19, 40, 49–50, 51, 58–59

equivalence across all spheres, as self-defeating, 46

equivalent concepts, in different languages, 19

Errington, Joseph, 130

essentialism, 49, 53–54, 185

ethical imperatives, languages and, 2

Ethiopia, 82, 244–257

Ethiopian and Eritrean languages, study of Zaugg on, 26–27, 244–257

Ethiopian Orthodox Tewahedo Church, 259, 260

Ethiopic characters, multiple levels of meaning in, 259–260

Ethiopic script, 245, 246, 250–253, 251, 254; orthographic tradition of, 259–260

ethnolinguistic groups, erasure of, 185

Ethnologue (database), 126, 149n1, 280

ethnonationalism, 21

EU. *See* European Union

Europe, hosting of refugees by, 103

European Union (EU), asylum and, 99, 102–104, 117nn1–2, 118n4

European Union Agency for Asylum, 117nn1–2

European values, human rights documents translations and, 55

Evers, Claudia, 77

everyday communication, by Miami people, 144

evolutionary development theory, Roman script and, 25

examiner question, about Pakistani geography, 114

EXIT (art exhibit), 274, 275–277, 282, 290–291

Facebook: comments in Ethiopia language choice in, 254–255, 255, 256, 257, 258–259; lack of content moderation in minority languages of, 264–265; pages popular in Ethiopia, 254

Family Code, of Algeria, 209

Fanon, Frantz, 200, 201–202

fear, necessity of proof of during asylum interview, 113

"February" (poem), 66; Chinese version of, 67; Bei Dao, 66

Fekhar, Kamel Eddine, 212n40

feminist group, incident with during hirak, 209n48

Firdyiwek, Yitna, 253

first country rule, 104, 120n16

first generation, of human rights, 37–38

first-language digital supports, for new scripts, 257

Fleming, Luke, 175

FLN. *See* Front de libération nationale

flood study, of Kurgan, 284, 286, 291–292

fluidity, language justice and, 196

fonts, apps for, 234

forced assimilation, of American Indians, 132

forced migration, language change and, 17, 166–167

foreign hand *(main de l'étranger)*, 205–206

France: attempted connection of Kabyle ethnic group with, 206, 212n29, 260–261; migrant miners in, 199; migrant workers in, 199

freedom, difference of in translation of term, 58

Freeman, Michael, 44

French: attitude in Algeria toward, 199–200, 204–206; influence on Miami language of, 140; UDLR in, 55, 56–58, 60n6; version of *Aide-Mémoire*, 108

French colonial era, in Algeria, 198

French Rights of Man and Citizen, 37–38

"Frère Jacques." ("Are You Sleeping?") (song), 139–140

Friday marches, of hirak, 207

Front de libération nationale (FLN), 199, 202

full-stack support, of languages, 247, 260–261

INDEX

function creep, 263–264
Fuocoammare (documentary), 112
fusha (Modern Standard Arabic), 200, 204–205

Gaïd Sālaḥ, Ahmed, 203, 206–207, 208–209
games, at Miami summer camp, 139
garbling, of scripts not in Unicode, 222, 223
Garifuna language, small boy and, 183
Gboard keyboard, 225, 234, 255
GDP. *See* gross domestic product
gender disparities, in education, 74
generations of immigrants, views of dialects of, 170–171
geographic diversity, of Miami people, 138
Giordano, Cristiana, 108–109
Girona Manifesto, 60n12
Glendon, Mary, 43
global asylum order, 108
global development goals, 69
global digital divide, 23
Global Education Monitoring Report (UNESCO), 82
Global English, 21–26, 27–28, 249
global flow of information, exclusion of Africa from, 74
Global Forest Watch, 278
global growth, needed sharing of benefits of, 86
globalization, 154n31
Global Justice for Indigenous Languages symposium, 7–8, 29n10
global language justice, 6
global megaphone, English as, 22
Global North, 98–99, 100–102
Global Positioning System (GPS), use in language activism of, 281
Global South, 99
Global Task Force for Making a Decade of Action for Indigenous Languages, of United Nations, 2
Global Trends (UN Refugee Agency), 11
global wealth, ownership of, 85
globe, planet contrasted with, 29n8
"Go!" *(ayaalo)* game, 143
Goodfellow, Anne, 127–128
Google Chrome, 230, 240n35
Google Input Tools, 240n35
Google searches, prejudices and, 261–262

government: crackdown, on hirak, 203–204; support for minority languages rights-based approach and, 246
GPS. *See* Global Positioning System
greetings and goodbyes, use of *myaamia* in, 145
Gridded Population of the World data set, 287, 288, 289, 290, 290
gross domestic product (GDP), needed increase of, 86
group rights, individual rights and, 14, 16–17
Guidelines on The Assessment of Credibility, 119n10
Gurage language, 253

Habermas, Jürgen, 17
Haddad, Malek, 211n21
Haketia language, 179
Haller, Herman, 171
Hanif, Shahana, 77
Hanifi Rohingya script, 224
Hanzi script, in East Asian languages, 22–23, 24–25, 257, 259
Harrison, K. David, 265–266
Hausa, 73–74
Hear Them Speak (art exhibit), 275–276
Heath, Jeffrey, 176
hegemonic power, insistence on equal participation in UDLR and, 56
Herderian formula, 176, 188n30
hierarchies: of digital inclusion of languages, 244; recalibration of, 18–19
hierarchization of versions, of translated documents, 106–107, 107, 121n28
high language varieties, low and, 170
high-resource scripts, digital support for, 249
Hill, Jane, 130, 151n9
Hindu and Urdu, different scripts of, 24
hirak (prodemocracy movement of Algeria), 18–19, 194–195, 205–206; collective sense of opposition and, 204; Covid-19 and, 203–204; Friday marches of, 207; government crackdown on, 203–204; incident with feminist group during, 209n48; linguistic pluralism of, 199; political coalitions from, 208–209; protests of, 198; slogans of, 198, 204, 212n31, 260–261

INDEX

historical relations, of domination, 14
hizb frança, "the party of France," 200, 211n20
Hobbes, Thomas, 41; on humanity language and, 42
Holpuch, Amanda, 184
Holy Trinity (እግዚአብሔር), 260
home of Applicant K., demonstrated attachment to, 113–114
home-region language ideologies, in immigrant communities, 170
homophonous characters in Ethiopic script, incorrect substitution of, 260
hotspots, of biodiversity, 69–70
human existence, language and, 14; Hobbes on, 42
Human immunodeficiency virus (HIV): risks of women in Africa, 76; sub-Saharan Africa and, 76
humanitarian protection, of Italian government, 106, 121n24, 121n26
humanitarian surveillance, 263–264
human-machine interfaces, English use in, 22–23
human rights, linguistic diversity and, 12–13, 15–16, 37–40, 194–195
Hurston, Zora Neale, 30n17

"I Am Not Your Data" (poem), 125
Ibn Badis, Abdelhamid, 199–200
ICLS. *See* Institute for Comparative Literature and Society
identity: of Algeria, 127–128m 134, 150n5, 201–202; American culture collective and, 47, 60n14; assumptions about, 127–128, 134, 150n5; embodied, 18; groups of Algeria, 202; relational, 18
illiteracy, cost of, 75–76
immigrants: dialectal lingua franca among Italian, 171; "Italianization" of Italian, 170–171; tacit trilingualism of Italian, 171; views of dialects of generations of, 170–171
immigration: to New York, 166–170; policy of Italy, 105
impartiality, Western notions of equality and, 37
imperialist campaigns, Western philosophy of individual and, 43

Incheon Declaration, 80, 81–82
India, English in, 20
Indiana and Oklahoma, concentration of Miami people in, 138
Indian boarding schools, 132, 152n16
Indians in Unexpected Places (P. Deloria), 126–127
indigenous languages, in large cities, 6
Indigenous languages: dominant discourse on, 127–135, 136, 147–148; doubts on vocabulary inclusion of, 137, 148; ecosystems and, 70; English influence of, 136, 153n30; language loss and, 132–133, 166–167; of Mexico reluctance to report on Census of, 171; perceived appropriate use of, 136, 146–147; restrictions on use of, 128, 136, 148; rise of English and, 21; social hierarchies and, 172; technology and, 27, 145, 244–245; in unexpected places, 128–129, 135, 149, 154n31; Western perceptions of, 134, 135, 136, 148; Western scholars on, 130, 134, 151n10; Western scholars on "legitimate" use of, 128, 148, 153n30
Indigenous Latin Americans in United States, linguistic erasure of, 171–172
Indigenous Mexicans, in New York, 181–182
Indigenous people, agency of, 5, 47–50, 133–134, 184–185
Indigenous purism, 176
individual, collective and, 56–57
individualism, 47–49, 62n31
individual rights: absolutism of, 43–44; collective rights and, 43–44, 56–57
Indonesia, palm oil plantations in, 278
inequality: climate change and, 70, 86, 290–292; of dominant economic world order, 85; economic growth and, 85–86; environment and, 87; language and, 14, 85–87, 197; of *in Plain Sight*, 290–291
information technology: linguistic diversity and, 22, 244–245; skills necessity of for digital inclusion, 221, 229
infrastructure: light of, 287; minority languages and, 37; technological infrastructure of script, 25; of informatics, 26

INDEX

In Plain Sight (art exhibit), 276, 286–287, *287*, *288*, *289*; inequality displays of, 290–291
Institute for Comparative Literature and Society (ICLS), 276–277
institutional language, 119n11
intake form, for refugees to Italy (C-3 form), *103*, 106–107, 121n34
intelligibility during asylum process, problems with translation and, 115–116
internal group variation, 49
International Declaration of Language Rights, 210n2
International Organization for Migration, 11–12
international protection: application process for, 111, 120n20; demand strain on system of, 104
international refugee law, 98–101, 119n6, 119n9
Internet Corporation for Assigned Names and Numbers, 247, 267n8
interoperability, of ideographic scripts, 259
interpreter, in asylum interview, 111, 122n36
intersecting disadvantages, minority languages and, 69, 247
Italian border control, increase of, 105, 120n22
Italian education, lack of foreign languages in, 104
"Italianization," of Italian immigrants, 170–171
Italian language: distinction between dialects of, 169–170; international status of, 104
Italian population, of New York, 170
Italian Supreme Court (Corte di Cassazione), 105, 120n22
Italo-Romance languages *(dialetti)*, 170
Italy, 99, 104; applicant narrative and, 109; asylum process of, 104–117, 117n3; asylum requests in, 105, 120n19; immigration policy of, 105; intake form for refugees to, *103*, 106–107, 121n24, 121n34; migrant detention measures in, 105–106; monolingualism of, 99, 104–105

Jelly-Shapiro, Joshua, 177, *178*, 179, 186n3
Jish sh'ab khawa ("the Army, the People are brothers, brothers" chant), 206–207

Jogues, Isaac, 166
journalists, use of ELA map of, 184
Just and Unjust Wars (Walzer), 61n22
justice, language loss and, 1–3, 36–37

Kabyle ethnic group: attempted connections with France of, 206, 212n29, 260–261; demonstrations of, 211n25; as migrant workers in France, 199
Kabylia, Algeria, 199–201
Kannada language, 159
Kaufman, Daniel, 13, 17, 77, 166–185, 249–250; New York language map of, 281
Kensington neighborhood, of New York, 77
keyboard: for Amharic language, *256*, *257*; downloadable Ethiopic, 255, *256*, *257*; QWERTY, 248–249, 255, 258–259; for script, 234, 240n33
Keyman software, 234
Khin, Tun, 224
kiinteelintaakana (computers), use of by Miami people, 145
Kornai, András, 250, 268n20
Kpelle script, 230, *231*, 239n26; destruction of written materials in, 231
Kroskrity, Paul, 133–134, 176
Krueger, Anne, 85
Kurgan, Laura, 17, 266, 275–276; flood study of, 284, 286, 291–292; *EXIT*, xiv, xv, 275, 277, 279, 283, 286; *In Plain Sight*, 288–290
Kusy, Miroslav, 37–38
Kwak'wala language, 127–128
Kymlicka, Will, 38–39, 57, 194–195

Laclau, Ernesto, 62n31
lacrosse *(pakitahaminki)*, 141
Ladino language, 179
land rights, language rights and, 45–46
language, distinction between dialect and, 169–171, *178*, 179, 186n15
language activism, colonial influence, 195
language attrition, language change contrasted with, 134, 155n42
language authenticity, 5, 126–129, 143
language bias, in digital sphere, 248–249
language borders, as arbitrary, 173
language change, language attrition contrasted with, 134, 143

INDEX

language communities, 3–4, 45; communication with proposal authors, 231–232; inclusion in work on languages of, 266; networks among, 221, 228–229
language contact, 143
language disinvention, 174–177
language extinction, 4–5, 29n11, 69–70, 126–127, 132; technology and, 245; turning points in, 152n18
language goals, of Miami people, 129–131
The Language Guy (blog), 130, 151n8
language identification, Indigenous views on, 175–176
language loss: ancestral habitat loss and, 7, 29n9, 132–133; asylum seekers and, 12, 27–28, 29n9; digital inclusion and, 27; ecological devastation and, 1–2, 6, 27–28, 29n9; economy and, 11, 14–15, 29n9; Indigenous languages and, 132–133; justice and, 1–3, 29n9; migration and, 11, 29n9, 166–167
language mixing: in actual language practice, 173–174; with colonial languages, 4–5, 144, 146–147, 153n30; Nheengatú speakers and, 175–176; "translanguaging," 13, 173–177, 187n16, 187n19
language policy, 38–39; marginalized poor and, 68–69; mother tongue education and, 79–83
language-power hierarchies, 244–245
language purity, biased expectations for, 126–128
language reclamation, 5, 129–130, 147–148; measurement of success of, 131; term language revitalization contrasted with, 133, 149, 152n20, 187n19
language shift, of Indigenous languages, 132–133
language skepticism, 173
Languages of New York (ELA), *178*, 179–185
language-specific data, Unicode scripts and, 234–235
language transmission, contested ideas about, 130–131, 151n12
Latin American Indigenous language speakers: medical care and, 171–172; view on dialects of, 172–173

Latin-based writing systems, digital support for, 249
Latinization campaigns, in China, 24, 30n32
Latin script, 24–25; Amharic in, 254–255, 255, 259; ease of encoding into Unicode, 221, 222, 223; number of languages used for, 257–259; Western-designed communication technologies and, 258–259; romanization, 24, 30–31n32, 258
Lefebvre, Henri, 207
legal cases, linguistic rights and, 51, 72n39
legal equality, for women in Algeria, 209
legal infrastructure, of international protection, 100
legislation, linguistic diversity and, 14
"legitimate" use of Indigenous languages, Western scholars on, 128, 148, 153n30
Lenape language, 166
Lenape people, 7–8
Leonard, Wesley, 4–5, 126–143, 146–149, 187n19; Miami auction Western name of and, 144–145, 155n43
liberal-constitutional theory, 196–197
Liberia, number of English speakers in, 77
"La Liberté" (song), 205
lifeworld, of languages, 1–8, 11, 21, 195–196
light, of infrastructure, 287, *288*, *289*, 290, *290*
lingua franca: across world, 22–23; shift in, 21
linguistic analysis, in terms of languages familiar to researcher, 130–131
linguistic asymmetry, 7
linguistic community: drafting of UDLR and, 41; Hobbes on, 44
linguistic competence, 131–132, 152n15
linguistic development, true development and, 72–73
linguistic diversity, 3–4; Census undercount areas and, 168–169; information technology and, 22, 244–245; justice and, 12–13, 59, 87; of New York, 167–168, *168*, 177, *178*, 179–185, 249–250; through prism of English, 13
Linguistic Diversity and Social Justice (Piller), 9–10
linguistic equality, 37–39
linguistic exogamy, 175

linguistic justice, 39; Algerian protests and, 207–208; during asylum process, 100, 119n11; equal rights and, 19, 40, 49–50, 51, 58–59; mother tongue education and, 78–82
linguistic pluralism, 52; of hirak, 199
linguistic recognition, during asylum process, 99
linguistic reinvention, of Bird, 53
linguistic relationship, between state and asylum seeker, 104
linguistic rights, attempt to protect, 15, 38, 40. *See Also* Universal Declaration of Linguistic Rights
linguistic values, digital representation and, 236
linguists, approach of describing languages of, 173
listening, translation and, 108–109
literacy, minority languages and, 74–75, 78–81
Littlebear, Richard E., 151n12
liturgical languages, in ELA database, 180–181
Liu, Lydia, 60n6, 61n26, 98–99, 194–195, 259; on technological infrastructure of languages, 249; *Tokens of Exchange* by, 61n22
locale data, 235, 240n39
Locke, John, 16, 41–42, 45–46
logos, 8–9, 28
logos, oikos, and techné, 6, 25, 28
Loowit language, 52–53
low language varieties, high and, 170
low-resource languages: difficulties in digital communication in, 247–248; NLP tools for, 247

MacDonald, Peter, 41, 45
machine-readable dictionaries, for spellcheckers, 235
Maghrebi Arabic, 200
main de l'étranger (foreign hand), 205–206
MAK. *See* Mouvement pour l'autodétermination de la Kabylie
Makihara, Miki, 176
"making do," in translation, 17
Makoni, Sinfree, 174–175
Malay, 62n34

Mambwe, 80–81
Mandarin, 62n34
Mande language group, 180, 229
Mandinka language, 183
Manfredini, Tommaso, 12–13, 39–40, 60n14, 98–99, 182; work with refugees of, 282
map, of New York languages, 177, *178*, 179
mapping, objections of Indigenous community to, 281
Marshall, T. H., 15–16
Martelli law, 105
Maryns, Katrijn, 122n35
Mayan: hieroglyphs, 227; interpreters asylum seekers and, 172; workshop with speakers of, 227
McClurg, Martha Una, 136
MDGs. *See* United Nations Millennium Development Goals
Mead, Margaret, 30n21
Médecins Sans Frontières (Doctors without Borders), 77
Medellin, Colombia, 284
Meek, Barbra, 131
Mellon Foundation, Architecture, Urbanism, and the Humanities program of, 283–284
melting pot theory, 47
Mexico, views on dialects in, 171
Meziane, Raja, 207–208
Miami auction, Western name of Leonard and, 144–145, 155n43
Miami counting song, 139
Miami *eewansaapita* language and cultural immersion camp, 137–141, 145
Miami games, 140–141
Miami greeting song, 139–140
Miami Indian Stories (McClurg), 136
Miami kinship terms, 144
Miami *(myaamia)* language, 4–5, 26, 126–139, 150n2; chess piece names in, 141–142, 155n38; computer-mediated communication in, 144–146; cultural value of, 144, 147–149; French in surnames of, 140; influence of French on, 140; introduction into conversations of, 144; modern language practices of, 129–147, 154n31; names increase of, 144–145; restrictions on use of, 128, 136, 148; short spontaneous songs in, 140; use in

INDEX

chess game of, 142–143, 155n37; use of during lacrosse game, 141
Miami Nation of Indians of the State of Indiana, 150n7
Miami people, 5, 126–130, 150n2; counting song of, 139; creation of space for, 143; differences in appearance of, 134–135, 153n23; diversity of, 129, 134–135; everyday communication by, 144; biased assumptions on appearance of, 135; language goals of, 130; multiculturalism of, 141–142; songs of, 138–139, 154n35
Miami Removal, of 1846, 151n7
Miami Tribe of Oklahoma Language Committee, 129, 137–138, 151n7
migrant detention in Italy, strict measures for, 105–106
migrant miners, in France, 199
migration, language loss and, 11
Millennium Development Goals and Education for All Goals, of United Nations, 9, 68–69, 83–85
Milliband, Ed, 69
Minniti, Luca, 117n3
Minniti, Marco, 120
Minniti law, 105
minority girls, disadvantages of, 74–75
minority-language communities, scripts and, 223–224
minority languages: access to education in, 84; attempted support for, 20–21; intersecting disadvantages and, 69, 247; scripts of, 228–229
minority-language script users, difficulty of calculation of, 236
Minority language technology users, low literacy rate areas and, 236
Missing Scripts project, of Atelier National de Recherche Typographique, 234
mistrust, of Census, 169
"Mixteco es un lenguaje" (song), 186n8
Mixteco (Tu'un Savi) language, 179–180, 186n8
modern Indigenous languages, 5, 127–137
modern life, American Indians and, 127–137
modern Miami language practices, 129–147, 154n31
Modern Standard Arabic (fusha), backlash against, 200, 204–205

MODIS satellite, of NASA, 286–287
monetary resources, of minority communities, 236–237
Mongolia, 227
Mongolian language, multiple scripts used for, 257
Mongolian script: education in, 227, 239n16; inclusion in Unicode of, 227; malfunction of, 222; variations of in Mongolian language, 257
Monokutuba speaker, at festival, 182–183
monolingualism of Italian state, 99, 104–105
Mossang, Lakhum, 236–237
mother tongue–based multilingual education (MTBMLE), 80; lack of access to, 73–74, 76, 81; social justice and, 78–82
mountain example, of Bird, 52
Mouvement pour l'autodétermination de la Kabylie (MAK), 201, 206, 211n25
MTBMLE. See mother tongue–based multilingual education
Mufwene, Salikoko, 174–175
multiculturalism, of Miami people, 141–142, 146–149, 150n2
multilingual education, cost of English-language education contrasted with, 21
multilingualism: in *myaamia* community, 143, 150n5; negotiation of, 105; as norm, 21–22, 87
multilingual protests, in Algeria, 205–207
multiple idiolects, respect for, 174
multiple levels of meaning, in Ethiopic characters, 259–260
multiplicity of cultures, equal rights and, 14, 87
multistakeholder efforts, creative resistance and, 251–252, 266
mutual intelligibility: language enumeration and, 175; work of translator and, 109–110
Myanmar, Rohingya refugees and, 264

Nahuatl names, Hispanicized versions of, 170–187
named languages, understanding of, 172–177
narration in asylum process, linguistic hierarchy and, 13

INDEX

NASA. *See* National Aeronautics and Space Association
National Aeronautics and Space Association (NASA), 286–287
nation and state, Hobbes on, 42–43
Native American agency, 5, 47–50, 133–134
native language: abandonment of, 7, 132–133, 148; English-language learning and, 10, 79–80; shame in, 132–133, 148
natural language processing (NLP) tools, 247, 263
nature, current use of, 86
Navajo sheep example, 137
Nchare, Nji Oumarou, 224–225
"Neelamma" (poem), 161, 162
Nelson, Fraser, 85
Neoliberal developmentalism, 11
neoliberal growth models, Third-World countries and, 20
Nettle, Daniel, 8
New Amsterdam, 166
New Oriental Education and Technology Group, 26
new scripts, older mobile devices and, 235
newspaper readership, electoral participation and, 80–81
New York: African languages in, 180; Arabic dialects in, 181; Bangladeshi neighborhoods of, 77; endonyms on language map of, *178*, 179; impact of Covid-19 on Indigenous Latin Americans in, 184; Indigenous languages in, 179–182, 249–250; Indigenous Mexicans in, 181–182; Kensington neighborhood of, 77; language map of Kaufman and Perlin in, 281; linguistic diversity of, 17, 167–168, *168*, 177, *178*, 179–185, 249–250; map of languages of, 177, *178*, 179; tacit trilingualism of Italian immigrants in, 171; visibility of Indigenous languages in, 184–185; West African languages in, 180; wide differences between *creole* languages in, 179
Nheengatú speakers, language mixing and, 175–176
Nigeria, 74
Njoya, Ibrahim, 224, 238n12
N'ko script, 183, 229

NLP. *See* natural language processing
Nolan, Rachel, 172
Ñomndaa (Amuzgo) language, 179–180
nonnormative language cultures, language users contrasted with, 14
Nonstop Metropolis (Solnit and Jelly-Shapiro), 177, *178*, 179, 186n3
non-Unicode coding, garbled text and, 233
Northeast Amazonia, 175–176
Noto font project, of Google, 225, 233–234, 239n27
Nougaret, Claudine, 275–276
Nyagchu River valley, Tibet, 170

Occupy Movement, 207
Odell, Jenny, 52, 53
official interview transcript *(verbale)*, 106–107, *107*, 109–114; status of Italian version of, 108
oikos (home), 8; etymon for eco-, 9; *logos* and, 11–12, 25, 28
Oklahoma and Indiana, concentration of Miami people in, 138
Ol Chiki script, 223–224
older mobile devices, new scripts and, 235
Old Hungarian script, 223–233, *233*
1%, amount of wealth of, 85
online language choices, 245
Open Font License, of SIL, 233–234
original of translated document, higher status of, 108
orthographic changes, changes in meaning and, 259–260
Osage language, 227; script of, 26, *228*
Osage Nation, 26, 227
Ouyang Jianghe, 216; "Between English and Chinese" (poem), 216–219
Ouled al-Bahja football club, 205, 208n38
"outer galaxy," of refugee status, 107–108
out-of-school children: classroom languages and, 68, 73; disadvantages of, 74–75
Oxfam, on global wealth and poverty, 85

Pact for a Democratic Alternative, PAD (Pacte de l'Alternative démocratique), 209
Pact for Migration and Asylum, 120n17
PAD. *See* Pacte de l'Alternative démocratique

INDEX

Pakistan: Azad Jammu and Kashmir Pakistan (AJK), 112; examiner question about geography of, 114; floods of, 292
pakitahaminki (lacrosse), 141
palaanikaani, "eight building" (Super 8 Motel), 143
palm oil plantations, in Indonesia, 278
Parijs, Philippe Van, 21–22
parity, across difference, 19
"part Miami," disuse by Miami governance of, 134–135
"the party of France" *(hizb frança)*, 200, 211n20
pathways for Africa, outcomes contrasted with, 83
Patten, Alan, 38–39, 57
Paz, Moria, 51, 62n39
pedestrian streets *(strade pedonali)*, mistranslation of answer of Applicant K. as, 114, 122n37
PEN International, 15, 36, 41, 54, 60n12; minority language efforts of, 195
Pennycook, Alastair, 174–175
Perlin, Ross, 13, 17, 77, 166–185, 249–250; New York language map of, 281
"The Perplexities of the Rights of Man," (Arendt), 60n14
Peterson, Leighton, 149
Pettit, Philip, 42
phenotypic diversity, of Miami people, 134–135, 153n23
phones, loading of fonts onto, 234
physical writing *(techné)*, 25
Piller, Ingrid, 9–10
pinyin alphabet, 30n32
planetary perspective, to global poverty, 70–71
political activism, wariness of Algerians of, 207
political coalitions, from hirak, 208–209
political considerations, proposed freedom of languages from, 175
political equality, 40–41, 59
political processes, language and, 3, 172–173, 186n15, 195–196
"Political Refugees and Forced Migration" (art exhibit), 283
politics in Algeria, culturalization of, 201–202

"Population Shifts" (art exhibit), 274, 284, 286
postcolonial Africa, language policy in, 79–80
poverty: concentrated regions of, 68; goals for reduction of, 84–86; linguistic diversity and, 9–10
power structures: American Indians and, 127; minority languages and, 263–264
primary school education: completion in Africa of, 79–80; rates of, 74; state and, 21
"Printed English" code, 25–26
private ownerships, philosophers on, 15
private tutoring, in China, 20, 30n23
prodemocracy movement, of Algeria (hirak), 18–19, 194–195, 205–206; collective sense of opposition and, 204; Covid-19 and, 203–204; Friday marches of, 207; government crackdown on, 203–204; incident with feminist group during, 209n48; linguistic pluralism of, 199; political coalitions from, 208–209; protests of, 198; slogans of, 198, 204, 212n31, 260–261
proof of danger, of asylum seeker, 101–102
property rights, 16; common property private property and, 45–46
protests, of hirak movement, 198
protezione speciale (special protection), 106
"Protocol to Ensure Language Rights" (Unrepresented Nations and Peoples Organization), 60n12
public policy, economics as mother tongue of, 71–72
Pular language, 226–227
pure cultural identity, biased assumptions about, 127–128, 134, 150n5

Qu, Xing, 2
quality education, mother tongue instruction and, 80
Queens, Asian languages in, 180
QWERTY keyboard, 248–249, 255, 258–259

racial exclusion, language rights and, 18
Rahal, Malika, 202
Ramapough Lenape Nation, 7–8
Rao, Anupama, 98–99, 194–195, 249

Rapa Nui people, 176
rational thought, Hobbes on language and, 42
Raworth, Kate, 9, 71
receiving countries, for displaced people, 103
reciprocity, equality contrasted with, 51, 57
reflexive democracy, 196
refugees: hosting by Europe of, 103; intake form to Italy (C-3 form), *103*, 106–107, 121n34; mapping of flow of, 282–283, *283*, 291; Rohingya Myanmar government and, 264; rules for determination of population of, 282–283; top countries for, 103; work of Manfredini with, 282
refugee status: "outer galaxy" of, 107–108; requirements for, 101–102, 106; temporary protection of, 100
refugee status determination interview (RSD), 106; arbitrariness of, 116; needed proof of fear during, 113–114; preparation for, 110–111, 122n37
regular communication, in Indigenous languages, 143–144
Reinventing the Enemy's Language (Bird), 52
relational identity, 18
religious characters, exclusion from Amharic of, 259–260
religious meaning, of Ethiopic script, 259
religious orientation, of *Ethnologue*, 280
Reported Internally Displaced People, of Colombia, 285
representation: democracy and, 208; inclusion in Unicode and, 26–27
rich script traditions, encoding of, 259–260, 269n40
rights: group individual and, 14, 16–17; linguistic diversity and, 12–13, 15–16, 37–40, 194–195; particular contexts of, 39–40; in political system discourse over, 209; prioritization and, 39; to translation for asylum seekers, 99–100
rights-based system: V. Deloria, on, 50–51; justice-based approach contrasted with, 246
rights-bearer: collective as, 49; linguistic community as, 41, 44
rights discourse: against marginalized people in early American history, 43; in social contract theory, 40–41

rights of solidarity, 38
right to the city ("*droit de la ville*"), 207
rigid policing, in Europe, 43
Riley, Charles, 238n12
rituals, acceptance of Indigenous languages by European population during, 144
road construction, in Cameroon, 278
Roche, Gerald J., 30n17, 177
Rohingya refugees, Myanmar government and, 264
Romaine, Suzanne, 8–9, 50, 52, 68–69, 172–173; on ecological and language diversity, 245, 266, 277
romanization, 24, 30n32, digital tech and, 258; Latin script, 24–25
Rousseau, Jean-Jacques, 41–42, 196
RSD. *See* refugee status determination interview
rural-urban migration, due to conflict, 284

Mount St. Helens, 52
Saldarriaga, Juan, 283–284
Salvini, Matteo, 105–106, 120n22
Sango language, 221, 222
San Jacinto Mountains, 53–54
Sanskrit language, 159
Santali language, 24, 223–224
satellite images, of *In Plain Sight*, 286–287, *287*
script: Amharic language in, 254–255, *255*, 259; Anderson on, 257; Arabic and, 248; Arabizi, 248; for Azerbaijani language, 257–258; Bamum, 224–225, *225*, 238n12; Bété, 231–232, *232*; bias of, 258–259; bias toward alphabetic, 259; complex, 230, *230*, 239n24; Cyrillic, 227; deconstruction of systems of, 25; difficulty in finding details of, 230; digital support for high-resource, 249; encoding off rich, 259–260, 269n40; Ethiopic in Unicode, 253–254, *254*; evolutionary development theory Roman or Latin and, 25; first-language digital supports for new, 257; garbling when not in Unicode of, 222, 223; Hanifi Rohingya, 224; Hanzi, 257, 259; of Hindu and Urdu, 24; incorrect substitution of homophonous characters in Ethiopic, 260; integrity of, 257–258;

INDEX

interoperability of ideographic, 259; keyboard for, 234, 240n33; Kpelle, 230, 231, *231*, 239n26; language-specific data Unicode and, 234–235; Latin, 24–25, 221, 222, 223–224, 254–255, 255, 257–269, 259; Latin colonialism/colonization, 258–259; minority inclusion on social media of, 235, 240n40; minority-language communities and, 223–224; of minority languages, 228–229; Mongolian, 222, 227, 239n16, 257; for Mongolian language, 257; N'ko, 183, 229; Ol Chiki, 223–224; older mobile devices and, 235; political complications in Unicode inclusion of, 233; proposal minority communities and, 228–229; religious meaning of Ethiopic, 259; significance for encoding of, 221, 222, 223; Tai Tham, 233; tech companies and, 236–237, 247; of Urdu and Hindi, 24; use of different for similar languages, 257–258; viable market for, 236; Western-designed communication technologies Latin and, 258–259; writing systems contrasted with, 24, 220–221, 238n5, 257–258

Script Encoding Initiative (SEI), 26, 221, 249, 266

SDG. *See* Sustainable Development Goals

second generation, of economic rights, 37–38

SEI. *See* Script Encoding Initiative

self-determination, of American Indians, 133–134

self-fulfilling prophecy, poverty and linguistic diversity as, 10

semantic requirement, of refugee Convention, 102

Senegal: bilingual education and, 80–81; debate over varieties of Baïnounk in, 182–183

sensational content, social media platforms and, 262

sensitive data, questions about use of, 264

Serres, Thomas, 206–207

shame, in native language, 132–133, 148

Shannon, Claude, 25–26

sharanas (Shiva worshippers), 159

Shiva (Hindu God), 159

Shivaprakash, H. S., 159

short spontaneous songs, in Miami, 140

Sierra Leone, 77

signature of composers *(ankita)*, 159

SIL. *See* Summer Institute for Linguistics

silent disappearances, 1, 99

Silverman, Charlotte, 266, 275–276

similar languages: different names for, 179; use of different scripts for, 257–258

simultaneous translation, problems with, 113

Singapore, 62n34

Sioux dialects, of Dakota Lakota and, 30n21

Sitting Bull, 49–50; eagle and cow example of, 51

Sky News Arabia interview, 204

sleeping languages, preference of term over "extinct," 134, 149, 152n20

slogans, of hirak movement, 198, 204, 212n31

small communities, challenges with Unicode of, 228–229

Soaring Hawk, Clara, 7–8, 29n10

social activity, approach to language as, 195–196

social citizenship, 15–16

social contract theory, 41–43, 44, 50, 53–54

social contradictions, 18

social existence, language and, 39–40

social foundation, of humanity, 71

social goods, Walzer on, 46, 195

social hierarchies, Indigenous languages and, 172

social media: inclusion of minority scripts on, 235, 240n40; *myaamia and*, 145; YouTube language advocacy and, 262. *See Also* Facebook

social practice, view of language of, 209–210

social rights, 37–38

Solnit, Rebecca, 177, *178*, 179, 186n3

Soolking (musical artist), 205

South Africa, 79

southern Asia, out-of-school children in, 74–75

Spanish, UDLR in, 55, 57–58, 63n45, 63n50

special protection *(protezione speciale)*, 106

The Spectator (magazine), 85

"Speechless Deforestation" (art exhibit), 276–280, *277*, 286, 290–291

INDEX

spellcheck features in Amharic, use of, 260
Spheres of Justice (Walzer), 39
Spivak, Gayatri Chakravorty, 116, 177
square word calligraphy, 243
standard language, as one register, 173
Standard Procedures on the Identification and Referral of Victims, 117n3
Standard Tibetan written tradition, 170
state and asylum seeker, linguistic relationship between, 104
state-sponsored digital surveillance, 262, 266–267
story, of Applicant K, 111–114
strade pedonali (pedestrian streets), mistranslation of answer of A.K. as, 114, 122n40
strategic essentialism, 17, 177
street-level citizen movement in Algeria, conditions for, 207
stroke, of Bouteflika, 203–204
sub-Saharan Africa: HIV/AIDS, 76; illiteracy in, 75, 76; out-of-school children in, 73–75; southern Asia and, 68
subsidiary protection, 106, 119n14
subversive tool, language as, 53
"successful" narrative, strict imposition of, 109
Summer Institute for Linguistics (SIL), 233–234
Super 8 Motel (*palaanikaani*, "eight building"), 143
surveillance capitalism, 261–262
surveys on classroom instruction language, necessity for, 82
Sustainable Development Goals (SDGs), of United Nations, 70, 74, 76, 79–87
sustainable economic system, languages and, 9, 69, 80–87
s-wedge (š), 26, 146
syllabic scripts, 259

tacit trilingualism, of Italian immigrants, New York, 171
Tai Tham script, 233
Tamazight language, 198–199; Arabic and, 200–201, 211n23
targets: for language reclamation, 130; need for specificity of in UN, 83–84

Taylor, Charles, 194–195
Tebboune, Abdelmadjid, 203–204, 208–209, 212n31
tech companies: extended internet reach efforts of, 246–247; minority script inclusion of, 236–237, 247
techné (of inscription), 25
technological infrastructure, of Global English, 249; of informatics, 25–26; of scripts, 24, 26, 221–237
techno-optimism, under-resourced languages and, 246–247
Tewa language, 176
textual residue, 110, 124n35
textual steps, of asylum process, 116
theories of language, work of Hobbes and Rousseau as, 42
"They must all go!" slogan (*Yetnahaw gaâ!*) (يتنحاو قاع), 204–205
"This Old Man" (song), 139
Tibetan language, variety of dialects of, 170
Tifnagh alphabet, 201
Tiwa people, 142
Tokens of Exchange (Liu), 61n22
Torner, Carles, 41, 45, 54
torture, protection from, 106, 121n26
translanguaging (*trawsieithu*), 13, 173–177, 187n16, 187n19
translation: for asylum seekers, 98–99, 106–117 107, 121n34, 122n36; challenges muting of, 110; human rights documents and, 40–41, 54–55, 61n26; institutional process of, 99–100; of language and dialect in immigrant community, 169–170; as method, 19, 195; as nontransactional, 17; of same word differences, 61n26; trust and, 108–109; of UDLR, 40–41, 54–59, 60n12; of *verbale* during asylum process, 114–116
tribal citizenship: blood quantum requirement for, 134–135, 153n25; Miami governance on, 134–135, 153n25
tribunali ordinari (courthouses), 120n22
tropics, high concentration of languages in, 4, 69–70
Trump administration, attempted citizenship question on Census of, 169, 281–282

INDEX

Tuchscherer, Konrad, 224–225, 238n12
Turki, Sofiane Bakir, 204–205
Tu'un Savi (Mixteco) language, 179–180, 186n8
typeface design program, of University of Reading, 234, 240n30

UDHR. *See* Universal Declaration of Human Rights
UDLR. *See* Universal Declaration of Linguistic Rights
Una Isu. *See* Villegas Ventura, Miguel
undercount areas of Census, linguistic diversity and, 168–169
under-resourced languages, techno-optimism and, 246–247
undersea cables, 247, 267n7
UNESCO. *See* United Nations Educational, Scientific and Cultural Organization
UNHCR. *See* United Nations High Commissioner for Refugees
Unicode, 23–24, 26, 220–221, 222, 223–224; code points for, 233; complications in approval for, 232–233, *233*; delays in, 229; Ethiopic script in, 253–254, *254*; first version of, 227–228, 249–250; malfunction of, 223; political complications in approval of script for, 233; procedure for proposal for, 228–233, *229*, 239n21; Pular language and, 226–227; Standard for, 238n1; success of language and, *225*, 225–226, *226*; tech companies and, 235–237; technical knowledge and English skills needed for, 232–233, 266
Unicode Common Locale Data Repository (CLDR), 235
Unicode Consortium, 227, 238n1
United Nations (UN): Framework Convention on Climate Change of, 276; Global Task Force for Making a Decade of Action for Indigenous Languages of, 2; High Commissioner for Refugees of (UNHCR), 102–103, 282–283, *283*; Millennium Development Goals (MDGs), 68, 69; Millennium Development Goals and Education for All Goals of, 9, 83–85; Permanent Forum on Indigenous Issues, 2, 28nn2–3;

Sustainable Development Goals (SDGs) of, 70, 74, 76, 79–87
United Nations Educational, Scientific and Cultural Organization (UNESCO), 3, 28n3, 54, 195; education report of, 82; exhibit, 277–280, *279*
United Nations Framework Convention on Climate Change, 276
United Nations High Commissioner for Refugees (UNHCR), 102–103; data set of, 282–283, *283*
United States: context of human rights of, 43; Declaration of Independence of, 37–38; Empire of, 25–26; erasure of Indigenous Latin Americans in, 171–172
Universal Declaration of Human Rights (UDHR), 38, 59n4, 222
Universal Declaration of Linguistic Rights (UDLR), 15, 36–38, 40, 54–55, 59n3; in Catalán, 54–55, 63n45; deliberate choice *(délibéré)* in, 56–57, 58; of English-language learning, 55–56; in French, 55, 56–58, 60n6; hegemonic power equal participation and, 56; translation of, 40–41, 54–59, 60n12; treatment of term "assimilation" in, 56–58; Western European translations, of, 55
universalization, 58
universal primary education, 68, 73, 74–75
universal secondary education, 83–84
University of California, Berkeley, 26, 221
University of Reading, England, 234, 240n30
unmarked graves, in Canada, 7
Unrepresented Nations and Peoples Organization, 60n12
Urdu and Hindi, different scripts of, 24
users of marginalized languages, treatment of, 14

vachanas (Kannada poems), 159–160
"The Vachanas" (translation by M. Devadevan), 19, 159
"La valutazione di credibilità del richiedente asilo" (L. Minniti), 117n3
Vanishing Voices (Nettle and Romaine), 8
verbale (official interview transcript), 106–107, *107*, 109–114, 121n35

viable market, for script support by tech companies, 236
Victims Register, of Colombia, 283–284
Villegas Ventura, Miguel (Una Isu), 186n8
Vince, Natalya, 201–202
Virilio, Paul, 275–276, 291
visibility, of Indigenous languages in New York, 184–185
voiceless postalveolar fricative, 26, 126

Waldron, Jeremy, 49
Walzer, Michael, 39, 45–46, 61n22, 61n26, 195
Webster, Anthony, 137, 149
Wee, Lionel, 49, 57, 62n34, 195, 209–210
weekihkaaminki-meehkintiinki (ball games and games of chance), 139
Welsh language teaching, translanguaging and, 173–174
West African languages, in New York, 180
Western culture, reaction to nature of, 53–54
Western-designed communication technologies, Latin script and, 258–259
Western European translations, of UDLR, 55
What's Wrong with Rights (D'Souza), 43
White, Orlando, 35
Wikipedia articles, literacy rates and, 73–74
Williams, Cen, 173–174, 187n16
Wittgenstein, Ludwig, 73–74
wooden lacrosse sticks, at Miami camp, 141, 155n36
Woodward, David, 85–86
"Words" (poem), 192; Arabic version of, 193; Bennis, 192

work of translator, mutual intelligibility and, 109–110
workshop, with Mayan speakers, 227
World Bank, 81
World Education Forum, of 2015, 80
World War II, 25–26, 104
worst off, improvement of position of, 78
writing systems, 249; as language specific, 24–25; scripts contrasted with, 24, 220–221, 238n5, 257–258
written corpus, of *myaamia* language, 132

Xaxa, Abhay, 125
Xu Bing, 243

Yacine, Kateb, 211n21
Yetnahaw gaâ! (يتنحاو قاع) "They must all go!" slogan, 204–205
yishi (consciousness), 58
yizhi (completely consistent participation), 56
Young, Iris Marion, 18
young people: beliefs on language use of, 245; in Miami community, 137–142, 147–149
YouTube, language advocacy and, 262

Zambia, 80–81
Zaugg, Isabelle, 23, 74, 185, 225; study on Ethiopian and Eritrean languages of, 26–27, 244–257; on technology, 244–245
Zhai Yongming, 96; "Becoming a Child," 96–97
Zhuang ethnic minority, 30n32

GPSR Authorized Representative: Easy Access System Europe, Mustamäe tee 50, 10621 Tallinn, Estonia, gpsr.requests@easproject.com